VISIT US AT

YNGRESS®

CONFIGURING

SonicWALL
Firewalls

Chris Lathem
Benjamin W. Fortenberry
Kevin Lynn
Daniel H. Bendell
Joshua Reed

Bradley Dinerman   Technical Editor
Lars Hansen   Technical Editor

KEY	SERIAL NUMBER
001	HJIRTCV764
002	PO9873D5FG
003	829KM8NJH2
004	P762ABL8D2
005	CVPLQ6WQ23
006	VBP965T5T5
007	HJJJ863WD3E
008	2987GVTWMK
009	629MP5SDJT
010	IMWQ295T6T

PUBLISHED BY
Syngress Publishing, Inc.
800 Hingham Street
Rockland, MA 02370

Configuring SonicWALL Firewalls

Transferred to Digital Printing 2012

ISBN-13: 978-1-59749-250-8
ISBN-10: 1-59749-250-7

Publisher: Andrew Williams
Acquisitions Editor: Jaime Quigley
Technical Editor: Lars Hansen, Brad Dinerman
Copy Editors: Amy Thomson, Beth Roberts

Page Layout and Art: Patricia Lupien
Indexer: J. Edmund Rush
Cover Designer: Michael Kavish

Distributed by O'Reilly Media, Inc. in the United States and Canada.
For information on rights, translations, and bulk sales, contact Matt Pedersen, Director of Sales and Rights, at Syngress Publishing; email matt@syngress.com or fax to 781-681-3585.

Acknowledgments

Syngress would like to acknowledge the following people for their kindness and support in making this book possible.

Syngress books are now distributed in the United States and Canada by O'Reilly Media, Inc. The enthusiasm and work ethic at O'Reilly are incredible, and we would like to thank everyone there for their time and efforts to bring Syngress books to market: Tim O'Reilly, Laura Baldwin, Mark Brokering, Mike Leonard, Donna Selenko, Bonnie Sheehan, Cindy Davis, Grant Kikkert, Opol Matsutaro, Steve Hazelwood, Mark Wilson, Rick Brown, Tim Hinton, Kyle Hart, Sara Winge, C. J. Rayhill, Peter Pardo, Leslie Crandell, Regina Aggio, Pascal Honscher, Preston Paull, Susan Thompson, Bruce Stewart, Laura Schmier, Sue Willing, Mark Jacobsen, Betsy Waliszewski, Kathryn Barrett, John Chodacki, Rob Bullington, Aileen Berg, and Wendy Patterson.

The incredibly hardworking team at Elsevier Science, including Jonathan Bunkell, Ian Seager, Duncan Enright, David Burton, Rosanna Ramacciotti, Robert Fairbrother, Miguel Sanchez, Klaus Beran, Emma Wyatt, Chris Hossack, Krista Leppiko, Marcel Koppes, Judy Chappell, Radek Janousek, and Chris Reinders for making certain that our vision remains worldwide in scope.

David Buckland, Marie Chieng, Lucy Chong, Leslie Lim, Audrey Gan, Pang Ai Hua, Joseph Chan, and Siti Zuraidah Ahmad of STP Distributors for the enthusiasm with which they receive our books.

David Scott, Tricia Wilden, Marilla Burgess, Annette Scott, Andrew Swaffer, Stephen O'Donoghue, Bec Lowe, Mark Langley, and Anyo Geddes of Woodslane for distributing our books throughout Australia, New Zealand, Papua New Guinea, Fiji, Tonga, Solomon Islands, and the Cook Islands.

Brandon McIntire and Jason Acosta at CDW for their support.

Lead Author

Chris Lathem (CSSA, Network+) is currently working as a Network Engineer for Consultrix Technologies. Consultrix, based in Ridgeland, MI, specializes in network management and security services, structured cabling, and application development. Prior to joining Consultrix, Chris was a Security/Network Engineer for NSight Technologies, now based in Tampa, FL. While at Nsight, Chris specialized in the support and configuration of firewall appliances from multiple vendors, as well as network design and architecture. While working for NSight, Chris gained extensive knowledge of SonicWALL firewall appliances and' achieved certification as a Certified SonicWALL Security Administrator. It was during his tenure at Nsight that Chris first worked with Syngress Publishing as a contributing author to the book *Configuring NetScreen Firewalls*. Before joining Nsight, Chris held the position of Network Engineer for SkyHawke Technologies, a technology start-up company in the recreational GPS industry, where he spent a great deal of time configuring NetScreen security appliances. Chris currently resides in Sebastopol, MI, with his wife, Susann, and son Miller.

Contributing Authors

Benjamin Fortenberry (CISSP, CSSA, CCSE-4x) is Manager of Security Services with Consultrix Technologies, of Jackson, MI. His responsibilities include development, design, implementation, and senior-level support for all security services provided to Consultrix clients. Benjamin has been involved with the installation, configuration, and ongoing support of 200-plus SonicWALL appliances for clients, ranging in size from five to several thousand users. His specialties include SonicWALL security appliances, LAN/WAN switching, penetration testing, security consulting services, and incident response services. Benjamin has also developed and presented numerous seminars and training classes related to network security.

Joshua Reed (CISSP, CCSA/CCSE/+, CCNA, CCNP, MCP) works for a leading firewall and security vendor, with solutions securing all of the Fortune 100 and 99% of the Fortune 500. Joshua has a decade of experience in information technology and security as both staff and architect. He is a consultant in various sectors including the largest public university in the world, the sixth largest financial services/insurance provider in the world, a well-known Bay Area Internet search engine, and a leading aerospace/defense concern. Joshua received a bachelor's degree from the University of California at Berkeley, and holds a CISSP, as well as numerous other industry certifications, is a member of and regular speaker for ISSA, and has lectured and taught courses on information technology and security topics for over 7 years. Joshua currently lives in Long Beach, CA, and can be regularly found hiking the Sierra Nevada and the Mojave Desert.

Daniel H. Bendell (BA, CNE) is the Founder and President of Assurance Technology Management, Inc. (ATM), a full-service consulting practice specializing in providing complete business technology guidance to small and medium-sized companies. ATM's unique consulting approach takes into consideration all of a company's technology systems and combines that with a clear understanding of the client's business goals and practices. With over 20 years of experience in the industry, Daniel combines his breadth of technical knowledge with an ability to understand his clients' business needs. He has published widely on a number of topics, including technical systems documentation and remote systems management. He also delivers customized presentations and educational seminars to organizations and groups of small business owners on how to better manage the technology systems they have invested in. Dan was the Technical Editor of *How to Cheat at Microsoft Windows Small Business Server 2003* (Syngress Publishing, ISBN: 1932266801). Prior to founding ATM, Daniel worked as a senior-level consultant for CSC Consulting, where he specialized in client/server technologies, and as a Healthcare Information Systems Consultant with Superior Consultant Company. Daniel lives in Framingham, MA, with his wife, Phyllis, and daughters Melissa and Jessica.

Daniel J. Gordon (MCSE # # 2455250, CNA 12/95) is Principal and Founder of Gordon Technical Consulting LLC. Gordon Technical Consulting was founded in November of 2000, and is a technical consulting firm specializing in computer networking, design, implementation and support. Daniel has been employed for many years in the networking technologies field with over 14 years of experience. Prior to founding his own firm, Daniel worked for many years at the University of California at San Francisco and Berkeley as a network manager responsible for over 1,500 network connections, numerous applications, and servers. He also worked at various private firms prior to founding his own company. His specialties include Microsoft Windows Server, Exchange design and implementation, strategic network planning, network architecture and design, and network troubleshooting. Daniel currently resides with his family in Berkeley, CA.

Kevin Lynn (CISSP) is a network systems engineer with Unisys Kevin's more than 12 years of experience has seen him working a variety of roles for organizations including Cisco Systems, IBM, Sun Microsystems, Abovenet, and the Commonwealth of Virginia. In addition to his professional work experience, Kevin has been known to give talks at SANS and teach others on security topics in classroom settings. Kevin currently resides in Rockville, MD with his lovely wife Ashley.

Technical Editor

Brad Dinerman combines a rare blend of security, high-end systems architecture and application development skills with a unique sense of humor. On top of these, he adds a strong scientific background that he draws upon to analyze and troubleshoot complex IT problems. Brad currently serves as the vice president of information technology at MIS Alliance in Newton, MA, to provide MIS and IT solutions to companies in the greater Boston area. He has taught classes in Active Server Pages, JavaScript, HTML, and the Theory of Relativity. He is a Microsoft MVP in Windows Server Systems (Networking), one of only 50 worldwide to possess the award in this category. He also possesses an MCSE and MCP+I, is a Certified SonicWall Security Administrator, and holds a Ph.D. in physics from Boston College. Brad is a frequent contributor to various online TechTips sites and gives user group/conference presentations on topics ranging from spam and security solutions to Internet development techniques. He also published numerous articles in international physics journals in his earlier, scientific career.

Brad is the founder and president of the New England Information Security Group, the former chair of the Boston Area Exchange Server User Group, and a member of the FBI's Infragard Boston Members Alliance.

Lars Hansen also contributed to the technical editing of this book. Lars is a technology consultant living in Boston, MA, with his wife and daughter.

Additional Contributors

Rob Cameron (CCSA, CCSE, CCSE+, NSA, JNCIA-FWV, CCSP, CCNA, INFOSEC, RSA SecurID CSE) is an IT consultant who has worked with over 200 companies to provide network security planning and implementation services. He has spent the last five years focusing on network infrastructure and extranet security. His strengths include Juniper's NetScreen Firewall products, NetScreen SSL VPN Solutions, Check Point Firewalls, the Nokia IP appliance series, Linux, Cisco routers, Cisco switches, and Cisco PIX firewalls. Rob strongly appreciates his wife Kristen's constant support of his career endeavors. He wants to thank her for all of her support through this project.

CJ Cui (CISSP, JNCIA) is Director of Professional Services for NetWorks Group, an information security consulting company headquartered in Brighton, Michigan. NetWorks Group provides information security solutions that mitigate risk while enabling secure online business. CJ leads the technical team at NetWorks Group to deliver information security services to customers ranging from medium-sized companies to Fortune 500 corporations. These services touch every part of the security life cycle—from enterprise security management, security assessment and audit to solution design and implementation—and leverage leading-edge technologies, including firewall/VPN, intrusion prevention, vulnerability management, malicious code protection, identity management, and forensics analysis. CJ holds an M.S. degree from Michigan State University and numerous industrial certifications. He is a board member of ISSA Motor City Chapter and serves as the Director of Operations for the chapter.

Thomas Byrne is a Code Monkey with NetScreen Technologies (now Juniper Networks). He currently does design, planning, and implementation on Juniper's Security Manager, the company's next-generation network management software. Tom's background includes positions as a UI Architect at ePatterns, and as a senior developer and consultant for several Silicon Valley companies, including Lightsocket.com and Abovenet. Tom is an active developer on several open-source projects and a voracious contributor to several on-line technology forums. Tom currently lives in Silicon Valley with his wife, Kelly, and children, Caitlin and Christian.

Dave Killion (NSCA, NSCP) is a senior security research engineer with Juniper Networks, Inc. Formerly with the U.S. Army's Information Operations Task Force as an Information Warfare Specialist, he currently researches, develops, and releases signatures for the NetScreen Deep Inspection and Intrusion Detection and Prevention platforms. Dave has also presented at several security conventions, including DefCon and ToorCon, with a proof-of-concept network monitoring evasion device in affiliation with several local security interest groups that he helped form. Dave lives south of Silicon Valley with his wife, Dawn, and two children, Rebecca and Justin.

Kevin Russell (JNCIA-FWV, JNCIA-IDP) is a system engineer for Juniper Networks, specializing in firewalls, IPSEC, and intrusion detection and prevention systems. His background includes security auditing, implementation, and design. Kevin lives in Michigan with his wife and two children.

Chris Cantrell (NetScreen IDP) is a Director of System Engineering—Central Region for the Security Products Group at Juniper Networks. His career has spanned over 12 years, the last eight focused on network and application security. Chris joined OneSecure in late 2000 where he was an active member of the team who designed and was responsible for the introduction of their intrusion prevention product, the IDP. In 2002, OneSecure was acquired by NetScreen Technologies and most recently acquired by Juniper Networks, where Chris continues to manage the security sales engineering team for the Central Region. Chris attended Auburn University at Montgomery, where his focus was on business and management information systems. Chris lives in Denver, CO, with his wife, Maria, and two children, Dylan and Nikki.

Kenneth Tam (JNCIS-FWV, NCSP) is Sr. Systems Engineer at Juniper Networks Security Product Group (formerly NetScreen Technologies). Kenneth worked in pre-sales for over four years at NetScreen since the start-up days and has been one of many key contributors in building NetScreen as one of the most successful security companies. As such, his primary role has been to provide pre-sale technical assistance in both design and implementation of NetScreen solutions. Kenneth is currently covering the upper Midwest U.S. region. His background includes positions as a Senior Network Engineer in the Carrier Group at 3Com Corporation, and as an application engineer at U. S. Robotics. Kenneth holds a bachelor's degree in computer science from DePaul University. He lives in the suburbs of Chicago, IL, with his wife, Lorna, and children, Jessica and Brandon.

Johny Mattsson (NCSA, NCSP, SCJP, SCJD) is a senior engineer in Ericsson Australia's IP Centre, where he has been working with NetScreen firewalls for over three years. The Ericsson IP Centre provides global integration and support services for a wide range of IP-based telecommunications solutions, including DSL broadband and 3G IP Multimedia Subsystems (IMS). Johny's main areas of specialization are IP network security and several cutting-edge 3G mobile services built on IMS. In addition to making sure things are always working on the technical plane, he is the main interface towards Juniper/NetScreen, working to ensure that the support channels are functioning optimally. Before taking up the role in the Ericsson IP Centre, Johny worked as a system designer for Ericsson in Sweden.

Ralph Bonnell (CISSP, LPIC-2, CCSI, CCNA, MCSE: Security) is a senior information security consultant at Accuvant in Denver, CO. His primary responsibilities include the deployment of various network security products and product training. His specialties include NetScreen deployments, Linux client and server deployments, Check Point training, firewall clustering, and PHP web programming. Ralph also runs a Linux consulting firm called Linux Friendly. Before moving to Colorado, Ralph was a senior security engineer and instructor at Mission Critical Systems, a Gold Check Point partner and training center in South Florida.

Contents

## Chapter 1

Networking, Security, and the Firewall

Solutions in this chapter:

- **Understanding Networking**

- **Understanding Security Basics**

- **Understanding Firewall Basics**

☑ **Summary**

☑ **Solutions Fast Track**

☑ **Frequently Asked Questions**

Introduction

Every enterprise requires at least one firewall to provide the backbone for its network security architecture. Firewalls are the core component of your network's security. The risks today have greatly increased, so the call for a stronger breed of firewall has been made. In the past, simple packet-filtering firewalls allowing access to your internal resources have helped to mitigate your network's risk. The next development was stateful inspection allowing you to monitor network sessions instead of single packets. Today's risks are far greater and require a new generation of devices to help secure our networks' borders from the more sophisticated attacks.

Firewalls police your network traffic. A firewall is a specialized device that allows or denies traffic based upon administratively defined policies. They contain technologies to inspect your network's traffic. This technology is not something that is exclusive to firewalls, but firewalls are designed specifically for inspecting traffic and therefore do it better then any other type of device. Any network can have millions of packets transverse it in a short period of time. It is impossible for a human to directly interact with the network. Even if you were to use a tool to look at the traffic directly it would be impossible for you to decide which traffic is good and which is bad. The need for a specialized device to enforce traffic restrictions has grown over the years. Because security is of such high importance, a specialized device was required to ensure the security of network traffic.

SonicWALL firewall appliances have answered this call for a secure enterprise. The SonicWALL firewall product line has complete offerings from the home office to the enterprise networks. In this chapter we will review networking basics. Security requires a strong basic knowledge of networking protocols. In our first section, "Understanding Networking," we will look at networking from a top-down approach. This section starts with the basic ideas of networking models and then works into full networking communications. We will also discuss the components and prerequisites of IP addresses and how they are divided up to make networks.

We will next look at networking in general by breaking it down to a layered approach. This will help you understand the flow of networking. Each specific layer in the networking model has a purpose. Working together, these layers allow for data to seamlessly pass over the network between systems. An example of browsing a Web site will be used. You will see all of the effort it takes just to fetch a Web page. We will focus then on the TCP/IP protocol suite. This is the most commonly used networking protocol and it is the protocol of the Internet. Finally in this chapter, we will look at network security. There are many important concepts to be aware of for information security. This will help you understand some network design considerations and the background behind them.

Understanding Networking

To understand networking is to understand the language of firewalls. A firewall is used to segment resources and limit access between networks. Before we can really focus on what a firewall does for us, we need to understand how networking works. Today in most environments and on the Internet, the protocol suite TCP/IP (Transmission Control Protocol/Internet Protocol) is used to transport data from here to there. We will begin this chapter by looking at networking as a whole with a focus on the Open System Interconnection (OSI) model.

The OSI Model

The OSI model was originally developed as a framework to build networking protocols on. During the time when then Internet was being developed, a protocol suite named TCP/IP was developed. TCP/IP was found to meet the requirements of the Internet's precursor, ARPANET. At this point, TCP/IP was already integrated into UNIX and was quickly adopted by the academic community as well. With the advent of the Internet and its widespread usage, TCP/IP has become the de facto standard protocol suite of internetworking today.

The OSI model consists of seven distinct layers. These layers each contain the fundamental ideas of networking. In Figure 1.1 we can see the way that the seven layers stack on top of each other. The idea is that each upper layer is encapsulated inside of each lower layer. So ultimately, any data communications are transformed into the electrical impulses that pass over the cables or through the air that surrounds us. Understanding the OSI model is understanding the core of networking. In many places throughout this book, the OSI model is used to create a visual representation of networking.

The reality, however, is that the OSI model is just a reference model that protocols are based upon. The next section, called "Moving Data Along With TCP/IP," demonstrates how some of the layers blur together. All in all, the OSI model is a great tool to help anyone understand networking and perform troubleshooting. Over the years, the OSI model has served as a reference for all protocols that have been developed. Almost every book, manual, white paper, or Web site that talks about networking protocols references the OSI model. It is important to have a baseline when discussing every topic.

For example, let's compare cars and trucks. They are effectively the same device. Both are used to get from here to there, but they are designed very differently. A truck has a sturdier frame to allow it to tow heavy loads. A car is smaller and is designed to be a transport for people. While these devices are very different, they still have common components. They both have wheels, doors, brakes, and engines. This is much like the different components of a network protocol, which is essentially a vehicle for data. Networking protocols have components to help get the data from here to there, like wheels. They have components to control the flow of data, like brakes. These are all requirements of any protocol. Using and understanding the OSI model makes protocol usage and design easier. Whether TCP/IP or IPX/SPX, most protocols are built around the same framework (model).

Figure 1.1 The Seven-Layer OSI Model

---

7. Application Layer
6. Presentation Layer
5. Session Layer
4. Transport Layer
3. Network Layer
2. Data Link Layer
1. Physical Layer

Layer 7: The Application Layer

The application layer contains application data. This is the layer at which applications communicate to one another. The reason for all of the other layers is essentially to transport the messages contained at the application layer. When communicating with each other, the applications use their own language, as specified by that application's standard. A perfect example of an application protocol is Hypertext Transfer Protocol (HTTP). HTTP is used to send and receive Web content. When HTTP is used to pass data from server to client, it employs something called HTTP *headers*. HTTP headers are effectively the language of HTTP. When the client wants to request data from a server, it issues a request to get the content from the server. The server then responds with is headers and the data that was requested. All of this is an example of application layer communications. Other examples of application layer protocols are File Transfer Protocol (FTP), Domain Name Service (DNS), Telnet, and Secure Shell (SSH).

Layer 6: The Presentation Layer

The presentation layer controls the presentation or formatting of the data content. At this point in the OSI model there is no data communications per se. The focus of this layer is having a common ground to present data between applications. For example, let's take image files. Billions of image files are transferred every day. Each of these files contains an image that ultimately will be displayed or stored on a computer. However, each image file must be the proper specified file format. This way, the application that reads the image file understands the type of data and the format that is contained in it. A JPEG file and a PNG file may contain the same image, but each uses a separate format. A JPEG file cannot be interpreted as a PNG and vice versa. Additionally, file-level encryption occurs at the presentation layer.

Layer 5: The Session Layer

The session layer controls sessions between two systems. It is important to have sessions, as it is the core of any communications for networking. If you did not have sessions, all communications would run together without any true idea of what is happening throughout the communication. As you will see below, TCP/IP has no session layer, really. In TCP/IP the session layer blends together with the transport layer. Other protocols such as NetBIOS, used on Microsoft networks, use the session layer for reliable communications.

Layer 4: The Transport Layer

The transport layer provides a total end-to-end solution for reliable communications. This layer provides the mechanisms for reliable communications. TCP/IP relies on the transport layer to effectively control communications between two hosts. When an IP communication session must begin or end, the transport layer is used to build this connection. The elements of the transport layer and how it functions within TCP/IP are discussed in more detail later in the chapter. The transport layer is the layer at which TCP/IP ports listen.

Layer 3: The Network Layer

When packets have to get between two stations on a network, the network layer is responsible for the transportation of these packets. The network layer determines the path and the direction on the network in order to allow communications between two stations. The IP portion of TCP/IP rests in this part of the OSI model. IP is discussed in detail in the following section.

Layer 2: The Data Link Layer

Layer two, or the data link layer, is the mechanism that determines how to transmit data between two stations. All hosts that communicate at this level must be on the same physical network. The way in which the transmission of data at this level is handled is based upon the protocol used. Examples of protocols at the data link layer are Ethernet, Point-to-Point Protocol (PPP), Frame Relay, Synchronous Data Link

Control (SDLC), and X.25. Protocols such as Address Resolution Protocol (ARP) function at the Data Link Layer.

Layer 1: The Physical Layer

The last but most important layer of the OSI model is the physical layer. The physical layer consists of the objects that connect stations together physically. This layer is responsible for taking the bits and bytes of the higher layers and passing them along the specified medium. There are many examples of the physical layer that you should already have heard of, such as Cat5 cable, T1, and wireless.

Moving Data Along with TCP/IP

On the Internet and most networks, TCP/IP is the most commonly used protocol for passing network data. At the time of its development, TCP/IP used a very advanced design. Decades later, TCP/IP continues to meet the needs of the Internet. The most commonly used version of IP used today is version 4, the version covered in this book. The next generation IP, version 6, is starting to be used much more throughout the world. Many vendors, including Juniper Networks, Cisco, Microsoft, and Apple, are developing software that supports the new IP version 6 standard.

Over the course of this section, we will cover how systems use TCP/IP to interact, and we will review the IP and how its protocol suite compares to the OSI model. We will also discuss how IP packets are used to transmit data across networks, and we will examine the transport layer protocols TCP and User Datagram Protocol (UDP) and how they are used to control data communications in conjunction with IP. Finally, we will wrap up the discussion of TCP/IP with information about the data link layer.

Understanding IP

The Internet Protocol is used to get data from one system to another. The IP sits on the third layer of the OSI model, the network layer. When you need to send data across a network, that data is encapsulated in a packet. A packet is simply a segment of data that is sent across the network. In TCP/IP however, there are not seven true layers as there are in the OSI model (see Figure 1.2 for a comparison of TCP/IP and OSI model layers).

When an application needs to pass its communication to another system on the network, it passes its information down the protocol stack. This is the process that creates an IP packet.

Figure 1.2 OSI Model Layers versus TCP/IP Layers

OSI Model	TCP/IP Model
7. Application Layer	5. Application Layer
6. Presentation Layer	
5. Session Layer	4. Transport Layer
4. Transport Layer	
3. Network Layer	3. Network Layer
2. Data Link Layer	2. Data Link Layer
1. Physical Layer	1. Physical Layer

Let's look at an example of IP connectivity. We will be referencing the TCP/IP model, as it will be easier to understand for this example. Remember that the TCP/IP model is a condensed version of the OSI model. Use Figure 1.2 to reference the steps of the OSI model on the left to the TCP/IP model on the right. You can use your Web browser to connect to www.syngress.com and view the series of events that occur during a network (in this case, the Internet) connection. We will look at the course of action that happens for the first packet that is created for this connection.

First, enter the address in the Web browser and then press **Enter**. The browser will make a request to get the data from the server. This request is then given to the transport layer where it initiates a session to the remote machine. To get to the remote machine, the transport layer sends its data to the network layer and creates a packet. The data link layer's job is to get the packet across the local network. At this point, the packet is called a *frame*. At each junction point between systems and routing devices, the data link layer makes sure that the frame is properly transmitted. The physical layer is used during the entire connection to convert the raw data into electrical or optical impulses.

When the end station receives the packet, that station will convert the packet back to the application layer. The electrical impulses are changed at the physical layer into the frame. The frame is then unencapsulated and converted to individual packets. Because the packet is at its end destination, the network layer and transport portions of the packet are removed and then the application data is passed to the application layer. That sounds like a lot of work for just one packet to transverse the Internet, but all of this happens on a broadband connection in 30 milliseconds or less. This, of course, is the simplified version of how all of this happens. In the following sections, we will expand on this example and show you what happens behind the scenes when two stations have a network conversation.

The following list provides a rundown of the phases of connectivity:

1. The URL www.syngress.com is entered into the browser.
2. The user presses **Enter** and forces the browser to connect to the Web site.
3. The browser makes a request to the server.
4. The browser request is handed to the transport layer.
5. The transport layer initiates a session to the remote server.
6. The transport layer passes its request to the network layer.
7. The network layer creates a packet to send to the remote server.
8. The data link layer takes the packet and turns it into a frame.
9. The frame is passed over the local network by the physical layer.
10. The physical layer takes the frame and converts it into electrical or optical impulses.
11. These impulses pass between devices.
12. At each junction point or router, the packet is transformed to the data link layer.
13. The packet is taken from the data link layer to the network layer.
14. The router looks at the packet and determines the destination host.
15. The router forwards the packet to the next and all subsequent routers until it reaches the remote system.
16. The end station receives the packet and converts it back through the layers to the application layer.
17. The remote system responds to the client system.

IP Packets

As discussed in the previous sections, IP is essentially used to get data from one system to another. The anatomy of IP is very straightforward. In Figure 1.3 you can see what exactly makes up an IP packet header. An IP packet contains the very important application data that needs to be transported. This data is contained in the last portion of the packet. The IP portion of a packet is called the IP header. It contains all of the information that is useful for getting the data from system to system. The IP header includes the source and destination IP addresses.

Figure 1.3 IP Packet Header Contents

Version	Header Length	Type of Service	Length		
Identification			Flags		Fragment Offset
TTL		Protocol	Header Checksum		
Source IP Address					
Destination IP Address					
Options					
Data					

So the question remains, "how do IP packets actually get from system to system?" Let's reference our previous example of browsing to www.syngress.com. When the IP packet is formed, it includes the source IP address (the IP address of the client system making the request). This is like the return address on an envelope it tells the recipient where to send return mail to. The packet also receives the destination address of the Web server being contacted. There are other parts that are set in the IP header, but are not germane to this discussion. After the packet is created, it is sent to the originating system's routing table. The routing table is referenced and then the operating system determines which path to send this packet to. In routing, each system that receives the packet determines the next location or *hop* to send the packet to. So when sending information or requests across the Internet, there may be 15 hops or routers to go through before you get to the final system you are trying to connect to. Simply stated, a router is a system whose primary function is to route traffic from one location to another. As each router receives a packet it determines the next best location to send it to.

This, of course, is very simplified, as there are millions of routers on the Internet. Once the destination system receives the IP packet, it formulates a response. This is then sent back to the client system. The IP header contains the source address of the server that received the first packet and then the destination address of the initiating client machine. This is the fundamental basis of IP communications.

One of the confusing things about IP is that IP packets are not just used to transport data; the IP protocol suite does more than that. If you refer to Table 1.1, you can see a field called *protocol*. This determines which IP protocol the packet is using. All of the available IP protocols are specified in RFC 1700. Table 1.1 is a short reference of the IP protocols we will be discussing in this book. For example, if the packet was UDP, it would be using IP protocol 17, and if the packet was IP Security (IPSec) ESP, it would be using IP protocol 50.

Table 1.1 The IP Protocol Suite

Protocol Number	Name	Protocol
1	ICMP	Internet Control Message Protocol
4	IP	IP to IP Encapsulation
6	TCP	Transmission Control Protocol
17	UDP	User Datagram Protocol
50	ESP	Encapsulating Security Payload
51	AH	Authentication Header

One of the most important protocols in the IP protocol suite is the Internet Control Messaging Protocol (ICMP). ICMP is used as a messaging protocol to give information to the source or destination machine that is engaging in IP communications. Table 1.2 lists all of the commonly used ICMP types and codes. To give an example of ICMP, let's look at the common application *ping*. Ping is an application that is on pretty much any operating system, including SonicOS. It is used to test if a host is responsive from a network perspective. When you ping a host, an IP packet is generated that has the source IP address of the requesting system and the destination IP address of the system you are trying to contact. This packet then has an ICMP type of eight and a code of zero. The destination system then would receive the packet and recognize that the IP packet is *echo* or *echo request packet*. It then creates an ICMP packet that is a type zero code zero. This is an *echo reply packet*, acknowledging the original request.

Devices use ICMP for other reasons as well. If a system had a route in its routing table that specified a host could be found at a location that did not exist, the router it points to would send an ICMP message to the initiating host. That router would send a type three code zero or code one message specifying that the network or host is not available. Now apply that to the Internet and all of those millions of routers out there. This makes the ICMP protocol very helpful for notifying users when there is a problem with getting IP packets from one location to another.

Table 1.2 ICMP Types and Codes

Type	Name
0	Echo Reply

Codes	Name
0	No Code

Type	Name
3	Destination Unreachable

Codes	Name
0	Network Unreachable
1	Host Unreachable
2	Protocol Unreachable
3	Port Unreachable

What Does an IP Address Look Like?

IP addresses are 32 bits in length. They consist of four eight-bit numbers. An example of an IP address is 1.2.3.4. This looks like a very simple format, but it has a great deal of meaning. Each of the four numbers can contain a value from 0 to 255. IP addresses are allocated in blocks or subnets. A subnet is a grouping of IP addresses based upon a subnet mask. There are three major types of IP address blocks, class A, B, and C. Each class is determined based upon the three leading bits for each number. The class A grouping of IP addresses all start with the binary digit 0. The class B grouping of IP addresses all start with 10. Finally, the class C grouping of IP addresses all start with 110. In Table 1.3 you can see all of the ranges of IP addresses based upon class. There are two other classes of IP addresses, classes D and E, which have special functions that are not covered in this book.

Table 1.3 IP Address Ranges by Class

Class	Address Range
A	0.0.0.0 to 127.255.255.255
B	128.0.0.0 to 191.255.255.255
C	192.0.0.0 to 223.255.255.255
D	224.0.0.0 to 239.255.255.255
E	240.0.0.0 to 255.255.255.255

You can also use your own local computer to look at your IP address. We will use both a Windows system and a UNIX-based system as an example. Open up a DOS window on your Microsoft Windows system, then enter the command **ipconfig**. An example of this is shown in Figure 1.4. You can also do the same thing on a UNIX-based system by using the command **ifconfig**. An example of this is shown in Figure 1.5.

Figure 1.4 Microsoft Windows ipconfig Output

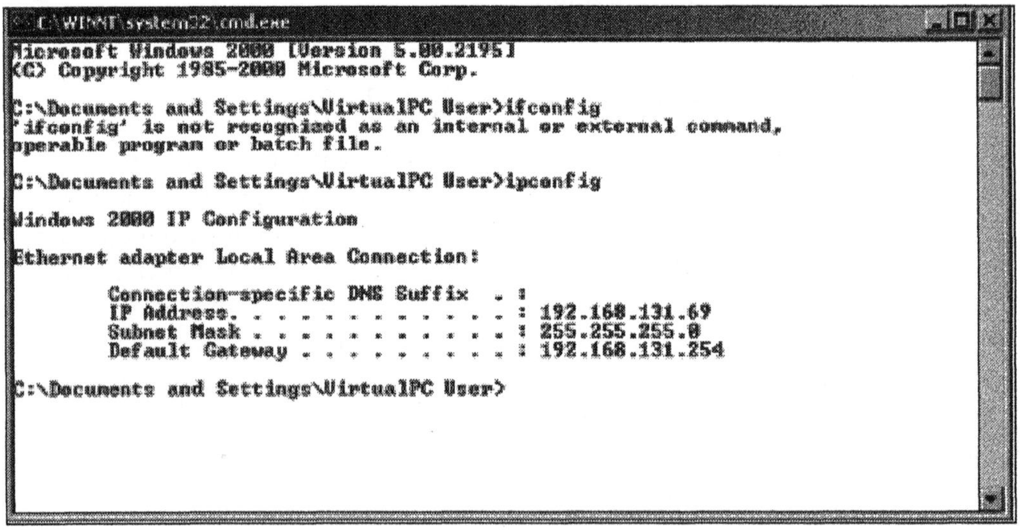

Figure 1.5 UNIX ifconfig Output

```
en1: flags=8863<UP,BROADCAST,SMART,RUNNING,SIMPLEX,MULTICAST> mtu 1500
        inet 10.6.0.123 netmask 0xffffff00 broadcast 10.6.0.255
        ether 00:0d:93:8c:62:2e
        media: autoselect status: active
        supported media: autoselect
```

IP Address Allocation

When you are creating a network, deciding on IP address allocation is very important. But with billions of options, how does one decide? The Internet Assigned Numbers Authority, or IANA, is responsible for allocating IP addresses. They determine which organizations get which IP address ranges. They are also responsible for conserving IP addresses and planning for future uses for IP addresses. Does this mean that you need to contact them to get IP addresses? Unless you are starting your own Internet Service Provider (ISP) the size of Qwest or SBC, you do not need to contact them. Your ISP will always assign any Internet or public IP addresses, and for private IP address networks you would use the IP addresses that are specified in RFC 1918. See Table 1.4 for a list of the private IP address ranges. A non-Internet routable IP is an IP address that is not routed on the Internet. If a packet was to leave your network with a source or destination IP address in one of these ranges, it would not get very far.

Table 1.4 RFC 1918 IP Address Ranges

Class	Address Range
A	10.0.0.0 to 10.255.255.255
B	172.16.0.0 to 172.31.255.255
C	192.168.0.0 to 192.168.255.255

NAT and Private IP Addresses

Most companies need to access Internet resources while preserving IP addresses. The solution is Network Address Translation, or NAT. NAT is used to hide your private IP address behind a public IP address. This allows private IP-addressed systems to access publicly addressed systems. NAT also provides a layer of security by hiding the real IP addresses of your internal network. A gateway device such as a SonicWALL firewall performs NAT for IP packets that pass through the device. Once the firewall receives an IP packet with the source IP address, it changes the private IP address into a public IP address. When the SonicWALL firewall receives the return packet, it translates the new destination address to the private IP address. There are two types of NAT: NAT source, and NAT destination.

TCP Communications

The Transmission Control Protocol is used to control the creation and form of data transfer connections. TCP is one of two transport layer protocols that are used as part of the TCP/IP protocol suite. TCP is designed to provide many functions mostly based on reliability. TCP is used for applications that require reliability over speed. When talking about speed at this level, we are talking about calculations of milliseconds or less. TCP functions as a stateful protocol. This means that during the communications, the connection has specific states in which it functions. There is a clear beginning, middle, and end of a TCP connection.

When a TCP session begins, it goes through a three-way handshaking process. Inside of a TCP header, options (called flags) are set. These flags identify the type of TCP message that has been sent. The three-way handshake process is shown in Figure 1.6. Let's continue to use our earlier example of using your Web browser to access www.syngress.com. When your web browser attempts to make its connection to the Web server, it attempts to open a connection to TCP port 80. A port is a specific communications channel specific to a particular application. TCP port 80 is the default port for HTTP.

The first packet that is sent to the Web server is a SYN packet. A SYN packet is used to synchronize a connection between two hosts. This packet is also sent with a sequence number that is used to identify the packet inside of this connection. This sequence number is to be used for the initiating systems packets. Next, the Web server receives the packet acknowledges it. To do this, the server creates and sends a packet with the TCP flags SYN and ACK. A packet that has the ACK (or acknowledgement) flag set is sending a message to the other system that says, "I have received your packet". A sequence number is also given to this packet that is independent of the sequence number that is associated with the initiating system's sequence number. The system that initiated the connection now sends an ACK packet to acknowledge the connection. The ACK packet has a sequence number that is incremented, as it is the second packet that has been sent from this system. The TCP session has now been created and the requested data from the Web server can begin to pass to the client.

The data that was requested is divided into packets by TCP. The client sends a TCP packet with the ACK flag for each part of the data. Again, each packet that is sent from the client has a sequence number that is incremented by one. The sequence number is used to identify all of the packets of a TCP exchange. If, for example, a client receives packets with sequence numbers 6, 7, 8, and 10, but never receives packet 9, the client will request that packet nine be resent from the server. On the client, all of the packets would be reordered before passing the data back to the application. When the connection is completed, the server system would send a packet with the FIN flag. This indicates that the connection is finished. The client would then send an ACK packet back to the server acknowledging that the conversation has completed.

Figure 1.6 TCP Session Initialization

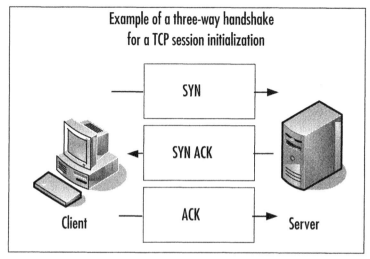

UDP Communications

The User Datagram Protocol is a connectionless protocol that is designed to stream data. When a UDP connection occurs, there is no beginning, middle, or end to the conversation. Data simply begins to flow between the two systems. UDP is a very simple protocol and is used when speed is an issue. UDP packet receipt is not verified. An example of a use of UDP is DNS queries. When you attempt to use your Web browser to access www.syngress.com, it must first resolve the name to an IP address. This would require a DNS query. The query is sent over a single UDP packet. The DNS server would then respond by telling the originating system the IP address of the Web server. Because the UDP response is faster than setting up a TCP session, UDP makes sense in these situations. Another example of using UDP is voice over IP (VoIP). The downfall, of course, is the lack of reliability, so you may have to employ other methods to guarantee delivery.

What Is a Port?

Both TCP and UDP support the use of ports. But what exactly is a port? Let's look at an example that can help further explain this. When you turn on your television, you get a picture and sound. Every time you change the channel, each new channel contains different content. This is much like a TCP or UDP port. Each port contains a specific type of content or application. When you tune to that port, you can access those specific resources. Theoretically, you can put any application on any port, but by specifying specific ports for specific applications, you can always be assured of the type of content you will find on a specific port.

This is why a specification of well-known ports has been established. Table 1.5 lists well-known TCP and UDP ports. Using our earlier television example, you can see that this is much like a channel lineup. If television programming could appear on any television channel, there would be a lot of confusion about which programming you were watching. When you use your television, the service provider gives you a channel lineup. This lineup is specified so that you know which channel is which. Most Web servers serve data over port 80. Again, they can serve the data over any port, but it would be very hard to get the content if you did not know which port to use.

Table 1.5 Well-Known TCP and UDP Ports

Well-Known TCP Ports		Well-Known UDP Ports	
FTP	21	DNS	53
SSH	22	DHCP-Relay	67
Telnet	23	TFTP	69
SMTP	25	NTP	123
HTTP	80	IKE	500
IMAP	143	Syslog	514
HTTPS	443	H.323	1719

Data Link Layer Communication

The last part of networking we are going to discuss is the data link layer, or layer two. This layer is essentially the protocol that operates on the specific physical medium. Each of the following function differently on the data link layer: Ethernet, ATM, Frame Relay, HDLC, SDLC, PPP, and Serial Line Internet Protocol (SLIP) to name a few. In this section how Ethernet functions will be focused on. As of the time of this writing the main layer two protocol that is used by SonicWALL firewalls is Ethernet.

Ethernet is the most commonly used medium today in corporate networks. It is inexpensive to use, easy to set up, and can operate at incredible speeds. The data link layer is used to communicate across the local medium. Figure 1.7 shows the breakdown of the use of layers and where they take place during system-to-system communication. When systems need to talk over Ethernet, they cannot use IP addresses, because Ethernet is at a lower level and it is used to move IP between layer three devices. So each device on an Ethernet segment uses a Media Access Control (MAC) address. When a station needs to have a conversation, the source and destination systems use their MAC addresses to identify each other. Each manufacturer is assigned a range to use when creating Ethernet adapters. Then each individual adapter is given a unique number to create the MAC address.

Figure 1.7 A Layered Look at Network Communications

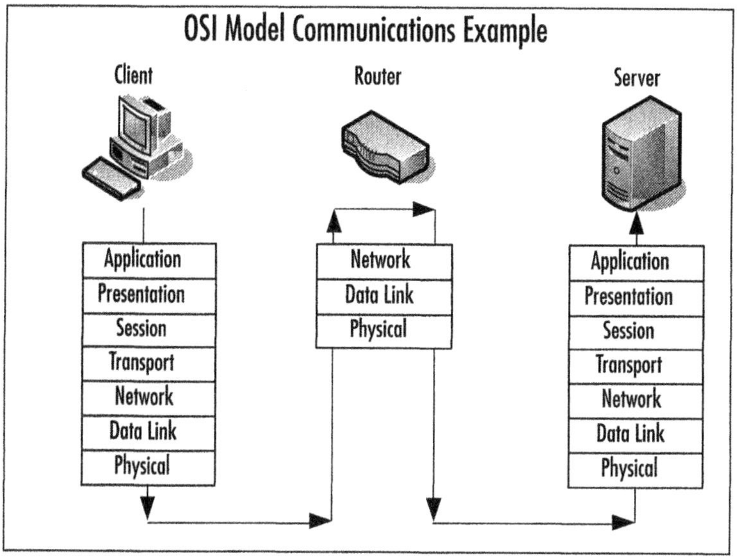

Because systems communicate via IP, but need to talk over Ethernet (which requires the use of MAC addresses), there has to be a way to resolve an IP to a MAC address. The method used is called the Address Resolution Protocol, or ARP. For example, if system A, which has an IP address of 192.168.1.10, wanted to view the Web pages on system B, which has an IP address of 192.168.1.25, before the communications can begin, system A must learn the MAC address of system B. System A broadcasts a request over the local broadcast domain asking who has the IP address 192.168.1.25. A broadcast is a communication that is sent out to every system that is within a broadcast area. All of the systems in the broadcast area get this request and the system with the requested IP address responds with a unicast message that specifies it has the IP address of 192.168.1.25 and also provides its MAC address.

Because almost everyone uses a computer today, a typical company can contain at least twenty computers or more. There are many ways to connect computers together. If you have just two systems, you can connect them with just a crossover Ethernet cable. A crossover cable is an Ethernet cable that allows two systems to directly connect to each other. If you have two to four computers, you could use a hub or bridge. If you have four or more computers, you will likely want to use a switch. A hub or bridge is a device that connects several systems together. When two systems want to access the Ethernet media to transfer data, their communications take up the use of the media while they are talking. If a third system wants to talk over the network, it simply starts talking and the data frames will collide with those of the already ongoing communication. An Ethernet segment where the media is shared between is called a *collision domain*. Switches, however, do not have this problem. When two systems begin a network conversation on a network with a switch, the packets are isolated and the switch prevents packets from colliding. If a system was to broadcast, however, the broadcast would be sent to every system connected to the switch. When the switch sends the data between two hosts, it sends it such a way that other network conversations are not interrupted.

Understanding Security Basics

The key to understanding network security is understanding networking. We hope the previous section has started you on the path to understanding networking. Just be patient with yourself while reading this book. There may be many new concepts that you have never heard of before. Working with these technologies over time well help solidify your knowledge. In this section, we discuss basic security concepts that will prepare you for the final section about firewalls. In this section, we focus on some of the different aspects of what it takes to have a secure organization. As you will see, there are no hard-and-fast rules about what it really takes to make your network secure. I have been to many organizations that would fall well below the line I would say is good security. However, some of those same organizations have gone years without a security breach. On the other hand, I have seen other companies spend much more on their security and have more problems with break-ins and data loss. Much like everything in the world, a balance is the best thing you can have for your network.

The Need for Security

Enterprise security is the hottest technology trend today. Every aspect of a company's data infrastructure has the need for security. With ever–growing, ever-evolving networks in every organization, managing security has become harder. For many organizations, the operating budget for security is less than one percent of there total company budget. When it comes down to purchasing security products, firewalls are the core product used to secure the enterprise network. However, firewalls should by no means be the only method used to secure your network, but used effectively, they can mitigate the risks of network security breaches and data loss. With integrated technologies such as anti–virus, deep packet inspection, Uniform Resource Locator (URL) filtering, and virtual private networks (VPNs), the firewall can provide a host of security applications all in one system. As the old saying goes, however, you should never put all of your eggs in one basket.

Introducing Common Security Standards

Security and network professionals use a number of currently accepted procedures and standards to conduct business and ensure that we are following the accepted practices for security and access. Although we have a responsibility as network and systems administrators to try to attain perfection in the availability and integrity of our data, we also have constraints placed on us in accomplishing those tasks. These constraints include budgets, physical plant capability, and training of users and technicians to maintain the security and integrity of the data. These constraints do not relieve us of our responsibility of maintaining the data safely and securely. To that end, we currently employ some accepted standards for security that help us perform our tasks to the best possible level. In this section, we remind you of the common security standards and briefly discuss them:

- **Authentication, authorization, and auditing (AAA)** AAA use is required in security operations for creating and maintaining the method of authenticating users and processes, and validating their credentials prior to allowing access to resources. It is also the method we use to grant access or deny access to the resource. Auditing of activity is a crucial part of this function.

- **Confidentiality, integrity, and availability (CIA)** CIA is the originally defined process that establishes the goals that we have used to try to protect our data from unauthorized view, corruption, or unauthorized modification, and to provide constant availability. Over the past few years, the CIA processes have expanded to include a more comprehensive guideline that also includes the process of defining risk and use of risk management tools to provide a more complete method of protection.

■ **Least privilege** This concept is used by the security planners and teams to define the levels of access to resources and the network that should be allowed. From a security standpoint, it is always preferable to be too restrictive with the capability to relax the access levels than to be too loose and have a breach occur.

Remember, too, that the security process involves a three-tiered model for security protection:

■ **Computer security**, including the use of risk assessment, the expanded CIA goals, and enterprise planning that extends throughout the entire enterprise, rather than to just a portion of it.

■ **Physical security**, in which we must build and include physical access systems and coordinate them with our network access systems.

■ **Trusted users**, who become an important cog in maintaining the integrity of our security efforts.

Common Information Security Concepts

A generic dictionary definition of *security* (taken from the American Heritage Dictionary) is, "freedom from risk or danger; safety." This definition is perhaps a little misleading when it comes to computer and networking security, because it implies a degree of protection that is inherently impossible to achieve in the modern connectivity-oriented computing environment.

For this reason, the same dictionary provides another definition specific to computer science: "The *level to which* a program or device is safe from unauthorized use" (emphasis added). Implicit in this definition is the caveat that the objectives of security and accessibility—the two top priorities on the minds of many network administrators—are, by their very nature, diametrically opposed. The more accessible your data, the less secure it is. Likewise, the more tightly you secure your data, the more you impede accessibility. Any security plan is an attempt to strike the proper balance between the two.

Defining Information Security

Over the last couple of decades, many companies began to realize that their most valuable assets were not only their buildings or factories, but also the intellectual property and other information that flowed internally as well as outwardly to suppliers and customers. Company managers, used to dealing with risk in their business activities, started to think about what might happen if their key business information fell into the wrong hands, perhaps a competitor's.

For a while, this risk was not too large, due to how and where that information was stored. *Closed systems* was the operative phrase. Key business information, for the most part, was stored on servers accessed via terminals or terminal emulators and had few interconnections with other systems. Any interconnections tended to be over private leased lines to a select few locations, either internal to the company or to a trusted business partner.

However, over the last five to seven years, the Internet has changed how businesses operate, and there has been a huge acceleration in the interconnectedness of organizations, systems, and networks. Entire corporate networks have access to the Internet, often at multiple points. This proliferation has created risks to sensitive information and business-critical systems where they had barely existed before. The importance of information security in the business environment has now been underscored, as has the need for skilled, dedicated practitioners of this specialty.

We have traditionally thought of security as consisting of people, sometimes with guns, watching over and guarding tangible assets such as a stack of money or a research lab. Maybe they sat at a desk and watched via closed-circuit cameras installed around the property. These people usually had minimal training and sometimes did not understand much about what they were guarding or why it was important. However, they did their jobs (and continue to do so) according to established processes, such as walking around the facility on a regular basis and looking for suspicious activity or people who do not appear to belong there.

Information security moves that model into the intangible realm. Fundamentally, information security involves making sure that only authorized people (and systems) have access to information. Information security professionals sometimes have different views on the role and definition of information security

The three primary areas of concern in information security have traditionally been defined as follows:

- **Confidentiality** Ensuring that only authorized parties have access to information. Encryption is a commonly used tool to achieve confidentiality. Authentication and authorization, treated separately in the following discussion, also help with confidentiality.

- **Integrity** Ensuring that information is not modified by unauthorized parties (or even improperly modified by authorized ones!) and that it can be relied on. Checksums and hashes are used to validate data integrity, as are transaction-logging systems.

- **Availability** Ensuring that information is accessible when it is needed. In addition to simple backups of data, availability includes ensuring that systems remain accessible in the event of a denial of service (DoS) attack. Availability also means that critical data should be protected from erasure—for example, preventing the wipeout of data on your company's external Web site.

Often referred to simply by the acronym *CIA*, these three areas serve well as a security foundation. To fully scope the role of information security, however, we also need to add a few more areas of concern to the list. Some security practitioners include the following within the three areas described above, but by getting more granular, we can get a better sense of the challenges that must be addressed:

- **Authentication** Ensuring that users are, in fact, who they say they are. Passwords, of course, are the longstanding way to authenticate users, but other methods such as cryptographic tokens and biometrics are also used.

- **Authorization/access control** Ensuring that a user, once authenticated, is only able to access information to which he or she has been granted permission by the owner of the information. This can be accomplished at the operating system level using file system access controls or at the network level using access controls on routers or firewalls.

- **Auditability** Ensuring that activity and transactions on a system or network can be monitored and logged in order to maintain system availability and detect unauthorized use. This process can take various forms: logging by the operating system, logging by a network device such as a router or firewall, or logging by an intrusion detection system (IDS) or packet-capture device.

- **Nonrepudiation** Ensuring that a person initiating a transaction is authenticated sufficiently such that he or she cannot reasonably deny that they were the initiating party. Public key cryptography is often used to support this effort.

You can say that your information is secure when all seven of these areas have been adequately addressed. The definition of *adequately* depends, however, on how much risk exists in each area. Some areas may present greater risk in a particular environment than in others.

Insecurity and the Internet

The federation of networks that became the Internet consisted of a relatively small community of users by the 1980s, primarily in the research and academic communities. Because it was rather difficult to get access to these systems and the user communities were rather closely knit, security was not much of a concern in this environment. The main objective of connecting these various networks together was to share information, not keep it locked away. Technologies such as the UNIX operating system and the TCP/IP networking protocols that were designed for this environment reflected this lack of security concern. Security was simply viewed as unnecessary.

By the early 1990s, however, commercial interest in the Internet grew. These commercial interests had very different perspectives on security, ones often in opposition to those of academia. Commercial information had value, and access to it had to be limited to specifically authorized people. UNIX, TCP/IP, and connections to the Internet became avenues of attack and did not have much capability to implement and enforce confidentiality, integrity, and availability. As the Internet grew in commercial importance, with numerous companies connecting to it and even building entire business models around it, the need for increased security became quite acute. Connected organizations now faced threats that they had never had to consider before.

When the corporate computing environment was a closed and limited-access system, threats mostly came from inside the organizations. These *internal threats* came from disgruntled employees with privileged access who could cause a lot of damage. Attacks from the outside were not much of an issue since there were typically only a few, if any, private connections to trusted entities. Potential attackers were few in number, since the combination of necessary skills and malicious intent were not at all widespread.

With the growth of the Internet, *external threats* grew as well. There are now millions of hosts on the Internet as potential attack targets, which entice the now large numbers of attackers. This group has grown in size and skill over the years as its members share information on how to break into systems for both fun and profit. Geography no longer serves as an obstacle, either. You can be attacked from another continent thousands of miles away just as easily as from your own town.

Threats can be classified as structured or unstructured. *Unstructured threats* are from people with low skill and perseverance. These usually come from people called *script kiddies*—attackers who have little to no programming skill and very little system knowledge. Script kiddies tend to conduct attacks just for bragging rights among their groups, which are often linked only by an Internet Relay Chat (IRC) channel. They obtain attack tools that have been built by others with more skill and use them, often indiscriminately, to attempt to exploit vulnerability in their target. If their attack fails, they will likely go elsewhere and keep trying. Additional risk comes from the fact that they often use these tools with little to no knowledge of the target environment, so attacks can wind up causing unintended results. Unstructured threats can cause significant damage or disruption, despite the attacker's lack of sophistication. These attacks are usually detectable with current security tools.

Structured attacks are more worrisome because they are conducted by hackers with significant skill. If the existing tools do not work for them, they are likely to modify them or write their own. They are able to discover new vulnerabilities in systems by executing complex actions that the system designers did not protect against. Structured attackers often use so-called *zero-day exploits*, which are exploits that target vulnerabilities that the system vendor has not yet issued a patch for or does not even know about. Structured attacks often have stronger motivations behind them than simple mischief. These motivations or goals can include theft of source code, theft of credit card numbers for resale or fraud, retribution, or destruction or disruption of a competitor. A structured attack might be neither blocked by traditional methods such as firewall rules nor detected by an IDS. It could even use non-computer methods such as social engineering.

NOTE

Social engineering, also known as *people hacking*, is a means of obtaining security information from people by tricking them. The classic example is calling up a user and pretending to be a system administrator. The hacker asks the user for his or her password to ostensibly perform some important maintenance task. To avoid being hacked via social engineering, educate your users that they should always confirm the identity of any person calling them and that passwords should never be given to anyone over e-mail, instant messaging, or the phone.

Another key task in securing your systems is closing vulnerabilities by turning off unneeded services and bringing them up-to-date on patches. Services that have no defined business need present an additional possible avenue of attack and are just another component that needs patch attention. Keeping patches current is actually one of the most important activities you can perform to protect yourself, yet it is one that many organizations neglect.

The Code Red and Nimda worms of 2001 were successful primarily because so many systems had not been patched for the vulnerabilities they exploited, including multiple Microsoft Internet Information Server (IIS) and Microsoft Outlook vulnerabilities. Patching, especially when you have hundreds or even thousands of systems, can be a monumental task. However, by defining and documenting processes, using tools to assist in configuration management, subscribing to multiple vulnerability alert mailing lists, and prioritizing patches according to criticality, you can get a better handle on the job.

One useful document to assist in this process has been published by the U.S. National Institute of Standards and Technology (NIST), which can be found at http://csrc.nist.gov/publications/nistpubs/800-40/sp800-40.pdf (800-40 is the document number).

Also important is having a complete understanding of your network topology and some of the key information flows within it, as well as in and out of it. This understanding helps you define different zones of trust and highlights where re-architecting the network in places might improve security—for example, by deploying additional firewalls internally or on your network perimeter.

Identifying Potential Threats

As you prepare your overall security plan and de-militarized zone (DMZ), it is important that you identify and evaluate the potential risks and threats to your network, systems, and data. You must evaluate your risks thoroughly during the identification process to assign some sort of value to the risks in order to determine priorities for protection and likelihood of loss resulting from those risks and threats if they materialize. In this vein, you should be looking at and establishing a risk evaluation for anything that could potentially disrupt, slow, or damage your systems, data, or credibility. In this area, it is important to assign these values to potential threats such as:

- Outside hacker attacks
- Trojans, worms, and virus attacks
- DoS or Distributed Denial of Service (DDoS) attacks

- Compromise or loss of internal confidential information
- Network monitoring and data interception
- Internal attacks by employees
- Hardware failures
- Loss of critical systems

This identification process creates the basis for your security plan, policies, and implementation of your security environment. You should realize that this is an ongoing evaluation that is subject to change as conditions within your company and partners, as well as employee need for access, change and morph over time. We have learned that security is a process and is never truly "finished." However, a good basic evaluation goes a long way toward creating the most secure system that we can achieve.

Using VPNs in Today's Enterprise

Ensuring that your data arrives safe and sound when it passes through a network is something everyone wants to have. In an ideal world, your data's integrity and confidentiality would be guaranteed. If you believe this all sounds like nothing more then a fantasy, you are wrong. These types of guarantees can be made when you use IPSec VPN technologies. When you use an IPSec connection either between two networks or a client and a network you can ensure that no one looked at the data and no one modified it. Almost every company today uses VPN technologies to secure its data as it passes through various networks. In fact there are many regulations that specify that a VPN connection must be used to pass specific types of data.

IPSec provides integrity checking to ensure that your data was not modified. It also provides encryption ensuring that no one has looked at the data. When two sides create a VPN connection, each side is authenticated to verify that each party is who they say they are. Combined with integrity checking and encryption, you have an almost unbeatable combination.

The Battle for the Secure Enterprise

This book covers the SonicWALL firewall product line and focuses on that specific product and technology. A firewall is the core of securing your network, but there are other products out there that should also be implemented in your network. These additional devices help ensure a network that has security covered from all angles. The following technologies are usually the minimum that companies should implement to provide security in the organization.

A *firewall* can contain many different types of technology to increase its importance in your network. Many firewall products today can integrate several different technologies. Almost all firewalls today provide VPN services. This allows secure streams of data to terminate to your firewall. This is usually over the Internet, but also be over other unprotected networks. When the traffic gets to your secured network it no longer requires encryption. You can also force users to authenticate before accessing resources through the firewall. This commonly used practice denies access to systems until the user authenticates. When doing this, clients cannot see the resource *until authentication has occurred.*

URL filtering is another requirement in many organizations. URL filtering provides a way to accept or reject access to specific Web sites. This allows companies to reduce liability by users accessing inappropriate Web content. Many firewalls can integrate with this type of scanning when used with another product.

Anti-virus is a requirement for any organization today. With more viruses being written, the last thing you want to have happen in your network is a virus outbreak. The Windows operating system is built to provide so many different functions that there are many ways that it can be exploited. In recent months, Microsoft has done a great job of coming out with security patches when or before an exploit is discovered. Typically though, when vulnerability is discovered an anti-virus company has a way to stop it much faster than Microsoft. An outbreak on your network can mean disaster, data loss, or loss of your job. Data is a company's most valuable asset today and loss of that data or access to it can cost companies millions of dollars or more per day. Firewalls can be used to perform virus scanning. These devices are usually deployed in a central area on the network. A tiered anti-virus solution is a requirement for any organization.

You should have anti-virus scanning on all of your desktops and servers to stop infections at the source. This will help prevent most virus outbreaks. Also, you should have anti-virus scanning on your Simple Mail Transfer Protocol (SMTP) mail forwarder and should be resident directly on your mail server. Your chances for a virus outbreak should be small as long as you keep all of those devices up to date with the appropriate virus definitions. There are also new technologies such as inline virus scanning in firewalls and other network appliances that can provide extra protection from viruses.

Patch management has become a truly Herculean effort with all of the software that an organization needs to run today. Patching operating systems and applications as soon as a vulnerability occurs is a must. With limited staff and increased software deployed, this task is almost impossible to accomplish. However, by providing an anti-virus system, you can provide a first level of defense against the spreading of malicious software or malware.

No matter what device or security you provide, everything usually comes down to some type of access token, usually a username and password. Using static user names and passwords is not enough anymore. Even fifteen to thirty days may be too long to keep the same password. Two-factor authentication, digital certificates, and personal entropy are leading the march to provide a stronger non-static type of authentication that is hard to break.

Your network has millions of packets traversing it every day. Do you know what they are all doing? This is where an intrusion detection or intrusion detection and prevention device comes into play. These devices detect application- and network-based attacks. Intrusion detection devices sit on your network and watch traffic. They provide alerts for unusual traffic as well as TCP resets to close TCP sessions. The newer technology of intrusion detection and prevention provide the ability to stop malicious traffic altogether as well as to alert on it. However, heavy tuning of the products is required to make it effective.

Access into your network should be encrypted whenever possible. This ensures that parties that are not authorized to see your data do not get access to it by any means. IPSec VPN clients are one of the most popular ways to do this. This type of client provides strong encryption of your data as well as access to your internal resources without having them be publicly accessible. A new trend in VPN solutions is the Secure Sockets Layer (SSL) VPN. These products allow you to put more behind them and do not require pre deployment of a VPN client.

Making Your Security Come Together

In today's security battlefield it almost seems impossible to win. You must identify the best products and procedures for your organization. If you have all of the suggested security solutions, but not enough staff to manage it, then the solutions may not be effective enough. Simply having the appropriate products is not going to resolve all of your problems; you must effectively understand how to use and configure the products. There is no easy solution regarding the best way to go about securing your organization. This is why companies all over the world spend hundreds of millions of dollars on consulting companies to come in and make security decisions for them.

Understanding Firewall Basics

A firewall is a device that is part hardware, part software and is used to secure network access. Throughout this book, we will cover every aspect of the SonicWALL firewall product line, its usage, and configuration. Before we begin to look at the various aspects of the SonicWALL firewall, we need to look at some general firewall information. This will give you a better perspective on the pros and cons of the SonicWALL firewall. Firewalls have come a long way since the original inception of the idea.

In the first part of this section we discuss the firewall in today's network. We look at the types of firewalls and how its importance has increased as well as there increased deployments in each network. Next, the many types of firewalls are discussed and contrasted and compared. Finally, we will review some common firewall concepts that will be used throughout the book.

Types of Firewalls

In the past, an organization may have had one firewall that protected the edge of the network. Some companies did not have their network attached to the Internet, or may have had perhaps one or two stations that would dial up to the Internet or to another computer that they needed to exchange data with. After the late 1990's, however, the need for the Internet, its information, and e-mail was undeniable.

With the requirement for instantaneous e-mail access comes the requirement for an always-on Internet connection. At first, companies would place their systems directly on the Internet with a public IP address. This, of course, is not a scalable solution for the long term. With limited IP addresses and unlimited threats, a better solution is required. At first, the border router that connected the Internet medium to the local network was used to provide a simple layer of access control between the two networks. With the need for better security, new types of firewalls were developed to meet the new needs for an Internet-enabled office. Better security, the ability for the firewall to provide more secured segments, and the need to thwart newer styles of attacks brought firewalls to where they are today.

Packet Filters

The most basic firewall technology is the packet filter. A packet filter is designed to filter packets based on source IP, destination IP, source port, destination port, and on a packet-per-packet basis to determine if that packet should be allowed through.

The basic security principles of a packet filter, such as allowing or denying packets based upon IP address, provide the minimum amount of required security. So then, where does the packet filter go wrong? A packet filter cannot determine if the packet is associated with any other packets that make up a session. A packet filter does a decent enough job of protecting networks that require basic security. The packet filter does not look to the characteristics of a packet, such as the type of application it is or the flags set in the TCP portion of the packet. Most of the time this will work for you in a basic security setting. However, there are ways to get around a packet filter. Because the packet filter does not maintain the state of exactly what is happening, it cannot determine the proper return packets that should be allowed through the connection.

For example, if you wanted to permit outbound access to DNS on UDP port 53, you would need to allow access for the return packet as well. A packet filter cannot determine what the return packet will in order to let it in. So now you have to allow access inbound for that DNS entry to return. So its source port would be UDP 53 and the inbound destination port would be the source port, which could be 1024-65535. Now add that up with all of the other applications you need to allow through the firewall and you can see the problem. Because the packet filter has no way to dynamically create an access rule to allow inbound traffic, the packet filter is not effective as a security gateway.

Application Proxy

Application proxies provide one of the most secure types of access you can have in a security gateway. An application proxy sits between the protected network and the network that you want to be protected from. Every time an application makes a request, the application proxy intercepts the request to the destination system. The application proxy initiates its own request, as opposed to actually passing the client's initial request. When the destination server responds back to the application proxy, the proxy responds back to the client as if it was the destination server. This way the client and the destination server never actually interact directly. This is the most secure type of firewall because the entire packet, including the application portion of the packet, can be completely inspected.

However, this is not dominant technology today for several reasons. The first downfall of the application proxy is performance. Because the application proxy essentially has to initiate its own second connection to the destination system, it takes twice the amount of connections to complete its interaction. On a small scale the slowdown will not be as a persistent problem, but when you get into a high-end requirement for many concurrent connections this is not a scalable technology. Furthermore, when the application proxy needs to interact with all of today's different applications, it needs to have some sort of engine to interact with the applications it is connecting to. For most highly used vanilla applications such as Web browsing or HTTP this is not a problem. However, if you are using a proprietary protocol, an application proxy might not be the best solution for you.

Stateful Inspection

Stateful inspection is today's choice for the core inspection technology in firewalls. Stateful inspection functions like a packet filter by allowing or denying connections based upon the same types of filtering. However, a stateful firewall monitors the "state" of a communication. So, for example, when you connect to a Web server and that Web server has to respond back to you, the stateful firewall has the proper access open and ready for the responding connection. When the connection ends, that opening is closed. Among the big three names in firewalls today, all of them use this reflexive technology. There are, as mentioned above, protocols such as UDP and ICMP that do not have any sort of state to them. The major vendors recognize this and have to make their own decisions about what exactly constitutes a UDP or ICMP connection. Overall though, most uses of stateful technology across vendors have been in use for some time and have worked the bugs out of those applications.

Many companies that implement stateful inspection use a more hybrid method between application proxy and stateful inspection when inspecting specific protocols. For example, if you were to do URL filtering on most firewalls, you may need to actually employ application proxy-type techniques to provide the proper inspection. This, much like application proxy firewalls, does not scale and is not a good idea for a large amount of users. Depending on the vendor and function, your mileage may vary.

Firewall Incarnate

A firewall can function many different ways, but always has the same basic requirements. A firewall is part hardware and part software, and the combination of each makes a huge difference. In this section we will look at the differences between an appliance-based firewall and a standard operating system (OS) running a firewall as an application.

First we will look at the firewall application that sits on an OS. In this case, there is an underlying operating system that runs on a standard computer system. The computer system consists of a processor, memory, and hard disk drive. The operating system will most likely be used for other functions without the firewall application. The operating system may be a multifunction operating system such as Microsoft Windows, Red Hat Linux, or Sun Solaris. To provide the utmost security, the operating system will have to be stripped down either by the end user or the manufacturer before it will be suitable for use as a secure gateway. The firewall software is then installed on top of the operating system. Generally, if you were to choose this kind of firewall, you would want the system to do nothing but act as a firewall. Enabling any other services, even acting as a print server, could result in a potential security vulnerability.

The other scenario is an operating system that has the firewall application integrated with it. In this case, the operating system is not used for any purpose other than to provide the firewall application. The device has a processor, memory, and flash memory for long-term storage. This device is an appliance.

In the first scenario, the firewall application is also limited based upon the limits of the specified hardware it is running upon, as well as the underlying OS. For example, if you wanted to add additional interfaces, it is limited to the specific type of hardware you are running. In most cases you can upgrade your hardware and then simply reinstall your application to upgrade the system.

In the second scenario we have an appliance whose sole purpose is to provide a firewall that will pass packets in and out as fast as possible while inspecting them based upon the defined security policy. The device's hardware is specialized for providing that single application. However, the device may have some specific limitations, such as limited memory or physical interfaces, and in many cases the only way to upgrade the device is to do a forklift upgrade and replace the entire device.

Firewall Ideologies

No matter which type of firewall you choose there are some basic design considerations involved. Placement is usually the biggest question. Where is the most effective location to place my firewall to maximize its effectiveness? Is one firewall enough? How do I protect the servers that I need to make publicly accessible? These and many other questions come to mind when discussing firewall effectiveness. Unfortunately, the answers to all of these questions are beyond the scope of this section.

DMZ Concepts

The use of a DMZ and its overall design and implementation can be relatively simple or extremely complex, depending on the needs of the particular business or network system. The DMZ concept came into use as the need for separation of networks became more acute when we began to provide more access to services for individuals or partners outside the LAN infrastructure. One of the primary reasons that the DMZ has come into favor is the realization that a single type of protection is subject to failure. This failure can arise from configuration errors, planning errors, equipment failure, or deliberate action on the part of an internal employee or external attack force. The DMZ has proven to be more secure and to offer multiple layers of protection for the security of the protected networks and machines. It has also proven to be very flexible, scalable, and relatively robust in its ability to provide the protection we need. DMZ design now includes the ability to use multiple products (both hardware- and software-based) on multiple platforms to achieve the level of protection necessary, and DMZs are often designed to provide failover capabilities as well.

When we are working with a DMZ, we must have a common ground to work from. To facilitate understanding, we examine a number of conceptual paths for traffic flow in the following section. Before we look at the conceptual paths, let's make sure that we understand the basic configurations that can be used for firewall and DMZ location and how each of them can be visualized. In the following figures, we'll see and discuss these configurations. Please note that each of these configurations is useful on internal networks needing protection as well as protecting your resources from networks such as the Internet. Our first configuration is shown in Figure 1.8.

Designing & Planning...

Know What You Want to Secure First

As you begin your DMZ design process, you must first be clear about what your design is intended for. A design that is only intended to superficially limit internal users' access to the Internet, for instance, requires much less planning and design work than a system protecting resources from multiple access points or providing multiple services to the public network or users from remote locations. An appropriate path to follow for your predesign path might look like this:

- Perform baseline security analysis of existing infrastructure, including OS and application analysis
- Perform baseline network mapping and performance monitoring
- Identify risk to resources and appropriate mitigation processes
- Identify potential security threats, both external and internal
- Identify needed access points from external sources
- Public networks
- VPN access
- Extranets
- Remote access services
- Identify critical services
- Plan your DMZ

Figure 1.8 A Basic Network with a Single Firewall

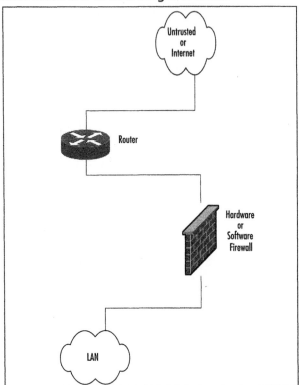

In Figure 1.8, we can see the basic configuration that would be used in a simple network situation in which there was no need to provide external services. This configuration would typically be used to begin to protect a small business or home network. It could also be used within an internal network to protect an inner network that had to be divided and isolated from the main network. This situation could include payroll, finance, or development divisions that need to protect their information and keep it away from general network use and view.

Figure 1.9 details a protection design that would allow for the implementation and provision of services outside the protected network. In this design, it would be absolutely imperative that rules be enacted to not allow the untrusted host to access the internal network. Security of the bastion host machine would be accomplished on the machine itself, and only minimal and absolutely necessary services would be enabled or installed on that machine. In this design, we might be providing a Web presence that did not involve e-commerce or the necessity to dynamically update content. This design would not be used for provision of virtual private network (VPN connections, FTP services, or other services that required other content updates to be performed regularly.

Figure 1.9 Basic Network, Single Firewall and Bastion Host (Untrusted Host)

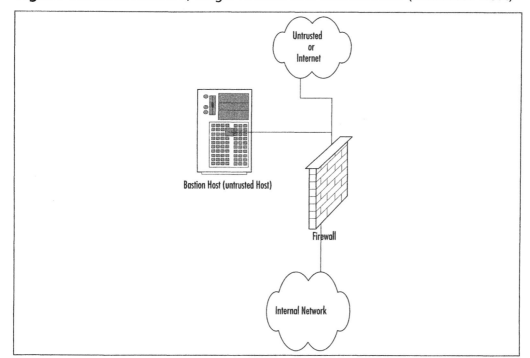

Figure 1.10 shows a basic DMZ structure. In this design, the bastion host is par-
tially protected by the firewall. Rather than the full exposure that would result to the
bastion host in Figure 1.9, this setup would allow us to specify that the bastion host
in Figure 1.9 could be allowed full outbound connection, but the firewall could be
configured to allow only port 80 traffic inbound to the bastion host (assuming it was
a Web server) or others as necessary for connection from outside. This design would
allow connection from the internal network to the bastion host if it was necessary.
This design would potentially allow updating of Web server content from the
internal network if allowed by firewall rule, which could allow traffic to and from
the bastion host on specific ports as designated.

Figure 1.10 A Basic Firewall with a DMZ

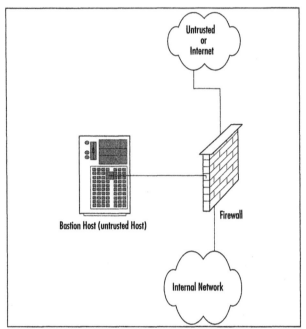

Figure 1.11 shows a generic dual-firewall DMZ configuration. In this arrangement, the bastion host can be protected from the outside and allowed to connect to or from the internal network. In this arrangement, like the conditions in Figure 1.10, flow can be controlled to and from both of the networks away from the DMZ. This configuration and method is more likely to be used if more than one bastion host is needed for the operations or services being provided.

Figure 1.11 A Dual Firewall with a DMZ

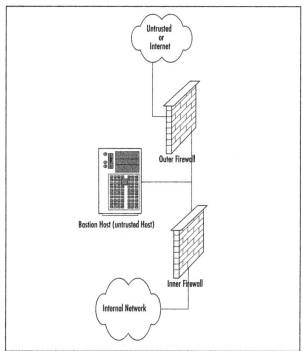

Traffic Flow Concepts

Now that we've had a quick tour of some generic designs, let's take a look at the way network communications traffic typically flows through them. Be sure to note the differences between the levels and the flow of traffic and protections offered in each of them.

Figure 1.12 illustrates the flow pattern for information through a basic single-firewall setup. This type of traffic control can be achieved through hardware or software and is the basis for familiar products such as Internet Connection Sharing (ICS) and the NAT functionality provided by digital subscriber line (DSL) and cable modems used for connection to the Internet. Note that flow is unrestricted outbound, but the basic configuration will drop all inbound connections that did not originate from the internal network.

Figure 1.12 Basic Single-Firewall Flow

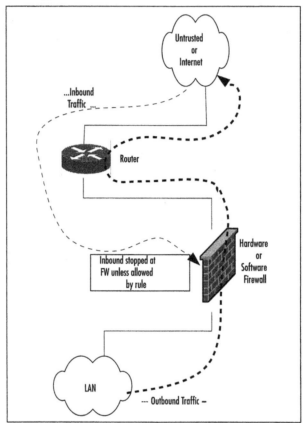

Figure 1.13 reviews the traffic flow in a network containing a bastion host and a single firewall. This network configuration does not produce a DMZ; the protection of the bastion host is configured individually on the host and requires extreme care in setup. Inbound traffic from the untrusted network or the bastion host is dropped at the firewall, providing protection to the internal network. Outbound traffic from the internal network is allowed.

Figure 1.13 A Basic Firewall with Bastion Host Flow

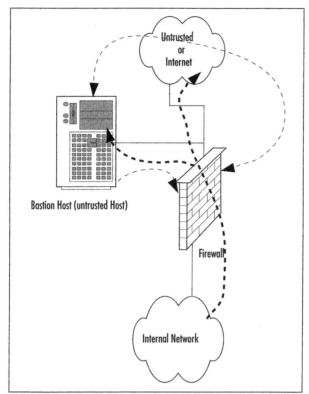

Figure 1.14 shows the patterns of traffic as we implement a DMZ design. In this form, inbound traffic flows through to the bastion host if allowed through the firewall and is dropped if destined for the internal network. Two-way traffic is permitted as specified between the internal network and the bastion host, and outbound traffic from the internal network flows through the firewall and out, generally without restriction.

Figure 1.14 A Basic Single Firewall with DMZ Flow

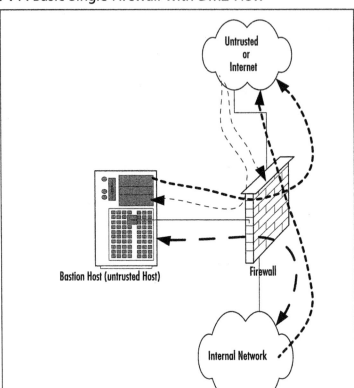

Figure 1.15 contains a more complex path of flow for information but provides the most capability in these basic designs to allow for configuration and provision of services to the outside. In this case, we have truly established a DMZ, separated and protected from both the internal and external networks. This type of configuration is used quite often when there is a need to provide more than one type of service to the public or outside world, such as e-mail, Web servers, DNS, and so forth. Traffic to the bastion host can be allowed or denied as necessary from both the external and internal networks, and incoming traffic to the internal network can be dropped at the external firewall. Outbound traffic from the internal network can be allowed or restricted either to the bastion host (DMZ network) or the external network.

Figure 1.15 A Dual Firewall with DMZ Flow

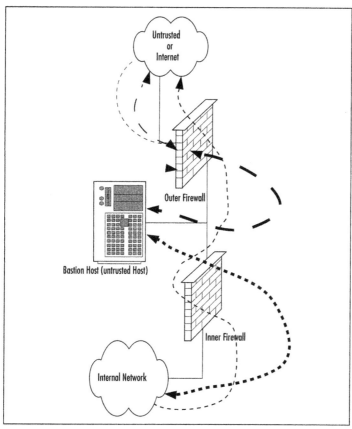

As you can see, there is a great amount of flexibility in the design and function of your protection mechanisms. In the sections that follow, we expand further on conditions for the use of different configurations and on the planning that it done to implement them.

Networks with and without DMZs

As we pursue our discussions about the creation of DMZ structures, it is appropriate to also take a look at the reasoning behind the various structures of the DMZ and when and where we'd want to implement a DMZ or perhaps use some other alternative.

During our preview of the concepts of DMZs, we saw in Figures 1.5 to 1.8 some examples of potential design for network protection and access. Your design may incorporate any or all of these types of configuration, depending on your organization's needs. For instance, Figure 1.5 shows a configuration that may occur in the case of a home network installation or perhaps with a small business environment that is isolated from the Internet and does not share information or need to provide services or information to outside customers or partners. This design would be suitable under these conditions, provided configuration is correct and monitored for change.

Figure 1.6 illustrates a network design with a bastion host located outside the firewall. In this design, the bastion host must be stripped of all unnecessary functionality and services and protected locally with appropriate file permissions and access control mechanisms. This design would be used when an organization needs to provide minimal services to an external network, such as a Web server. Access to the internal network from the bastion host is generally not allowed, because this host is absolutely subject to compromise.

Figure 1.7 details the first of the actual DMZ designs and incorporates a screened subnet. In this type of design, the firewall controls the flow of information from network to network and provides more protection to the bastion host from external flows. This design might be used when it is necessary to be able to regularly update the content of a Web server, or provide a front end for mail services or other services that need contact from both the internal and external networks. Although better for security purposes than Figure 1.6, this design still produces an untrusted relationship in the bastion host in relation to the internal network.

Finally, Figure 1.8 provides a design that allows for the placement of many types of service in the DMZ. Traffic can be very finely controlled through access at the two firewalls, and services can be provided at multiple levels to both internal and external networks.

In the next section, we profile some of the advantages and disadvantages of the common approaches to DMZ architecture and provide a checklist of sorts to help you to make a decision about the appropriate use (or not) of the DMZ for protection.

Pros and Cons of DMZ Basic Designs

Table 1.6 details the advantages and disadvantages of the various types of basic designs discussed in the preceding section.

Table 1.6 Pros and Cons of Basic DMZ Designs

Basic Design Utilization	Advantages	Disadvantages	Appropriate
Single firewall	Inexpensive, fairly easy configuration, low maintenance	Much lower security capabilities, no growth or expansion potential	Home, small office/home office (SOHO), small business without need to provide services to others
Single firewall with bastion host	Lower cost than more robust alternatives	Bastion host extremely vulnerable to compromise, inconvenient to update content, loss of functionality other than for absolutely required services; not scalable	Small business without resources for more robust implementation or static content being provided that doesn't require frequent updates
Single firewall with screened subnet and bastion host	Firewall provides protection to both internal network and bastion host, limiting some of the potential breach possibilities of an unprotected bastion host	Single point of failure; some products limit network addressing to DMZ in this configuration to public addresses, which might not be economic or possible in your network	Networks requiring access to the bastion host for updating of information
Dual firewall with DMZ	Allows for establishment of multiple service-providing hosts in the DMZ; protects bastion hosts in DMZ from both networks, allows much more	Requires more hardware and software for implementation of this design; more configuration work and monitoring required	Larger operations that require the capability to offer multiple types of Web access and services to both the internal and external networks involved

Continued

Table 1.6 continued Pros and Cons of Basic DMZ Designs

Basic Design Utilization	Advantages	Disadvantages	Appropriate
	granular control of resources and access; removes single point of failure and attack		

Configuring & Implementing...

Bastion Hosts

Bastion hosts must be individually secured and hardened because they are always in a position that could be attacked or probed. This means that before placement, a bastion host must be stripped of unnecessary services, fully updated with the latest service packs, hot fixes, and updates, and isolated from other trusted machines and networks to eliminate the possibility that its compromise would allow for connection to (and potential compromise of) the protected networks and resources. This also means that a machine being used for this purpose should have no user accounts relative to the protected network or directory services structure, which could lead to enumeration of your internal network.

DMZ Design Fundamentals

DMZ design, like security design, is always a work in progress. As in security planning and analysis, we find DMZ design carries great flexibility and change potential to keep the protection levels we put in place in an effective state. The ongoing work is required so that the system's security is always as high as we can make it within the constraints of time and budget while still allowing appropriate users and visitors to access the information and services we provide for their use. You will find that the time and funds spent in the design process and preparation for the implementation are very good investments if the process is focused and effective; this will lead to a high level of success and a good level of protection for the network you are protecting. In this section of the chapter, we explore the fundamentals of the design process. We incorporate the information we discussed in relation to security and traffic flow to make decisions about how our initial design should look. Additionally, we'll build on that information and review some other areas of concern that could affect the way we design our DMZ structure.

NOTE

In this section we look at design of a DMZ from a logical point of view. Physical design and configuration are covered in following chapters, based on the vendor-based solution you are interested in deploying.

Why Design Is So Important

Design of the DMZ is critically important to the overall protection of your internal network—and the success of your firewall and DMZ deployment. The DMZ design can incorporate sections that isolate incoming VPN traffic, Web traffic, partner connections, employee connections, and public access to information provided by your organization. Design of the DMZ structure throughout the organization can protect internal resources from internal attack. As we discussed in the security section, it has been well documented that much of the risk of data loss, corruption, and breach actually exists *inside* the network perimeter. Our tendency is to protect assets from external harm but to disregard the dangers that come from our own internal equipment, policies, and employees.

These attacks or disruptions do not arise solely from disgruntled employees, either. Many of the most damaging conditions that occur are because of inadvertent mistakes made by well-intentioned employees. Each and all of these entry points is a potential source of loss for your organization and ultimately can provide an attack point to defeat your other defenses. Additionally, the design of your DMZ will allow you to implement a multilayered approach to securing your resources that does not leave a single point of failure in your plan. This minimizes the problems and loss of protection that can occur because of misconfiguration of rule sets or access control lists (ACLs), as well as reducing the problems that can occur due to hardware configuration errors. In the last chapters of this book, we look at how to mitigate risk through testing of your network infrastructure to make sure your firewalls, routers, switches, and hosts are thoroughly hardened so that when you do deploy your DMZ segment, you can see for yourself that it is in fact secure from both internal as well as external threats.

Designing End-to-End Security for Data Transmission between Hosts on the Network

Proper DMZ design, in conjunction with the security policy and plan developed previously, allows for end-to-end protection of the information being transmitted on the network. The importance of this capability is explored more fully later in the chapter, when we review some of the security problems inherent in the current implementation of TCP/IPv4 and the transmission of data. The use of one or more of the many firewall products or appliances currently available will most often afford the opportunity not only to block or filter specific protocols but also to protect the data as it is being transmitted. This protection may take the form of encryption and can utilize the available transports to protect data as well. Additionally, proper utilization of the technologies available within this design can provide for the necessary functions previously detailed in the concepts of AAA and CIA, utilizing the multilayer approach to protection that we have discussed in earlier sections. This need to provide end-to-end security requires that we are conversant with and remember basic network traffic patterns and protocols. The next few sections help remind us about these and further illustrate the need to design the DMZ with this capability in mind.

Traffic Flow and Protocol Fundamentals

Another of the benefits of using a DMZ design that includes one or more firewalls is the opportunity to control traffic flow into and out of the DMZ much more cohesively and with much more granularity and flexibility. When the firewall product in use (either hardware or software) is a product designed above the home-use level, the capability usually exists to not only control traffic that is flowing in and out of the network or DMZ through packet filtering based on port numbers but often to allow or deny the use of entire protocols. For instance, the rule set might include a statement that blocks communication via ICMP, which would block protocol 1. A statement that allowed IPSec traffic where it was desired to allow traffic utilizing ESP or AH would be written allowing protocol 50 for ESP or 51 for Authentication Header (AH). (For a listing of the protocol IDs, visit www.iana.org/assignments/protocol-numbers.) Remember that like the rule of security that follows the principle of least privilege, we must include in our design the capability to allow only the absolutely necessary traffic into and out of the various portions of the DMZ structure.

Summary

In this chapter we reviewed the many different fundamental concepts that are important to networking. First we reviewed the OSI model. As you can see, the OSI model is very important to understand. It is used throughout this book and other documentation. In fact, almost any documentation referencing networking uses the OSI model as a base to explain how networking functions. An important fact to remember is that the OSI model is just that; a model. As you saw in the explanation of the TCP/IP model, the OSI model does not exactly fit together with TCP/IP. However, once you understand TCP/IP and how it works you will understand it for all platforms and applications.

If you were to truly have a book titled "Understanding Security Basics," it could easily span over a thousand pages. In this chapter we have brought together a concise version of that material to help you begin to understand the expansive world that is security. In the battle for the secure enterprise, the most important thing to remember is that there is no single solution to secure everything. Many products claim to have the silver bullet for securing your network, but this is nothing more than marketing. Each company has different restrictions on resources and has different security requirements.

In the last section we reviewed the basics of firewalls. The evolution of firewalls has been a long and harrowed path. As new threats come to light there will always be new technologies that will be created to stop these threats. The concept of a DMZ is an important one to understand. Segmenting your important hosts is one of the critical things you can do to secure your network.

Solutions Fast Track

Understanding Networking

- ☑ The OSI model is used as a reference for all networking protocols.
- ☑ TCP/IP is used as the core networking protocol today on both the Internet and in the enterprise.
- ☑ The TCP has clear defined points where a session begins and ends.

Understanding Security Basics

☑ Security is a process that is never finished; security needs are constantly changing as well as the needs for new technologies.

☑ There is no single product or solution that can be used to ensure your network's security.

☑ Each organization has its own specific needs to best help it minimize security risks.

Understanding Firewall Basics

☑ SonicWALL firewalls use stateful inspection to ensure the security of connections passing though the firewall.

☑ Firewall technology is constantly changing to meet the security needs of today's organizations.

☑ DMZ design depends on the designer's ability to accurately assess the actual risks in order to design an adequate structure.

Frequently Asked Questions

The following Frequently Asked Questions, answered by the authors of this book, are designed to both measure your understanding of the concepts presented in this chapter and to assist you with real-life implementation of these concepts. To have your questions about this chapter answered by the author, browse to **www.syngress.com/solutions** and click on the **"Ask the Author"** form.

Q: If the OSI model does not match the way in which TCP/IP functions, then why is it still used?

A: The OSI model is just that; a model. The OSI model was to be originally used as the model for the development of networking protocols. However, developers found the specifications too rigid for practical use. Most networking protocol suites do not follow the OSI model fully, but do follow the layered concept that was identified first during the development of the OSI model.

Q: Why would I want to use a SonicWALL firewall appliance when I could just use Red Hat Linux with iptables?

A: A SonicWALL firewall appliance is built with one thing in mind; security. It doesn't have to provide any other services. There are many more services and applications that run on conventional operating systems that can contain security vulnerabilities. Furthermore, SonicWALL does not have a hard drive. This is the most likely part to fail on a computer when running for an extended period of time. Finally, the SonicWALL firewall architecture runs on Application-Specific Integrated Circuit (ASIC) chips. These are specifically designed to perform special tasks providing more performance with less horsepower, while general purpose processors are not optimized for networking performance. This requires you to have more horsepower to provide the same function as a lower end SonicWALL firewall.

Q: You mention that each organization has different security needs. Why don't you provide a definite answer that can resolve my security issues?

A: Every organization has different types of requirements that they need to provide for their users. Some companies may have hundreds of Web servers, others just a few file sharing servers. There are some good baselines that have been outlined that do a good job of securing your resources, such as every organization's need for anti-virus. However, application-level protection may not be required for some organizations.

Q: Do I really need a DMZ? It only confuses my users.

A: Segregated networks are a requirement for any company that has resources that have to be accessible to the Internet or resources that everyone in the company does not need access to. The slight complexities that the DMZ creates simply do not outweigh its benefits.

Q: If I follow your guidelines for security, is this all I will ever need to secure my network?

A: Your organization's security requirements are something that should never be written in stone. You should always be on the lookout for new technologies and methodologies that can provide additional security to your environment.

Q: Why do I need to know so much about networking?

A: Knowing networking allows you to truly understand the risks that can occur in a network. When using networking, the more that you know about it, the more options you give yourself. For example, if you were trying to build a house to provide protection against a hurricane and all you knew was using sticks and straw to build with, your chances of building a successful house are close to zero. However, if you know about several construction styles then you would have more flexibility in choosing methods and materials that would provide you a better chance for creating a better house.

Chapter 2

Dissecting the SonicWALL

Solutions in this chapter:

- SonicWALL Security Product Offerings

- SonicWALL Firewall Core Technologies

- SonicWALL Product Line

☑ Summary

☑ Solutions Fast Track

☑ Frequently Asked Questions

Introduction

This chapter will introduce you to the SonicWALL firewall product. We'll begin by looking at all of the SonicWALL security products, exploring the wide range of products available, and allowing you to determine which is best suited for your security needs. A well-designed and properly implemented security infrastructure must be multitiered. SonicWALL offers three separate security product lines (discussed shortly) that can help mitigate your security risks.

SonicWALL delivers an integrated firewall and virtual private network (VPN) solution, the SonicWALL firewall. The firewall product line has several tiers of appliances and systems. This allows you to choose the right hardware for your network, giving the precise fit for your needs. Recently, SonicWALL also introduced a Secure Sockets Layer (SSL) VPN appliance. The SSL-VPN appliances offer a clientless remote access solution. With a clientless VPN approach, you remove the need for software deployment and management of the remote clients. You can easily deploy the SSL portal to thousands of users in mere hours. This is a great boon to any organization.

SonicWALL also offers a Content Security Manager. This appliance helps protect your network from a wide range of threats, including viruses, worms, Trojans, and spyware. It also provides URL (Uniform Resource Locator) filtering to block illicit or questionable websites.

We'll also be looking at the core technologies of the SonicWALL firewalls. These are the frameworks that are used through out this book. This discussion will give you an idea of the features of the SonicWALL firewall and will prepare you to actually implement these solutions on the SonicWALL firewall. We will look at fundamental concepts such as *zones*. Zones are used to logically separate areas of the network. This allows a more granular approach when you begin to write access rules to allow or deny network traffic.

In the last section of the chapter we will look thoroughly at the SonicWALL firewall products. The products range from small office devices that would allow for VPN connectivity into a central location, up to and including enterprise products that can carry as much as 2.4 gigabits per second (Gbps) of firewall traffic. This allows you to take your network to new heights with the options provided in the SonicWALL firewall product line.

The SonicWALL
Security Product Offerings

As mentioned earlier, SonicWALL offers a variety of firewall products designed to meet the needs of anyone from the home office to the enterprise. Since coming to the market in 1991, SonicWALL has become one of the top players in the industry. Today, with over a half million units in the field, they continue to be touted as one of the best firewall appliances on the market.

Firewalls

SonicWALL's premier security platform is its firewall product line. This product line provides integrated firewall and Internet Protocol Security (IPSec) VPN solutions in a single appliance. Antivirus and content filtering are also built into the SonicWALL firewalls. The core of the SonicWALL firewall is based upon the stateful inspection technology. This provides a connection-oriented security model by verifying the validity of every connection while still providing a high-performance architecture. The SonicWALL firewalls themselves are based on a custom-built architecture consisting of Application-Specific Integrated Circuit (ASIC) technology along with a main processor. ASIC is designed to perform a specific task and to do that task at a higher performance level than a general-purpose processor. ASIC connects over a high-speed bus interface to the core processor of the firewall unit a RISC (reduced instruction set computer) CPU.

Generally speaking, there are two distinct hardware architectures used by SonicWALL. In the home office and small business appliances such as the TZ 170, SonicWALL utilizes a SonicWALL security processor to handle the workload. Throughout the higher-end appliances, such as the SonicWALL PRO 3060, SonicWALL utilizes an Intel or x86-based main processor, along with a Cavium Nitrox cryptographic accelerator. The combination of the cryptographic accelerator and the x86 architecture has proven to be an effective hardware design, shown in the SonicWALL product line's overall stability and its high throughput in processing VPN and firewall traffic.

The firewall platform also contains additional technologies to increase your network's security. First, the products support deep inspection. *Deep packet inspection* is a technology that involves the inspection of traffic at the application level to look for application-level attacks. This can help prevent the next worm from attacking your Web servers, or someone trying to send illegal commands to your SMTP (Simple Mail Transfer Protocol) server. The deep inspection technology includes a regularly updated database. All of the appliances include the ability to create IPSec VPNs to secure your traffic. The integrated VPN technology has received the ICSA (wwwicsalabs.com) firewall certifications. This means that the IPSec VPN technologies have a good cross-compatibility as well as standards compliance. SonicWALL also offers three client VPN solutions to pair with the SonicWALL firewall. First, the SonicWALL VPN client provides the user with the ability to create an IPSec connection to any SonicWALL firewall or any IPSec compliant device. The second client product is the SonicWALL Global VPN Client. This custom-engineered software is designed to create tunnels with the SonicWALL firewall easily. It is designed for enhanced security as well as ease of management. Finally, the SonicWALL Global Security Clients work similarly to the Global VPN client, adding a software firewall to its functionality. The SonicWALL firewall product line also leverages a subscription-based antivirus software. This allows you to scan traffic as it passes directly through the firewall, thus mitigating the risks of viruses spreading throughout your network.

The SonicWALL firewall platform provides you with three management options:

- **Command-Line Interface (CLI)** The CLI is available only on certain SonicWALL models, and only with the use of a serial cable. Although SonicWALL has support for the CLI, it is not full-featured. You cannot set up access rules using the CLI. We will review more on the CLI later in this book.

- **Web User Interface (WebUI)** The WebUI is a streamlined Web-based application with a user-friendly interface that allows you to easily manage the SonicWALL appliance. This is the preferred method for configuring the SonicWALL appliance.

- **SonicWALL Global Management System (GMS)** A centralized enterprise-class solution that allows you to manage your entire SonicWALL firewall infrastructure. The GMS not only provides a central console to manage your firewalls, it also provides consolidated logging and reporting. This is a great option that allows you to see all of your network's activity from a central location.

SSL VPN

Many years ago accessing corporate resources and being productive while away from the office was a dream. With the advent of the IPSec VPN, accessing resources remotely became a reality. However, using IPSec VPNs to access resources resulted in more work for the network administrators. This was especially the case if a company had several hundred or even a thousand employees who all needed remote access. There was software to install and update and policies to create. Generally speaking, when you deploy IPSec client software you must also purchase licenses. This can become extremely costly if you have a fairly large user base. The ability to access a company's resources while on the go is now at an all-time high.

This is where SSL VPN comes into play. SSL VPN allows you to secure your internal resources behind a single entry point device. The remote users only require a Web browser capable of SSL encryption. The user connects to the SSL VPN gateway and begins his or her secure session. At this point the user can access many different types of resources. This provides secure ubiquitous client access, and because you don't have to deploy a client, you can easily deploy access to thousands of users in a matter of hours.

Content Security Manager

SonicWALL also offers an appliance-based content security management product. This appliance, the SonicWALL CF 2100, provides your network with an easy way to filter questionable content and increase employee productivity. Using its integrated antivirus, anti-spyware, and URL filtering, the SonicWALL 2100 CF can filter anything from Web traffic to peer-to-peer and IM application traffic. The Content Security Manager is deployed between your firewall and Internet router. The SonicWALL Content Security Manager 2100 CF also supports high availability to minimize possible network downtime.

The SonicWALL Firewall Core Technologies

SonicWALL makes use of several conventions and technologies throughout their entire product line. Throughout this book these conventions and technologies will be referenced and used to build concepts. By defining these technologies and concepts now you will have a fuller understanding when they are later referenced.

SonicOS

Sitting at the core of every SonicWALL appliance is SonicOS. SonicOS is the firmware developed by SonicWALL engineers that give the appliance its features and functionality. All SonicWALL appliances are built on and rely on SonicOS to do its job policing network traffic.

There are two modern versions of SonicOS: SonicOS Standard and SonicOS Enhanced. Often you will see the enhanced version listed with a trailing "e" signifying "enhanced." There are several major differences in SonicOS Standard and SonicOS Enhanced. Some of them include SonicOS Enhanced's ability to provide ISP (Internet Service Provider) failover, WAN (wide area network) load balancing, and zone-based management. Tables 2.1 and 2.2 list more detailed feature comparisons of SonicOS Standard and SonicOS Enhanced on some of the available SonicWALL models.

Notes from the Underground...

SonicWALL Firmware 6.x

We previously mentioned that there are two modern versions of SonicOS: SonicOS Standard and SonicOS Enhanced. However, there is another firmware revision used on some appliances. This previously unmentioned version, SonicWALL Firmware version 6.x (6.x is the current version number), is used on older appliances such as the TELE 2, TELE 3, SOHO 2, SOHO 3, PRO 100, and many other early generation SonicWALL appliances. SonicWALL Firmware version 6.x is not discussed in detail primarily because SonicWALL no longer produces and sells the product line that utilizes this code. Throughout this book, unless specifically noted otherwise, the information and procedures will be based on SonicOS Standard or SonicOS Enhanced, the modern predecessors of the old firmware.

If you're reading this book and have a SonicWALL appliance that operates using the older firmware, now is a good time to consider replacing that appliance. The newer products offered by SonicWALL provide several new feature enhancements designed to better protect your infrastructure from attacks, along with increasing throughput and availability. SonicWALL offers a secure upgrade program, which is designed to allow you to trade in or trade up from your old SonicWALL to a current SonicWALL appliance at a discounted price. For more information on the secure upgrade program, contact your SonicWALL retailer, or visit the SonicWALL Web site at www.sonicwall.com.

Table 2.1 Comparison of SonicOS Standard and SonicOS Enhanced on a SonicWALL TZ170

Feature	SonicOS Standard	SonicOS Enhanced
Zones	No Zone Support	20 Maximum
Policy-Based Firewall Access Rules	N/A	Yes
Address Objects/Groups	N/A	100 Objects / 20 Groups
User Objects/Groups	N/A	150 Objects / 32 Groups
Schedule Objects/Groups	N/A	50 Objects / 10 Groups
Service Objects/Groups	N/A	100 Objects / 20 Groups
VPN Zone Support and Rules per Security Association	N/A	Yes
Bandwidth Management on All Interfaces and VPN Tunnels	N/A	Yes
WAN/WAN ISP Failover and Load Balancing	N/A	Yes
User-Definable IKE Entries	N/A	Yes
Redundant Peer Gateway/ Secondary IPSec Gateway	Yes	Yes
Site-to-Site VPN Tunnels	Max. 10 with unlimited node license	Max. 10 with unlimited node license
DHCP Scopes/ Address Leases	2/255	2/255
Hardware Failover	N/A	N/A

Table 2.2 Comparison of SonicOS Standard and SonicOS Enhanced on a SonicWALL Pro3060

Feature	SonicOS Standard	SonicOS Enhanced
Zones	No Zone Support	20 Maximum
Policy-Based Firewall Access Rules	N/A	Yes
Address Objects/Groups	N/A	256 Objects / 64 Groups
User Objects/Groups	N/A	500 Objects / 64 Groups

Continued

Table 2.2 continued Comparison of SonicOS Standard and SonicOS Enhanced on a SonicWALL Pro3060

Feature	SonicOS Standard	SonicOS Enhanced
Schedule Objects/Groups	N/A	50 Objects / 10 Groups
Service Objects/Groups	N/A	100 Objects / 20 Groups
VPN Zone Support and Rules per Security Association	N/A	Yes
Bandwidth Management on All Interfaces and VPN Tunnels	N/A	Yes
WAN/WAN ISP Failover and Load Balancing	N/A	Yes
User-Definable IKE Entries	N/A	Yes
Redundant Peer Gateway/ Secondary IPSec Gateway	Yes	Yes
Site-to-Site VPN Tunnels	500	1,000
DHCP Scopes/Address Leases	2/1024	255/4096
Hardware Failover	N/A	Yes

If you've purchased a SonicWALL appliance with the standard OS and decide later you want the more feature-rich enhancements provided by SonicOS Enhanced, don't worry. SonicWall has made the process of upgrading an appliance to the enhanced OS very simple. Simply purchase the upgrade license to SonicOS Enhanced, download the new firmware, and follow the instructions to upgrade your appliance. We will cover the upgrade procedure later in this book.

Notes from the Underground...

SonicOS Standard?

With today's network security needs and architectures is there really a need to purchase a SonicWALL appliance with SonicOS Standard? To me the answer is clearly "no." Other than SonicWALL, no reputable security vendor still has a product with a pre-zone-based management architecture. The convention of zones makes firewall management a much easier task. Object-based management also makes access rules and traffic flow easier to follow and manage. When you combine these features with the other features provided in SonicOS Enhanced you can clearly see there is no reason to purchase an appliance with SonicOS Standard.

Both versions of SonicOS are managed through a Web-based GUI (graphical user interface). In order to manage SonicWALL appliances and ensure you have support for all management features, it is recommended you use a Java-enabled browser.

Zones

Originally SonicWALL's security model was to allow administrators to create rules based on traffic flowing in one physical interface and out another. In the earlier years of SonicWALL this approach may have worked well, but over time both networks and the Internet evolved. The realization set in that not only could attacks come from the outside, but attacks could also be assembled from within the local network.

Suppose Bill in Sales wanted to find out how his salary stacked up against the salaries of other salespeople. Since the local network would have been a flat network, Bill could easily initiate an attack on the HR and Payroll servers to try and access this information. Since nothing is in place to police the internal traffic, Bill's malicious traffic is not terminated. His malicious intent, for the most part, is unknown and his attempt to access restricted resources is successful.

With the release of SonicOS 2.0 enhanced firmware came the introduction of *zones* into the SonicWALL firmware. A *security zone*, or just plain "zone" for short, is nothing more than a logical method of grouping one or more interfaces or sub-interfaces and applying security rules to traffic as it passes between zones. To protect departments or more restricted resources from internal malicious intent, an administrator could enable zones, place different departments into different zones, and then create rules to police the traffic between the zones.

It is also important to note that the concept or usage of zones is not something unique to SonicWALL appliances. In fact, zones are used industry-wide in the firewall and networking world.

Interface Modes

When you first power up a SonicWALL and begin to deploy it, the default configuration is for the SonicWALL to utilize NAT (network address translation) and act as a router. In this instance, devices inside the firewall are assigned private IP (Internet Protocol) addresses that are not routable on the Internet. As traffic traverses the SonicWALL, the firewall creates a session and provides translation to ensure traffic is properly delivered.

However, there may be instances where you need to assign public IP addresses to servers or systems, but you still want to provide firewall filtering to the traffic. To do this, SonicWALL provides the ability to operate in transparent mode. When you operate a SonicWALL in transparent mode, the SonicWALL acts as if a bridge has been created between the WAN interface and one or more of the internal interfaces, assigning both interfaces the same address as is assigned to the WAN interface. Public addresses can then be assigned to devices behind the internal interface. When traffic is transmitted, no translation of addresses is performed.

Access Rules

An *access rule* is a statement that allows or denies traffic based upon a defined set of specifications. The base specifications are source IP address, destination IP address, source zone, destination zone, and service or port. With this information, you can create an access rule.

SonicWALL appliances have a couple of default access rules built into SonicOS. By default, there is a global access rule that denies any traffic from passing through the SonicWALL from the WAN to the LAN. So if the traffic is not implicitly allowed by another policy, it is denied. There is also a default access rule that allows any traffic generated and passing through the LAN interface to the WAN interface to be allowed.

Creating policies allows you to perform one of two actions on the traffic: allow the traffic or deny the traffic from passing. Allowing the traffic is the action you would want to use when the matching traffic is traffic you want to pass through the firewall. You would want to deny traffic when you want to prevent traffic from passing through your firewall. Each SonicWALL device has a limited number of policies. This is a license restriction, as well as a capacity restriction. You are not allowed to create new policies once you reach the maximum number of policies per device. This is set to ensure the performance numbers that are specified for the specification sheets. It would not make much sense to allow a low-end TZ 150 appliance to run 40,000 policies, only to have the performance at 1Mbps. These restrictions are not modifiable and are restrictions of each platform. There are many different elements involved in configuring an advanced policy. This includes traffic shaping, user authentication, NAT, alarms, URL filtering, and scheduling. This provides a great deal of configuration options.

Administering policies can be done in by of two methods: from the WebUI or by using the SonicWALL Global Management System. Each method creates the same end result, but performing each task is slightly different.

VPN

SonicWALL firewalls also provide VPN functionality and support. They can terminate most any kind of VPN tunnel, from site-to-site tunnels to dial-up VPNs. SonicWALL firewalls supports all of the standard elements you would expect a VPN device to include. It supports Internet key exchange (IKE), authentication header (AH), encapsulating security payload (ESP), tunnel mode, transport, aggressive mode, quick mode, main mode, MD5 (message-digest algorithm 5), SHA-1 (secure hash algorithm 1), DES (data encryption standard), 3DES (triple data encryption standard), AES-128 (advanced encryption standard), and Perfect forward secrecy to name a few. SonicWALL's appliances VPN capabilities are also interoperable, meaning they can be used to create VPN tunnels with most any other VPN appliance on the market.

Deep Inspection

Today's firewalls have to provide much more then just your regular Layer 3 and Layer 4 inspection. Filtering your ports, protocols, and IP addresses no longer provides the security necessary for preventing sophisticated attacks. Firewalls need the ability to look inside the packet for specific data that indicates an attack. A packet-level inspection product, such as an intrusion detection and prevention device, or IDP for short, is far more capable of pointing out potential attacks than a basic firewall. Typically, any device designed to specifically provide a service will do a much better job than a multifunction device. There are many instances where the implementation of Application Layer inspection can be a great benefit to a network.

A smaller network may not have the same management needs and financial means to gainfully install an IDP device. The integration of application-level inspection may be a better fit. Application-level scanning in an integrated device can also be used provide a second level of protection to your network by blocking specific attacks.

Deep inspection technology is the next step in the evolution of firewalls. Deep inspection allows you to inspect traffic at the Application Layer, relying on signatures to determine what content in a packet is malicious. SonicWALL incorporates this technology in its intrusion prevention system, or IPS. The SonicWALL IPS uses a database of signatures similar to those an antivirus software may use to scan files, except that it scans the packets as they traverse the firewall for possible matches to its signature database. When a match is detected, the SonicWALL can optionally log or reset the session and drop the packet – whichever you configure.

For example, if a worm spreading on the Internet attempts to exploit your IIS (Internet Information Server) Web server vulnerabilities by sending a specific string of characters to your Web server, a signature may be developed and released to identify that attack string. By applying the signature within the SonicWALL IPS, the traffic in that policy would be inspected for that specific string. Deep inspection is truly the next jump in evolution for the firewall. Look to the future to provide much more strength in this field for development.

Damage & Defense…

Application-Level Inspection

Firewalls have conventionally focused on Layer 3 and Layer 4 filtering. This means that the connection is only filtered based on IP addressing and TCP (Transmission Control Protocol) and UDP (User Datagram Protocol) ports and the options set at those layers. This can prevent systems that you do not intend to access your servers from accessing them. What do you do, though, when an attacker can use your firewall configuration against you? Suppose, for example, that your firewall is blocking all ports except for HTTP (Hypertext Transfer Protocol).

The attacker simply passes right through your allowed port and manipulates your Web application without you detecting it on your firewall. It is simply not aware of attacks at the application level. Now even though your Web server is on a separate DMZ (de-militarized zone) than your database server, the attacker uses your Web application to access the secured database and takes your customers' credit card information and identities. If you think that this is nothing but a good story, think again. Ever hear of SQL injection? If not, Google it. This type of attack goes on every day and many organizations are not aware of this kind of threat. Talented individuals who understand Web applications and their designs can easily snake through your applications and extract data from your database.

So does this mean that you need to disable access to your Web server and dismantle your e-commerce efforts? Of course not. You must, however, use security products that provide application-level inspection to attempt to identify these attacks. The best method is to first have a penetration test done on your

Continued

application to determine what type of vulnerabilities your applications may have. Next, begin implementing products that can determine what are attacks and what is normal traffic. The deep inspection software integrated into the SonicWALL firewall can help protect against many of the unstructured attacks that can be damaging to your Web server. However, structured attacks need a stronger tool such as the IDP to mitigate the risks of these attacks.

Using tools such as IDPs and the deep inspection technology is not something that you just turn on and hope for the best. Initially when implementing an IDP system, you may see many false positives. To make this type of application-level inspecting technologies work effectively you need to tune them for your network. This can take a great deal of effort and time to ensure that your network is using these devices effectively. Generally it's best to start with an IDP system configured with as stringent a ruleset as possible and the make changes as necessary to not disrupt the flow of normal traffic. Many times organizations purchase devices like this hoping that they will ensure that a poorly written application will be completely secured. Many times some simple programming techniques can enhance the security of your applications greatly.

Device Architecture

The engineers at SonicWALL developed the SonicWALL appliances with one thing in mind—designing a purpose-driven appliance with extreme speed and reliability. Developed from the ground up to provide exceptional throughput, the firewall engineers produced an amazing device that remains among the top vendors on the market. The SonicWALL product line is a layered architecture, designed to provide optimal performance for critical security applications.

The firewall connects all of its components together with a high-speed bus configuration to connect all of the components together. The SonicWALL product line utilizes a cryptographic accelerator to perform services such as encryption and decryption of VPN traffic. An ASIC is a chip that is designed for a single purpose. This allows that single purpose to be performed much faster then as if you were using a general-purpose microprocessor to compute the task. The SonicWALL firewall architecture has been designed to provide what a firewall running on a general-purpose operating system cannot. For example, utilizing a general-purpose box configured as a firewall decrypting VPN traffic generally causes a heavy load on the CPU. The SonicWALL contains ASICs and processors specifically designed to do the decryption at the hardware level, thus reducing the load across the system, and increasing throughput.

Tools & Traps...

Choosing the Right Tool for the Job

When you plan to purchase a SonicWALL appliance, you should put a great deal of thought into your network's needs. The hardware contained within the appliances cannot be upgraded. When purchasing an appliance you need to think about not just today, but tomorrow as well. Realistically, you should look at the life of the product over the next three years. Think about how your network will change and/or grow and make your purchasing decision based on the planned changes. This will provide you for the right amount of growth room for your network.

In many lower end networks where you have just an internal LAN (local area network) and an Internet connection, an extremely significant amount of throughput is not required. Even a SonicWALL TZ170 firewall appliance can easily handle even a hefty DS3 circuit to the Internet providing 45 Mbps. This said, choosing a firewall can be hard work. Because these devices lack the capability to be upgraded, many people looking at a device such as SonicWALL may think twice, and if they don't, they should. As you can see with the range of available products offered, a proper selection of the correct appliance can easily overcome your cognitive dissidence when choosing a SonicWALL firewall.

The SonicWALL Product Line

The SonicWALL product line is very diverse, with products designed for everything from home office use to enterprise-class networks. One of the great parts of the SonicWALL firewall product line is that no matter what tier of device, the configuration of each device remains similar. Once you become familiar with the architecture of one SonicWALL appliance, it is easy to understand and configure another SonicWALL model. All SonicWALL appliances support the same management options; the WebUI and the SonicWALL GMS. Additionally, some models include support for a CLI. Models that include limited management with the CLI are the SonicWALL TZ 170, SonicWALL Pro 2040, and the SonicWALL Pro 4060, all running the enhanced firmware.

The architecture on all of the platforms remains very similar, leveraging the power of a RISC processor and ASICs to provide a high-performance operating system. Many systems that you are familiar with, such as Intel-based Pentium systems, use the less efficient complex instruction set computer (CISC) processor. All of the devices use flash memory as the long-term storage option. None of the firewalls rely on a hard disk to run. Not relying on a hard disk eliminates moving parts and helps to decrease the chances of failure.

Product Line

In this section we will review all of the products in the current SonicWALL line, starting with the low-end devices, and finishing with the high-end products. At the end of the section we will review the enterprise management options that SonicWALL has to offer. Table 2.3 offers a quick glimpse at the line of firewalls available from SonicWALL, from lower-end appliances to higher end.

Table 2.3 Overview of the SonicWALL Product Line

Model	Product Class	Maximum Interfaces	Firewall Throughput	Estimated Price Range
TZ 150	SOHO	5 (includes 4 port switch)	30 Mbps	$330-400
TZ 150 Wireless	SOHO	5 (includes 4 port switch)	30 Mbps	$430-500
TZ 170	Remote / Branch Office	7 (includes 5 port switch)	90 Mbps	$370-1,300
TZ 170 SP	Remote / Branch Office	7 (includes 5 port switch) Analog modem	90 Mbps	$600-750
TZ 170 Wireless	Remote / Branch Office	7 (includes 5 port switch)	90 Mbps	$500-1,100
TZ 170 SP Wireless	Remote / Branch Office	7 (includes 5 port switch) Analog modem	90 Mbps	$825-1,100
PRO 1260	Midrange	26 (includes 24 port switch)	90 Mbps	$825-1,600
PRO 2040	Midrange	3 (4 with Enhanced OS)	200 Mbps	$1,675-2,700
PRO 3060	High Range / Enterprise	3 (6 with Enhanced OS	300 Mbps	$2,325-2,800

Continued

Table 2.3 continued Overview of the SonicWALL Product Line

Model	Product Class	Maximum Interfaces	Firewall Throughput	Estimated Price Range
PRO 4060	High Range / Enterprise	6	300 Mbps	$4,500-5,000
PRO 4100	High Range / Enterprise	10 (Gigabit)	800 Mbps	N/A
PRO 5060c / PRO 5060f	High Range / Enterprise	6 Copper (5060c) 4 Copper; 2 Fiber (5060f)	2.4 Gbps	$11,000-13,000
Content Security Manager 2100 CF	Content Filter	N/A	N/A	$2,000-10,000
SSL-VPN 200	SSL VPN Appliance	N/A	N/A	$575-700
SSL-VPN 2000	SSL VPN Appliance	N/A	N/A	$1,950-2,500
Global VPN Client	VPN Client	N/A	N/A	$50-*
Global Security Client	VPN Client / Security software	N/A	N/A	$250-*
Global Management System Software	SonicWALL Appliance Management	N/A	N/A	$2,000-*

* Pricing is based on the number of client licenses. The prices listed are the starting prices.

SonicWALL VPN Clients

In today's high-paced world, remote access to company resources is a requirement for successful organizations. However, company resources must also be secured to prevent unauthorized access or data loss. SonicWALL offers three software clients that do just that – the SonicWALL VPN client, the SonicWALL Global VPN Client, and the SonicWALL Global Security Client. All three clients are designed to maintain the balance between accessibility and security. All VPN clients are integrated with the rest of the SonicWALL product line.

The SonicWALL VPN Client provides an easy-to-use interface to configure and connect to IPSec gateway endpoints. You are not limited to client access of the SonicWALL VPN firewalls; the SonicWALL VPN Client is capable of connecting to any IPSec gateway. Providing standards-based IPSec connectivity is just part of the SonicWALL VPN client. The XAuth Extended Authentication protocol is also supported by the client. XAuth supports handing out an IP address and DNS (domain name system) settings to a virtual interface on the client. The SonicWALL VPN Client is capable of supporting up to one hundred concurrent IPSec VPN tunnels.

The SonicWALL Global VPN Client provides an interface that's easy to configure and connect to IPSec gateway endpoints. The XAuth Extended Authentication protocol is also supported by the SonicWALL Global VPN Client. XAuth supports handing out an IP address and DNS (domain name system) settings to a virtual interface on the client.

The SonicWALL Global Security Client has an integrated client firewall to protect the remote users system. This client allows the end user to connect securely to the enterprise network over the industry standard IPSec. The interface of the client allows the user to quickly configure a VPN connection. It also provides the administrator with the ability to create and then export a VPN policy that can be deployed to all remote users. The crowning feature of the Security Client is the integrated firewall. This firewall allows you to protect the end user's system from intrusions and network attacks. Not only does this protect the end user's system, but it also protects your company's network by preventing malicious attackers from connecting through a VPN client's system into the company's network. SonicWALL VPN and Security Clients provide easy, secured access to your mobile workforce.

Small Office/Home Office

Designed for remote locations or remote users with the need for a dedicated security appliance, the Small Office/Home Office (SOHO) line of SonicWALL firewall appliances provide enterprise-class security at a low cost entry point. These appliances work great for use for terminating a site-to-site VPN from a corporate office to a remote site for a small number of users. These devices still support the easy-to-use WebUI management interface that the high-end appliances and systems do. These appliances have a small footprint and can easily be stacked on a table or desk. It is important to note the throughput for the SOHO line when using IPS or Gateway Antivirus, as when these services are enabled, the appliance would not have the ability to support a DS3 circuit's full speed. The Small Office Home Office line of products is given in Table 2.4.

Table 2.4 Small Office/Home Office Appliances

	TZ 150	TZ 150 Wireless	TZ 170	TZ 170 SP	TZ 170 Wireless	TZ 170 SP Wireless
Interfaces	5	5	7	7	7	7
Max IP Address Behind	10	0	10, 25, or No limit*	10	10, 25, or No limit*	10
Maximum Throughput Firewall VPN**	30 Mbps 90 Mbps	10 Mbps 30 Mbps	30 Mbps 90 Mbps	10 Mbps 30 Mbps	90 Mbps 90 Mbps	30 Mbps 30 Mbps
Maximum Sessions	2,000	2,000	6,000	6,000	6,000	6,000
Maximum Site-to-Site VPN Tunnels	2	2	2/10/10*	2	2/10/10*	2
Maximum Client VPN Tunnels	2	2	5/50/50*	5/50/50*	5	5
Maximum Policies	20	20	100/250*	100/250*	100/250*	100/250*
Security Zones	No	No	Yes***	Yes***	Yes***	Yes
Object-Based Management	No	No	Yes***	Yes***	Yes***	Yes
Opt Port (DMZ Port)	No	No	Yes	Yes	Yes	Yes
Analog Modem (Integrated)	No	No	No	No	Yes	Yes
Advanced Features						
-ISP Failover	No	No	Yes*	Yes*	Yes*	Yes
-WAN/WAN Failover	No	No	Yes*	Yes*	Yes*	Yes
-Load Balancing	No	No	Yes*	Yes*	Yes*	Yes

Continued

Table 2.4 continued Small Office/Home Office Appliances

	TZ 150	TZ 150 Wireless	TZ 170	TZ 170 SP	TZ 170 Wireless	TZ 170 SP Wireless
Anti-virus Scanning Throughput	8 Mbps	8 Mbps	8 Mbps	8 Mbps	8 Mbps	8 Mbps
Intrusion Prevention Service Throughput	8 Mbps	8 Mbps	8 Mbps	8 Mbps	8 Mbps	8 Mbps
Can Be Upgraded to SonicOS Enhanced	No	No	Yes	Yes	Yes	Yes

* Based on installation of upgrade license

** Based on 3DES/AES VPN tunnel

*** With Enhanced OS

The SonicWALL TZ 150 is designed for very small office and home office users. The TZ 150 has an integrated four-port Auto-MDIX 10/100 switch. It supports up to 2000 concurrent sessions from a maximum of 10 nodes. Firewall throughput is around 30 megabits per second (Mbps), with VPN throughput around 10 Mbps. The SonicWALL TZ 150 supports two site-to-site VPN policies, and a maximum of two client VPN licenses. Like the midrange and higher-end models, the TZ 150's firewall utilizes deep packet inspection.

The SonicWALL TZ 150 Wireless contains many of the same features as the TZ 150, but it also provides support for 802.11b/g wireless networks. The TZ 150 Wireless has a built-in access point, and also provides wireless guest services and wireless intrusion detection and prevention.

Both the SonicWALL TZ 150 and TZ 150 Wireless ship with SonicOS Standard. It is important to note that neither of the TZ 150 series can be upgraded to SonicOS Enhanced. The inability to upgrade the OS is a good reason to step up one level and deploy the TZ 170.

The SonicWALL TZ 170 is an ideal solution for any small office or home office user. The base model is very versatile. The TZ 170 can be purchased with the ability to support ten, twenty-five, or an unlimited number of nodes. Note that *unlimited nodes* means there is no restriction built into the software on the appliance. The more nodes the SonicWALL is providing services for, the higher the load on the appliance, and the more the throughput will decrease.

The SonicWALL TZ 170 provides seven 10/100 interfaces, including a five-port switch. At 90 Mbps, the TZ 170 can easily support a DS3 circuit. The TZ 170 can also support up to 30 Mbps throughput for VPN traffic. The TZ 170 supports up to 10 site-to-site VPN policies, and a maximum of 50 client VPN tunnels. The SonicWALL TZ 170 can support a maximum of 6,000 concurrent sessions.

The SonicWALL TZ 170 is the lowest end model in the SonicWALL product line to support features such as WAN failover and load balancing, provided your TZ 170 is running SonicOS Enhanced. The TZ 170 also provides an OPT (optional) port, which is used to provide these services. It can also be used to provide your network with a DMZ.

The SonicWALL TZ 170 SP is the TZ 170 with an additional piece of hardware. The SonicWALL TZ 170 SP is designed to provide continuous uptime by utilizing an integrated analog modem as a failover device. This can provide continuous uptime in event of a failure of a broadband link. The TZ 170 SP, however, comes only as a 10-node appliance.

The SonicWALL TZ 170 Wireless adds an integrated wireless access point to the TZ 170's base hardware configuration. Using this access point, the TZ 170 Wireless can provide secure 802.11b/g wireless networking to your wireless devices. The TZ 170 Wireless can also provide guest wireless services. The TZ 170 Wireless also provides support for power over Ethernet.

Combining all of the TZ 170 features into one appliance is the TZ 170 SP Wireless. This product includes an integrated analog modem for a dial backup, and includes an integrated 802.11b/g wireless access point. Like the base model SonicWALL TZ 170 SP, the TZ 170 SP Wireless is only available in a ten-node model. Like the TZ 170 Wireless, the TZ 170 Wireless SP also supports the use of power over Ethernet.

Midrange

The SonicWALL PRO 1260 and SonicWALL PRO 2040 fall into the midrange category. These appliances are designed for use in branch and remote offices, or even in small or medium-sized businesses. They are designed to provide a solid gateway and firewall solution, as well as to provide secure VPN access. Both the SonicWALL PRO 1260 and PRO 2040 are rack-mountable appliances. Table 2.5 details the SonicWALL midrange appliances.

Table 2.5 Midrange SonicWALL Appliances

	PRO 1260	PRO 2040
Interfaces	26 (Includes 24 port switch)	3/4*
Max IP Address Behind	No Limit	No Limit
Maximum Throughput		
Firewall	90 Mbps	200 Mbps
VPN**	30 Mbps	50Mbps
Maximum Sessions	6,000	32,000
Maximum Site-to-Site VPN Tunnels	25	50
Maximum Client VPN Tunnels	50	100
Maximum Policies	150/300*	150/1,000*
Security Zones	Yes*	Yes*
Object-Based Management	Yes*	Yes*

Continued

www.syngress.com

Table 2.5 continued Midrange SonicWALL Appliances

	PRO 1260	PRO 2040
ISP Failover	Yes*	Yes*
WAN/WAN Failover	Yes*	Yes*
Load Balancing	Yes*	Yes*
Hardware Failover	No	Yes*
Anti-virus Scanning Throughput	8 Mbps	40 Mbps
Intrusion Prevention Service Throughput	8 Mbps	39 Mbps

* With Enhanced OS

** Based on 3DES/AES VPN tunnel

The SonicWALL PRO 1260 is designed with the idea of being the core of a small business or branch office network integrated into a single appliance. Not only does the PRO 1260 provide deep inspection firewall and VPN capabilities, it also provides a 24-port 10/100 Ethernet switch. The integrated switch also includes Auto-MDIX support. Although there is an integrated 24-port switch on the PRO 1260, the appliance can support an unlimited number of nodes behind the appliance. The SonicWALL PRO 1260 ships with SonicOS Standard and five VPN client licenses, with a maximum of 50 VPN clients.

The SonicWALL PRO 1260 has a unique feature called *PortShield architecture*. The SonicWALL PortShield architecture provides you with the ability to configure each port as an individual security zone. In reality, not only is traffic from the WAN being inspected and filtered, but by utilizing PortShield you can effectively filter traffic from other ports on the firewall, including the other LAN ports. It's as if each port has a firewall running on it.

Firewall performance provided by the PRO 1260 reaches 90 Mbps, with VPN throughput at just over 30 Mbps. The PRO 1260 also supports up to 6,000 concurrent sessions. The PRO 1260 can also support up to 25 site-to-site VPN policies.

The SonicWALL PRO 2040 is designed to be a midrange workhorse rather than an out-of-the-box core network solution. The PRO 2040 provides three available 10/100 interfaces, and supports an additional fourth 10/100 interface when utilizing SonicOS Enhanced. There is no built-in switch on the PRO 2040. Like the PRO 1260, the SonicWALL PRO 2040 provides a small or medium-sized business network with a deep inspection firewall as well as a VPN gateway. The PRO 2040 supports an unlimited number of nodes, with a maximum of 32,000 concurrent sessions. The PRO 2040 provides up to 200 Mbps of firewall throughput, and up to 50 Mbps of VPN throughput. The PRO 2040 supports up to 50 site-to-site VPN policies, and a maximum of 100 VPN client licenses. Unlike the PRO 1260, the SonicWALL PRO 2040 supports hardware failover when SonicOS Enhanced is installed.

Both the SonicWALL PRO 1260 and PRO 2040 support several advanced features, including WAN/WAN failover, ISP failover, and load balancing. Both appliances also come bundled with a 30-day subscription of services, including gateway antivirus, anti-spyware, intrusion prevention service, and the SonicWALL Premium content filter service.

Enterprise Class

Next, we will take a look at the large corporate and enterprise-class solutions that SonicWALL has to offer. These appliances are designed for use in large, complex networks, where higher throughput and additional segmentation of the network is needed. They are designed to provide a solid gateway and firewall solution, as well as to provide secure VPN access. All appliances in this class are rack-mountable appliances. Table 2.6 details the SonicWALL enterprise-class appliances.

Table 2.6 Large Business/Enterprise-Class Appliances

	PRO 3060	PRO 4060	PRO 4100	PRO 5060c	PRO 5060f
Interfaces	3/6* 10/100	6 10/100	10 Gigabit	6 Gigabit	6 Gigabit (4 Copper & 2 Fiber)
Max IP Address Behind	Unlimited	Unlimited	Unlimited	Unlimited	Unlimited
Maximum Throughput					
Firewall	300 Mbps	300 Mbps	800 Mbps	2.4 Gbps	2.4 Gbps
VPN**	75 Mbps	190 Mbps	350 Mbps	700 Mbps	700 Mbps
Maximum Sessions	128,000	500,000	600,000	750,000	750,000
Maximum Site-to-Site VPN Tunnels	500/1,000*	3,000	3,500	4,000	4,000
Maximum Client VPN Tunnels	500	3,000	5,000	6,000	6,000
Maximum Policies	300/3,000*	5,000	10,000	15,000	15,000
Security Zones	Yes*	Yes	Yes	Yes	Yes
Object-Based Management	Yes*	Yes	Yes	Yes	Yes
Hardware Failover	Yes*	Yes	Yes	Yes	Yes
Policy-Based NAT	Yes*	Yes	Yes	Yes	Yes
Advanced Features					
-ISP Failover	Yes*	Yes	Yes	Yes	Yes
-WAN/WAN Failover	Yes*	Yes	Yes	Yes	Yes
-Load Balancing	Yes*	Yes	Yes	Yes	Yes
Anti-virus Scanning Throughput	99 Mbps	182 Mbps	300 Mbps	339 Mbps	339 Mbps

Continued

Table 2.6 continued Large Business/Enterprise-Class Appliances

	PRO 3060	PRO 4060	PRO 4100	PRO 5060c	PRO 5060f
Intrusion Prevention Service Throughput	98 Mbps	170 Mbps	300 Mbps	79 Mbps	279 Mbps
Can Be Upgraded to SonicOS Enhanced	Yes	Standard	Standard	Standard	Standard

* Requires upgrade to SonicOS Enhanced

The SonicWALL PRO 3060, although at the lower end of the large business and enterprise-class appliances, is well suited for any complex environment. The SonicWALL PRO 3060 appliance comes standard with SonicOS Standard. The PRO 3060 appliance includes six customizable 10/100 network interfaces. Firewall throughput is provided at over 300 Mbps. The SonicWALL PRO 3060 also provides up to 75 Mbps of VPN throughput, and supports as many as 1,000 VPN policies when SonicOS Enhanced is installed. With support for up to 128,000 concurrent connections, the SonicWALL PRO 3060 is designed to handle a large amount of traffic without losing efficiency.

The SonicWALL PRO 4060 steps up the performance from the SonicWALL PRO 3060. It ships from SonicWALL with SonicOS Enhanced preinstalled, providing for object-based management out of the box, a must in today's world. Like the PRO 3060, the SonicWALL PRO 4060 provides six 10/100 user-configurable network interfaces capable of firewall throughput at over 300 Mbps. The SonicWALL PRO 4060 places more emphasis on acting as a VPN concentrator. In fact, VPN throughput is more than double that of the PRO 3060—the SonicWALL PRO 4060 provides VPN throughput at up to 190 Mbps. It also supports up to 3,000 site-to-site VPN policies, and up to 3,000 VPN clients. The SonicWALL PRO 4060 also has a larger connection table, supporting up to a half a million concurrent connections.

The SonicWALL PRO 4100 is designed for higher traffic environments with many network segments. The PRO 4100 provides 10 gigabit network interfaces and up to 800 Mbps of firewall throughput. The SonicWALL PRO 4100 can support up to 10,000 access rules, and is capable of handling as many as 600,000 concurrent connections. The PRO 4100 builds on the high-end VPN performance of the SonicWALL PRO 4060, providing up to 350 Mbps of throughput and supporting up to 3500 site-to-site VPN tunnels. The SonicWALL PRO 4100 provides gateway antivirus and intrusion prevention throughput at 300 Mbps.

The SonicWALL PRO 5060c and 5060f round out the SonicWALL firewall appliance offerings. Both the PRO 5060c and PRO 5060f have similar specifications. In fact, the major differences are the available interfaces. The PRO 5060c offer 6 copper interfaces, while the PRO 5060f offers four copper interfaces along with two fiber interfaces. These two appliances offer the utmost in network throughput. They can provide firewall throughput at a whopping 2.4 Gbps. In addition, the SonicWALL PRO 5060 series can provide VPN throughput at 700 Mbps, and supports as many as 4,000 site-to-site tunnels. The PRO 5060 can also support as many as 6,000 client VPN tunnels. The SonicWALL PRO 5060 series provides Gateway AntiVirus scanning and throughput at 339 Mbps, and intrusion prevention at 279 Mbps. The PRO 5060 series also comes standard with SonicOS Enhanced.

Enterprise Management

SonicWALL offers the easy-to-use WebUI integrated into SonicOS to manage SonicWALL appliances. The WebUI is an ideal solution to manage a small number of appliances, like four to five remote sites or perhaps a few telecommuters. However, what if your organization consists of tens or hundreds or branch offices? What if you are a service provider, managing hundreds or thousands of SonicWALL appliances for clients? Managing each individual firewall turns into a great chore. Furthermore, what about all of the logging from these devices? Is it practical to use a simple syslog server to managing all of those devices? This brings up a definite need for a centralized management console. This is where the SonicWALL Global Management System, or GMS, comes into the picture. The SonicWALL GMS is an all-in-one solution to manage many SonicWALL appliances from one easy-to-use interface and workspace. The SonicWALL GMS is the solution for your needs to control all of your devices. The SonicWALL Global Management System provides administrators with the following benefits:

- Unified management interface
- Lower administrative costs
- Centralized logging
- Simplified VPN deployment

Each individual device is entered into the GMS. Once the device has been imported you can manage each individual aspect of the firewall directly from the GMS. You can add and delete security zones, create new access rules, and tweak existing access rules. If, for example, you have dozens of locations that need to have the same policy, you can easily deploy that policy to all of those devices. If you then need to make a change to that policy, instead of accessing each device individually, you can simply make the change to the policy and then update all of the policies at once. This simplifies large-scale deployments and allows the administrator to gain more control over the enterprise's security as a whole. The GMS also brings together your logging to one central location to store it for historical purposes as well as monitor it in real time.

Deploying all of your devices into a tightly knit VPN solution can be complicated when you have many devices. Verifying that each device has the proper configuration on it can lead to big headaches, especially if you need to make changes to your configuration. If you use the GMS, however, deploying large-scale VPNs is a snap. This takes the guesswork out of determining what is happening to your secured infrastructure.

There are several scenarios in which you may want to use GMS to take total control over your SonicWALL infrastructure. For any SonicWALL deployment, small or large, the GMS can easily empower the administrator into gaining full control over your network.

Summary

In this chapter we looked at the various components that comprise a SonicWALL firewall. The SonicWALL security product line contains an amazing collection of security products. The SonicWALL product lines offer any customer, both small and large, a good selection of products for deployment on the network. The firewall product line offers a core set of products to secure your network's focal points. To minimize your network's risk, the integrated gateway antivirus and intrusion prevention service products enable you to intensely inspect your traffic. With the proper configuration you can block malicious traffic before it affects your systems, possibly compromising them and or creating data loss. The SonicWALL firewall product strays away from the traditional look of a firewall with its ability to act as a transparent device in your network, yet still providing full firewall features.

The SSL VPN product series is a new solution to an old problem. Remote access into the company's network has been a long journey to provide an easy-to-deploy, yet secure solution. The SSL VPN series solution can deploy to thousands of users without the deployment of a software client. This helps organizations because it does not require a large staff deployment to manage all of the software. These security products provide any company secure options for several facets of the company's needs.

We began to look at the core technologies that make up the SonicWALL firewall product line. We discussed the differences in SonicOS Standard and SonicOS Enhanced, their feature sets, and the options each supports. Zones are a core part of the SonicWALL firewall architecture on a go-forward basis. Now nearly every SonicWALL firewall appliance either supports zones out-of-the-box, or via a firmware upgrade. They allow the administrator to divide networks into logical separations. This allows you to simplify the policy creation process by clearly allowing or denying access to different network segments based upon their applied zones. Through the addition of zones, SonicWALL has proven they intend to take a proactive approach to simplify management and ease configuration.

Besides being a firewall gateway, the SonicWALL firewall is also a fully integrated VPN gateway, providing the ability to act as a site-to-site gateway and also provide remote VPN access to mobile users. The industry standard IPSec implementation provided by SonicWALL gives the enterprise a truly enterprise class VPN solution. Application-level security is a must for every organization today. It provides inspection of the Application Layer that otherwise could only be provided by a dedicated device such as an IDP product. The amazing design of the hardware architecture shows that the single purpose design can certainly provide for a high-end, high-performance firewall device.

The SonicWALL firewall product line provides a complete selection of firewall products that can cover any company's needs. Each product is tailored to provide exactly what you need for almost every possible solution for an enterprise's firewall needs. The GMS product brings all of your firewalls together to be managed under one single solution. It provides all of the various solutions any one would want to centrally manage all of your firewall products.

Solutions Fast Track

The SonicWALL Security Product Offerings

☑ The SonicWALL firewalls use deep packet inspection as part of their firewall packet-filtering technology.

☑ The implementation of VPNs on the SonicWALL product line is ICSA certified.

☑ The primary method for configuring SonicWALL firewalls is the WebUI integrated into SonicOS. Not all SonicWALL appliances support configuration via a CLI.

☑ The SSL VPN appliances are a clientless solution that does not require the pre-deployment of a software client.

☑ SonicWALL's integrated Gateway AntiVirus and Intrusion Prevention Service provide additional layers of security, allowing for inspection, detection, and blocking of attack attempts at the application level.

The SonicWALL Firewall Core Technologies

☑ SonicWALL appliances rely on one of two modern versions of SonicOS: SonicOS Standard or SonicOS Enhanced.

☑ SonicOS Enhanced adds features such as ISP failover, WAN load balancing, and zone-based management to the SonicWALL product line.

☑ You can use a SonicWALL firewall in transparent mode, which allows the firewall to act as a switch while still providing its normal firewall functions.

☑ An access rule, or policy, is used to instruct to the firewall on how it should handle traffic.

☑ By default SonicWALL appliances contain a rule that denies any traffic coming from the WAN attempting to enter into the LAN. They allow any traffic from the LAN to exit to the WAN.

☑ SonicWALL appliances also contain an integrated VPN, providing for both site-to-site and client, or dial-up, VPNs.

The SonicWALL Product Line

☑ The SonicWALL TZ 150 and TZ 150 Wireless makes a good VPN gateway for a telecommuter.

☑ The SonicWALL TZ 170 Wireless and TZ 170 Wireless SP can both be operated using power over Ethernet.

☑ The SonicWALL Global VPN client and Global Security Client are designed to run on Microsoft Windows.

☑ Of the Small Office/Home Office products offered by SonicWALL, the TZ 170 is the most versatile and full-featured firewall appliance offered.

☑ The SonicWALL PRO 1260 provides a "small network core in a box."

☑ The SonicWALL PRO 1260 utilizes a unique feature called PortShield architecture.

☑ The SonicWALL PRO 4060 provides additional emphasis on acting as a VPN gateway—it more than doubles the VPN throughput of the PRO 3060 and provides support for more than double the number of VPN tunnels.

Frequently Asked Questions

The following Frequently Asked Questions, answered by the authors of this book, are designed to both measure your understanding of the concepts presented in this chapter and to assist you with real-life implementation of these concepts. To have your questions about this chapter answered by the author, browse to **www.syngress.com/solutions** and click on the **"Ask the Author"** form.

Q: You mention several times that the SonicWALL firewall is ICSA certified. Why does this matter?

A: The ICSA certification ensures that the firewall device meets a certain level of criteria. This is important when determining interoperability between different vendors' devices. For example, automotive companies use a special network called the *automotive network exchange*, or ANX for short. They require that you use an ICSA-certified device to ensure that your device will be interoperable with other trading partners on that network.

Q: You mentioned that SonicWALL offers three VPN clients, but I cannot find the SonicWALL VPN client on the SonicWALL Web site. Why can't I locate this VPN client?

A: The SonicWALL VPN client is actually an application developed by a third party, SafeNet. SonicWALL has discontinued sales of the SonicWALL–branded version of the VPN client. If you insist and want to use this version of the client for configuring VPNs, you can get a version very similar to the SonicWALL version from SafeNet.

Q: Security zones seem like a bit of a confusing concept, and SonicWALL offers SonicOS Standard, which does not use security zones. Why are security zones important to me?

A: Security zones are an excellent concept to provide logical separation between multiple areas of your network. As you will see in later chapters, as we get deeper into firewall management, zones really simplify the process by helping to identify separate segments of your network. This, in turn, makes it much easier to create rules, as well as to visualize the flow of traffic through your network. This can prevent you from accidentally creating access rules that will allow access to sections of your network that you did not intend.

Q: You mentioned the SonicWALL command-line interface and said that it is somewhat limited in its management capabilities. When would I find this useful to use?

A: The command-line interface is an ideal way to get a quick look at interface statistics, or even to back up your preferences file from your SonicWALL appliance. It can also be useful in event that the Web interface stops operating properly, to help you regain access to your firewall.

Chapter 3

Deploying SonicWALL Firewalls

Solutions in this chapter:

- Managing the SonicWALL Firewall

- Configuring the SonicWALL Firewall

- Configuring Your SonicWALL for the Network

- Configuring System Services

☑ Summary

☑ Solutions Fast Track

☑ Frequently Asked Questions

Introduction

In this chapter we will look at the basics of deploying a SonicWALL firewall. The "basics" include a great deal of information. The SonicWALL firewall has a large number of configuration options. Before you can deploy a device, you must first understand how to manage it, so in the first section of this chapter we will look at the various methods of managing your SonicWALL firewall. Each option and best-known procedure is discussed. Strong system management is important, but no more so than preventing intruder attacks.

There are many management options available on the SonicWALL firewall. Of these options, there are two ways to manage the device directly. The first is using the command line interface (CLI). As mentioned previously, the CLI on SonicWALL appliances is limited in its capabilities. Some people prefer this method of device management for configuring interfaces and viewing interface statistics. Fully comprehending the command line interface allows you to better understand the SonicWALL firewall device.

The second firewall management option is the Web user interface (WebUI). This streamlined interface is user-friendly and intuitive, allowing anyone to jump in and manage your firewall with ease. Even command line junkies will use the WebUI to reference the configuration or to see a configuration more clearly.

Since a firewall is a core network component of the network, we will focus heavily on how to configure your device to interact with the network. This covers zone configuration and IP (Internet Protocol) address assignment. Properly configuring the network is crucial to the functionality of your network entity. Each type of zone and interface is documented to explain the different configuration options to you.

Finally, we will configure various system services. These services empower your firewall and stretch its possibilities.

Managing the SonicWALL Firewall

One of the most important aspects of securing your infrastructure with SonicWALL firewalls is knowing how to effectively manage them. In this section we will look at all of the various management options. Each option brings certain strengths and weaknesses to the table, so you should never rely on just one method. Instead, take advantage of the range of security options SonicWALL offers, and use multiple configurations.

All management access requires authentication, and it's critical that only autho- rized administrators are permitted to change your firewall's configuration. The last thing that you want to happen is to lose control of your firewall.

There may be times when you mistakenly erase parts of your configuration or lose your configuration altogether. We will review how to recover from these mistakes. Losing access to your device can be devastating. With so many different passwords to remember, you can easily forget how to gain access to your SonicWALL firewall. Even the most experienced administrators can find themselves in this situation.

Finally, we will look at how to update the operating system on your SonicWALL device. Staying current with software revisions is very important. It provides you with security-related fixes as well as new software enhancements. Each new release may also contain bug fixes or code changes that allow better interoperability with other devices. Some options may be more effective then others, depending on your needs. At the completion of this section you should be familiar with both the WebUI and CLI. Knowing this is a requirement for managing your SonicWALL firewall efficiently and correctly.

SonicWALL Management Options

Every SonicWALL management option centers around two forms of management: the WebUI and the CLI. SonicWALL also supports management via one other method. The SonicWALL Global Management System (GMS), an enterprise-class management interface, is designed to manage multiple SonicWALL appliances easily and efficiently through a single interface. The SonicWALL GMS will be discussed in more detail in Chapter 13 of this book.

Serial Console

SonicWALL security appliances offer a serial console for basic firewall setup and configuration. The *serial console* is a nine-pin female serial connection. This option gives you CLI access to the firewall. The serial console is used to initially connect to your device and to conduct *out-of-band management*. Out-of-band management is management that is not network–based, such as access via a modem or over Ethernet. When configuring over a serial port, you are not using any sort of network connectivity. In the case when you need to change IP addressing on the firewall and guarantee connectivity, using the serial console is an excellent option. With, and only with serial console can you view and interact with the booting process. This cannot be accomplished remotely because the OS has not started and it is unable to provide management services. Many devices from UNIX-type servers, as well as other embedded devices, use serial consoles to provide serial console management.

There are certain benefits to using a serial console that you do not get from using any other type of connection. The console provides secure, physical, and dedicated access to the SonicWALL appliance. Issues with network connectivity do not impact management using the serial console. Also, since your connection to the appliance is direct using a serial cable, your management is completely secured.

The command-line console provides an administrator the ability to manage interface setup and configuration, as well as to view statistical information regarding the appliance and its interfaces. The command line interface on a SonicWALL is only available when you are directly connected to the appliance using a serial cable. The CLI of the SonicWALL is not full-featured. Some management options cannot be set up using the CLI. For example, you cannot set up access rules using the CLI.

When connecting to a SonicWALL firewall for serial console management, use a null modem cable. When you purchase a SonicWALL, a null modem cable should be included in the packaging. Table 3.1 outlines the proper connection settings when connecting with a serial terminal and serial terminal emulation software.

Table 3.1 The Serial Terminal Settings

Setting	Value
Speed	115,200 (9,600 on TZ 170)
Character Size	8 Bit
Parity	None
Stop Bit	1
Flow Control	None

WebUI

The integrated WebUI offers an easy-to-use interface to manage SonicWALL appliances and access SonicOS. Because of its simple point-and-click nature, it gives the end user a great jumpstart into the management of the SonicWALL firewall. Figure 3.1 depicts the Web interface of a SonicWALL appliance. The left side of the screen provides you with clickable menus and submenus to access each area of configuration options. By default, the WebUI is configured to work over the Hypertext Transfer Protocol (HTTP). It can, however, be configured to work over Hypertext Transfer Protocol Secure (HTTPS). This provides a mechanism to secure your Web management traffic. The Web interface is the preferred method for configuring the SonicWALL appliance. Throughout this book concepts and examples will utilize the Web interface for configuration.

Damage & Defense...

Web Interface Management

Although the SonicWALL appliance line supports management via the HTTP protocol, you should try to avoid using it as much as possible. Rather, use the HTTPS protocol, which utilizes a Secure Sockets Layer (SSL) connection for management. When you communicate with a SonicWALL over SSL, the traffic is encrypted, thus preventing attackers from sniffing traffic. You can tell that you are using SSL to manage a SonicWALL by looking at the address line in Internet Explorer—the URL will start with "https:"

Figure 3.1 The SonicWALL Web Interface

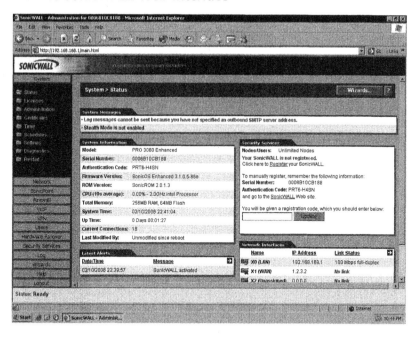

The SonicWALL GMS

The SonicWALL Global Management System is a separate tool that can be used to manage a SonicWALL firewall appliance. The SonicWALL GMS is an application that runs on either a Solaris server or a Windows XP Pro, 2000 (Pro or Server), or 2003

Server. It also requires the use of a database server—Oracle or MS SQL Server. The SonicWALL GMS requires a separate license, based on how many devices you want to manage. This product is used most effectively if you have several devices you need to manage at the same time. The GMS product is fully discussed in Chapter 13.

Administrative Users

Before you can perform any management functions, you must first authenticate to the SonicWALL appliance as an administrator. This holds true for management via the Web interface, serial console, or GMS. The SonicWALL default administrator account is the "admin" account. The admin account default password on all SonicWALL appliances is "password." You are allowed to change the name of the admin account to something more secure, up to 32 characters long. Note that the SonicWALL appliance does not see usernames as case-sensitive. The username "MillerT" and "millert" are the same name to the SonicWALL appliance. Only passwords are case-sensitive.

SonicWALL also allows you to create users that are known as *Limited Administrators*. Limited Administrators are allowed access to the following SonicWALL configuration pages:

- **General** Status, Network, and Time
- **Log** View Log, Log Settings, Log Reports
- **Tools** Diagnostics, except no permissions to Tech Support Report, Restart

Limited Administrators are only allowed management access to the SonicWALL from the LAN (local area network) zone, or via a VPN (virtual private network). Management from the WAN (wide area network) or any other zone is not permitted.

The Local File System and the Configuration File

Each SonicWALL firewall appliance has a similar design for its internal system components. Long-term storage on the device is stored in *flash memory*. Flash memory is a nonvolatile type of memory that retains information after the system is turned off. All of the component information that the SonicWALL appliance needs to store is stored in flash memory, including SonicOS log files, license keys, IPS (intrusion prevention system) databases, and virus definitions.

Each SonicWALL appliance also contains Random Access Memory (RAM). RAM is a volatile type of memory that is lost whenever the system is powered off or reset. When the SonicWALL device powers on, and after the power on self test (POST) is completed, the SonicOS image is loaded into RAM. After SonicOS is up and functional, it loads the saved configuration file from flash memory. The configuration that is stored in RAM is called the *running configuration.*

Using the Command-Line Interface

As mentioned earlier, the serial console can provide a stable and secure method to configure SonicWALL appliances. Although most administrators who only administer one or two SonicWALL firewalls never use the serial console for management, it is important to mention its features and capabilities.

To start using the SonicWALL serial console, connect a null modem cable to the port labeled "Console" on your SonicWALL appliance and attach the other end to a serial port on your computer. Start your preferred terminal emulation software, such as hyperterminal, and set the parameters for communications with the SonicWALL. For all SonicWALL appliances that support using the console other than the TZ 170, the settings are as follows: 115,200 baud, 8 data bits, no parity, 1 stop bit, and no flow control. For an appliance in the TZ 170 family use 9,600 baud, 8 data bits, no parity, 1 stop bit, and no flow control.

Once the connection has been established with the SonicWALL appliance, press the **Return** key. You should see a prompt appear within your console session showing the device name, followed by a prompt for your username. Enter the administrator username and press **Enter**. You will then see a prompt for the password. Type in your **current administrator password**, press **Enter**, and if the login credentials were entered correctly, you will be granted access to the management console. If you've entered invalid credentials, you will receive an error message and will be allowed to retry logging in. Note that SonicWALL appliances do not use any kind of account lockout mechanism for login attempts from the CLI. When an attempted login on the CLI is unsuccessful, a warning entry is generated in the SonicWALL log acknowledging the attempt. Figure 3.2 shows a successful login to the SonicWALL serial console.

Figure 3.2 SonicWALL Console Login

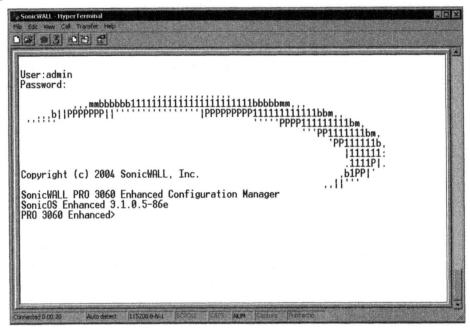

Once you've successfully logged into the serial console, you can begin using configuration commands to modify your SonicWALL appliance's current settings.

The SonicWALL command-line interface is very user-friendly and easy to operate. It includes several control keys that can be used to make tasks within the CLI easier. Table 3.2 lists the control-key combinations for the SonicWALL CLI and their purpose.

Table 3.2 SonicWALL CLI Control Keys

Keys	Function
Tab	Completes the word currently being typed
?	Displays a listing of possible command completions
Left Arrow	Moves cursor to the previous character
Right Arrow	Moves cursor to the next character
Up Arrow	Displays previous command from command history
Down Arrow	Displays next command from command history
Ctrl+A	Places cursor at beginning of the command line
Ctrl+B	Move cursor to previous character

Continued

Table 3.2 continued SonicWALL CLI Control Keys

Keys	Function
Ctrl+C	Exits Quick Start Wizard
Ctrl+E	Moves cursor to end of the command line
Ctrl+F	Moves cursor to the next character
Ctrl+K	Erases all characters from the current cursor position to the end of the line
Ctrl+N	Displays the next command from command history
Ctrl+P	Displays the previous command from command history
Ctrl+W	Erases the previous word

The SonicWALL CLI supports several features common to other command-line interfaces. You can use the Tab key to complete the command currently being typed, as well as using the ? key to list all possible command completions. Commands can also be abbreviated, so long as the abbreviation is unique to the command word. Figures 3.3 and 3.4 show examples of using command features.

Figure 3.3 Using Tab to Complete Commands

```
PRO 3060 Enhanced> show int [TAB]
show interface
```

As you can see in Figure 3.3, when typing the command *show interface*, the user pressed the **Tab** key. When the Tab key was pressed, the SonicWALL CLI knew that there was one command word starting with "int"—the word "interface," and as a result, completed the command for the user. As mentioned before, the user could have simply completed the rest of the command as *show int x0* and the SonicWALL CLI would have also interpreted this properly, since the only possible command starting with "int" is *interface*.

Figure 3.4 Using "?" to Get Possible Command Completers

```
PRO 3060 Enhanced> show ?

alerts            log               network           tech-support

arp               log-categories    processes          timeout

buf-memzone       log-filters       route              tsr

cpu               memory            security-services  web-management

device            memzone           sonicpoint         zone

gms               messages          status             zones

if                nat               syslog

interface         netstat           system
```

In Figure 3.4 we knew that we wanted to use the *show* command to display information, but we were uncertain of the next command word to use. By typing **show ?** the SonicWALL CLI returns a list of all the possible sub-commands that can be used for *show*.

The SonicWALL command-line interface uses the command and sub-command model for configuration. This means that under a given command context, there can be other commands that are only available under that context. For example, suppose you want to configure the LAN interface manually to 10 megabits, you could use the following commands:

```
PRO 3060 Enhanced> configure
(config[PRO 3060 Enhanced])> int x0
(config[PRO 3060 Enhanced]-if[X0])> speed 10
(config[PRO 3060 Enhanced]-if[X0])> end
(config[PRO 3060 Enhanced])> end
PRO 3060 Enhanced>
```

A quick *show int x0* shows us the interface information for x0, the LAN interface. Note the linkAbility field and its value of 10Mbps full duplex.

```
PRO 3060 Enhanced> show int x0


General data:

    type                  ifLan
    zone                  LAN


    linkAbility           10Mbps full duplex
    fragmentPackets       off
```

```
ignoreDontFragBit        off
mtu                      1500
proxyPcMacOnWan          off
bwmEnabled               off
bwmBandwidth             384


name                     X0
comment                  Default LAN

LAN data:

ip                       192.168.168.1
mask                     255.255.255.0
transparent              0
```

An excellent way to make use of the CLI is to back up the preferences file from your SonicWALL appliance. This can also be achieved from within the Web interface, but it can be quicker to do so via the CLI. SonicWALL appliances support the use of the ZModem protocol, and by default hyperterminal also supports receiving files using ZModem. To back up your preferences from the CLI, perform the following steps:

1. Connect to your SonicWALL appliance using a null modem cable and hyperterminal.

2. Authenticate to the SonicWALL with your administrator credentials.

3. Enter the command to export the preferences file via ZModem.

    ```
    PRO 3060 Enhanced> export preferences
    ```

4. The preferences file transfer using ZModem should begin. In just a short time, your preferences file will be backed up to the default location as set in hyperterminal. By default, the preferences file exported is named prefs.exp. Figure 3.5 shows an example of what the ZModem transfer looks like.

Figure 3.5 CLI Backup of the Preferences File

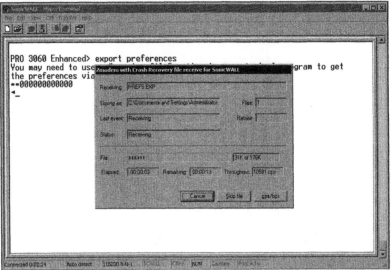

If an unforeseen event occurs and you lose the ability to manage your appliance through the Web interface, you can use the CLI and the command *restore* to restore your SonicWALL to its factory-default state. Afterward, however, you would need to reconfigure your appliance.

Managing the SonicWALL via the CLI can prove to be an efficient way to manage interface configuration. It can also be an excellent tool to look at statistics, alerts, and logs, as well as to back up your configuration.

Using the Web User Interface

The Web user interface is a simple tool to use for managing your SonicWALL firewall. It is very intuitive and allows even those with little firewall experience to easily control a SonicWALL appliance. As we continue through the book we will use the WebUI for our examples. You may see some examples for the CLI, but since the CLI does not provide you with full firewall management capabilities, the examples will be fewer. In Figure 3.1 , we looked at the main WebUI page following authentication. On the left side is the menu bar, where you can select the different configuration options. On the right-hand side of the screen is the current status of the device. The status display is divided into five different regions: System Messages, System Information, Security Services, Latest Alerts, and Network Interfaces.

Each of these boxes shows you the current events. The System Information box shows you several different bits of information, including the model number, serial number, firmware version, ROM version, CPU load, memory status, system time, uptime, number of connections, authentication code, and when the SonicWALL configuration was last modified. The Security Services box shows your device registration status, number of nodes the device allows, and installed license information. The System Messages box shows general configuration information and warning messages. The Latest Alerts box shows you some of the latest alert messages that have been logged. This may include messages relating to packets dropped or blocked by firewall rules or the IPS service as well as login attempts. If you look at the box labeled Network Interfaces you will see all of the interfaces and their link statuses. This is handy for determining which interfaces are up or down. Some boxes in the upper right-hand corner have a small blue arrow icon. This icon contains a hyperlink, and by clicking on you are taken directly to the detail page for each one of those items.

Securing the Management Interface

Now that you are beginning to understand the management of SonicWALL firewall appliances, it is time to secure the management access to your device. The last thing you want to do is leave the doors wide open for another individual to take over your device. There are some easy things that you can do to prevent this. First, as we mentioned earlier, you should change the root username and password. Everyone who owns a SonicWALL firewall is well aware of the default login and password to the device.

Use the following steps to change the root username and password via the WebUI:

1. Select **System | Administration**. A screen similar to Figure 3.6 will be displayed.

2. Type in the desired name for renaming the administration account. For our example we will use **Syngress**.

3. Enter the old password, and then enter the desired new password into the two corresponding blanks.

4. As an additional security option, you can also enable the administrator lockout feature on this same screen. To enable administrator lockout after failed login attempts, enable the **Enable Administrator/User Lockout** option. The default settings are to lock out a user or administrator if five invalid login attempts occur within one minute. The default time period for the lockout to last is five minutes.

Figure 3.6 WebUI Administration Screen

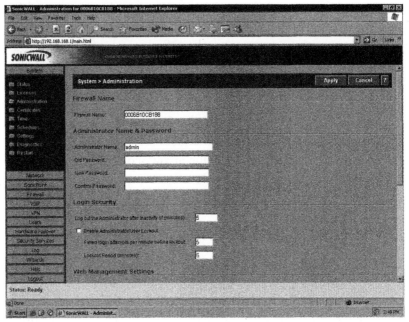

5. Click the **Apply** button on the top right side of the page. After the changes are completed, you will see the new administrator name in the Administrator Name field. Be sure you remember the updated administration information, as you will need this information in order to manage your SonicWALL.

Another option that you should configure is the idle timeout. By configure, I don't mean disable the feature. I have been to many locations where administrators would disable the idle timeout and you could simply connect to the console and have a privileged account ready and waiting for you. Anyone with a little know-how can cause trouble on your network this way. Be certain to set the idle timeout to something reasonable (the default is five minutes). If you find you are being logged out too often, then you can increase this number. However, to balance the scale between security and convenience, I would recommend at most 15 minutes.

The next step is to limit the systems that can access your firewall for management purposes. By restricting management to a specific short IP range or a single IP address, you can limit the chances and intruder may be able to gain access to your firewall. Once you enable this setting, it immediately takes effect, so if you are setting this up remotely, ensure that you add your own IP address and/or source network. Use the following steps to limit access to the management interface on your SonicWALL:

1. Select **Firewall | Access Rules**. A screen similar to Figure 3.7 will be displayed.

Figure 3.7 Access Rules Screen

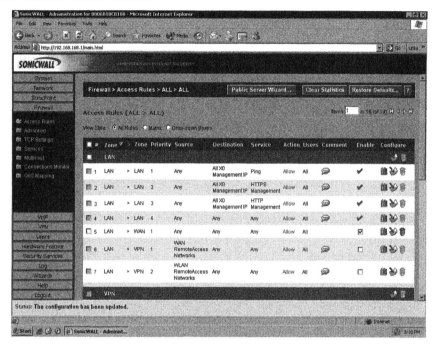

2. Locate the access rule with the service HTTPS Management. Click the **Configure** icon to the right of the rule. A window will open allowing you to modify the rule. Note that on the rules allowing management only the Source field can be modified.

3. Click the **arrow top**, open the drop-down menu, and then choose the option **Create New Network...** Another window will open allowing you to create an address object to apply to the rule. Enter the name for the **Address** object, and select the **Zone Assignment**, **Type**, and **IP address**. In our example, we call the object Manage IPs, and the zone is LAN. We are allowing a range of addresses for management. Figure 3.8 shows the object configuration.

Figure 3.8 Address Object configuration

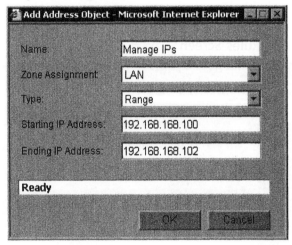

4. Click **OK** to save the address object, and then on **OK** to save the changes to the access rule. Your completed rule will then look similar to Figure 3.9. Note that if you hover your mouse over the Source for the rule Manage IPs, a box will be displayed showing what the Manage IPs address object is.

Figure 3.9 Modified Management Rule

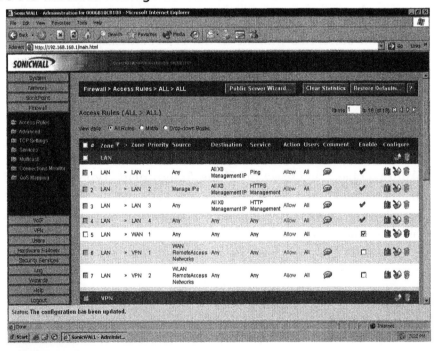

Now that we have the access restricted to specific hosts, there are yet several more options we can choose to enhance the security. The first task is to ensure that unnecessary management services are disabled. Management services are bound to individual interfaces. It is important to restrict them to the bare minimum. By default, SonicWALL does not allow management services from the WAN interface, or interfaces other than the LAN.

If you are taking over management of a SonicWALL previously managed by another person, it is highly recommend that you take a look at each interface to see which management options are enabled and disabled. If something is enabled that you will not be using, disable it. In this case, we are using a SonicWALL PRO 3060 with SonicOS Enhanced, and we will be modifying the WAN interface. We are going to disable the WebUI and WebUI using SSL as management options.

Use the following steps to disable unnecessary management services via the WebUI:

1. Select **Network | Interfaces**. A screen similar to Figure 3.10 will be displayed.

Figure 3.10 Network Interfaces Screen

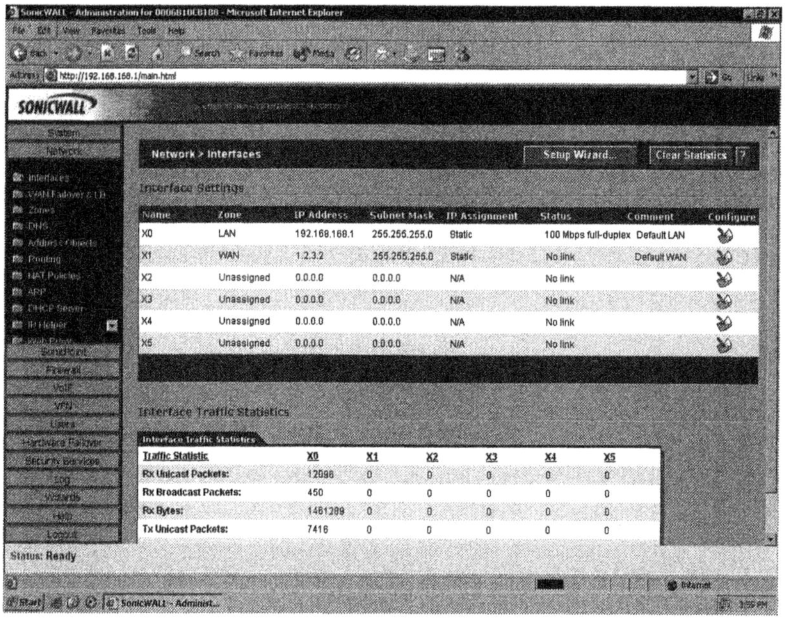

2. Locate the WAN interface and click the **Configure** option to the far right. The configuration for the WAN interface will open in a window similar to the one shown in Figure 3.11.

Figure 3.11 WAN Interface Management Window

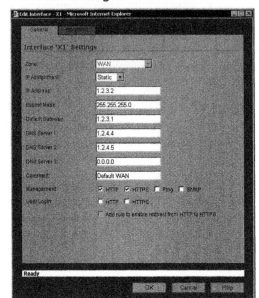

3. Disable the **HTTP** and **HTTPS** option and click **OK**. Now management via the WAN interface has been disabled.

You can follow the same steps for each interface on your SonicWALL to enable or disable management services.

Next, you can change the local port that your management services listen on. This can help prevent your services from being detected if someone was to do a scan looking for open services. Both HTTP and HTTPS management can be configured to listen on a different port. Use the following steps to change the ports via the WebUI:

1. Select **System | Administration**.

2. Scroll down and look under the heading **Web Management Settings**.

3. Modify the **HTTP Port:** and **HTTPS Port:** values to listen on the ports of your choice.

4. Click **Apply** to save your changes. Figure 3.12 shows the SonicWALL modified for HTTP Management on port 8081 and HTTPS management on port 4443.

Figure 3.12 Configuring the Management Ports

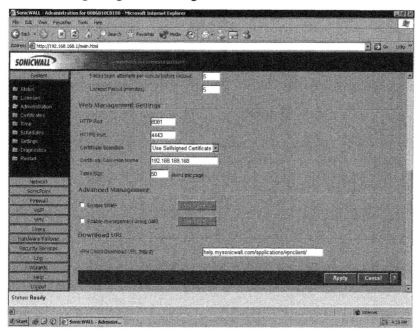

By default, SonicWALL appliances are configured to use a self-signed certificate for HTTPS management. SonicWALL firewalls also support the ability to import certificates.

The primary idea behind security is mitigating risks. By adding additional layers of protection such as those we've just discussed, you can reduce the chances you'll become a target for someone and also minimize the chances that security-related problems will arise. You may find that not all procedures fit within the guidelines for your organization's security. These guidelines are simply best practices, and although it is recommended that you use them, you can mix and match the configurations that work best in your environment to achieve the security level you desire.

Updating and Managing SonicOS

SonicWALL is committed to providing a secure and robust operating system for the SonicWALL firewall product line. From time to time SonicWALL publishes new versions of SonicOS. These may include security updates, feature enhancements, or both. It is very important that you keep the software on your firewall up to date. As a core component of your network security, your firewall has to be secure to perform its job properly. In fact, immediately after logging into a new SonicWALL, one of the first things I do prior to configuration is to verify it is running the most current version of SonicOS, and if not, I update it. This helps to ensure a smooth deployment and reduces the risk that something could go wrong after spending time customizing the configuration.

To check to see if your appliance has a firmware update available, login to your account on www.mysonicwall.com. Note that SonicWALL only provides you with 90 days of complimentary firmware updates. After the initial 90-day period, you will need to obtain a support contract in order to download new firmware releases.

Your SonicWALL appliance can also check for firmware updates and notify you if an update is available. To enable automatic checking for firmware updates:

1. Select **System | Settings**.

2. Enable the **Notify me when new firmware is available** option. Figure 3.13 shows an example of this setting.

Figure 3.13 Automatic SonicOS Update Notification

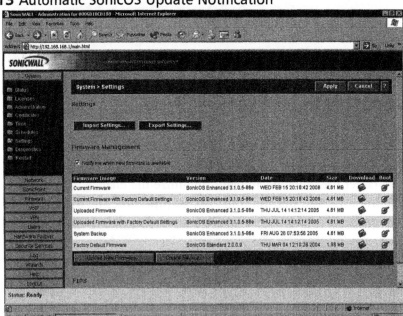

3. Click **Apply**.

When a firmware update is available, it can be applied through the Web interface. It is important, however, that you read any accompanying technotes for the release of firmware you intend to use. Often these notes will acknowledge changes made to the new firmware, including default behavior changes and any possible caveats in the new version. It is also important before updating your firmware that you back up your preferences file. Use the following procedure to back up and update your SonicWALL appliance's version of SonicOS:

1. Log in to your SonicWALL appliance. Click **System | Settings**.

2. Create a backup of your current firmware by clicking **Create Backup...** at the bottom of the screen. You will receive a warning message to verify that you want to overwrite your current backup if one exists.

3. Click **OK** to proceed with the backup. After a couple of seconds, notice the changes to the System Backup in the firmware listings. The version number should match the current running version. Also note the date the backup was created and ensure that it is correct.

4. Click **Upload New Firmware** A window like the one shown in Figure 3.14 will open.

Figure 3.14 Upload New Firmware Window

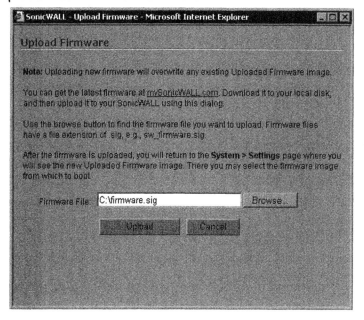

5. Browse to the path of the new firmware and select the file. Click **Upload** to start the upload process. The upload processes time to run depends on your network bandwidth. Once the upload is complete view the System | Settings window again. Note that the line labeled New Firmware should now show the version of SonicOS you just uploaded as well as today's date and time.

6. To reboot the SonicWALL with the newly uploaded version of SonicOS, Click the **Boot** icon to the right of the new firmware. You may be prompted to make a backup of your settings and old firmware prior to rebooting. Click **OK** to confirm and initiate the reboot sequence with the new firmware.

After the restart has completed and the SonicWALL appliance is running the new version of SonicOS, the browser window will refresh and take you back to the login page. You can now log back in to the SonicWALL Web interface and continue management of your appliance.

System Recovery

There comes a time in every administrator's life that it happens. You are modifying a system configuration, and somehow, during the modification you make a bad keystroke, mouse click, or worse, something locks up. It could even be as simple as a power outage, leaving you locked out of your device, or leaving the device unmanageable. It's time to perform a system recovery.

If you're having problems with accessing the Web interface, SonicWALL has provided a feature called *safe mode*. Safe mode can also be used in event the firmware on your appliance has become corrupted. Safe mode allows you to use one of several boot options including booting the current firmware with your preferences, booting the current firmware with factory default preferences, or uploading new firmware to the SonicWALL appliance. SonicWALL safe mode is available on all SonicWALL models except the SonicWALL TZW.

Accessing safe mode requires physical access to the appliance. To access safe mode, locate the hardware reset button on your SonicWALL appliance. The button is usually located in a recessed hole near the console port on the SonicWALL. Using a paperclip or similar tool, press and hold the reset button for five to seven seconds and let go. Allow the SonicWALL appliance time to reboot, and then open a Web browser. Enter the SonicWALL appliance's currently configured IP address, or enter the factory default IP address 192.168.168.168. Your browser should load the safe mode interface. Figure 3.15 shows a SonicWALL appliance booted in safe mode.

Figure 3.15 SonicWALL Safe Mode

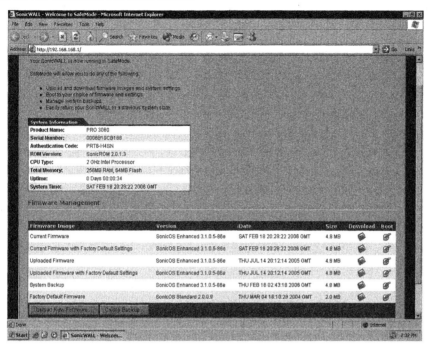

Occasionally, you may find that even after pressing the reset button you still cannot get the Web interface to load. If this occurs, you can use the SonicWALL CLI to restore your appliance to the factory default settings. Figure 3.16 shows using the CLI to restore a SonicWALL to the factory default settings.

Figure 3.16 Restoring Factory Settings via the CLI

```
User:Syngress
Password:
SonicWALL PRO 3060 Enhanced Configuration Manager
SonicOS Enhanced 3.1.0.5-86e
PRO 3060 Enhanced> restore
Are you sure you want to restore the device to factory defaults? (Y/N):y
restoring to factory defaults.
Are you sure you want to restart? (Y/N):y
Restarting the firewall
```

Zones, Interfaces, and VLANs

Before we get into the configuration of interfaces, access rules, and objects, we will first take a look at the zones and interfaces. By establishing what each zone and interface entails, it makes for understanding the configuration later. We will also review SonicWALL's support for VLANs. VLAN support is only available on the SonicWALL PRO 4060 and PRO 5060 model appliances.

Zones

As we've previously mentioned, zones logically group one or more interfaces together to make configuration and management simpler and more efficient. Out of the box, SonicWALL appliances come with several pre-defined zones. Each zone also has a security type defined. The security type specifies the level of trust given to that zone. The SonicWALL predefined zones cannot be modified from their factory configuration. The default zones are WAN, LAN, DMZ, VPN, WLAN (wireless LAN), and Multicast. Each zone is defined below:

> **WAN** The WAN zone can consist of up to two physical interfaces. This allows for the support of load balancing and WAN failover. By default, the WAN zone contains one interface. If you intend to use either of these services, you'll need to add a second interface to the zone. The WAN zone has the security type "untrusted," which means that without rules, no traffic from this zone is allowed to reach any other zone.

> **LAN** The LAN zone may consist of as many as five physical interfaces. Each interface is configured for a network subnet, with all interfaces being manageable as the LAN zone. The LAN zone has the security type "trusted," which allows any traffic from this zone to reach any other zone with restriction.

> **DMZ** The DMZ is designed to contain any servers and devices that will be publicly accessible or have an Internet-facing port, such as an MTA (message transfer agent) or Web server. The DMZ can consist of up to four physical interfaces. The DMZ falls into the security zone "public." The security type public really just says the zone has less trust than the LAN, but more than the WAN. By default, traffic from the DMZ can exit to the WAN, but cannot exit to the LAN.

VPN The VPN zone contains no physical interfaces. It is a virtual zone, used to provide secure remote network access. The VPN zone has a security type of "encrypted." All traffic flowing to and from the VPN zone is encrypted.

WLAN The WLAN zone is used to provide support for using *SonicPoints* on your network. SonicPoints are SonicWALL's wireless network product used for providing wireless network connectivity. On a TZ 170 Wireless or TZ 170 Wireless SP, the integrated SonicPoint falls into the WLAN zone. The WLAN zone falls into the security type "wireless," which is just a security zone where the wireless traffic is considered to reside.

Multicast The multicast zone provides support for IP multicasting. IP multicasting is a method for sending packets arriving from a single source to multiple destinations.

Even though you can assign multiple physical interfaces to a single zone to make management simpler, it is still important to remember that you can manage and apply access rules to each interface independently of its zone.

Another benefit of using the SonicWALL zones is that you can apply most of the SonicWALL security services to a specific security zone. For example, you can enable the SonicWALL intrusion prevention service across the entire LAN zone, and at the same time you could have this service disabled on the VPN zone.

If necessary, you can also create custom-defined zones on your SonicWALL appliance, applying the security type "trusted," "public," or "wireless," as well as the SonicWALL security service features to the traffic to your liking.

To add a custom zone:

1. Select **Network | Zones**.

2. Click **Add**. An add zone window will open.

3. Name the new zone and select the options for the services you want to enforce for the new zone.

4. Click **OK** to create the new zone. Figure 3.17 shows the addition of a zone.

Figure 3.17 Adding a Zone to the SonicWALL

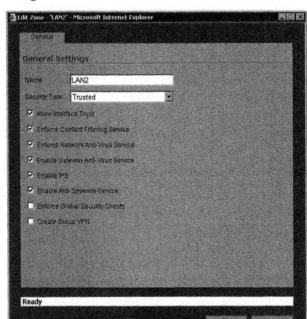

Interfaces

SonicWALL firewall appliances may contain several physical interfaces, including Ethernet, modem, or fiber, depending on the model you have. Interfaces go hand in hand with zones, because most zones rely on interfaces to be assigned to them for traffic to flow in and out. There are some exceptions, such as the VPN zone, which relies on a virtual interface rather than an actual physical interface.

On all SonicWALL appliances, the first two interfaces, x0 and x1, are permanently assigned to the LAN and WAN zones respectively. The TZ 170 may also have two special interfaces; one for the modem, and one for the wireless LAN. All remaining interfaces can be configured and bound to any zone type, depending on the model SonicWALL you have.

Some SonicWALL appliances have special interfaces. The SonicWALL Pro 1260 has a single LAN interface, but this interface includes all 24 numbered ports of the integrated switch, as well as the uplink port on the front of the firewall. The TZ 170 has a single LAN interface that includes all five of the ports in its integrated switch. These physical ports cannot be separated from the LAN interface and used in other zones.

The SonicWALL PRO 3060, PRO 4060, and PRO 5060 contain four user-definable interfaces, interfaces x2 through x5. The SonicWALL PRO 2040 contains two user-definable interfaces, x2 and x3. The SonicWALL PRO 1260 and TZ 170 contain a single user-definable interface—the interface labeled as OPT.

Binding an Interface to a Zone

Now that we've created our new zone, we need to bind an interface to the zone. Suppose that we want to assign interface x2 to the zone. We want this interface to be assigned the IP address 10.10.10.1. This network is a full class C network. We also want to allow management via HTTPS on this interface.

From the Web interface:

1. Select **Network | Interfaces**. Locate the x2 interface and click the **Configure** icon to the right. The Edit Interface window will open.

2. Choose the desired zone for the interface. In this case we are using LAN2. Upon making a selection, you will see additional interface configuration is required.

3. Enter the IP address **10.10.10.1** and verify the netmask is correct. Since we know that the network is a class C network, we know the netmask 255.255.255.0 is correct.

4. Enable HTTPS management on this interface. Note that by default, the option **Add rule to enable redirect from HTTP to HTTPS** is enabled.

5. Click **OK** to complete the addition of interface x2 to the LAN2 zone. Figure 3.18 shows the proper configuration of the interface.

Figure 3.18 Binding an Interface to a Zone

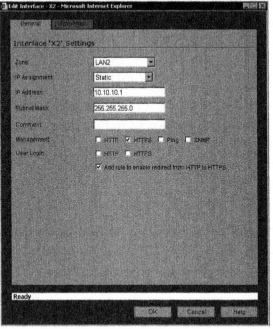

VLANs

The SonicWALL PRO 4060 and PRO 5060 also support the use of virtual interfaces, or VLANs. A virtual interface is a sub-interface of a physical interface. Virtual interfaces allow you to have more than one network on a single wire and physical connection. The virtual interfaces can provide services just as the regular interface can, including assignment to zones, the ability to act as a DHCP (Dynamic Host Control Protocol) server, and can provide NAT (Network Address Translation) and enforce access rules. SonicOS does not participate in any VLAN trunking protocols, and requires each VLAN to be configured and assigned appropriate security characteristics.

Trunk links are supported by adding the VLAN ID as a sub-interface on your SonicWALL and configuring it just as you would a physical interface. Any VLANs not explicitly defined will be disregarded by the SonicWALL. This allows the same interface to support traffic that is native traffic and to act as a normal interface would.

Advanced Features

SonicOS also provides several advanced features configurable for each interface. These features include such settings as manually setting link speed, bandwidth management, and creating a default NAT policy.

SonicOS Enhanced supports bandwidth management, allowing you to specify the amount of traffic that can flow across a link. SonicOS Enhanced can manage bandwidth both inbound and outbound. Inbound management is provided by using an ACK delay algorithm to control traffic flow. Outbound management uses class-based queuing (CBQ), which provides guaranteed and maximum bandwidth, to control the flow of traffic. CBQ works by queuing each packet into different priority queues, based on its priority. The packets are then delivered and transmitted by the quality of service scheduler based on the flow and available bandwidth on the link.

Configuring the SonicWALL Firewall

In this section we will look at configuring basic requirements to make your SonicWALL appliance functional on your network. In order to start configuring your SonicWALL, you will need some basic information about your network architecture. You will need information on the configuration of your connection to the Internet, which will be the WAN interface on the SonicWALL. This will include information such as the type of connection you are using, IP address or address range, netmask, gateway, and DNS (domain name system) servers. You will also need information about your local area network, which will be used to configure the LAN interface on the SonicWALL. This will include information such as your local IP address range and netmask.

There are two different methods for configuring a SonicWALL appliance for the first time. First, the SonicWALL appliance can be configured using the configuration wizard. Using the configuration wizard allows you to configure a SonicWALL with a basic configuration in about 10 minutes. Once you've completed the wizard, you should have network connectivity and traffic should be able to pass through the SonicWALL.

An alternative method for configuration is to cancel the setup wizard and log directly in to the Web interface. You can then manually configure all the necessary options to get the SonicWALL ready for your network. To get started using the configuration wizard:

1. Using an Ethernet cable, connect the SonicWALL to your computer and verify you have a network link light. If you do not have a link light, replace the Ethernet cable with a crossover cable.

2. Set your computer's IP address to something in the 192.168.168.0/24 range. I usually use the IP address 192.168.168.100.

3. Power the SonicWALL appliance on. Wait until the "Test" light goes off. Point your Web browser to http://192.168.168.168. This is the factory-assigned IP address of the SonicWALL appliance. Your Web browser will load the SonicWALL setup wizard, shown in Figure 3.19 Click **Next** to continue setting up your SonicWALL appliance.

Figure 3.19 SonicWALL Setup Wizard

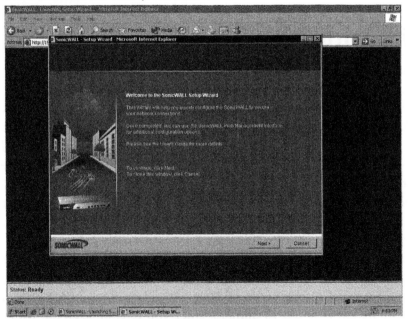

4. The first requirement is to change the default password. Input your desired password into the fields. The ideal password is something that is made up of letters, symbols, and numbers, and would be difficult for someone to guess. Be sure that you remember this password, as you will need it every time you want to make changes to your SonicWALL appliance! Once you've chosen your password, click **Next** to proceed.

5. Select the correct **Time Zone** for your location from the drop-down list. If desired, enable the **Daylight Savings Time** option. Since SonicWALL

appliances by default use NTP (Network Time Protocol) to keep time, it is not necessary to set the clock. Click **Next** to proceed.

6. The next screen configures the WAN interface for network connectivity. Here you are presented with four options. SonicWALL supports setting the WAN interface to a static IP address, to perform a PPPoE (Point-to-Point Protocol over Ethernet) login, to utilize DHCP to obtain its WAN configuration, or to use PPTP (Point-to-Point Tunneling Protocol). Figure 3.20 shows an example of configuring the SonicWALL to use statically set WAN addressing information. Once you've chosen the option for your needs, click **Next** to proceed.

Figure 3.20 WAN Interface Configuration

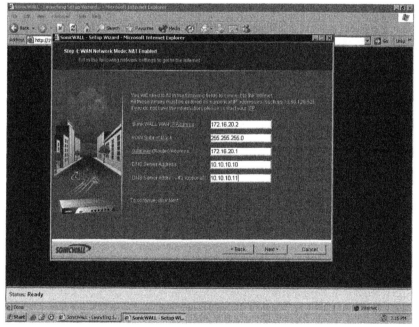

7. Depending on your choice from step six, proceed with the configuration. Since we are configuring a static IP scenario, we will enter the IP address, netmask, default gateway, and DNS server information. Configuration for the other methods will be discussed later in this chapter. Click **Next** to continue to the LAN configuration page.

8. The SonicWALL will now ask you for its LAN interface address and netmask. Input the desired network information and click **Next** to continue.

9. The final quickstart screen will appear, similar to the one in Figure 3.21. This screen allows you to review the configuration as you have entered into the SonicWALL. Check all values to ensure they are set as you want them. If anything is incorrect, click the **Back** button to go back and make any necessary changes. Once you've verified the configuration, click **Apply**. The SonicWALL Quickstart wizard will apply the configuration to your SonicWALL for you and then acknowledge completion. Click **Close** to end the Quickstart wizard and be redirected to the SonicWALL login page.

Figure 3.21 Final Configuration Review

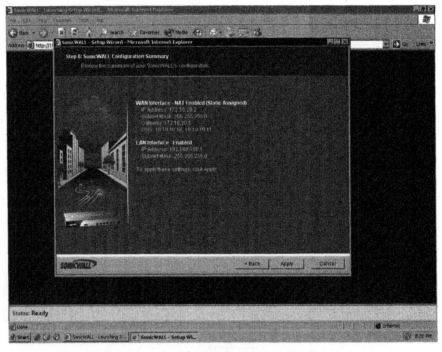

Congratulations! You've just completed the initial configuration of your SonicWALL appliance for your network. You can now log into the Web interface to work with other features that your SonicWALL has to offer.

Other Methods for Configuring the WAN Interface

Statically assigning network information to your SonicWALL appliance is only one method for configuring the WAN interface. SonicWALL appliances support additional methods for configuring the WAN interface. This includes configuration by DHCP, PPPoE, PPTP, and L2TP (Layer 2 Tunneling Protocol).

Configuring the DHCP Client

SonicWALL supports acting as a DHCP client to configure the WAN interface. In this mode, the SonicWALL sends a DHCP request out from the WAN interface, expecting to receive network configuration information including an IP address, netmask, default gateway, and DNS servers back from a DHCP server. This method is sometimes used when connecting the SonicWALL to a router that provides DHCP addresses, or a cable modem. To configure the SonicWALL for DHCP:

1. Click the **Network | Interfaces** tab. Locate the WAN interface and click the **Configure** icon.

2. Change **IP Assignment** to **DHCP**.

3. Click **OK** to complete the configuration.

Configuring PPPoE for the WAN interface

Most DSL (digital subscriber line) service providers require the use of PPPoE. PPPoE connects to the Ethernet network using a username and password. Once the device is authenticated, it is assigned an IP address. This requires additional configuration to the WAN interface. To configure the WAN interface for PPPoE:

1. Click the **Network | Interfaces** tab. Locate the WAN interface and click the **Configure** icon.

2. Change **IP Assignment** to **PPPoE**. The window will update with fields specific to PPPoE.

3. Enter your username and password in the **User Name** and **User Password** fields as provided to you by your DSL provider.

4. Click **OK** to complete the configuration.

You can also configure the PPPoE connection to terminate after a specified number of minutes of inactivity, although I don't know why one would want to use this feature. Just enable the **Inactivity Disconnect (minutes)** option and input the desired timeout. The default value is ten minutes.

Configuring PPTP

SonicWALL also supports using PPTP to obtain its WAN configuration. PPTP is seldom used for configuring the WAN, but is included. It is used to obtain network information from older versions of Microsoft Windows. To configure PPTP:

1. Click the **Network | Interfaces** tab. Locate the WAN interface and click the **Configure** icon.

2. Change **IP Assignment** to **PPTP**. The window will update with fields specific to PPTP.

3. Enter your username and password in the **User Name** and **User Password** fields. Enter the IP address of the PPTP server in the **PPTP Server IP Address** field.

4. Click **OK** to complete the configuration.

Configuring L2TP

SonicWALL supports L2TP as a method of WAN configuration. L2TP uses an encrypted IPSec connection to connect to the specified server, either Windows 2000 or Windows XP. Only the traffic passing between the server and the SonicWALL is encrypted. All traffic to other destinations is passed in the clear.

1. Click the **Network | Interfaces** tab. Locate the WAN interface and click the **Configure** icon.

2. Change **IP Assignment** to **L2TP**. The window will update with fields specific to L2TP.

3. Enter your username and password in the **User Name** and **User Password** fields. Enter the IP address of the L2TP server in the **L2TP Server IP Address** field. If the IP address is manually assigned, enter the values as required. If the IP is acquired through DHCP, change the **L2TP IP Assignment** to **DHCP**.

4. Click **OK** to complete the configuration.

Interface Speed Modes

By default, all of the ports on your SonicWALL firewall are auto-sensing. This means they negotiate the Ethernet settings such as speed and duplex automatically with the device they are connected to. This is great most of the time, but in an ideal world you may want to hard code these settings to ensure that you are getting the proper performance out of your network. Occasionally you may also see an instance where link speed or duplex mode will not properly negotiate, resulting in no link or traffic not flowing. Interface speed can be configured through both the serial console and the Web interface.

To set an interface's speed mode manually through the Web interface:

1. Select **Network | Interfaces**. Select the interface you want to hard code the interface speed for and click the **Configure** icon

2. Click on the **Advanced** tab.

3. Change the value of the field **Link Speed** to the setting you wish to use.

4. Click **OK** to save the settings.

Setting an interface's speed mode using the serial console looks something like this:

```
PRO 3060 Enhanced> configure
(config[PRO 3060 Enhanced])> int x0
(config[PRO 3060 Enhanced]-if[X0])> speed 100
(config[PRO 3060 Enhanced]-if[X0])> end
(config[PRO 3060 Enhanced])> end
PRO 3060 Enhanced>
```

Configuring System Services

On your SonicWALL firewall there are some other notable things to configure. We will first look at configuring the local clock on the device. Configuring the time is very important for being able to correlate information in the logs to a specific time.

SonicWALL firewalls contain a built in DHCP server. Typically, you can have a server on each interface. This allows you to manage your internal IP addressing in a single location. All SonicWALL firewalls are able to query DNS servers. This allows them to resolve hostnames to IP addresses just as normal systems do. It is important to have working DNS servers configured on your firewall so that URL filtering and other services that utilize hostnames can work properly.

There is a great deal of information generated by your firewall in the form of logs. Because all SonicWALL firewalls have very limited space for storing the logs, you may want to be able to send this logging information to a remote system. We will look at how to configure and use remote log repositories. Finally, we will examine how to unlock certain features of your firewall device with license keys and also how to update these keys.

Setting the Time

Every SonicWALL device contains an internal clock. This clock continually runs while the device is turned on. You can manually adjust the clock from within the WebUI on the System | Time page. The SonicWALL uses the clock for time-stamping logs, as well as for managing rules that are on a schedule. As previously mentioned, all SonicWALL firewalls are factory-configured to use an internal list of NTP servers to set and keep the time. The firewall periodically queries the time-servers to ensure that it has the proper time. You can also add your own preferred NTP server or servers for the SonicWALL to use for timekeeping purposes. The update interval for NTP is also configurable. The default NTP update interval is 60 minutes.

DHCP Server

SonicWALL appliances support the ability to act as a DHCP server for your network. This allows your firewall to manage and control IP address allocation to client devices on the network. The number of DHCP scopes and addresses that can be assigned varies depending on the model of SonicWALL appliance you are using. The DHCP server can give out IP addresses from a specified pool or from a reserved list based on MAC (media access control) addresses. An additional feature that SonicWALL supports is DHCP conflict detection. If the SonicWALL detects that there is another DHCP server handing out addresses on the network, it can auto-matically cease DHCP functionality. This can prevent IP address conflicts on your local network.

IP Helper

SonicWALL appliances provide functionality to act as an IP helper. Rather than the SonicWALL acting as a DHCP server on the local subnet and allocating addresses to client devices, the SonicWALL just listens for DHCP requests. When it receives a DHCP request, it forwards the request to a specified DHCP server on another subnet, which in turn, allocates an address for the client. The address is then passed back to the client device from the SonicWALL. This allows for centralized management of DHCP scopes from a single DHCP server, even when the DHCP server resides on a remote network.

DNS

Configuring the SonicWALL appliances for client DNS is a simple process. The Network | DNS page allows you to configure DNS settings manually. SonicWALL supports the ability to inherit DNS from the WAN zone. When this option is enabled, the DNS servers assigned to the WAN zone are the servers that the SonicWALL will use for DNS. If you prefer, or if you need to use a different DNS server or servers, choose the **Specify DNS Servers Manually** option, and input the desired values.

Licenses

Most SonicWALL security service features require proper licensing be configured on the appliance. This may include the number of allowed nodes, antivirus and anti-spyware filtering, content filtering, and VPN tunnel availability. All SonicWALL security licenses are centrally managed from the System | Licenses page.

For example, on the lower-end SonicWALL models such as the TZ 170, you can purchase the appliance with support for as few as 10 nodes. SonicWALL defines a node as a computer or device connected to your local area network that has an IP address. When this computer or device attempts to access the Internet through the SonicWALL, a node license is said to be in use. If you have only 10 node licenses available, when all 10 licenses are consumed by devices, the next device that attempts to access the Internet will be denied access, and an event will be logged to the SonicWALL system log. In the event that this happens, you have two possible solutions: you can exclude a node or nodes from connecting to the network, or you can purchase a node upgrade license for your SonicWALL appliance. Once the upgrade has been purchased, you simply install the upgrade license on your SonicWALL to activate the new functionality, in this case, additional node support. Figure 3.22 shows the System Licensing page on a SonicWALL appliance.

Licensing for your SonicWALL appliance is managed through your mysonicwall.com account. When you first set up your SonicWALL appliance, you create a mysonicwall.com account and enter your device serial number and authentication code to obtain the registration code for the appliance. After you enter this code into your SonicWALL, the appliance is registered. At this point you can install additional security service features for your SonicWALL.

Figure 3.22 SonicWALL Security Services Licensing

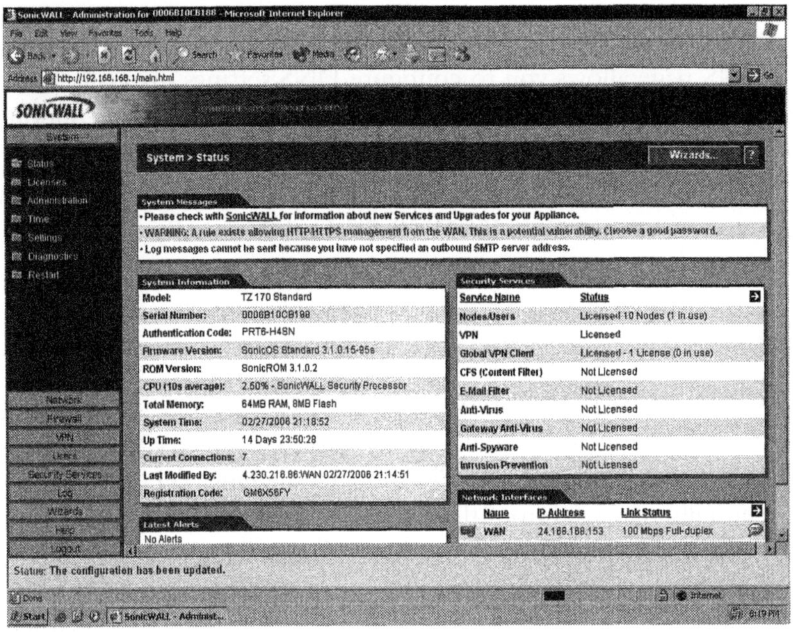

The Security Services Summary shows an overview of the currently activated security services, as well as the available features that are not currently active. The Status column indicates if a service has been activated (Licensed), can be activated (Not Licensed), or if the subscription to the service has expired (Expired). This chart also notes the node count supported by your SonicWALL appliance. The column labeled Expiration shows the expiration date of licensed services.

Once a day your SonicWALL firewall "phones home" to your mysonicwall.com account and updates your license information. You can also manually synchronize the licenses by clicking **To synchronize licenses with mySonicWALL.com click here**.

SonicWALL also offers free trial subscriptions of some of their security services, including the Content Filter Service and Network Antivirus. To activate any of the trial features, or to activate any other features, click the link to activate the service. You will be presented with the mysonicwall.com login page. You can then login to your account and complete the trial setup, or optionally purchase a security service subscription.

Sometimes you may need to deploy a SonicWALL firewall in a closed environment (an environment that cannot get access to the Internet). For this, SonicWALL offers the manual upgrade. The manual upgrade allows you to install license keys for security services when connecting to mysonicwall.com is not possible. To perform a manual upgrade, do the following:

1. Log in to the mysonicwall.com site.

2. Click the **registered appliance** for which you want to obtain security license keys.

3. Click the link **View License Keyset**. You will be presented with a text box that contains the license keyset. Copy the license keyset to your clipboard, and paste it into a text document.

4. If possible, paste the license keyset into the SonicWALL **Manual Upgrade** area on the System | Licenses page. If you cannot paste the license directly into the SonicWALL, print the license keyset and manually key the information into the SonicWALL.

5. Click **Submit** or **Apply** to update your SonicWALL.

After performing a manual upgrade, you will not see any registration or license information on the System | Licenses page. Also, you may see a "SonicWALL Registration Update Needed" warning message. If this occurs, you can simply ignore this message.

Syslog

By default, the SonicWALL stores event log information in its onboard memory on a "first in, first out" basis. Older events are the first to be overwritten. If you intend to keep your logs for a period of time or require the ability to audit or do reporting on your logs, it is recommended that you use a syslog server to perform logging.

The SonicWALL syslog captures and reports all log activity and includes source and destination addresses, number of bytes transferred, and IP service. Syslog support does require that you have a syslog server running on your network, and that the syslog daemon is running on UDP port 514. You can use a log analyzer such as SonicWALL's Viewpoint software, or WebTrend's Firewall Suite to analyze and graph the logged data. The SonicWALL appliances can support up to three syslog servers at a time.

Summary

Before you begin using your firewall, you must understand how to manage it.

There are two core types of management, the WebUI and the CLI. If you are using the serial console, you are using the CLI. The SonicWALL CLI is not full-featured, but can be a valuable tool to perform some management functions. The WebUI is easier to use, and provides you with full management capabilities. However, you will see that some advanced troubleshooting techniques can easily be carried out from the command-line interface. These techniques are invaluable for more advanced configurations. We also mentioned a third type of management called the Global Security Manager. The Global Security Manager product is an external source of management, and is covered in detail in Chapter 9.

This chapter also discussed configuring your SonicWALL firewall to run on the network. Zones have become a core part of the SonicWALL security infrastructure, and will remain so in the future. Each interface must be bound to a zone. In the next chapter we will focus on basic policy creation and policy theory. In that chapter you will see the application of security zones. In this chapter, we looked at all of the various types of interfaces that the firewall supports. The physical interface will be used on each type of SonicWALL device to interact with the network. The firewall can operate in two modes, Layer 3 and Layer 2. In this chapter we focused on the Layer 3 configuration of the device. In Chapter 8 we will focus completely on the Layer 2 mode, called *transparent mode*.

In the last section of the chapter we looked at configuring various system components. Ensuring that the time is properly adjusted on your device is critical. Time is the central reference point used to correlate all events on your firewall. If someone was to break in to your network and your logs were off by several hours or days, this could hinder your investigation of the break-in. Configuring your logs to be sent to a separate location is also important if you intend to keep your logs long term. The syslog server and WebTrends server are both great options to choose if you plan to keep your logs for a long time.

Solutions Fast Track

Managing the SonicWALL Firewall

☑ There are two methods that can be used to directly manage a SonicWALL appliance—the Web interface and the serial console.

☑ The SonicWALL serial console does not provide for rules management, but is a great tool for interface configuration or backing up your preferences.

☑ As often as possible, use HTTPS Management (SSL) over HTTP since the management traffic is encrypted and will be secured from possible sniffing.

☑ The SonicWALL Global Management System is a tool used to make management of several SonicWALL appliances unified and simple.

Configuring the SonicWALL Firewall

☑ Prior to making any configuration changes, always back up your current preferences file!

☑ Limited administrators can only manage a few select areas of the firewall, and can only do so from the LAN zone via a VPN.

☑ SonicWALL safe mode can assist you in gaining access to a firewall that you've been locked out of or have experienced problems accessing via the Web interface.

☑ SonicWALL security services such as anti-spyware and intrusion prevention service can be activated on a per-interface basis.

Configuring Your SonicWALL for the Network

☑ The SonicWALL WAN interface can be configured using several methods, including static IP assignment, DHCP, PPPoE, PPTP, and L2TP.

Configuring System Services

☑ It is important to ensure that your time zone is configured properly on your SonicWALL so that scheduled rules are in effect at the correct time, and the system log timestamps are accurate.

☑ If you need the ability to store your logs long-term for auditing or reporting, it is best that you configure the SonicWALL to send log messages to a syslog server.

☑ SonicWALL automatically inherits the WAN interface's DNS server settings, but you can manually specify DNS servers if there is need.

Frequently Asked Questions

The following Frequently Asked Questions, answered by the authors of this book, are designed to both measure your understanding of the concepts presented in this chapter and to assist you with real-life implementation of these concepts. To have your questions about this chapter answered by the author, browse to **www.syngress.com/solutions** and click on the **"Ask the Author"** form.

Q: What are the advantages of using SonicOS Enhanced instead of SonicOS Standard?

A: SonicOS Enhanced provides many additional features that are not available in SonicOS Standard. Some of these include security zones, rule scheduling, and support for hardware failover. In most corporate or small business environments today, these features can be crucial to maximizing resource availability and minimizing downtime. Many of the features in SonicOS Enhanced also aid in simplifying firewall and access rule management.

Q: Why does SonicWALL use zones on interfaces? I have used this type of configuration on other devices and I did not find it to be very effective.

A: Zones are designed to segment areas of the network from each other. On a SonicWALL firewall, using security zones during policy creation allows or disallows traffic from one zone to another. This simplifies policy creation by specifying which zone traffic can leave from and go to. Furthermore, it removes the chance that you accidentally configure access from one system to another. This can easily happen if you use a firewall that does not support zones.

Q: You cover securing the management interface extensively. Are all of those options really required?

A: Because the firewall is such a critical part of your network, you need to ensure its own security as well. Each option may be used in your network, or perhaps a combination of all of the options makes the most sense in your environment. By understanding all of the options, you will have the ability to pick and choose among all of them.

## Chapter 4

Policy Configuration

Solutions in this chapter:

- Theory of Access Control
- BWM
- QOS
- Advanced Options for Firewalls
- SYN Flood Protection Overview

☑ Summary

☑ Solutions Fast Track

☑ Frequently Asked Questions

Introduction

Imagine a world without any rules, regulations, or consequences; where everyone did exactly what they wanted to do, when they wanted to do it. It would be dangerous and chaotic; nothing would be safe.

Networks live in a similar world. Even though laws have been passed, new regulations are being enforced, and the consequences are more severe, networks are still being scanned daily for weaknesses. A single weak point in your perimeter defense can cause you to lose valuable data.

This chapter covers the components that access rules require, and covers how to best plan, implement, and maintain a secure set of rules to protect your private network(s). It also discusses the Advanced Firewall settings and the BWM features available on the SonicWALL.

Theory of Access Control

The theory behind access control is simple: allow access to the required resources and deny everything else. On a SonicWALL firewall, access to any zone from the Wide Area Network (WAN) is denied, and access from the Local Area Network (LAN) to any zone is allowed. This makes the initial installation of the SonicWALL as simple as providing the interfaces with proper Internet Protocol (IP) address information, and then physically plugging the unit in. At this point, the rules required to restrict traffic into and out of a network can be implemented.

The official SonicWALL definition of access rules is, "Access rules are network management tools that allow you to define inbound and outbound access policy, configure user authentication, and enable remote management of the SonicWALL security appliance." Simply put, access rules are used to grant or deny access to resources on a network.

Access Rule Components

Access rules are composed of several key elements that are used to specify the interfaces, zones, address objects, services, and Network Address Translation (NAT) policies that will be used for each rule created on the SonicWALL. Each of the elements should be created and configured before beginning to add any access rules.

The recommended order that each element should be configured in is shown in Table 4.1.

Table 4.1 Configuration Tasks

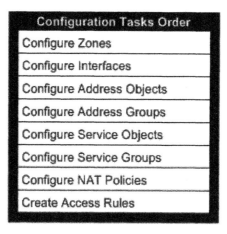

Zones

Zones are used to provide logical groupings of interfaces with additional flexibility when configuring NAT policies and rules (e.g., to provide enhanced security for a certain department, create a zone for that department, and then assign the appropriate interface or interfaces to the new zone). This provides the capability to configure individual rules that apply directly to the specific department.

Predefined Zones

By default, SonicWALL appliances contain predefined zones (see Figure 4.1).

Figure 4.1 Predefined Zones on TZ170 Wireless Appliance

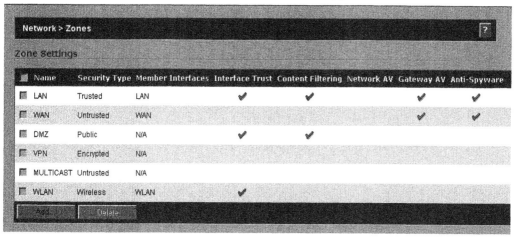

- **WAN** This zone contains either one or two interfaces. If WAN Failover is used, a second interface must be configured and applied to the WAN zone.

- **LAN** This zone can consist of up to five interfaces, each with their own unique subnet. When assigned to the LAN zone, they are managed as a single entity.

- **Demilitarized Zone (DMZ)** This zone can consist of up to four interfaces and is usually applied to networks that contain publicly accessible devices (e.g., Web servers, File Transfer Protocol (FTP) servers, and so on).

- **Virtual Private Network (VPN)** The VPN zone is a virtual zone that is used to simplify securing remote connectivity to the internal resources. This is the only zone that does not have a physical interface assigned to it.

- **Wireless Local Area Network (WLAN)** Depending on the platform, this zone serves different purposes. On SonicWALL PRO Series appliances, it is used to support SonicWALL SonicPoints. On TZ170 or TZ170-SP wireless appliances, it works with the built-in 802.11b/g antennas assigned to the WLAN interface and does not apply to SonicPoint devices.

- **Multicast** This zone is used to support multicasting. Multicasting is used to simultaneously send IN packets from a single source to multiple hosts.

User-Defined Zones

In addition to the predefined zones, administrators can also define custom zones. An example of this would be to separate data center resources from the rest of the LAN. Referring back to Figure 4.1, the following configuration options are available for each zone on the appliance.

- **Name** The name of the zone; should be indicative of what the zone is.

- **Interface** Trust A checkbox in this field indicates that interface trust has been enabled. This informs the SonicWALL to automatically create the access rules necessary to allow traffic to pass from this interface to other interfaces of equal or less trust levels.

- **Content Filtering** A checkbox in this field indicates that content filtering is enforced on this zone.

- **Network AV** A checkbox in this field indicates that the network anti-virus is enabled on this zone.

- **Gateway AV** A checkbox in this field indicates that the gateway anti-virus service should be enabled on this zone.

- **Anti-spyware** A checkbox in this field enables the anti-spyware services on this zone.nIPS A checkbox in this field indicates that the Intrusion Prevention Services (IPS) should be applied to this Zone.

- **GSC** A checkbox in this field indicates that Global Security Clients (GSCs) will be connecting to this zone.

Creating Zones

Before creating custom zones, careful planning is required. The following questions should be answered for each zone that you plan to create:

- What purpose will the zone serve?

- What interfaces will be assigned to the zone?

- What level of trust (security type) will be assigned to the zone?

- What additional security services will be applied to the zone?

A sample zone planning template is shown in Figure 4.2.

Figure 4.2 Zone Configuration Template

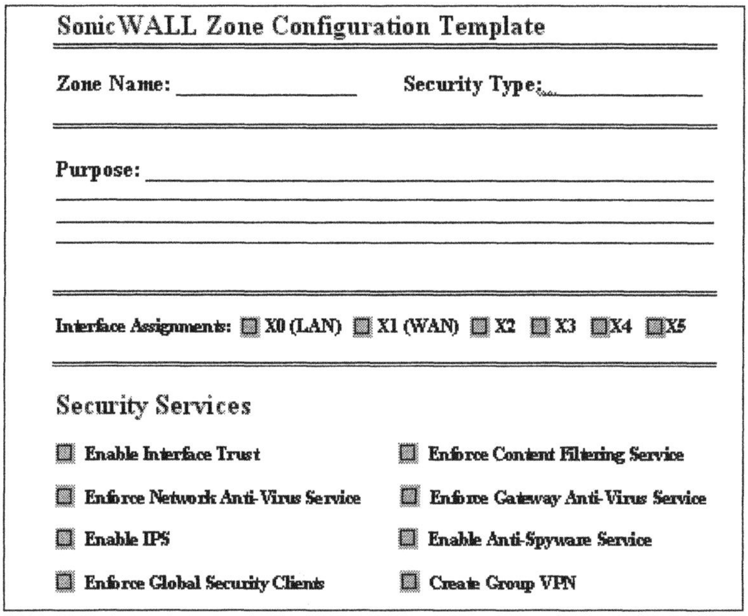

SonicWALL Zone Configuration Template

Zone Name: _____   Security Type: _____

Purpose: _____
_____
_____
_____

Interface Assignments: ☐ X0 (LAN) ☐ X1 (WAN) ☐ X2 ☐ X3 ☐ X4 ☐ X5

Security Services

☐ Enable Interface Trust   ☐ Enforce Content Filtering Service
☐ Enforce Network Anti-Virus Service ☐ Enforce Gateway Anti-Virus Service
☐ Enable IPS   ☐ Enable Anti-Spyware Service
☐ Enforce Global Security Clients   ☐ Create Group VPN

After planning for the additional zones, you need to create them. To do this, navigate to the **Network | Zones** page and click the **Add** button, which displays the Add Zone window (see Figure 4.3). We created the Data Center zone to illustrate the procedure.

Figure 4.3 Add New Zone Dialog

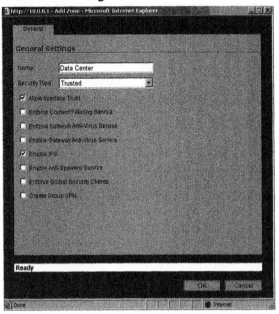

Enter **Data Center** for the Name of the Zone and select **Trusted** for the Security Type. The optional services that we will enable are:

- Allow Interface Trust
- Enable IPS

Click **OK** to complete the creation of the Data Center Zone. It is now displayed in the list of available zones (see Figure 4.4).

Figure 4.4 Data Center Zone

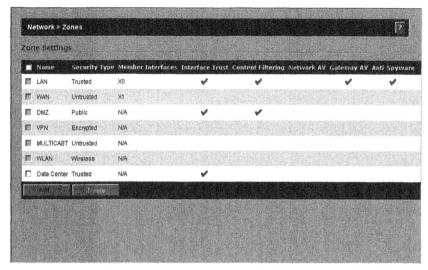

This process is repeated for each zone created. Once the zones have been created, the appropriate interfaces need to be added to each of them.

Interfaces

When discussing interfaces, most of us think about a physical port on a switch or router, or maybe a Network Interface Card (NIC) in a server or PC. Interfaces on a SonicWALL appliance can either be a physical port, wireless port, or a virtual port.

The number of physical interfaces is dependent on the SonicWALL appliance (see Table 4.2).

Table 4.2 Platforms and Physical Interfaces

Platform	Interfaces
PRO 5060c	(6) x 10/100/1000 Copper Ports
PRO 5060f	(2) x SX/SC Fiber Ports and (4) x 10/100/1000 Copper Ports
PRO 4100	(10) x 10/100/1000 Copper Ports
PRO 4060	(6) x 10/100 Copper Ports
PRO 3060	(6) x 10/100 Copper Ports Enhanced / (3) Standard
PRO 2040	(4) x 10/100 Copper Ports Enhanced / (3) Standard
PRO 1260	(27) x 10/100 Copper Ports
TZ 170 SP Wireless	(7) x 10/100 Copper Ports (1) x WAN, (5) x LAN, (1) x OPT
TZ 170 Wireless	(7) x 10/100 Copper Ports (1) x WAN, (5) x LAN, (1) x OPT
TZ 170 SP	(7) x 10/100 Copper Ports (1) x WAN, (5) x LAN, (1) x OPT
TZ 170	(7) x 10/100 Copper Ports (1) x WAN, (5) x LAN, (1) x OPT
TZ 150 Wireless	(5) x 10/100 Copper Ports (1) x WAN, (4) x LAN
TZ 150	(5) x 10/100 Copper Ports (1) x WAN, (4) x LAN

Interfaces are configured on the **Network | Interfaces** page of the SonicWALL. Depending on which appliance you are using, the list of interfaces will be different. Figure 4.5 shows an example of the available interfaces on a SonicWALL TZ170 Wireless appliance; Figure 4.6 shows an example of the available interfaces on a SonicWALL 3060 appliance).

Figure 4.5 SonicWALL TZ 170 Interfaces

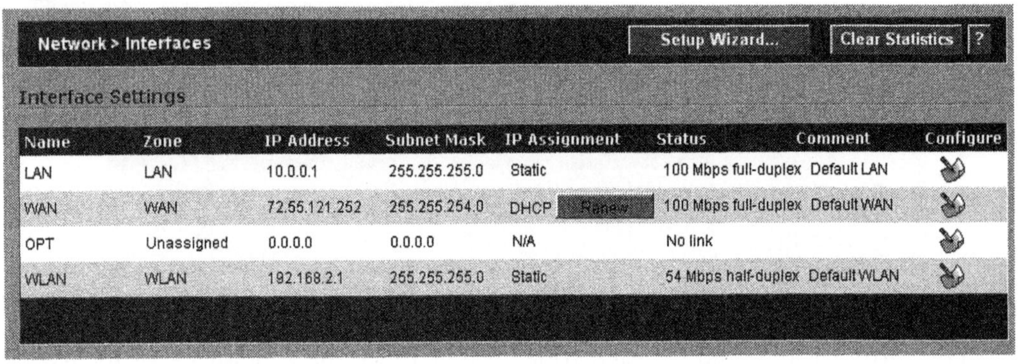

Figure 4.6 SonicWALL PRO 3060 Interfaces

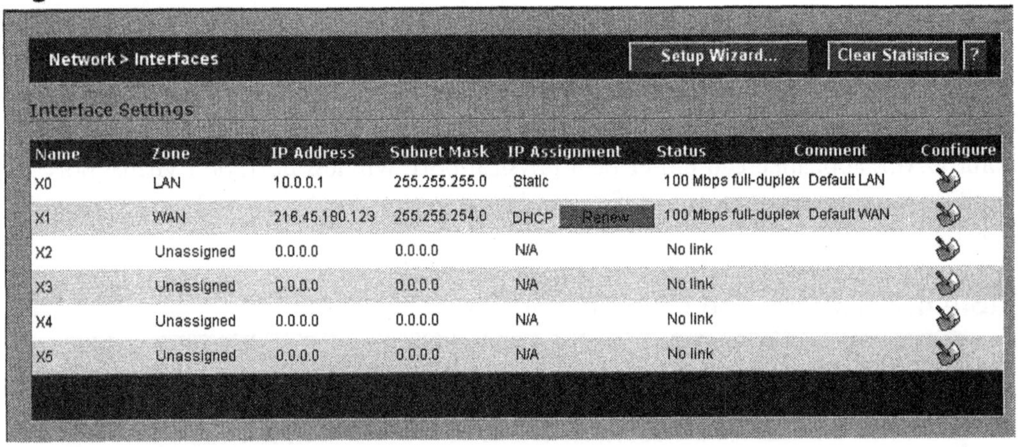

To configure an interface, click the icon under the **Configure** column, which will display the Interface Properties window. If the interface has not been assigned to a zone, the administrator is prompted to select a zone from a drop-down menu.

To continue with the Data Center example, browse to the **Network | Interfaces** page and click the configure icon to the right of the X2 interface. Since you have not assigned a zone to this interface yet, you will immediately be prompted to select one from a drop-down menu (see Figure 4.7).

Figure 4.7 Selecting the Data Center Zone

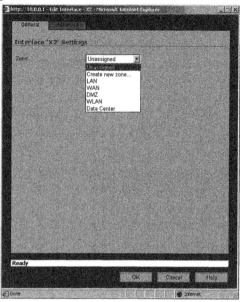

After selecting the Data Center Zone from the drop-down menu, the Edit Interface window is displayed (see Figure 4.8).

Figure 4.8 Edit Interface Dialog

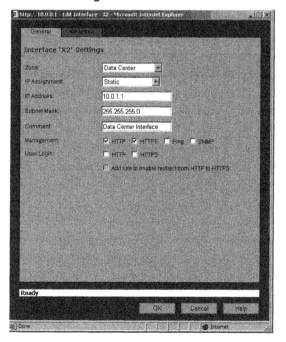

The interface configuration includes the following settings:

- **Zone** Select the zone that the interface will be assigned too.

- **IP Assignment** Select either Static or Transparent. Transparent mode is used to configure the interface in bridge mode. Static mode is used to assign the interface a specific IP address.

- **Subnet Mask** The subnet mask defines the scope of the network (e.g., 255.255.255.0 (CLASS C) allows for 254 different devices on the network).

- **Comment** A short descriptive comment, used to help identify the purpose of the interface (e.g., entering IPNET-01 is not very descriptive; however, Data Center Interface is.

- **Management** Each interface can be configured to allow or block specific types of management-based traffic that originates from devices within the same subnet (see Table 4.3).

Table 4.3 Interface Management Options

Option	Purpose
HTTP	Allows devices behind the Interface to manage the SonicWALL via HTTP.
HTTPS	Allows devices behind the Interface to manage the SonicWALL via HTTPS.
PING	Allows devices behind the interface to PING the IP address of the interface.
SNMP	Allows the interface to be managed via Simple Network Management Protocol (SNMP)

- **User Login** To enable users with limited management privileges, either Hypertext Transfer Protocol (HTTP), Hypertext Transfer Protocol Secure sockets (HTTPS), or both must be enabled.

- **Add Rule to Enable Redirect from HTTP to HTTPS** Enabling this option will ensure that access to the SonicWALL Management uses HTTPS to secure the traffic.

Now, you need to create address objects for devices, IP address ranges, networks, and Media Access Control (MAC) addresses that will be used in your rule base.

Address Objects

NAT policies and access rules are created using a combination of objects and groups. Address objects allow entities to be defined once and then reused throughout the firewall configuration.

Address objects are not restricted to access rules; they can be used on any applicable configuration page within the firewall, such as NAT policies and routing policies. An address object can be one of four classes:

- Address
- User
- Service
- Schedule

The address and service classes are used more frequently than the user and schedule classes. The address class is divided into four address types: host, range, network, and MAC. Each of these address types are discussed below.

- **Host** Host address objects are used to define a single device via its IP address. When creating host address objects, the subnet address will be 255.255.255.255 to indicate that this is a single device.

- **Range** Range address objects define a list or range of contiguous IP addresses (e.g., 10.0.0.100 through 10.0.0.150 encompass all IP addresses between 100 and 150 inclusive). Range objects do not use a subnet mask.

- **Network** Network address objects are used to define entire subnets (e.g., 10.0.0.0 with a subnet mask of 255.255.255.0 encompasses 10.0.0.1 through 10.0.0.254).

- **MAC Address** MAC address objects are typically used to define wireless client devices. This type of object uses the hardware address (MAC address) to define what devices are allowed to pass through the firewall.

Address Groups

In addition to the ability to create address objects, administrators can also create address object groups. Address groups combine any combination of host, range, or network address objects into a single entity. Access rules are then created for the group, instead of individual objects.

It is important to note that while MAC address objects can be added to groups, it is recommended that they be grouped separately from other address object types. This recommendation is based on the fact that address groups are also used to create NAT policies where MAC address object types are ignored.

Creating Address Objects and Address Groups

To illustrate how address objects and groups are created, we continue with the Data Center example. Figure 4.9 shows the example Data Center network diagram. Table 4.4 lists network IP address assignments.

Figure 4.9 Network Diagram

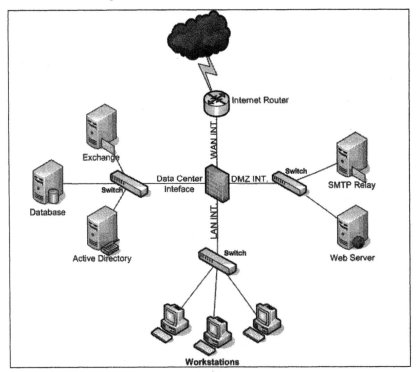

Table 4.4 Network IP Address Assignments

Device	IP Address	Subnet Mask
Internet Router	172.24.1.1	255.255.248.0
Firewall – WAN Interface	172.24.1.2	255.255.248.0
Firewall – DMZ Interface	192.168.1.1	255.255.255.0
Firewall – LAN Interface	10.0.0.1	255.255.255.0
Firewall – Data Center Interface	10.0.1.1	255.255.255.0
SMTP Relay Server	192.168.1.50	255.255.255.0
Web Server	192.168.1.51	255.255.255.0
Exchange Server	10.0.1.100	255.255.255.0
Database Server	10.0.1.101	255.255.255.0
Active Directory Server	10.0.1.102	255.255.255.0

We will assume that the zones and interfaces have been configured on the SonicWALL prior to proceeding. Your first challenge is to determine which objects need to be created. It is not necessary to define an object for each single device on your network. Understanding when to create an object and when not to create an object takes experience. The Internet router's Ethernet interface is specified as the default gateway for the SonicWALL under the WAN interface settings. With that said, no object is required for the router. In contrast, look at the Simple Mail Transfer Protocol (SMTP) relay server. In order for e-mail (SMTP) traffic to function, this server must accept SMTP traffic from the Internet. With that said, a host address object needs to be created for the server.

Why do we create a host address object and not a range or network address object? The reason for creating a host address object is to restrict traffic coming into the SMTP relay server only. If you had defined a range or network object for the DMZ instead of a host address object, your access rules would apply to all devices contained within the range or for the entire DMZ network. In other words, a rule to allow SMTP would apply to every device in the range or network. Using a host address object allows specific access rules or NAT policies to be configured for the individual device only.

The Web server also requires a host address object to allow HTTP and HTTPS traffic to the Web server. In addition to the objects for the DMZ, an object for the Exchange server on the LAN must be created. The purpose of this object is to allow the SMTP relay server to forward e-mail from the DMZ to the Exchange server.

What additional address objects need to be created for the example network? It depends. If Allow Interface Trust is not enabled for the data center and/or the LAN interfaces, objects will need to be created for the database and active directory servers so that access rules can be created to allow traffic from the LAN to these servers and vice versa. Also, you do not have to create address objects for the individual firewall interfaces; there are predefined objects already created for each interface.

Predefined Address Objects and Address Groups

The predefined address objects and address groups are dependant on the hardware platform. For the sake of brevity, we cover the SonicWALL PRO 3060, which includes the majority of the predefined objects and groups available. Table 4.5 lists the predefined address objects.

Table 4.5 Predefined Address Objects

Object	IP Address
LAN Primary IP	IP Address of the X0 (LAN) interface
LAN Primary Subnet	All IP addresses within the X0 interface's subnet.
WAN Primary IP	IP address of the X1 (WAN) interface
WAN Primary Subnet	All IP addresses within the X1 interface's subnet.
X2 Primary IP	IP address of the X2 (User Defined) interface
X2 Primary Subnet	All IP addresses within the X2 interface's subnet
X3 Primary IP	IP address of the X3 (User Defined) interface
X3 Primary Subnet	All IP addresses within the X3 interface's subnet
X4 Primary IP	IP address of the X4 (User Defined) interface
X4 Primary Subnet	All IP addresses within the X4 interface's subnet
X5 Primary IP	IP address of the X5 (User Defined) interface
X5 Primary Subnet	All IP addresses within the X5 interface's subnet
Default Gateway	The WAN Internet Router defined under the WAN interface settings
Secondary Default Gateway	Additional WAN interface's Internet Router

In addition to the address objects, predefined address groups are also included in the Enhanced OS. Tables 4.6 and 4.7 list the address groups that are predefined on a SonicWALL 3060 appliance.

Table 4.6 Predefined Address Groups

Group	Members
LAN Subnets	LAN Primary Subnet
Firewalled Subnets	LAN, WLAN, and DMZ Subnets
LAN Interface IP	LAN Primary IP
WAN Subnets	WAN Primary Subnet
WAN Interface IP	WAN Primary IP
DMZ Subnets	No Members by Default
DMZ Interface IP	No Members by Default
WLAN Subnets	No Members by Default
WLAN Interface IP	No Members by Default
All WAN IP	WAN Primary IP
All Interface IP	LAN, WAN, X2, X3, X4, X5 Primary IPs
All X0 Management IP	LAN Primary IP
All SonicPoints	No Members by Default
All Authorized Access Points	No Members by Default
Node License Exclusion List	No Members by Default

Table 4.7 Predefined Address Groups (cont.)

Group	Members
RBL User White List	No Members by Default
RBL User Black List	No Members by Default
Default SonicPoint ACL Allow Group	No Members by Default
Default SonicPoint ACL Deny Group	No Members by Default
All X1 Management IP	WAN Primary IP
Guest Authentication Servers	No Members by Default

At this point, you should be familiar with how zones, interfaces, address objects, and address groups are related. The next element required for access rules is service objects and service groups.

Service Objects and Service Groups

Service objects and service groups are used to define services that will be used in access rules for allowing or denying traffic for the network. SonicWALL appliances are shipped with the most commonly used services already predefined, such as HTTP, SMTP, and FTP.

Some applications may require the use of ports that may not be listed in the pre-defined services and/or groups. Administrators can create custom services and/or groups from the **Firewall | Services** page (see Figure 4.10).

Figure 4.10 Service Groups and Services

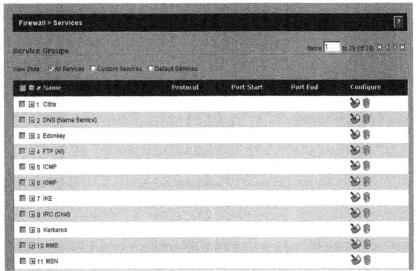

The View Style options for services allow administrators to view All Services, Custom Services, or Default Services. The Services page is divided into two sections: the top lists the service groups and the bottom lists the individual services.

Assume you have a custom Web application named GeoMech running on the Web server. GeoMech communicates with clients using Transfer Control Protocol (TCP) ports 8088 for handling initial client requests and 8099 for returning data back to the client. These two ports are not listed in the predefined services, so they must be created by the administrator. To do this, browse to the **Firewall | Services** page. To minimize the information displayed, choose **Custom Services** from the View Style options (see Figure 4.11).

Figure 4.11 Custom Services View

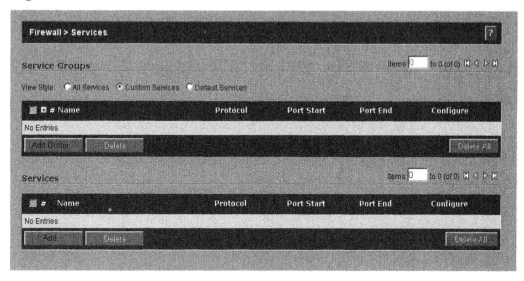

Click the **Add** button under the Services section. The Add Service page is displayed (see Figure 4.12).

Figure 4.12 Add Service Dialog

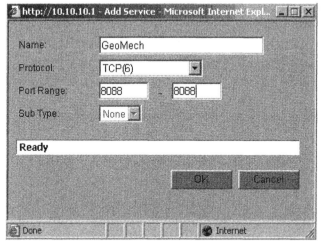

For this example, we will create the two GeoMech services for TCP ports 8088 and 8099. For the 8088 port, enter GeoMech-8088 in the Name: field. Click the drop-down menu and select **TCP** from the available protocols. In the Port Range: field, enter **8088** in both boxes. This informs the SonicWALL that this service uses a single port. If our services used ports 8088 and 8089, we would have entered 8088 in the first box and 8089 in the second.

With the services created, you need to create a group that contains the two GeoMech services. To do this, click the **Add** button under Service Groups (see Figure 4.13).

Figure 4.13 Add Service Group Dialog

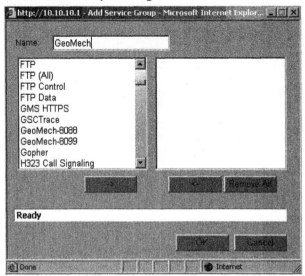

To add the two GeoMech services, highlight them and click the button with the right-pointing arrow. To remove a specific service from the group, highlight the service and click the button with the left-pointing arrow (see Figure 4.14).

Figure 4.14 Example Custom Service Group and Services

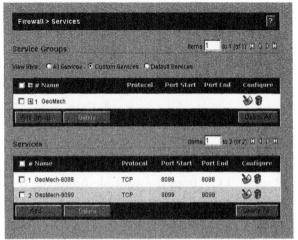

NAT Policies

We need to touch on the basics of how NAT relates to address objects and access rules. Prior to SonicOS Enhanced, administrators could not control how NAT was configured on the SonicWALL. The firewall configured the NAT policies automatically. While this approach simplified the configuration process, it also reduced the flexibility of the firewall. The NAT policies are fully exposed in SonicOS Enhanced, allowing administrators to enforce extremely granular control of how addresses are translated (see Figure 4.15).

Figure 4.15 Example Network Diagram

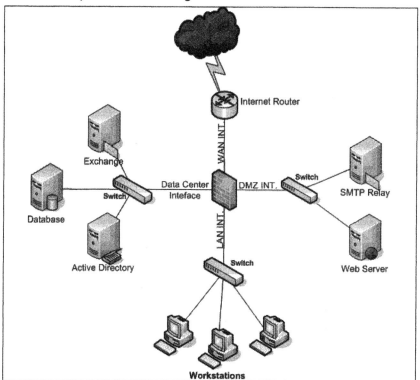

Internet users need to be able to access this server using HTTP and/or HTTPS. The WAN interface on the SonicWALL is assigned 172.24.1.2 and the Web server is assigned 192.168.1.51 (see Table 4.8).

Table 4.8 IP Assignments

Device	IP Address	Subnet Mask
Internet Router	172.24.1.1	255.255.248.0
Firewall – WAN Interface	172.24.1.2	255.255.248.0
Firewall – DMZ Interface	192.168.1.1	255.255.255.0
Firewall – LAN Interface	10.0.0.1	255.255.255.0
Firewall – Data Center Interface	10.0.1.1	255.255.255.0
SMTP Relay Server	192.168.1.50	255.255.255.0
Web Server	192.168.1.51	255.255.255.0
Exchange Server	10.0.1.100	255.255.255.0
Database Server	10.0.1.101	255.255.255.0
Active Directory Server	10.0.1.102	255.255.255.0

In order for Internet devices to communicate with devices protected by the SonicWALL, NAT policies must be configured that are used to translate private, *non-routable*, IP addresses to public, *routable*, IP addresses. To do this, you need two address objects for the Web server; one for the private address and one for the public address. Note that while the 172.24.1.0 network is actually part of the private Class B network range, for this example, we assume that it is a public range that is routable across the Internet.

According to the subnet mask, IP addresses for the WAN include 172.24.1.1 through 172.24.1.6. The internet router and firewall are assigned 172.24.1.1 and 172.24.1.2, respectively, and 172.24.1.3 through 172.24.1.6 are available for use. For this example, we assign the Web server address 172.24.1.3.

You need to create the address objects for the Web server. First, create the host address object for the Web server's DMZ address (name it "DMZ-WEB-01")," which reflects that it is part of the DMZ and the first server of its type. Secondly, create the host address object for the Web server's public IP address (name it "WAN-WEB-01")," to indicate that this particular object is located on the WAN interface and is assigned to the WEB-01 server.

After you define the address objects, the next task is to define any custom services needed for proper operation of the server. For this example, we only allow

HTTP and HTTPS to this server; therefore, no custom service objects need to be created. However, to simplify configuration, you will create a service group that contains these two services. The name assigned to the group will be "Trusted Web Services." Considering that the majority of Web servers require either HTTP or HTTPS, it makes sense to group them together to eliminate the need for multiple NAT policies and access rules.

To create the NAT policies required in order to translate the public address to the private address and vice versa, browse to the **Network | NAT Policies** page (see Figure 4.16).

Figure 4.16 NAT Policies Showing All Policies

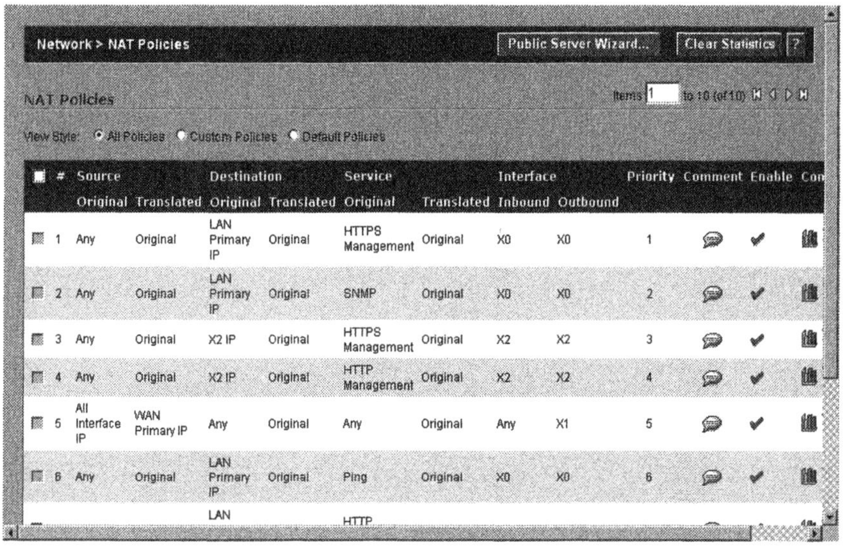

Click the **Custom Policies** radio button for the View Style option. This displays any custom policies that were created on the appliance and hides all of the default NAT policies from view (see Figure 4.17).

Figure 4.17 NAT Policies Showing Only Custom Policies

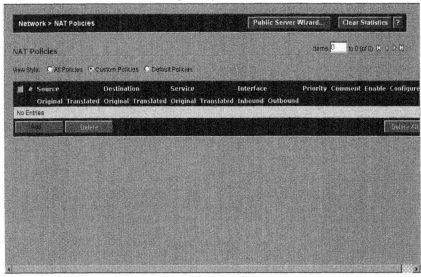

Click the **Add** button on the bottom of the page. The Add NAT Policy page is displayed (see Figure 4.18).

Figure 4.18 Add NAT Policy Dialog

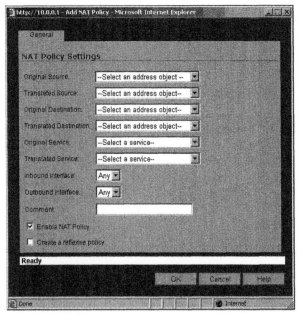

Two NAT policies are needed to configure the Web server; one for translating the external IP to the DMZ IP, and one to translate the DMZ address to the external IP. We start with translating the WAN (Public) IP to the DMZ (Private) IP. The Original Destination will be WAN-WEB-01 and the Translated Destination will be set to DMZ-WEB-01. Finally, the original service object will be set to the trusted web services group, and the translated service object will be set to original. For this example, we leave the inbound and outbound interfaces configured as Any. Enter a brief comment that states the purpose of this policy. For this example, you will enter **Inbound Access to DMZ-WEB-01**. Make sure that the Enable NAT Policy option is checked, then click **OK** to complete the configuration.

So, what does all of this mean? The Source fields refer to the device that is making the connection. In this case, it is any device that is attempting to contact DMZ-WEB-01 using one of the services defined in the Trusted Web Services group. By selecting **Original** for the Translated Source field, you enable the SonicWALL to leave the source IP address unchanged. In contrast, the original destination, configured as WAN-WEB-01, must be translated to the private IP address of the Web server. With the configuration that was entered for this policy, traffic with a destination of WAN-WEB-01 will actually be going to DMZ-WEB-01. The Service Translation configuration instructs the SonicWALL that this policy should only be applied for traffic that is attempting to connect to the server using a service listed in the Trusted Web Services group. All other traffic will not be translated and therefore will be blocked by the SonicWALL.

What about the opposite direction? Assume that your Web server needs to be able to contact the Internet for updates. As of now, there is no policy to translate the DMZ (private) IP address of the DMZ-WEB-01 server to the WAN (public) IP address. As a result, the Web server, itself, cannot access the Internet. There are two methods that can be used to resolve this. The first method is to create a new NAT policy that would translate the private IP to the public IP. The second method is to allow the SonicWALL to automatically create the NAT Policy (refer back to Figure 4.18). The option to Create a Reflexive Policy is used to accomplish this task. By enabling this option, a policy is automatically created to translate the DMZ-WEB-01 server's DMZ IP to the proper WAN IP, assuming that the traffic is using a service contained in the Trusted Web Services group.

SonicWALL Access Rules

This section explains how to create and manage access rules on the SonicWALL. As you know, the components that make up the rules require a lot of planning and configuration. It is equally important to ensure that the access rules you create are also well planned and carefully configured. It would be a shame to spend a lot of time configuring zones, address objects, services, and NAT policies only to create rules that do not use them efficiently and/or properly; or in some cases completely bypass them.

As mentioned in the beginning of this chapter, access rules are used to grant or deny access to your network resources. This section is broken into two parts. The first part covers the different windows and settings that are used to configure access rules, and the second part walks through several examples of creating, modifying, and deleting rules.

Access Rules—Part 1

We cover each of the options available for access rules and how they are used. First, we cover the different view styles that are used to apply display filters to the rule base to simplify management. Next, we cover the different configuration settings available on the General tab of each rule. Then, we cover the basics of the bandwidth and quality of service (QOS) settings, which can be configured on a per-rule basis. Finally, we review the default SonicWALL rule base.

Access Rule Views

To view, create, modify, and delete access rules, browse to **Firewall | Access Rules** (see Figure 4.19).

Figure 4.19 Access Rules View

The View style radio buttons are used to change how rules are displayed. There are three options available: All Rules, Matrix, and Drop-Down Boxes.

Figure 4.19 shows the All Rules View style. This view displays rules for all zones and, by default, is sorted by zone name. The list of rules can be sorted by Rule Number (#), From Zone name, To Zone name, Priority, Source, Destination, Service, Action, or Users by clicking the name of the column (e.g., if you want to sort the rules by priority, click the Priority column header [see Figure 4.20]).

Figure 4.20 Sorted by Priority

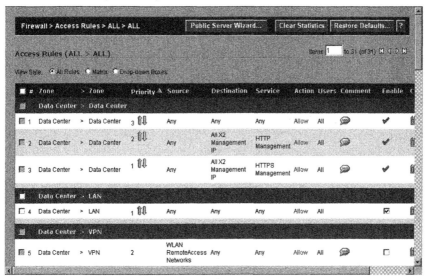

The column by which the list is sorted will have either an icon with an Up Arrow or with a Down Arrow to the right of the column name. The Up Arrow indicates that the list is sorted with the last item shown first, and the down arrow indicates the opposite (e.g., Figure 4.20 shows the results of sorting the rules by priority, and the Up Arrow indicates that the rules are listed by least priority first and the highest priority last).

The Matrix View style lists the zones in a From/To matrix (see Figure 4.21).

www.syngress.com

Figure 4.21 Matrix View Style

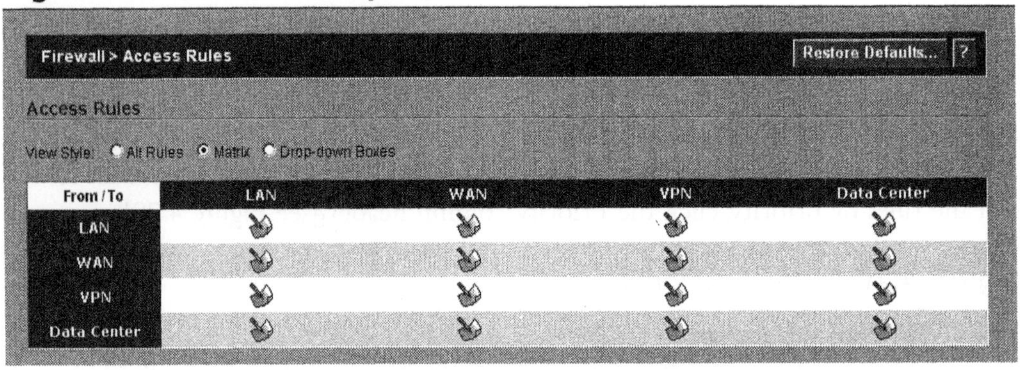

Using the Matrix View style is fairly straightforward. To list the access rules that are enforced on traffic originating from the WAN and destined for the LAN, click the **Configure** icon to the right of WAN (From Zone) and under LAN (To Zone). The corresponding access rules will be displayed (see Figure 4.22).

Figure 4.22 Rules View for WAN to LAN

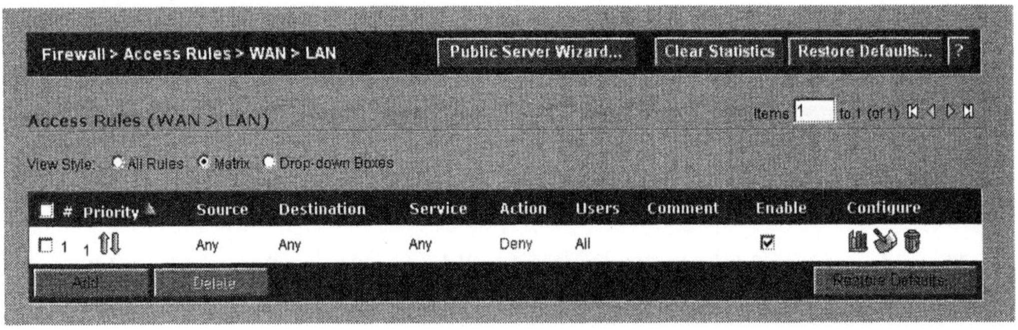

The Drop-down Boxes View style displays a page similar to that shown in Figure 4.23.

Figure 4.23 Drop-down Boxes View

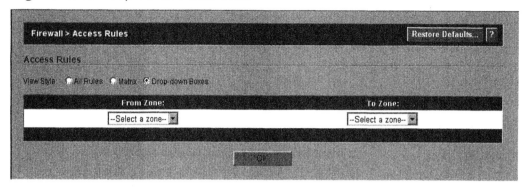

To view the rules associated with traffic originating from the WAN and destined to the LAN, first click the **From Zone** drop-down menu and select **WAN** and then click the **To Zone** drop-down menu and select LAN. The result will look identical to that shown in Figure 4.22. Figure 4.24 is an example of an access rule.

Figure 4.24 Example Access Rule

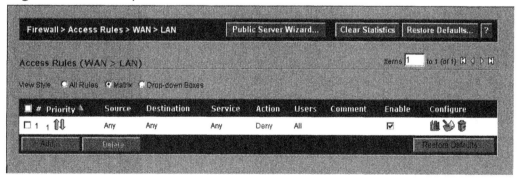

The following items are displayed for each rule:

■ **Priority** The priority of a rule indicates when that rule will be applied to traffic (e.g., a priority of –1 is the highest priority a rule can have). Traffic is processed by the SonicWALL one rule at a time, starting with rules that have the highest priority and continuing through the low-priority rules.

■ **Source** The source of the traffic that the rule pertains to.

■ **Destination** The destination of the traffic that the rule pertains to.

■ **Service** The Service or Service Group that the rule will be applied to.

■ **Action** The action used to allow, deny, or discard traffic matching the rule.

- **Users** The User or User Group that the rule will be applied to.

- **Comment** A short description explaining what the rule is for.

- **Enable** Enables or disables the rule. A check mark in this box indicates that the rule is enabled.

- **Configure** The Configure column contains three icons (see Table 4.9).

Table 4.9 Configure Column Icons

🏛	Holding the mouse pointer over this icon displays statistics related to the individual access rule.
👆	Modify existing access rules.
🗑	Delete existing access rules.

Notes from the Underground…

Deny vs. Discard

To understand the difference between the Deny and Discard actions on the SonicWALL, look at the packet captures shown in this sidebar. Assume that you have created a rule on the SonicWALL that blocks inbound Telnet access to the SonicWALL's WAN interface. The first set of packets shows the response from the SonicWALL when the action for the rule is set to Deny.

```
172.24.16.2 172.24.16.1  TCP   3869 > telnet [SYN] Seq=2166652584 Ack=0 Win=64512 Len=0 MSS=1460
172.24.16.1 172.24.16.2  TCP   telnet > 3869 [RST, ACK] Seq=0 Ack=2166652585 Win=0 Len=0
```

The first entry shows the synchronous (SYN) packet being sent to the SonicWALL's WAN interface. The second packet shows the reset (RST)/acknowledgement (ACK) packet being sent back to the client.

Next, look at the same test with the action set to Discard.

```
172.24.16.2 172.24.16.1  TCP   3871 > telnet [SYN] Seq=1560802127 Ack=0 Win=64512 Len=0 MSS=1460
172.24.16.2 172.24.16.1  TCP   3871 > telnet [SYN] Seq=1560802127 Ack=0 Win=64512 Len=0 MSS=1460
```

Continued

Notice that the SYN packet was sent to the SonicWALL's WAN interface; however, we never received a reset packet. That is the difference between a Deny action and a Discard action on the SonicWALL.

From an attacker's point of view, using the Deny action allows for strategic tests to be performed against the SonicWALL to map out the rule base. Each service (port) can be tested to determine if it is being blocked and if so, what are the details regarding the device that blocked it?

Creating Access Rules

To add access rules, the following 12 steps must be followed:

1. Select the **From and To Zones** from either the Matrix View or Drop-down View.

2. Click the **Add** button on the bottom of the Access Rules table.

3. In the Add Rule page, select the action that will be performed on traffic matching the rule. The available options are Allow, Deny, and Discard.

4. Select the appropriate service or service group from the Services drop-down menu.

5. Select the source network, IP address range, or host address object from the Source drop-down menu.

6. Select the destination network, IP address range, or host address object from the Destination drop-down menu.

7. Select the user or group of users that the rule applies to, if any.

8. Select the schedule to use for the rule if it will only be enabled during specific times.

9. Enter a descriptive comment for the rule that explains its purpose.

10. Typically the "Allow Fragmented Packets" option is not changed. Enabling this feature poses a security threat from malicious users. Fragmentation is often used in Denial-of-Service (DOS) and Distributed-Denial-of-Service (DDOS) attacks.

11. Configure the Advanced options for the rule by clicking the **Advanced** tab.

12. Click **OK**.

Editing, Deleting, Enabling, and Disabling Access Rules

To edit an existing access rule, click the **Configure** icon to the right of the rule, which displays the Edit Access Rule window. Make any necessary changes and then click **OK.** To delete an existing access rule, click the **Trashcan** icon to the right of the rule. A confirmation window will be displayed to ensure that you really want to delete the rule. Click **OK** to complete the access rule deletion process.

In many cases, rules are added for temporary testing purposes. Administrators can enable or disable a specific rule without deleting it from the rule base, by clicking the checkbox next to the rule. A check mark indicates that a rule is enabled, and a blank checkbox indicates a disabled rule.

Resetting the Rule Base for a Specific Zone

To reset access rules back to factory default settings for a specific zone, click the **Restore Defaults** button on the bottom of the page.

Viewing Traffic Statistics for Specific Access Rules

Traffic statistics for each access rule are gathered by the SonicWALL appliance. This information can be used to determine the amount of traffic that a specific rule is receiving. The following information is displayed for each access rule:

- Rx Bytes
- Tx Packets
- Tx Bytes
- Rx Packets

Traffic statistics are displayed by holding the mouse pointer over the Graph icon to the right of the rule (see Figure 4.25).

Figure 4.25 Access Rule Statistics

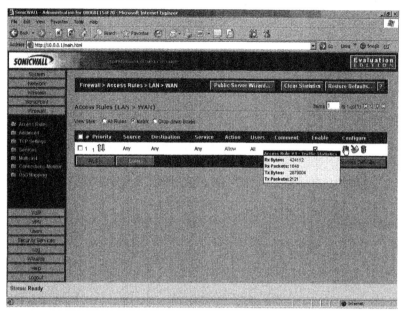

Advanced Rules Options

The **Advanced** tab located on each access rule provides the ability to configure the TCP and User Datagram Protocol (UDP) timeout values and to set the "Connection Limiting" feature. Figure 4.26 shows an example of the advanced tab window.

Figure 4.26 Edit Rule Dialog

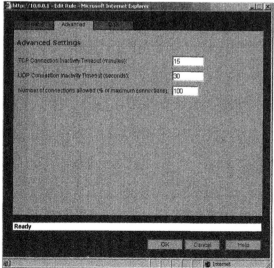

The TCP and UDP default timeout values are inherited from the TCP settings under the Firewall options. The TCP timeout value is specified in minutes and the UDP timeout value is specified in seconds.

Certain circumstances may require the default TCP timeout to be adjusted. An example of this would be AS400 Client Access connections. Users commonly leave a session open to the server for extended periods of time. If no activity is detected during these sessions before the expiration of the timeout value, the session is dropped. Use caution when setting this value. It is applied on a per-session basis and setting it too high could result in exhausting the connection cache, thereby preventing additional connections to the firewall.

It is recommended that the UDP timeout value be left at its default setting of 30 seconds.

The Number of connections allowed (% of maximum connections) field is used to limit the number of connections for a specific rule. Table 4.10 lists the Maximum Connection Cache sizes for the different SonicWALL appliances.

Table 4.10 Number of Connections Allowed

Appliance	Max Connection Cache
TZ 150	2,048
TZ 170	6,144
PRO 1260	6,144
PRO 2040	32,768
PRO 3060	131,072
PRO 4060	524,288
PRO 5060	750,000

The value entered in this field, X, instructs the SonicWALL to allow the rule to consume X percent of the maximum connection cache. Once the threshold is met, additional connections will be refused. This provides the ability to control the rapid spreading of viruses or worms.

BWM

SonicOS Enhanced provides the capability to control bandwidth to both ingress (inbound) and egress (outbound) traffic on WAN interfaces. SonicWALL uses Class Based Queuing (CBQ) to manage the egress bandwidth and an ACK delay algorithm for ingress traffic.

CBQ includes the capability to provide guaranteed and maximum bandwidth QOS for the SonicWALL. Each packet with the destination of the WAN interface is queued in the appropriate priority queue. The scheduler is then responsible for processing the queues and sends the packets out depending on the guaranteed bandwidth for the specific flow and the available bandwidth on the link.

To configure Bandwidth Management (BWM) on the SonicWALL appliance, navigate to **Network | Interfaces** and select **edit** next to the WAN interface. The BWM section is used to enable or disable control over the bandwidth. The ingress and egress connection speeds are defined on this page (see Figure 4.27).

Figure 4.27 Advanced Interface Options

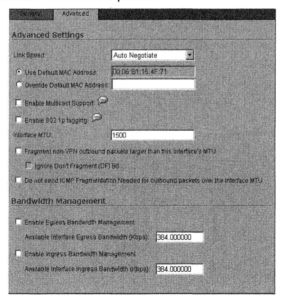

To enable either the egress or ingress BWM, place a check in the box for the appropriate option. Make sure to define the available bandwidth for each of the interfaces that you enable.

Once the bandwidth settings have been applied for the WAN interface, an additional tab is available on access rules (see Figure 4.28).

Figure 4.28 Access Rule BWM Settings

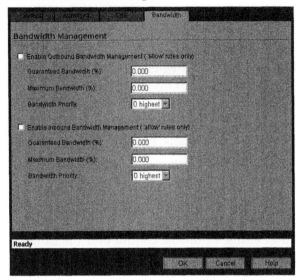

As shown in Figure 4.28, both outbound and inbound BWM are available. This, however, is dependent on what was configured for the WAN interface (e.g., if you did not enable ingress BWM on the WAN interface, the Enable Inbound BWM option would not show on the access rules BWM options.

Let's look at an example of how BWM works. Assume that we have the following access rule configured on a SonicWALL (see Figure 4.29).

Figure 4.29 BWM General Settings

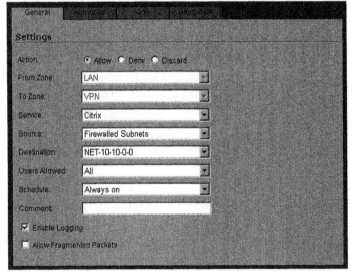

Now, assume that the following bandwidth configuration is applied to this access rule (see Figure 4.30).

Figure 4.30 BWM Bandwidth Settings

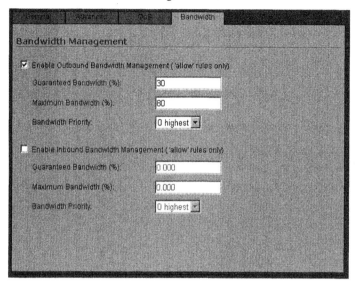

Finally, assume that no other access rules are configured to use BWM. We have accomplished a guarantee of 20 percent of the available outbound bandwidth, which in this case is 30 percent of the available 384 Kbps (or 77 Kbps) for Citrix traffic originating from the LAN and destined for the VPN network with the subnet of 10.10.0.0. At the same time, we restricted the Citrix services to the remote subnet to a maximum of 40 percent of the available 384 Kbps (or 154 Kbps. This leaves 230 Kbps available for other traffic.

QOS

Besides simple BWM features, SonicWALL QOS provides additional control over network traffic. While the technical details of how QOS and its associated components work are beyond the scope of this document, a brief overview is provided to describe how QOS is applied to traffic.

The QOS features of the SonicWALL are composed of three pieces:

- Classification

- Marking

- Conditioning

Classification is used to identify traffic that needs to be managed and access rules are used to configure the classification of certain traffic. This approach provides the maximum flexibility and management over how specific services are controlled. SonicOS 3.1 Enhanced and higher provides the ability for the SonicWALL to recognize, map, modify, and generate industry-standard external Class of Service (COS) designators, DiffServ Code Point (DSCP), and 802.1p.

Marking is used to tag traffic that has been classified as requiring management. The tag is used by external systems that support COS to ensure that the traffic is handled properly and to control per-hop behaviors. DSCP is used as the marking method and is considered safe, because there is no risk of incompatibility. In a worst case scenario, the DSCP tag will be stripped from the packet or just plain ignored; however, the actual data packet will be unaffected. RFC 2598 enhances DSCP by providing expedited forwarding levels within classes. The levels identified within the RFC are Gold, Silver, and Bronze.

Finally, conditioning is used to manage the traffic through the use of any available policing, queuing, and shaping methods.

Default Access Rules

By default, SonicWALL appliances are configured to drop all inbound traffic to the LAN. In contrast, all outbound traffic will be allowed. To further explain the default rule base configuration, refer to Table 4.11.

Table 4.11 Default Rule Base

Action	Service	Source	Destination	Comment
Allow	Any	LAN, WLAN	DMZ, OPT, WAN	Allow all traffic from LAN or WLAN to Public and Untrusted networks and/or devices.
Allow	Any	DMZ, OPT	WAN	Allow objects configured on the DMZ or OPT interface access to the WAN
Deny	Any	WAN	DMZ, OPT	Deny all traffic originating from the WAN that has a destination of the DMZ or OPT interface

Continued

Table 4.11 continued Default Rule Base

Action	Service	Source	Destination	Comment
Deny	Any	WAN, DMZ, or OPT	LAN, WLAN	Deny all traffic originating from the WAN, DMZ, or OPT interface with a destination of the LAN or WLAN.

All traffic originating from an interface that is not trusted is blocked by the SonicWALL. While the default rule base is acceptable for many organizations, it is not considered by most as the secure by default. Secure by default means that no traffic is allowed inbound or outbound from the firewall unless explicitly stated in the rule base. This approach is the recommended method for configuring any security appliance that is implemented in a high security environment. Table 4.12 shows how the rules would look for a Secure-by-Default configuration. Caution, you must have at least one access rule that allows for the management of the SonicWALL appliance. As shown in Table 4.12, address objects defining firewall management hosts are created, placed in an FW_Admin group, and then added to a single access rule.

Table 4.12 Secure-by-Default Rule Base

Action	Service	Source	Destination	Comment
Allow	HTTPS	FW_ADMIN (LAN)	LAN Management IP Address	Allow Firewall Administrators HTTPS Management of appliance
Deny	Any	DMZ, OPT	WAN	Allow objects configured on the DMZ or OPT interface access to the WAN
Deny	Any	WAN	DMZ, OPT	Deny all traffic originating from the WAN that has a destination of the DMZ or OPT interface

Continued

Table 4.12 continued Secure-by-Default Rule Base

Action	Service	Source	Destination	Comment
Deny	Any	WAN, DMZ, or OPT	LAN, WLAN	Deny all traffic originating from the WAN, DMZ, or OPT interface with a destination of the LAN or WLAN.
Deny	Any	LAN, WLAN	DMZ, OPT, WAN	Deny all traffic originating from the LAN or WLAN to the DMZ, OPT, and WAN interfaces

Access Rules—Part 2

We will now turn our attention from theory and configuration settings to actually creating rules on the SonicWALL. Three examples will be used to help explain exactly how access rules are created, as well as how certain settings affect the configuration options available.

Getting Ready to Create Access Rules

A solid rule base is critical to the effectiveness of your firewall. Over the past several years, the following methodology has been developed and can be applied to any firewall. The methodology follows *x* number of simple steps which are detailed below.

1. Create a network diagram that depicts all devices and networks that will be protected by the firewall.

2. Create a list of device names and IP addresses for devices, IP address ranges, and/or networks that you will create access rules for.

3. Create a list of services that will be allowed inbound and outbound from each network and/or device.

Access Rule Example 1—Firewall Management Rules

We start by creating our firewall management rules, which allow only authorized devices access to the SonicWALL's management console. However, first we need to create the address objects for the management devices (refer to Figure 4.31).

Figure 4.31 Firewall Management Diagram

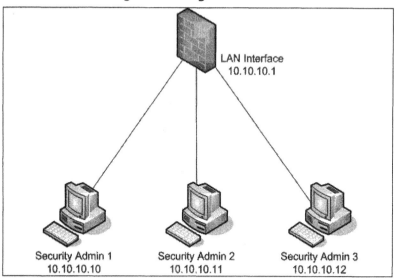

First, create the address objects for the devices that will be used for firewall management. We will use a range and name it FW_ADMIN. If the devices did not have IP addresses that were in sequence, we would create individual host address objects for the devices and then create an address group and assign them to it. Next, we browse to **Firewall | Access Rules** and click the **Matrix View Style** option. From the matrix, you need to modify the existing rules that pertain to firewall management under **LAN | LAN** (see Figure 4.32).

Figure 4.32 LAN-to-LAN Default Rules

#	Priority	Source	Destination	Service	Action	Users	Comment	Enable	Configure
1	1	Any	All X0 Management IP	Ping	Allow	All		✔	
2	2	Any	All X0 Management IP	SSH Management	Allow	All		✔	
3	3	Any	All X0 Management IP	HTTPS Management	Allow	All		✔	
4	4	Any	All X0 Management IP	HTTP Management	Allow	All		✔	
5	5	Any	Any	Any	Allow	All		✔	

Firewall > Access Rules > LAN > LAN   Public Server Wizard...   Clear Statistics   Restore Defaults... ?

Access Rules (LAN > LAN)   Items 1 to 5 (of 5)

View Style: All Rules Matrix Drop-down Boxes

Add   Delete   Restore Defaults...

As shown in Figure 4.32, any source is allowed to access the management interface of the SonicWALL via HTTP or HTTPS Management. This is obviously not recommended and needs to be modified. Click the **Configure** icon to the right of HTTPS Management. The dialog shown in Figure 4.33 will be displayed.

Figure 4.33 Default HTTPS Management Rule

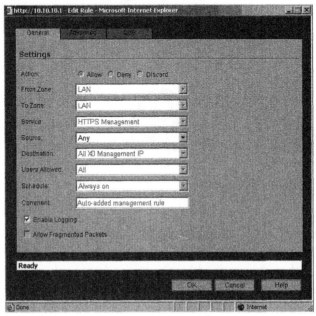

Since this is a default rule, the only option that can be changed is the source. Click the drop-down menu and select **FW_ADMIN** from the list. Click **OK** to complete the modification. Looking at the **LAN | LAN** rules again, we can see that the HTTPS Management rule only applies to the *FW_ADMIN* object (see Figure 4.34).

Figure 4.34 FW_ADMIN HTTPS Management Rule

#	Priority	Source	Destination	Service	Action	Users	Comment	Enable	Configure
1	1	Any	All X0 Management IP	Ping	Allow	All		✔	
2	2	Any	All X0 Management IP	SSH Management	Allow	All		✔	
3	3	FW_ADMIN	All X0 Management IP	HTTPS Management	Allow	All		✔	
4	4	Any	All X0 Management IP	HTTP Management	Allow	All		✔	
5	5	Any	Any	Any	Allow	All		✔	

The same process is repeated for Secure Shell (SSH) Management and HTTP Management. Why can't the last rule that states Allow Any Source to Any Destination using Any Service be set to Deny or Discard? This rule was automatically created by the SonicWALL due to Allow Interface Trust being enabled for the zone. To remove this rule, browse to **Network | Zones** and click the **configure** icon next to the LAN zone. On the Edit Zone dialog box, clear the Allow Interface Trust option and click **OK**. When you go back to the access rules and view the **LAN | LAN** rules, you see that our rules now only allow PING from the LAN to the SonicWALL LAN interface and all management rules are restricted to the FW_ADMIN Range object (see Figure 4.35)

Figure 4.35 Completed Firewall Management

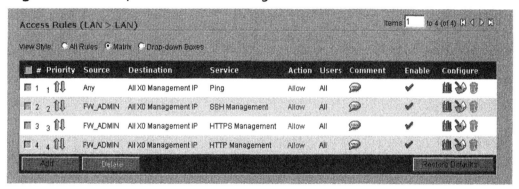

Access Rule Example 2— Restricting Outbound Traffic

This example continues with the Secure-by-Default approach and restricts outbound traffic from the LAN to the WAN. Choose the "Drop-Down Boxes View" style and select LAN as the From Zone and WAN as the To Zone. The resulting list of rules will look similar to that shown in Figure 4.36.

Figure 4.36 Default LAN-to-WAN Rules

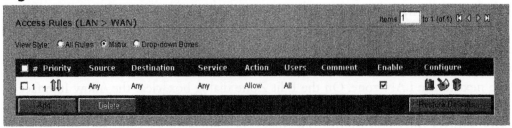

All traffic from the LAN is allowed to any destination on the WAN. While this may suffice for most organizations, from a security standpoint, it is recommended to restrict the outbound traffic to specific services. To do this, you need to first define a group of services that will be allowed outbound from the LAN. Browse to the **Firewall | Services** page and choose the **Custom Services View** style. Under Service Groups, click the **Add** button and name the group Allowed Outbound Services. For this example, we will allow HTTP, HTTPS, FTP, TELNET, and GEOMECH. Figure 4.37 shows the Allowed Outbound Services group and the services that are assigned to it.

Figure 4.37 Allowed Outbound Services Group

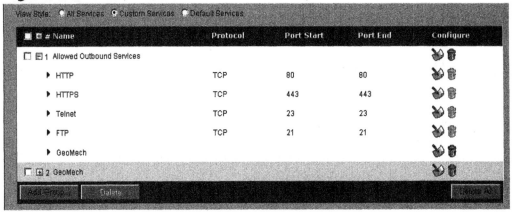

With the Service group created, you can now configure the required rules to restrict outbound traffic from the LAN. Return to the **Firewall | Access Rules | LAN | WAN** and click the **Configure** icon next to the Allow rule. The Edit Access Rule dialog will be displayed (see Figure 4.38).

Figure 4.38 Example 2 Edit Rule Dialog

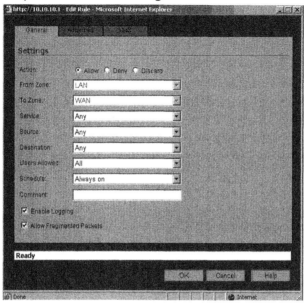

Change the action to Deny and click **OK** to complete the rule modification. Access from all the devices on the LAN is now denied to resources on the WAN. While this is a security administrator's dream, it is not reality. In reality, devices are allowed to WAN resources; however, you can limit the types of traffic that will be allowed. Click the **Add** button on the bottom of the **LAN | WAN** rules page. The Add Access Rule dialog box is displayed (see Figure 4.39).

Figure 4.39 Allow Outbound Services

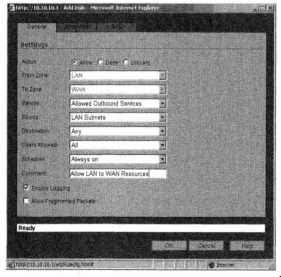

The action for our rule is Allow, the service is configured to use the Allowed Outbound Services group, and the source is LAN subnets. This rule applies to all traffic originating from the LAN with a destination on the WAN, so the destination is configured as Any. The final set of rules is shown in Figure 4.40.

Figure 4.40 LAN-to-WAN Rules

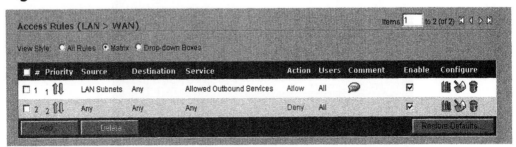

As you look at Figure 4.40, notice that the entries under the Source and Service columns only show the objects and not the actual values for the entries. Holding the mouse pointer over the Service Group lists the individual services that are part of the group (see Figure 4.41). The same is true for the Source object.

Figure 4.41 Viewing Service Group Members

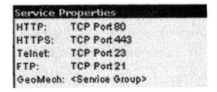

When testing the aforementioned rule, you will notice that you cannot browse the Internet. The reason is a common overlooked service is missing from our Allowed Outbound Services group, DNS. This was intentionally omitted from the group to illustrate the power of using objects in your configuration. Browse to **Firewall | Services** and click the **Configure** button next to the Allowed Outbound Services group. Scroll through the list of predefined services and select **DNS**. After adding DNS to the group, click **OK**. Since the rule is configured to use the Allowed Outbound Services group, it will automatically be updated when the group is changed. With that said, no further configuration changes are required and you can browse the Internet.

Access Rule Example 3—Allowing Inbound SMTP Traffic and Web Traffic

As discussed earlier in this chapter, NAT is used to translate public IP addresses to private IP addresses and vice versa. This example explains how NAT is used to translate SMTP and Web traffic that is received by a single public IP address to two different servers on the DMZ (see Figure 4.42).

Figure 4.42 Example 3—Network Diagram

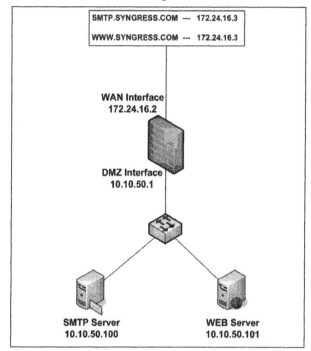

First, you need to create the address objects. This can be accomplished with three objects:

- DMZ-SMTP-01—10.10.50.100
- DMZ-WEB-01—10.10.50.101
- WAN-SMTP_WEB—172.24.16.3

However, in an effort to keep the NAT Policies and Access Rules as easy to understand as possible, we will create four objects:

- DMZ-SMTP-01—10.10.50.100

- WAN-SMTP-01—172.24.16.3

- DMZ-WEB-01—10.10.50.101

- WAN-WEB-01—172.24.16.3

The objects required for this example are shown in Figure 4.43.

Figure 4.43 Three Address Objects

WAN-WEB-01	172.24.16.3/255.255.255.255	Host	WAN
DMZ-WEB-01	10.10.50.101/255.255.255.255	Host	DMZ
WAN-SMTP-01	172.24.16.3/255.255.255.255	Host	WAN
DMZ-SMTP-01	10.10.50.100/255.255.255.255	Host	DMZ

Both the SMTP and Web server are configured to use the same external IP address, 172.24.16.3. We need to configure two NAT policies to accomplish the required translation. Browse to the **Network | NAT Policies** page and select **Custom Policies** as the View Style. Click the Add button to display the Add NAT Policy dialog window. For this example, enter the information shown in Figure 4.44 and click **OK**.

Figure 4.44 Map SMTP Traffic to DMZ-SMTP-01 Server

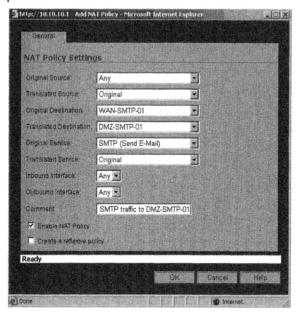

Do not enable the Create a Reflexive Policy option. We will create a policy for used for this purpose manually. Repeat the same procedure for the Web server, with the exception of the service. Instead of using a single service, configure a service group with HTTP and HTTPS assigned to it. The name of the group will be Web Services.

Instead of creating the service group by browsing to **Firewall | Services**, click the drop-down box next to Original Service and select **Create New Group**. This will display the Add Service Group dialog box. Enter **Web Services** for the name of the group, add HTTP and HTTPS to the group, and then click **OK** to complete the process. This will return you to the NAT policy and the Original Service will now show Web Services (see Figure 4.45).

Figure 4.45 Map Web Services to DMZ-WEB-01 Server

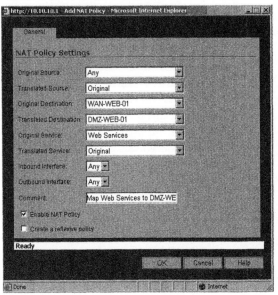

Click **OK** to complete the NAT policy. To further explain these policies, we are using a combination of NAT and Port Address Translation (PAT). First, the public IP address is contacted by a client device on the Internet. If the client is requesting Web services (HTTP or HTTPS), the public IP is translated to the private IP of the Web server. If the traffic was SMTP, the public IP is translated to the private IP of the SMTP server. The PAT takes place based on the traffic type.

After you create the inbound NAT policies, the outbound policies need to be created. To do this, click **Add** on the bottom of the NAT policies window. The "Add NAT Policy" dialog box will be displayed. Configure the policy to look like Figure 4.46.

Figure 4.46 Outbound SMTP NAT Policy

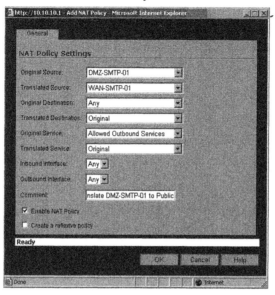

Again, do not enable the Create a Reflexive Policy option. Click **OK** to complete the policy. Repeat the procedure for the Web server. Finally, the access rules need to be created to allow the inbound and outbound traffic from these servers. Browse to **Firewall | Access Rules** and choose **Drop Down Boxes** as the view style. Select WAN as the From Zone and DMZ as the To Zone. Click the **Add** button on the bottom of the page. The Add Rule dialog is displayed in Figure 4.47.

Figure 4.47 Access Rule to Allow Inbound SMTP Traffic

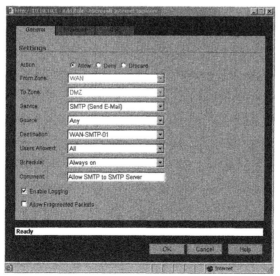

Enter the information as shown in Figure 4.47 and click **OK** to create the rule. Repeat the procedure for the Web server using the Web Services group. With the inbound rules defined, we need to create the outbound rules for the DMZ. Again, by default, all traffic on the DMZ is allowed outbound. Click the **Configure** icon to the right of the default rule and change the action to Deny.

Finally, we need to create the Outbound access rule. We will add a rule that will apply to all devices on the DMZ network in an effort to keep the rule base as short as possible. Click the **Add** button to display the Add Rule dialog box, and enter the information shown in Figure 4.48.

Figure 4.48 Outbound Access for DMZ Network Resources

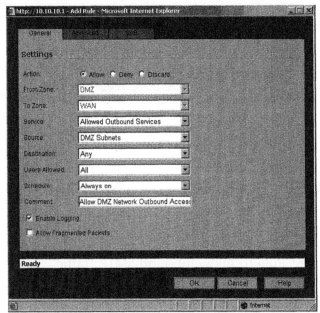

That completes the configuration for your rules. You should now understand how access rules are created and how the individual elements they are composed of fit together.

Advanced Options for Firewalls

The advanced options available for the firewall include options for Detection Prevention, Dynamic Ports, Source Routed Packets, Connections, Access Rule Service Options, IP and UDP Checksum Enforcement, and UDP Timeout values.

Detection Prevention

Detection prevention is used to essentially hide your SonicWALL from attackers. There are two options that you can set to accomplish this: Stealth Mode and Randomize IP ID.

By default, when a connection request is sent to the SonicWALL or a node that is protected by it, the firewall responds as either Blocked or Open. The concern with this behavior is that a "Blocked" response sends a reset packet back to the client and then drops the connection. If the request comes from a malicious user, the reset packet will tell them that there is a device on the IP address that they were attempting to connect to.

However, it is recommended that the SonicWALL be configured to drop connections without sending a reset packet back to the originating client. To do this, you need to check the **Enable Stealth Mode** option on the SonicWALL. When you enable the stealth mode on the SonicWALL, you have basically made the unit invisible to attackers.

Notes from the Underground…

Stealth Mode

Stealth mode has a similar effect on traffic with the destination of the SonicWALL's interface, as the Discard action has on rules. The capture shown below shows the SonicWALL's response when stealth mode is disabled. The request is being made to port 3389 (RDP).

```
172.24.16.2 172.24.16.1  TCP    3874 > 3389 [SYN] Seq=1553106819 Ack=0 Win=64512 Len=0 MSS=1460
172.24.16.1 172.24.16.2  TCP    3389 > 3874 [RST, ACK] Seq=0 Ack=1553106820 Win=0 Len=0
```

The SonicWALL sends a Reset packet back to the client, which in today's malicious world, is like painting a target on your chest and walking out onto a battle field.

Look at the same test with Stealth Mode enabled:

```
172.24.16.2 172.24.16.1  TCP    3874 > 3389 [SYN] Seq=1553106819 Ack=0 Win=64512 Len=0 MSS=1460
172.24.16.1 172.24.16.2  TCP    3389 > 3874 [RST, ACK] Seq=0 Ack=1553106820 Win=0 Len=0
```

Continued

www.syngress.com

> No response from the SonicWALL. To an attacker it looks as if there is no device configured on this particular IP address and he or she will move on to more interesting targets. Stealth Mode is equivalent to putting on camouflage and then walking out onto the battle field.

Dynamic Ports

Dynamic ports are typically used as source ports by clients communicating with a remote server on a well-known port such as HTTP. These ports change on a per-connection basis, hence the name dynamic ports. Some services, such as Oracle SQLNet, Windows Messenger, and Real Time Streaming Protocol, use dynamic ports for communication. The SonicWALL provides the capability to support these services (see Figure 4.49).

Figure 4.49 Dynamic Ports

Dynamic Ports

☑ Enable support for Oracle (SQLNet)

☑ Enable support for Windows Messenger

☑ Enable RTSP Transformations

- **Enable Support for Oracle (SQLNet)** This option should be enabled if you have Oracle applications on your network

- **Enable Support for Windows Messenger** Enabling this option provides support for special Session Initiation Protocol (SIP) messaging used in Windows Messenger on Windows XP clients.

- **Enable Real-time Streaming Protocol (RTSP) Transformations** This option should be enabled to support on-demand delivery of real-time data, such as audio and/or video. RTSP is the application level protocol that is used to control the delivery of data with real-time properties.

Source-Routed Packets

Source routing is an IP option that allows the capability to specify the route that a packet will take to a host, and the path the packet will follow while returning to the originator. Source routing is commonly used for troubleshooting purposes. As with most other tools, there is a dark side to this tool. Hackers can use source routing to trick a device into thinking that it is talking to a different device, when in fact they are talking to a third-party malicious host.

Source routing is disabled by default on SonicWALL appliances. If you need to enable source routing, simply clear the check box. Keep in mind that this should only be done if there is a specific need. It is recommended that source routing be disabled.

Connections

In high-traffic situations or if you have dedicated intrusion prevention devices on your network, it is beneficial to configure the firewall to perform strictly firewall functions. SonicWALL provides the capability to disable the Gateway Antivirus and IPS'. This is accomplished by checking Disable Gateway AV and IPS Engine. By checking this option, the maximum number of connections available on the SonicWALL will be increased.

Access Rule Service Options

In strict security configurations, it is beneficial to restrict all traffic, both inbound and outbound. However, services such as FTP commonly use a specific inbound port and remap the outbound traffic to a dynamic port. To disable this functionality (specifically for FTP), enable the option to force inbound and outbound FTP data connections to use default port 20.

TCP Settings

TCP statistics for the SonicWALL can be viewed by navigating to the TCP Settings under the **Firewall** tab. The TCP Settings page is divided into four sections:

- TCP Traffic Statistics
- TCP Settings
- Layer 3 SYN Flood Protection
- Layer 2 SYN Flood Protection

TCP Traffic Statistics

The TCP Traffic Statistics contain valuable data that can assist with troubleshooting the SonicWALL (see Figure 4.50).

Figure 4.50 TCP Traffic Statistics

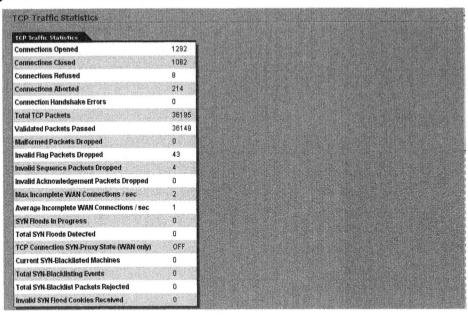

The following statistics are displayed by the SonicWALL:

- **Connections Opened** This number is incremented for each TCP connection client that sends a SYN or for each TCP connection server that receives a SYN.

- **Connections Closed** Incremented when a TCP connection is closed when both the client and server have sent a FIN packet and received an ACK packet.

- **Connections Refused** Each time the firewall receives a RST packet and the server is in a SYN_RCVD state.

- **Connections Aborted** If the server is not in a SYN_RCVD state and a RST packet is received, this number is incremented.

- **Total TCP Packets** This number is incremented with every TCP packet that is processed by the SonicWALL.

- **Validated Packets Passed** This number is incremented when the following conditions are met:

  - TCP packet passes checksum validation while TCP checksum validation is enabled.

  - A valid SYN packet is encountered while SYN Flood protection is enabled.

  - A SYN cookie is successfully validated on a packet with the ACK flag set, while SYN Flood protection is enabled.

- **Corrupted Packets Dropped** This number is incremented when the following conditions are met:

  - TCP packet failed checksum validation while TCP checksum validation is enabled.

  - The TCP Selective Acknowledgement (SACK) option is encountered, but the calculated option length is incorrect.

  - The TCP Maximum Segment Size (MSS) option is encountered, but the calculated option length is incorrect.

  - The TCP SACK option data is calculated to be either less than the minimum of 6 bytes or modulo incongruent to the block size of 4 bytes.

  - The TCP option length is determined to be invalid.

  - The TCP header length is calculated to be less than the 20-byte minimum.

  - The TCP header length is calculated to be greater than the packet's data length.

- **Invalid Flag Packets Dropped** This number is incremented under the following conditions:

  - If a non-SYN packet is received that cannot be located within the connection-cache when SYN flood protection is enabled.

  - If a packet with flags other than SYN, RST+ACK, or SYN+ACK is received during the session establishment when SYN Flood protection is enabled.

- TCP XMAS Scan will be logged if the packet has FIN, URG, and PUSH flags set.

- TCP FIN Scan will be logged if the packet has the FIN flag set.

- TCP NULL Scan will be logged if the packet has no flags set.

- If a new TCP connection initiation is attempted with something other than just a SYN flag set.

- If a packet with the SYN flag set is received within an already established TCP session.

- **Invalid Sequence Packets Dropped** This number is incremented when the following conditions are met:

  - If a packet within an already established connection is received, where the sequence number is less than the connection's oldest acknowledgement sequence.

  - If a packet within an already established connection is received where the sequence number is greater than the connection's oldest unacknowledged sequence plus the connection's last advertised window size.

- **Invalid Acknowledgement Packets Dropped** This number is incremented when the following conditions are met:

  - If a packet is received with the ACK flag set and neither the RST nor the SYN flags are set, but the SYN cookie is determined to be invalid when SYN Flood protection is enabled.

  - If a packet's ACK value, adjusted by the sequence number randomization offset, is less than the connection's oldest unacknowledged sequence number.

  - If a packet's ACK value, adjusted by the sequence number randomization offset, is greater than the connection's next expected sequence number.

TCP Settings

The TCP Settings page allows additional TCP packet checks to be enabled on the SonicWALL (see Figure 4.51). These settings vary depending on the model of SonicWALL that is implemented.

Figure 4.51 TCP Settings

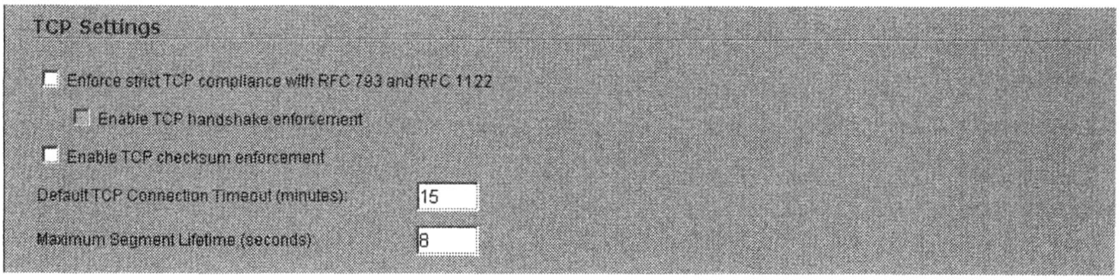

- **Enforce Strict TCP Compliance with RFC 793 and RFC 1122** This option forces all TCP connections to strictly adhere to the following setup requirements:
- Client → SYN → server
- Client ← SYN/ACK ← server
- Client → ACK → server
- Session established

After the initial SYN, clients can send a RST or a SYN or a server can send a SYN-ACK or a RST. All other TCP flags are considered invalid or malicious in nature. When the Enable TCP Stateful Inspection option is enabled, any traffic that violates these rules is dropped by the firewall.

- **Enable TCP Checksum Validation** Packets with invalid TCP checksums will be dropped.

- **Default TCP Connection Timeout** This value is the default time assigned to access rules for TCP connections. If a TCP session is active for a period of time in excess of this value, the TCP connection will be cleared by the SonicWALL. This value can be set between a minimum of 1 minute and a maximum of 999 minutes. Note, increasing this number too high could result in exhausting the connection cache and cause additional connections to be dropped.

- **Maximum Segment Lifetime (Seconds)** This option is used to set the amount of time (in seconds) that any TCP packet is valid. After this time expires the packet expires. This value is also used to determine the amount of time that an actively closed TCP connection should remain in the TIME_WAIT state to ensure that the proper FIN/ACK exchange has occurred to properly close the TCP connection. The default value is set to 8 seconds; it can be set to a minimum of 1 second and a maximum of 8 seconds.

SYN Flood Protection

To understand how SYN flood protection functions, you need to understand the three-way TCP handshake. In a typical TCP connection, the client first sends a SYN packet with a 32-bit sequence number referred to as (SEQc) to a server. If the service that the client is requesting is available on the server, it will respond to the request with a SYN/ACK to acknowledge that it received the sequence. The actual ACK packet that is returned to the client is equal to (SEQc + 1) and a random 32-bit sequence number (SEQs). In addition to responding to the client with the SYN/ACK, the server now maintains state awaiting the final ACK from the client. The next packet from the client, ACK, should contain the next sequence (SEQc + 1) in addition to an acknowledgement of the sequence it received from the server. The client sends an ACK packet equal to (SEQs + 1).

As shown in Figure 4.52, the client sends SYN (SEQc=751040435, ACK=0) to the server.

Figure 4.52 SYN Packet

```
⊟ Transmission Control Protocol, Src Port: 2854 (2854), Dst Port: http (80), Seq: 751040435, Ack: 0, Len: 0
     Source port: 2854 (2854)
     Destination port: http (80)
     Sequence number: 751040435
     Header length: 28 bytes
```

The server responds with SYN/ACK (SEQs=3292159804, ACKs=SEQc + 1 = 751040436) to the client (see Figure 4.53).

Figure 4.53 SYN/ACK Packet

```
⊟ Transmission Control Protocol, Src Port: http (80), Dst Port: 2854 (2854), Seq: 3292150804, Ack: 751040436, Len: 0
     Source port: http (80)
     Destination port: 2854 (2854)
     Sequence number: 3292150804
     Acknowledgement number: 751040436
     Header length: 24 bytes
```

As shown in Figure 4.54, the client responds with ACK (SEQc + 1=751040436, ACK=SEQs + 1=3292150805).

Figure 4.54 ACK Packet

```
⊟ Transmission Control Protocol, Src Port: 2854 (2854), Dst Port: http (80), Seq: 751040436, Ack: 3292150805, Len: 0
     Source port: 2854 (2854)
     Destination port: http (80)
     Sequence number: 751040436
     Acknowledgement number: 3292150805
     Header length: 20 bytes
```

Assume that the following scenario is encountered: the client sends SYN (SEQc=751040435, ACK=0) to the server (see Figure 4.55).

Figure 4.55 SYN Packet

```
⊟ Transmission Control Protocol, Src Port: 2854 (2854), Dst Port: http (80), Seq: 751040435, Ack: 0, Len: 0
    Source port: 2854 (2854)
    Destination port: http (80)
    Sequence number: 751040435
    Header length: 28 bytes
```

The server responds with SYN/ACK (SEQs=3292159804, ACKs=SEQc + 1 = 751040436) to the client (see Figure 4.56).

Figure 4.56 SYN/ACK Packet

```
⊟ Transmission Control Protocol, Src Port: http (80), Dst Port: 2854 (2854), Seq: 3292150804, Ack: 751040436, Len: 0
    Source port: http (80)
    Destination port: 2854 (2854)
    Sequence number: 3292150804
    Acknowledgement number: 751040436
    Header length: 24 bytes
```

However, the client never sends the final ACK packet to complete the three-way handshake—this is known as a "half-open connection." Since the server is responsible for maintaining state on half-opened connections, a situation could present itself where the number the SYNs received are occurring faster than the server can process or clear them. In essence, the server would deplete its memory and no longer be able to process legitimate connections. Welcome to the world of SYN flood attacks.

If a SonicWALL appliance is between the client and server, the SonicWALL proxies the TCP connection between the client and the server. With this in mind, the SonicWALL can provide protection for hosts behind it from DOS and DDOS attacks that attempt to exhaust available resources. These attacks may occur under two different scenarios.

1. Sending TCP SYN packets to a valid host using invalid or spoofed IP addresses

2. Excessive half-opened TCP connections are created in excessive numbers

The SonicWALL considers a SYN Flood attack to be in progress if the number of SYN/ACK packets sent by the firewall exceeds the threshold set in the "Flood rate until attack logged" field. In other words, if the unanswered SYN/ACK packets per second exceed this threshold, the SonicWALL assumes that there is a SYN Flood attack in progress and takes action. The default threshold value is 20; however, it can be set to a minimum of 5 and a maximum of 999,999.

SYN Flood Protection Overview

Beginning with SonicOS Enhanced 3.1, SonicWALL uses stateless SYN cookies to provide SYN Flood protection. This approach increases the reliability of SYN Flood detection and also improves overall resource utilization on the SonicWALL. By using stateless SYN cookies, the SonicWALL does not have to maintain the state of half-opened connections. As opposed to randomness, SonicWALL uses a cryptographic calculation to arrive at SEQs.

SonicWALL provides the capability to protect against SYN Flood attacks that originate from the LAN or the WAN. Attacks on the LAN are generally caused by devices that are infected with a virus, while attacks originating from the WAN are usually directed to one or more servers behind the firewall.

To provide protection against both types of attacks, LAN and WAN, there are two separate SYN Flood protection mechanisms built into the SonicWALL: one for Layer 3, WAN attacks and another for Layer 2, LAN attacks.

Layer 3 SYN Flood Protection

The SYN Proxy (Layer 3) mechanism provides protection for servers behind the SonicWALL by providing a SYN Proxy to verify the WAN clients before their connections are forwarded to the actual server. This functionality applies to WAN interfaces only. To configure Layer 3 protection, navigate to the **Firewall** tab and select **TCP Settings**.

SYN Flood Protection Mode

The three levels of Layer 3 SYN Flood Protection are listed below.

- **Watch and Report Possible SYN Floods** This option enables the SonicWALL to monitor all SYN traffic activity on all interfaces. Suspected SYN Floods are then logged to the event log if the packet count exceeds the configured threshold. This level of protection does not enable the SYN Proxy feature.

- **Proxy WAN Client Connection When Attack is Suspected** This option enables the SYN Proxy feature of the SonicWALL. Again, this only applies to the WAN interface. Protection is applied if the number of incomplete connection attempts per second exceeds the configured threshold value. This level of protection ensures that the device under attack will still process valid traffic and that its performance will not degrade during the attack. Proxy mode will remain active until the SYN Flood ceases or until the SonicWALL blacklists all of the devices responsible for the flood. This option should be enabled if there is a suspected SYN Flood taking place on either the LAN or WAN.

- **Always Proxy WAN Client Connections** In specific high-risk environments, it may be beneficial for the SonicWALL to always proxy SYN packets. This ensures that all spoofed SYN packets will be dropped by the firewall preventing them from ever reaching the protected server(s). Use caution when selecting this option, as the SonicWALL will respond to port scans on all TCP ports. Obviously, this can lead to degraded performance and may generate false positives.

SYN Attack Threshold

This value is used to determine the limits for SYN Flood activity before action is taken to provide protection. The initial value is computed automatically by the SonicWALL based on statistics gathered on the WAN TCP connections. The statistics gathered include the maximum, average maximum, and incomplete WAN connections per second.

- **Use the 300 Value Calculated from Gathered Statistics** Enabling this option sets the threshold for the number of incomplete connection attempts per second to 300. If the number of incomplete connection attempts exceeds this value, the SonicWALL begins dropping the connections.

- **Attack Threshold (Incomplete Connection Attempts/Second)** Enabling this option allows you to set a specific threshold for the number of incomplete connection attempts. If the number of incomplete connection attempts exceeds this value, the SonicWALL will begin dropping the connections. The value for this field can be set to a minimum of 5 and a maximum of 999,999.

SYN-Proxy Options

When the SonicWALL applies a SYN-proxy to a TCP connection, the appliance responds to initial SYN packets with a manufactured SYN/ACK packet and waits for the final ACK before forwarding the connection to the legitimate server. During a SYN Flood attack, devices never respond to the SYN/ACK packet, which makes it easy for the SonicWALL to identify the attack and block the spoofed connection attempts. While this type of protection appears to be great, the fact that the

SonicWALL manufactures a SYN/ACK packet response without knowing how the server will respond to the options normally provided on SYN/ACK packets posses a potential problem. To compensate for this, SonicWALL has additional controls that can be enforced when the unit is in SYN Proxy mode.

- **SACK** Selective Acknowledgement (SACK) controls whether or not a packet or series of packets can be dropped and if a notification from the SonicWALL can be sent to the client informing it which data has been received and were holes may exist in the data.

- **MSS** The Minimum Segment Size (MSS) sets the threshold that restricts the size of TCP segments to be below this value (e.g., when using Secure Internet Protocol (IPSec), the MSS may need to be limited to ensure space is provided for the IPSec headers. When SYN Proxy is enabled, the firewall is unable to predict the MSS value of the server when it sends the manufactured SYN/ACK packet to the client. The ability to control the size of a segment provides the capability to dictate the MSS value that is sent to WAN clients.

SYN Proxy Threshold

- **All LAN/DMZ Servers Support the TCP SACK Option** This option should only be enabled if all servers that are accessed from the WAN support the SACK option. Enabling this option instructs the firewall that packets can be dropped and that the client device will respond with which packets it has received.

- **Limit MSS Sent to WAN Clients (When Connections are Proxied)** This value sets the maximum MSS segment size, (1460 by default) and indicates that segments of this size or smaller will be sent to the client in the SYN/ACK cookie. Caution should be used when modifying this setting, as a value too low can impact performance and a value too high can break connections if the server responds with a smaller MSS value.

- **Maximum TCP MSS Sent to WAN Clients** This is the actual value of the MSS.

It is important to keep in mind that the options we just covered only apply when SYN Proxy mode is enabled. With that said, make sure that the values chosen are conservative. Proper configuration ensures that legitimate connections are processed appropriately during an attack.

Layer 2 Protection

Internal SYN Flood protection is accomplished using MAC Blacklisting. If a device exceeds the SYN Blacklist attack threshold, its MAC address is added to the black-list, which instructs the SonicWALL to block any traffic from the device early in the packet inspection process. This feature enables the firewall to process increased amounts of these packets. This provides a defense against attacks originating on the LAN, while also providing a second-tier level of protection for WAN networks.

The following options are used to configure Layer 2 SYN Flood protection on SonicWALL appliances:

- **Threshold for SYN Flood Blacklisting (SYNs/Secs)** This value indi-cates the maximum number of SYN packets allowed per second. The default setting is 1000. The value for this field should be larger than the SYN Proxy threshold value, because blacklisting attempts to thwart more vigorous local attacks or severe attacks from a WAN network.

- **Enable SYN Flood Blacklisting on All Interfaces** This enables the blacklisting capabilities on all interfaces.

- **Never Blacklist WAN Machines** When you enable this feature, WAN machines will not be blacklisted. This ensures that communications to and from the firewall's WAN interfaces will not be interrupted. It is recom-mended that this option be enabled.

- **Always Allow SonicWALL Management Traffic** To ensure that the management and routing protocols are allowed, the SonicWALL's WAN IP addresses are allowed through a blacklisted device. Enabling this feature is recommended to ensure that you do not lock yourself out of the firewall.

In addition to the TCP statistics covered earlier, there are numerous SYN Flood statistics that are also displayed.

- **Max Incomplete WAN Connections per Second** Indicates the number of pending embryonic half-open connections recorded since the firewall has been online or since the last time the statistics were manually cleared.

- **Average Incomplete WAN Connections per Second** Average number of pending embryonic half-open connections based on the total number of samples since the firewall has been online, or since the last time the statistics were manually cleared.

- **SYN Floods in Progress** Indicates the number of forwarding devices that are currently exceeding either SYN Flood threshold.

- **Total SYN Floods Detected** The total number of events in which a forwarding device has exceeded the lower of either of the SYN Flood threshold limits.

- **Total Connection SYN-Proxy Sate (WAN Only)** Indicates whether or not Proxy mode is currently enabled on the WAN interfaces.

- **Current SYN-Blacklisted Machines** Number of devices currently recorded in the blacklist.

- **Total SYN-Blacklisting Events** Running the total of devices that have been placed on the blacklist.

- **Total SYN-Blacklist Packets Rejected** Running the total of packets that have been rejected by the SonicWALL due to blacklisted devices.

Multicast

Multicast is used to deliver services such as multimedia presentations and videoconferencing. A multicast server sends a single IP packet to multiple hosts at the same time. SonicWALL allows administrators to configure individual settings to tune services that use multicasting.

Summary

The SonicWALL firewall provides many features that allow administrators complete control over traffic enforcement. This chapter covered everything from access control theory to access rule creation and TCP traffic statistics to SYN flood protection at Layer 2 and Layer 3. We reviewed the components required to create access rules, their purpose, and how they are all related. Three example scenarios were presented and walked through on a step-by-step basis to create the required NAT policies and rules to restrict both inbound and outbound traffic.

Solutions Fast Track

Theory of Access Control

☑ Zones are used to provide logical groupings of interfaces to provide additional flexibility when configuring NAT policies and rules.

☑ SonicWALLs ship with several predefined zones. In addition to the predefined zones, user-defined zones can be created to meet the needs of even the most complex networks.

☑ There are four classes of objects that can be configured on the SonicWALL: Address, Schedule, Service, and User.

☑ Address objects can be configured for a single host, a range of IP addresses, a network, or MAC addresses.

☑ Address objects are used throughout the SonicWALL configuration and are not limited to access rules.

☑ Address groups are used to group common address objects into a single entity. Instead of creating rules for individual objects, the address group can be specified.

☑ Service objects are used to define what types of traffic will be allowed, denied, or discarded by the SonicWALL.

☑ Service groups are used to group specific services into a single entity that can be used in access rules. This eliminates the need to create individual rules for each service that applies to a specific address object or address group.

☑ SonicWALL appliances ship with over 120 predefined services, including the most commonly used.

☑ NAT is used to translate public IP addresses to private IP addresses and vice versa.

☑ When using SonicOS Enhanced, administrators have full control over how NAT policies are enforced on the SonicWALL appliance.

☑ In addition to NAT, PAT can be configured to map IP addresses by service.

☑ Access Rules are used to either grant or deny access to specific resources protected by the SonicWALL.

☑ Rules are created for each set of Zones for inbound and outbound traffic.

☑ BWM and Quality of Service can be enforced on a per-rule basis.

☑ Access Rules are enforced by the Rule Priority.

☑ The number of access rules should be kept as short as possible to increase performance.

☑ Statistics can be viewed for each access rule by holding the mouse pointer over the Graph icon to the right of the rule.

BWM

☑ SonicOS Enhanced provides the capability to control bandwidth to both ingress (inbound) and egress (outbound) traffic on WAN interfaces.

☑ SonicWALL uses Class Based Queuing (CBQ) to manage the egress bandwidth and an ACK delay algorithm for ingress traffic.

☑ CBQ includes the capability to provide guaranteed and maximum bandwidth QOS for the SonicWALL.

QOS

☑ The QOS features of the SonicWALL are composed of three pieces: classification, marking, and conditioning.

☑ By default, SonicWALL appliances are configured to drop all inbound traffic to the LAN. In contrast, all outbound traffic will be allowed.

☑ A solid rule base is critical to the effectiveness of your firewall.

Advanced Options for Firewalls

☑ Detection prevention is used to hide the SonicWALL appliance from potential attackers by ignoring packets that are sent to directly to its WAN interface.

☑ Dynamic ports provide support for applications such as Oracle, Windows Messenger, and RTSP.

☑ Source-routed packets can be blocked or allowed.

☑ The SonicWALL Gateway Anti-Virus, Anti-Spyware, and IPS engine can be disabled if they are not being used. This eliminates the overhead of these services and allows the SonicWALL to perform strictly as a firewall.

☑ The TCP traffic statistics contain valuable data that can assist with troubleshooting the SonicWALL.

☑ Strict compliance with RFC 793 and 1122, as well as TCP checksum validation, can be enforced by the SonicWALL to enhance security.

☑ Layer 3 SYN Flood protection reduces the risks involved with DOS and DDOS attacks from the WAN.

☑ Layer 2 SYN Flood protection reduces the risks involved with DOS and DDOS attacks originating from the LAN.

SYN FLood Protection Overview

- ☑ Multicasting is used to send a single packet to multiple IP addresses at the same time.

- ☑ Multicasting is used for applications such as multimedia presentations and videoconferencing.

Frequently Asked Questions

The following Frequently Asked Questions, answered by the authors of this book, are designed to both measure your understanding of the concepts presented in this chapter and to assist you with real-life implementation of these concepts. To have your questions about this chapter answered by the author, browse to **www.syngress.com/solutions** and click on the **"Ask the Author"** form.

Q: Do I have to create address objects for each individual device on my network for them to be protected by the SonicWALL?

A: No. The predefined objects, NAT policies, and rules will cover all of the devices on your network. However, if you need to allow or block specific traffic to or from a specific device, it will need an address object.

Q: What is the maximum number of rules that I should have on my SonicWALL?

A: As few as possible. Each rule is processed in order by priority. The more rules that traffic has to be compared with, the more overhead the SonicWALL will have. It is also important to confirm that the most commonly matched rules be listed at the top of the rule base. This is done by viewing the rules priority.

Q: How does the SonicWALL know what order to put the rules in?

A: The SonicWALL orders rules by how granular they are. In other words, a rule that denies traffic to a specific device from a specific source and for a specific service will be listed above a rule that denies all traffic to any destination from any source.

Q: How does SonicWALL process rules with the same priority?

A: The priority can be the same for multiple rules; however, rule number 1 is always processed first, and then number 2, and so on.

Q: What is the highest priority that I can configure a rule to have?

A: The highest priority for a rule is -1.

Q: What is the difference between Deny and Discard actions for rules?

A: The Deny action sends a RST packet back to the client to notify it that the connection was dropped. The Discard action simply ignores the packet and does not respond to the client.

Q: Can I configure both Layer 2 and Layer 3 SYN Flood protection?

A: Yes, it is actually recommended. Caution should be used to ensure that servers are not blacklisted by the SonicWALL.

Chapter 5

User Authentication

Solutions in this chapter:

- **Types of users**
- **User databases**
- **External Auth Servers**

Introduction

User authentication is one of the most important aspects of the SonicWALL firewall. Without a method of providing for the authentication of users, the firewall would lack the ability to limit who has access to administrative features or virtual private networks (VPNs). By providing a set of strong user authentication capabilities, the SonicWALL firewall helps secure your network. The SonicWALL firewall also provides a balance between security and ease-of-use via the many features supported in its authentication mechanisms.

User authentication on the SonicWALL firewall can at first seem like a daunting task. It has three ways to store the users, and five default groups for assigning permissions.

In this chapter, we will discuss the types of users and how they should be used. We will discuss the types of authentication servers, the features that each authentication user has, and what limitations you should be aware of. Finally, we will show you how to set up users, authentication servers, and more.

Types of Users

The SonicWALL authentication system has the following types of users: *Local Users* and *Guest Accounts*. Each of the types of users has specific capabilities associated with its use. In the next section, we will discuss the types of users further and what their uses can or should be.

Local Users

Local users are users that must authenticate to the firewall before being given authorization to access either the firewall or systems behind the firewall. Local users store their authentication credentials on the firewall rather than external hosts, as found in RADIUS or LDAP authentication. Storing the credentials on the firewall is an excellent way to get started with user authentication with SonicWALL firewalls. However, when using multiple firewalls and network devices, it may be a good idea to use one of the centralized authentication schemes such as LDAP or RADIUS. The Local Users Database on the SonicWALL can support a maximum of 1,000 user accounts. If more than 1,000 users will be required, a RADIUS or LDAP server must be used.

To configure local users, browse to **Users | Local Users**. The Local Users table will be displayed as shown in Figure 5.1. Click the **Add User** button to display the Add User Dialog.

Figure 5.1 Local Users

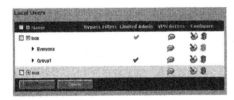

Figure 5.2 Add User Groups Dialog

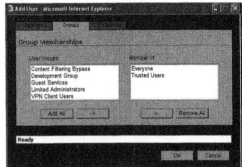

Type the User name, password and a brief comment for the new user and then click the Groups tab. The Groups tab, shown in Figure 5.2, is used to assign this user account to a Group. Access is then granted or denied on a group level instead of on the individual user account level.

Finally, the VPN Access tab is used to specify what resources this user can access if using a VPN client connection. The VPN Access tab is shown in Figure 5.3.

Figure 5.3 Add User VPN Access Dialog

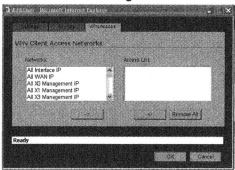

Local Groups

In addition to creating Local Users, Local Groups can also be created. Figure 5.4 shows the Local Users page and its associated entries.

Figure 5.4 Local Groups

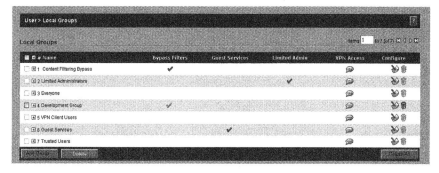

Click the **Add Group** button to display the Add Group Dialog page. Enter a name for the group and a brief comment, such as Development Team. Click the **Members** tab. The Add Group Members dialog will be shown (See Figure 5.5). Select the **Non-Member Users** and **Groups** from the left hand column that will be added to the new group, and then click the icon with the arrow pointing to the right. The selected users and groups will now be displayed under the Member Users and Groups column. After adding the appropriate members, click the **VPN Access** tab to display the VPN Access Dialog as shown in Figure 5.6.

Scroll through the list of available networks in the left hand column, and select the appropriate objects that the new group will have access to. Click the icon with the arrow pointing to the right to add the selected objects to the Access List column.

Figure 5.5 Add Group: Members Dialog

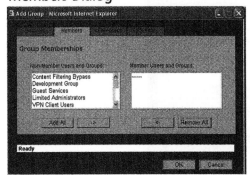

Figure 5.6 Add Group: VPN Access Dialog

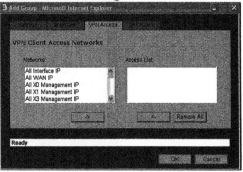

The CFS Policy tab is used to configure what Content Filtering Policy will be applied to this particular group. Select the policy and the appropriate options and then click the **OK** button to create the Group.

Guest Accounts

Guest accounts are used to allow guests to access specific resources. For example, if your company provides training facilities for customers and they need access to the Internet. A Guest Account could be created to allow this. Guest accounts are temporary and will be removed after the expiration date configured by the firewall administrator.

Guest Services

Before adding a new Guest Account, you should configure the Guest Services. To do this, browse to **Users | Guest Services**. The Guest Services screen will be displayed as shown in Figure 5.7.

Figure 5.7 Guest Services Screen

The Default Profile is used as a catch all. To modify the profile, click the configure icon to the far right. The Edit Guest Profile dialog will be displayed as shown in Figure 5.8.

Figure 5.8 Edit Guest Profile

Let's look at each of the settings in the Default Guest Services Profile.

- **Profile Name:** The name of the profile.
- **User Name Prefix** Every Guest Account that is created will contain this prefix. For example LAB001.
- **Auto-Generate User Name** The SonicWALL can auto-generate user accounts which will be comprised of the prefix plus a two or three digit number which is used to keep the accounts unique.
- **Auto-Generate Password** Passwords can also be auto-generated by the SonicWALL. The password will be a unique eight character alphabetic string.
- **Enable Account** Check this option to ensure that all accounts generated from this profile are enabled and ready to use. Clearing the check mark disables all accounts created by this profile, and the administrator will be required to enable the individual accounts before they can be used.
- **Auto-Prune Account** This option instructs the SonicWALL to remove the account after the account lifetime has expired.
- **Enforce Login Uniqueness** Enabling this option restricts simultaneous logins with the same account name. Disabling this feature allows multiple users to login using the same account name.
- **Account Lifetime** The lifetime for the account. Upon expiration of the value configured for this setting and assuming Auto-Prune Account is enabled, the account will be removed from the SonicWALL. If Auto-Prune is disabled, the account will be disabled after the expiration value, however, the account will remain intact on the SonicWALL.
- **Session Lifetime** Defines the maximum lifetime for a session. After the expiration of this value, the users session will be terminated.
- **Idle Timeout** This field defines the maximum period of time that a guest services session can remain with no activity. If no activity is detected before the expiration of the timeout value occurs, the session is terminated.
- **Comment** A brief description of the Profile.

To create a new Guest Services Profile, browse to **Users | Guest Services** and click the **Add** button under the Guest Profiles section. The same information covered for the default profile is available for all custom profiles. Configure the appropriate settings for the new profile and click the **OK** button to add the profile to the SonicWALL.

Guest Accounts

Guest Accounts are created from the Guest Accounts Page on the SonicWALL. Browse to Users | Guest Accounts. The Guest Accounts page is shown in Figure 5.9.

Figure 5.9 Guest Accounts

By default, no Guest Account is configured for the SonicWALL. To add a Guest Account, click the Add Guest button. The Add Guest Account dialog will be shown.

Select profile that will be used to generate this account. Next, enter a Name for the account or click the Generate button to automatically create the account name. Enter a brief comment describing the account and finally enter the password to be used. Once these settings have been entered, click the Guest Services tab.

The Guest Services options are identical to the Guest Services Profile that was selected for the account. The only option that we have not covered yet is the Enable Guest Services Privilege. This is the same as the Enable Account option for the profile. Enabling this option instructs the SonicWALL to enable this account immediately following its creation. After configuring the settings, click **OK** to complete the new Guest Account creation.

You may have noticed the option to Generate on the bottom of the Guest Accounts page, which is shown in Figure 5.9. Clicking this option will generate multiple accounts at once. Figure 5.10 shows the Generate Guest Accounts Dialog.

Figure 5.10 Generate Multiple Accounts

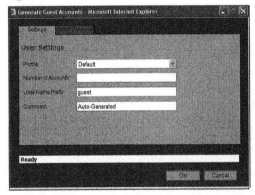

The settings for both User and Guest Services are identical to that for adding a single account, with the exception of Number of Accounts, which defines the number of accounts to create at once, and User Name Prefix, which is used to define the prefix which will be included for all accounts. For example, say we needed to add (10) guest accounts for a Lab name LAB-001. We would enter 10 for the Number of Accounts and LAB-001 for the Prefix and then click OK.

User Settings

The User Settings page is used to configure the nuts and bolts of how User Authentication, Session Settings, Global User Settings, and the Acceptable Use Policy Settings are configured on the SonicWALL. We will divide the **User | Settings** page into four sections. The first section will discuss **User Login Settings**, the second will cover the **User Session Settings**, the third will address the **Other Global User Settings**, and the fourth will explain the **Acceptable Use Policy Settings**.

User Login Settings

There are three configuration options available under the User Login Settings. First, the Authentication Method should be selected and configured. The available options are listed below.

- **Local Users** Select this option for Authentication to be performed by the SonicWALL's local user database only.
- **RADIUS** Select this option for Authentication to be performed by an external RADIUS server.
- **RADIUS + Local Users** Select this option for Authentication to be provided by both RADIUS and the SonicWALL's local user database.
- **LDAP** Select this option for Authentication to be performed by an external LDAP server, such as Microsoft Active Directory.
- **LDAP + Local Users** Select this option for Authentication to be performed by both an external LDAP server and the SonicWALL's local user database.

Second, the **Show authentication page for (minutes):** value specifies how long the authentication page should be displayed before being closed. If the timeout expires, a dialog stating that the user must click the link in order to login.

Finally, the option to redirect users from HTTPS to HTTP on completion of login is used to return the user to a standard, non-SSL HTTP session. HTTPS is required for all user authentication to the SonicWALL. While this seems backwards, it is actually correct.

Figure 5.11 User Login Settings

Figure 5.11 shows the User Login Settings Dialog window and the configuration options that we just covered. We will discuss the options for each of the Authentication Methods later in this chapter.

User Session Settings

The User Session Settings provides control over multiple timeout values that pertain to User Sessions. We will briefly cover what each of the settings is used for.

- **Inactivity timeout (minutes):** The value in this field determines how long a session is allowed to remain in an idle state before being terminated. The default value is five minutes.
- **Enable login session limit:** A checkmark in this field enforces the Login Session Limit feature on a per session basis.
- **Login session limit (minutes):** The value in this field determines the length of time that a session can be active. Upon the expiration of the value configured, the session will be terminated.
- **Show user login status window:** A checkmark in this field determines if a status window will be displayed during the users' sessions. This window contains a Logout button that the users can click to end their sessions.
- **User's login window sends heartbeat every (seconds):** The value configured for this field is used to send a heartbeat signal. The signal is checked every XX seconds, where XX is the value entered in the field, to determine if the user's session is still valid.
- **Enable disconnected user detection:** A checkmark in this field enables the SonicWALL to determine if a user has disconnected from the session, as opposed to logging out properly. If a session is in disconnected state, the SonicWALL will terminate the session.
- **Timeout on heartbeat from user's login status window (minutes):** This value determines the length of time without a reply from the heartbeat signal before the user's session is terminated.

Other Global User Settings

The Other Global User Settings option is used to specify certain URLs that can be accessed by users without having to authenticate (see Figure 5.12).

Figure 5.12 Other Global User Settings

To add a URL to the list, click the Add button. A dialog box will open that prompts for the URL that will be added to the list. Enter the URL that will be added to the list using the top level URL for the site that can be accessed. In other words, if users will be able to access www.mircosoft.com and all subdirectories under this, such as www.microsoft.com/downloads/details.aspx?FamilyID=435bfce7-da2b-4a6a-afa4-f7f14e605a0d&displaylang=en, then you would enter www.microsoft.com for the URL. To restrict access to only the Microsoft Downloads area, enter www.microsoft.com/Downloads

Wildcard matching can be used for both the prefix and/or suffix of the URL, for example, (*.microsoft.com) and (*.microsoft.com…), without the ( ).

After adding the URL to exclude from authentication, click **OK**. Repeat this process for each URL that will be excluded.

Acceptable Use Policy

The final section of the User Settings page is the Acceptable Use Policy, shown in Figure 5.13.

Figure 5.13 Acceptable Use Policy

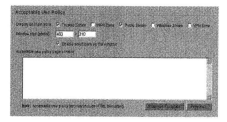

The Acceptable Use Policy can be displayed on a per zone basis by placing a checkmark next to the appropriate Zone name for the **Display on login form:** settings. The size of the window that is displayed can be configured to a custom size and can include Scroll bars to allow users to view the entire policy. The Example Template and Preview buttons are used to configure the format of the policy to be displayed and to preview how it will look to the end-users, respectively. By clicking the Example Template, the Acceptable use policy page content field will be populated with a pre-defined template that can then be modified to include the content of your company's Acceptable Use Policy.

Authentication Methods

There are five authentication methods available on SonicWALL appliances. They are Local Users, RADIUS, RADIUS + Local Users, LDAP, and LDAP + Local Users.

Local Users

The Local Users Authentication Method uses the SonicWALL's built in Local User Database to provide user authentication. In other words, all user authentication is performed locally on the SonicWALL. The Local User accounts which have been defined on the SonicWALL use this method to authenticate by default. This method is ideal for smaller networks. While the SonicWALL will support up to 1000 users, creating this many accounts is problematic. With that said, it is recommended to only use the Local

Users Authentication method when dealing with a handful of users. If the number of users exceeds 20 or so, one of the other Authentication methods might be worth pursuing.

RADIUS

RADIUS provides an extra layer of security for authentication. In certain environments where Microsoft Active Directory has not been implemented or some other LDAP directory exists, RADIUS is the solution to managing all user authentication tasks.

To configure RADIUS, browse to the **Users | Settings** page and click the drop-down menu next to Authentication Methods. Select **RADIUS** or **RADIUS + Local Users** from the available options. Click the **Configure** button to the right of the drop-down menu. The RADIUS configuration page will be displayed. There are three tabs on this page, which are used to configure the RADIUS Authentication: **Settings**, **RADIUS Users**, and **Test**. We will cover all three of the tabs and their associated settings.

RADIUS Settings Tab

The Setting tab contains the settings that apply to the RADIUS server. Figure 5.14 shows the Settings tab and its associated configuration options.

The RADIUS Server Timeout (seconds) value determines how long the SonicWALL will wait for a response from the RADIUS server, and how many times it will retry the connection before the authentication attempt is terminated. The timeout defaults to five seconds and three retries. The value for the timeout field can be from 1 to 60 seconds and the value for the retries field can be from 0 to 10 seconds. It is highly recommended that this value be left at three.

Figure 5.14 RADIUS Configuration Settings

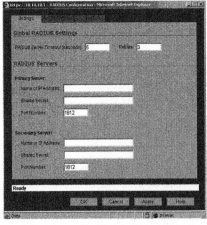

The SonicWALL allows two RADIUS servers to be specified to provide fault tolerance for authentication. The fields for the primary and secondary servers are used to specify the IP address or host name of the RADIUS server, the Shared Secret, and the port number to use for Authentication. The Shared Secret must be the same that was provided on the RADIUS server. The default port number should be left as 1812 unless the RADIUS server has been configured to use an alternative port number.

After entering the appropriate information for the primary and secondary (if used) servers, click the **RADIUS Users** tab.

RADIUS Users Tab

The Users Tab, shown in Figure 5.15, contains the configuration settings for specifying what users will be required to authenticate via the RADIUS server.

Figure 5.15 RADIUS Users Tab

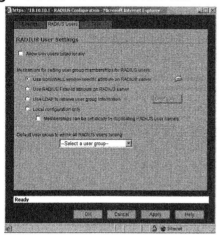

If only local users, defined on the SonicWALL, will be authenticating via RADIUS, enable the **Allow only users listed locally** checkbox. The options for **Mechanism for setting user group memberships for RADIUS users** include:

- Use SonicWALL Vendor-Specific attribute on RADIUS server.
- Use RADIUS Filter-ID attribute on RADIUS server.
- Use LDAP to retrieve user group information.
- Local Configuration only.

Depending on the configuration of the RADIUS server, the mechanism for setting user group memberships for RADIUS users will vary and is outside the scope of this book. The **Default user group to which all RADIUS users belong** drop down menu lists the groups that have been configured on the SonicWALL under the Local Groups page. Select the group to which users that will authenticate via RADIUS are members. Click the **Test** tab.

RADIUS Test Tab

To test the RADIUS configuration and ensure that it is functioning properly, administrators can perform test authentication against the RADIUS server. To do this, enter a valid RADIUS login name and password and select the type of test to perform from Password authentication, CHAP, or MSCHAP. If the test authentication is successful, the Test Status field will change from **Ready** to **Success**. If the test fails, the status will display **Failure**. If the RADIUS server returns user attributes, they will be displayed in the Returned User Attributes field. The Test tab and its associated settings are shown in Figure 5.16.

LDAP

SonicWALL appliances can act as a LDAP client and query against Microsoft Active Directory for user authentication. There are several prerequisites required for LDAP implementations. First, you need to install a certificate on your LDAP server. Secondly, you will need a Certificate Authority certificate for the issuing CA on the SonicWALL. To do this in an Active Directory Environment, follow the steps below.

Figure 5.16 RADIUS Test Tab

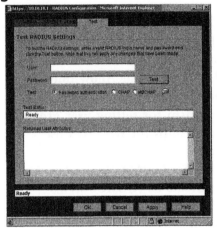

Install Certificate Services on a Active Directory Server
1. Browse to the control panel and select **Add / Remove programs**
2. Select **Add / Remove Window Components**
3. Click **Certificate Services**
4. When prompted, select **Enterprise Root CA**
5. Enter the information requested for the remaining setup
6. Click **Start, Run, dompol.msc**, and press **Enter**
7. Open **Security Settings** and choose **Public Key Policies**
8. Right click **Automatic Certificate Request Settings**
9. Select **New** and choose **Automatic Certificate Request**
10. Walk through the wizard and choose **Domain Controller** from the list

Export the CA from the Active Directory Server
1. Click **Start, Run, type certsrv.msc**, and press **Enter**
2. Right click the CA created in step 1 and select **properties**
3. On the General Tab, click the **View Certificate** button
4. Select **Copy to File** on the **Details** tab
5. Walk through the wizard and choose the Base-64 Encoded X.509 (.cer) format
6. Specify the path and filename to save the certificate

Import the CA Certificate on the SonicWALL
1. Browse to **System > CA Certificate**
2. Click **Add new CA Certificate**.
3. Browse to the path and where you saved the certificate from step 2 and select the **Certificate**.
4. Click the **Import Certificate button**
5. Continue with configuring the LDAP settings on the SonicWALL.

To configure LDAP on the SonicWALL, browse to **Users | Settings** and select **LDAP** or **LDAP + Local Users** from the Authentication Method drop-down menu. Click the **Configure** button to the right of the drop-down menu. The relevant configuration options for LDAP will be displayed. The LDAP configuration settings are composed of six separate tabs.

LDAP Settings Tab

The Settings Tab, shown in Figure 5.17 contains the configuration information required for the LDAP server, such as its IP address or name, the port number, timeout value, username and password, protocol version, and the option to use TSL (SSL) with the certificate that we generated above.

Figure 5.17 LDAP Configuration

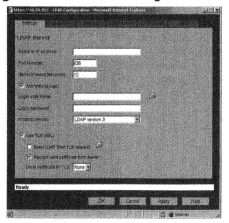

Figure 5.18 LDAP Schema Tab

LDAP Schema Tab

The Schema Tab, shown in Figure 5.18, defines the type Schema to be used for the LDAP communications and the form of the User Group Objects.

LDAP Directory

The LDAP Directory tab contains the configuration settings for the User Directory information, such as the Primary Domain name and the Organizational Unit that contains the user accounts in the directory tree.

LDAP Users

The LDAP Users tab, shown in Figure 5.19, is used to configure what groups of users will be required to authenticate to the LDAP server.

LDAP Relay

The LDAP Relay tab, shown in Figure 5.20, can be used to configure the SonicWALL to support remote SonicWALLs that do not support LDAP by acting as a RADIUS Server and relaying information from the remote appliances to the LDAP server and vice versa.

Figure 5.19 LDAP Users Tab

Figure 5.20 LDAP Relay

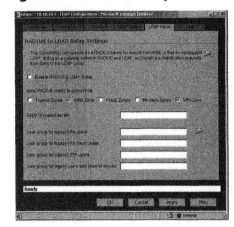

LDAP Test

The LDAP Test tab, shown in Figure 5.21, allows administrators to test LDAP authentication from the SonicWALL to ensure proper operation.

Figure 5.21 LDAP Test Tab

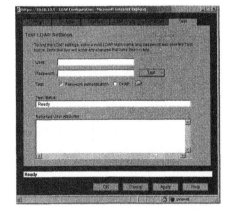

Summary

In this chapter, we have learned about the types of users and when each user type should be used. We have gone over the types of user database, the uses of the different user database types, the differences between them, and the features or limitations inherent with each. We have learned how to change the default authentication server used, and when you should choose to change the default authentication server. Subsequently, we learned how to set up RADIUS and LDAP authentication on the SonicWALL appliance.

Chapter 6

Routing

Solutions in this chapter:

- Routing Information Protocol (RIP)
- Open Shortest Path First (OSPF)

☑ Summary

☑ Solutions Fast Track

☑ Frequently Asked Questions

Introduction

Routing is a fundamental part of any IP (Internet Protocol)-based infrastructure. Every device on an IP-based network uses routes to determine the next hop or location it needs to access the desired host. In many cases, firewalls are just glorified routers. They provide firewall features, but are still a core routing component in many organizations' networks. Routers themselves are usually capable of providing a stateful firewall.

There are two routing protocols that can be used with a SonicWALL firewall. The first protocol, Routing Information Protocol (RIP), is an older protocol, but it is the most commonly supported protocol. The second protocol, Open Shortest Path First (OSPF), is an extremely robust protocol. OSPF is an open standard protocol and is used by many organizations for their internal networks.

Routing Information Protocol (RIP)

The routing information protocol (RIP) is one of the oldest dynamic routing protocols still in wide use today. The first version of RIP was contained in BSD as *routed* when released in 1982, but some of the basic algorithms within the protocol were used on the ARPANET as early as 1969. RIP is a widely used protocol within small to medium-sized networks because it is relatively easy to set up and is generally compatible among different device manufacturers. RIP began as an EGP but is now almost exclusively used as an IGP. RIP is a distance vector protocol, which means that it compares routes mathematically using a value that represents distance, in hops, to a destination. The term *hops* is used to describe how many networks a particular packet of data must traverse before arriving at the destination network.

The RIP sends update messages at regular intervals and when the network changes. This makes RIP a "chatty" routing protocol because it constantly sends information out to the network. RIP uses only one single mechanism to determine the best route. RIP counts a hop or how many hops away a network is. RIP has a limitation of using up to 15 hops of distance. If a route's metric reaches 16 hops, the destination is considered unreachable.

Some key pieces of information to remember about the RIP include:

- RIP is a distance vector protocol.

- RIP is an open protocol described in RFC 1058.

- RIP updates use UDP on port 520.

- RIP updates are sent every 30 seconds by default.

- RIP allows a router to request updates from its neighbors when it comes online.

- The maximum size of a network that is using RIP is 15 hops.

Networking with RIP

RIP defines the best route as the route having the shortest path to the destination network regardless of the specifications of your link or connection such as capacity or latency. RIP determines which path reaches a network via the shortest distance by comparing a distance metric, which is associated with each path in the route table. This distance metric is calculated by adding 1 for every hop between two routers along the path to a destination. To prevent routing loops, which are discussed later in this section, and other problems, the distance metric in the RIP is limited to 15 hops. A distance metric of 16 denotes a network that is unreachable. Routers using RIP exchange routing updates with their neighbors to build a complete table of all routes in the network. These routing updates are composed of each router's entire routing table, which includes a list of networks and distance metrics for each of those networks. When a router receives an update, it must choose whether to enter each route in the update into its routing table. RIP uses the following rules to determine if received route updates should be kept or discarded. Using these rules, routers running RIP populate their route tables and are able to make routing decisions.

The routes in updates will be entered into the route table if:

- The network in the update is not currently in the routing table and the metric is less than 16.

- The network in the update is currently in the routing table, but the metric is lower.

- The network in the update is currently in the routing table, the metric is higher, but the update has come from the same neighbor from which the original update came.

The routes contained in updates will be discarded if:

- The network in the update is already in the route table, but the distance metric in the update is larger.

- The network in the update is already in the route table, and the distance metric in the update is the same. (In some manufacturers' implementations of RIP, routes to the same destination with the same distance metric to different neighbors will be included in the route table and traffic will be load-balanced across up to four routes.)

Once RIP is running and all routers have populated their route tables, any changes or failures in the network mean that all routers must receive updates. This *convergence* process starts when a network change occurs and ends when all routers have the correct network information. The time it takes for a network to recover from any change depends on timers that are a part of RIP and are generally a part of most distance vector protocols. These timers are associated to each individual route:

- **Update timer** The update timer is the amount of time to wait between sending updates. The default for this timer is 30 seconds.

- **Invalid timer** The invalid timer has a default limit of 180 seconds and is reset to 0 every time an update is received for a route. If the route has not been updated in 180 seconds, then the route is marked as invalid. This, however, doesn't mean that the router stops forwarding traffic to the next hop for that route.

- **Hold-down timer** The hold-down timer is also set at 180 by default and is set on a route when the invalid timer expires. When the hold-down timer expires, a route is put in a hold-down state and can't be updated. A route is also put into a hold-down state when an update is received for that route with a metric of 16, meaning that the route is unreachable.

- **Flush timer** The flush timer has a default of 240 seconds and is set each time an update for a route is received. If the timer expires, the route is flushed, even if the route is in a hold-down state.

RIP has built-in methods to speed convergence and help prevent routing problems like routing loops from creeping into the routing tables. Routing loops can occur when incorrect information gets into the routing table and gets updated throughout the network. One of the means by which a router speeds convergence is flushing all routes learned through an interface that it detects as down. This bypasses all timers and speeds convergence of the network. Routers also send updates to their neighbors immediately when they detect a change in metric for a route. This is called a triggered update and can dramatically speed convergence. Poison reverse is another method used by routers for speeding convergence. With poison reverse, if a router detects a downed link, it automatically sends an update with a metric of 16 for those routes to its neighbors. Its neighbors will automatically put those routes in hold-down and not propagate those routes to the rest of the network.

Routers also do not send updates back through interfaces from which they were received. Split horizon, as it is known, resolves the problem where if one router were to lose the connection to a network on one of its interfaces, its neighbor router could then send it an update for the same network. This would create an endless loop where each router would re-update its neighbors with the network it just learned from them with a higher metric. Each router would keep the route with the higher metric because the update is being received from the original router from which the update was originally received. Without split horizon, this routing loop would continue until the metric in the update reached 16 and the route update would no longer be accepted.

Along with providing methods for accelerating convergence, RIP also supports features that simplify configuration and ease protocol overhead. As a basic means of simplifying configurations within a RIP-enabled network, RIP supports the config-uration of a default route. A default route simplifies configurations because it allows routers to forward traffic to a default next hop if a specific route to a destination can't be found. To reduce the amount of traffic used in route updates, RIP also sup-ports route summarization. Route summarization is the process by which multiple routes are represented by a single more general route in route updates. In this way, updates representing multiple routes can be contained in a single update.

Another important thing to note about RIP updates is that route updates don't contain subnet mask information. The subnet mask to associate with a particular net-work in an update must be determined by the router receiving the update. If a router receiving an update has an interface on the network for which it receives an update, then the router will automatically assume the same subnet mask for the net-work in the update as it has on its own interface. If the router does not have an interface on the network for which it is receiving an update, the router will assume the subnet mask that is naturally associated with the network number. Because of this, networks using RIP cannot use variable-length subnet masks anywhere in their network. This means that all networks in an environment connected by routers run-ning RIPv1 must use the same subnet masks. This might cause problems on some networks with segments of varying sizes and will likely result in IP address space not being used very economically.

When to Use RIP

RIP is a very reliable protocol, and is well suited to small and medium-sized networks. However, there are a couple of things to consider before deciding on RIP as the protocol for your network. The first consideration relates to the types of connections within your network. Are they all similar in capacity? Are all of your connections the same size in terms of bandwidth? What about latency and reliability? Are all of your connections a similar speed and similar media? If the answers to all these questions are yes, then RIP could be sufficient for your dynamic routing needs. If your network has disparities among its various connections, RIP might not be well suited for your network because RIP's distance metric does not consider any of a connection's attributes. To RIP, a 56Kbps serial line is considered equal to a 1.54Mbps T-1. Another consideration would be network size. Does any path on your network contain more than 15 hops? If so, RIP is definitely not for you. RIP can only handle networks with paths that contain fewer than 15 hops. Even if your network doesn't contain a path with more than 15 hops, in large networks, routing information updates every 30 seconds can mean network utilization at an unacceptable level and in some cases convergence can take too long.

RIP as It Applies to SonicWALL

SonicWALL firewalls support both RIPv1 and RIPv2 for routing. You should choose the version of RIP for your network based on what your routers support and their capabilities. RIPv1 has fewer features, and sends packets via broadcast. RIPv2, however, uses multicast to send packets. RIPv2 advertisements also provide information regarding VPN tunnel status. SonicWALL RIPv2 packets are backward-compatible and can be accepted and used by some RIPv1 implementations, provided they can listen for multicast packets. SonicWALL also supports broadcasting RIPv2 packets, in case you have a mixed network that supports both RIPv1 and RIPv2 routers.

To configure RIP for an interface on a SonicWALL:

1. Click the **Configure** icon for the desired interface. You will see the **Route Advertisement Configuration** window.

2. Select the version of RIP advertisement you want to use.

3. Choose if you want to advertise the default route of the SonicWALL. This can be configured to never advertise, always advertise, or only advertise if the WAN is up.

4. Enable **Advertise Static Routes** and **Advertise Remote VPN Networks** if you want to advertise these networks.

There are several other features that you can customize when using RIP. The default advertisement value is 30 seconds. By changing the **Change Damp Time** value, you can increase or decrease the interval as which route updates are broadcast. You can also enable RIPv2 authentication, which allows you to authenticate that the RIP packet originated from the source it says it came from.

Open Shortest Path First (OSPF)

OSPF is a link state protocol and is considered one of the best protocols to run for your internal network. The open in OSPF represents that it is an open standard protocol. OSPF will only send out periodic updates and is not considered to be a chatty protocol. It is extremely efficient and is supported by most modern routing equipment.

Networking with OSPF

In addition to being a dynamic routing protocol, OSPF is the first link-state protocol we will look at. The Open in OSPF represents the fact that the protocol is an open standard developed by the Internet Engineering Task Force (IETF) and described in RFC 2328. It was designed as an IGP to route within a single autonomous system (AS), but with the Internet environment in mind. OSPF can tag routes that come into the AS from outside the network. The Shortest Path First in the name refers to the algorithm the protocol uses to compute the shortest path to every destination in the route table. OSPF can be an extremely complex protocol in very large networks, so in this section we will only examine the basics of the protocol functionality. Some basic details to remember about OSPF include:

- OSPF is an open protocol described by RFC 2328 and is generally compatible between devices from different vendors.

- OSPF is a link-state protocol.

- OSPF exchanges information with Link State Advertisements (LSAs). All information exchange is authenticated.

- OSPF updates are directly encapsulated in IP with the protocol field set to 89.

- OSPF is scalable. There is no hop count limit on the size of the network, and OSPF is designed hierarchically so that networks are divided into areas for easier management.

- OSPF supports VLSM.

- OSPF requires a lot of processor and memory resources on your router.

How OSPF Works

OSPF determines the best path from itself to other destinations by maintaining a map of its network area in memory and computing the best path using that map. When a router is configured to run OSPF, it broadcasts hello packets from each interface configured with OSPF. It finds other OSPF routers by listening for OSPF hello packets. When another OSPF router is identified, the two routers authenticate and exchange configuration information before they exchange link-state advertisements (LSAs). Link-state databases are built by LSAs that are flooded to the entire network. LSAs describe each of the connections on a given router. LSAs contain information on each connection to a router, which includes a cost for each connection. This cost is a number based on details of the connection, including throughput, latency, and reliability. OSPF deals with network changes by flooding the network with LSAs whenever there is a status change within the network. When the link-state database is complete, the router can then calculate the best path from it to the rest of the network using the Shortest Path First (SPF) algorithm. In this way, routers using OSPF no longer have to rely on possibly bad routing information from other routers. They only have to ensure the accuracy of their own link-state databases to be able to find the best path to any destination on the network.

Because OSPF is a very processor-intensive protocol, it is designed to simplify large networks by creating different areas. Routers within each area are then only responsible for maintaining a link-state database of the topology in their local area. In this way, OSPF can scale to accommodate extremely large networks. Each area then summarizes its routes into what is called a *backbone area*. This backbone area then summarizes routes to all areas attached to it. All traffic going from one area to another must go through the backbone area.

When to Use OSPF

OSPF is great protocol for large to extra large networks. Because it is hierarchical, OSPF allows networks to grow by simply dividing large areas into smaller ones. However, OSPF can be very CPU and memory intensive; computing the shortest path first algorithm on a large link-state database can require a large amount of CPU resources, and the size of the link-state database can tax memory resources. OSPF is also a slightly complex protocol that can require extensive experience and training to design and operate properly

Basic OSPF Configuration on a SonicWALL

Now that we've covered the basics of networking with OSPF, let's review some of these concepts as they relate to the SonicWALL. These concepts are common throughout the configuration of OSPF and also across various vendors' devices. Routers are grouped into *areas*. By default, all routers participating in OSPF are grouped in to area **0**, also known as area **0.0.0.0**. There will be occasions when you will want to want to divide your network into multiple areas. This is typically done in large networks.

Each router that participates in an OSPF network is classified as one of four types of routers:

- **Internal Router** A router with all interfaces belonging to the same area.
- **Backbone Router** A router that has an interface in the backbone area. The backbone area is also known as area **0**.
- **Area Border Router** A router that connects to multiple areas.
- **AS Boundary Router** A router that borders another autonomous system (AS).

Summary

Routing is a powerful tool for any network. In this chapter we presented an overview of routing on a SonicWALL firewall using RIP and OSPF

RIP is an open-standard dynamic routing protocol used to exchange routing information in small to midsized networks. Windows Server 2003 supports RIP versions 1 and 2. Although RIP is simple to configure, it suffers from a few drawbacks. RIP is limited to a hop count of 15. This means that an advertisement can pass through only 16 routers before the route is considered unreachable. Also, RIP is considered slow to recover when there is a change in the network topology. One other problem with RIP, along with the slow recovery times, is the possibility of routing loops. Routing loops are advertisements that send IP traffic through the same series of routers until the maximum hop count is reached. Basically, RIP does not scale well for use in large networks because of the reasons mentioned here.

RIPv1 operates through broadcast announcements. It follows classful routing characteristics. This means that route advertisements in RIPv1 do not carry subnet mask information. Consequently, only network addresses that use their default subnet masks, following their classful boundaries, will work properly in an RIPv1 configured environment.

OSPF is an open-standard dynamic routing protocol used to exchange routing information in large to very large networks. Compared to RIP, OSPF is more difficult to configure and administer but it tends to be much more efficient than RIP even in very large networks. OSPF requires very little network overhead, even in complex networks.

OSPF uses the shortest path first (SPF) algorithm to determine routes that should be added to the routing table. OSPF routers maintain a map of the internetwork called the link state database. This database is synchronized by all OSPF routers and the information contained in the link state database is used to compute routing table entries. Each OSPF router forms an adjacency with its neighboring routers. Any time a change occurs in the internetwork, information about the change is flooded to the entire network.

OSPF is an excellent protocol for you to use inside of your network. It is extremely efficient and provides a very robust routing infrastructure. Unfortunately, it has a few downsides. First, it requires additional processing power and additional memory to compute its complex algorithms, and second, it is complex to configure.

Solutions Fast Track

Routing Information Protocol (RIP)

- ☑ RIP is a distance vector protocol.

- ☑ RIP is considered a chatty protocol because it is constantly sending updates.

- ☑ Using RIP is the easiest of all of the dynamic routing protocols supported by the SonicWALL firewall.

- ☑ RIPv2 is an open protocol that implements some of the features lacking in RIP, such as variable-length subnet masks and authentication. It is also generally backward compatible with RIP, which makes it an easy upgrade.

Open Shortest Path First (OSPF)

- ☑ OSPF is an efficient routing protocol.

- ☑ OSPF is a link state protocol.

- ☑ OSPF is more complicated to configure than RIP.

- ☑ OSPF is a link-state protocol and is *open*, meaning that it is based on an open standard. It is a fairly complicated protocol with many features. It is extremely useful in large complex networks.

For a bonus chapter on SonicWALL's advanced routing features, please visit the Syngress Solutions page.

Chapter 7

Address Translation

Solutions in this chapter:

- The Purpose of Address Translation
- SonicWALL NAT Overview
- Policy-Based NAT
- NAT Policy Basics

☑ Summary

☑ Solutions Fast Track

☑ Frequently Asked Questions

Introduction

Address translation has become a staple of enterprise networking, and its development has allowed users of the Internet to forestall its collapse under the weight of the explosion of Internet devices and the basic limitation of IPv4 addresses.

Network Address Translation (NAT) has become one of the most common firewall functions, and its simplicity has allowed the number of devices that can use the Internet to expand exponentially. It is the one key function that has provided home users with the capability to allow every member of a household to have his or her own computer and share a single Internet connection from a broadband ISP. In addition, its implicit nature to isolate individual devices from the general Internet public provides a very powerful firewall against malicious outsiders.

In the corporate environment, NAT offers the same benefits and, as implemented by the SonicWALL SonicOS, extends the features to allow network administrators to carefully control the inbound and outbound traffic they need to support.

The SonicOS software offers the network administrator the ability to perform IP address translations, IP protocol or port translations, and a combination of both at the same time. These translations can be performed in a number of ways:

- From a single address to a single address—One-to-One NAT
- From a single address to multiple addresses—One-to-Many NAT
- From multiple addresses to a single address—Many-to-One NAT
- From multiple addresses to a pool of other multiple addresses—Many-to-Many NAT

In this chapter, we discuss the uses of these variations and how to configure your SonicWALL appliance to take advantage of them.

The Purpose of Address Translation

High-level NAT is the ability to disguise one IP address from another, a function completely transparent to the users. For example, Figure 7.1 shows a host on network 192.168.10.0 traversing through a NAT device. The NAT device translates the source packet from host 192.168.10.105 to address 61.90.35.130 and retransmits it to the desired destination, a method known as *source NAT*.

Figure 7.1 Source NAT

The NAT process simply replaces the actual source address and/or port number of the originating device with one assigned by the firewall, and retransmits it to the intended destination. Modifying just the port number is referred to as *port address translation* (PAT), and changing both the IP address and the port is referred to as *NAPT*.

The destination host receives the packet and responds using the firewall's IP address and the unique port number the firewall assigned. When the firewall receives the packet, it looks up the port number in its table and replaces the destination IP address with the original LAN device's address and port number.

Advantages of Address Translation

The tremendous growth of the Internet in the past decade caused a shortage of IPv4 addresses, so NAT was developed to provide an immediate solution to this depletion. Request for Comment (RFC) 1631 was written in 1994 as the short-term solution to address the problem—the long-term solution was IPv6.

Other ways NAT is useful include:

- **Security** NAT can provide a hidden identity for host(s).

- **Addresses RFC 1918 private address usage on a routable network** A NAT device can translate an existing nonpublic routable subnet to a public routable address(es). Most companies use RFC 1918 addresses for their corporate networks to helps conserve their routable Internet Assigned Numbers Authority (IANA) public addresses. RFC 1918 addresses are:

- 10.0.0.0 to 10.255.255.255 (10/8 prefix)
- 172.16.0.0 to 172.31.255.255 (172.16/12 prefix)
- 192.168.0.0 to 192.168.255.255 (192.168/16 prefix)

- **Addresses overlapping networks** NAT can provide a masquerade of different networks when two duplicate networks must be merged.

- **Helps maintain a cohesive network** Provides a method of maintaining one cohesive network when needed to communicate with different extranets.

Both the source and destination packets can be translated using the SonicWALL's NAT functionality.

Disadvantages of Address Translation

When using address translation, certain scenarios come with certain concerns. The most common issues when using NAPT include:

- **Secure Internet Protocol (IPSec) usage through a NAT device** See Chapter 12, "VPN Usage," for more information on why NAT causes IPSec to break. There are two workarounds to this:
  - Create a one-to-one NAT and disable PAT.
  - Use NAT Traversal.

- **Protocol that requires dynamic port allocation** For example, passive File Transfer Protocol (FTP), Sun Remote Procedure Call (RPC), MS-RPC, Domain Name System (DNS), Voice over Internet Protocol (VoIP), Serial Interface Protocol (SIP), and so on. There are workarounds available. Most firewalls implement a feature called application level gateway (ALG) to address applications that require dynamic port opening.

- **Legacy application or custom application requires that the original packet information be maintained** This varies from requiring the network address to the port to remain the same. In some cases, disabling NAT, PAT, or both will address this issue. It is generally recommended to disable PAT first, because the majority of these applications relate to restrictive ports.

SonicWALL NAT Overview

The most commonly used NAT function is to allow all of the internal LAN devices to be privately addressed using one of the three nonroutable address ranges and have all outbound traffic passed through the firewall and re-assigned a single public address, usually that of the firewall's WAN interface. This is the same mechanism that all residential "routers" use to allow homeowners to run many computers off one DSL or cable connection.

NOTE

When broadband Internet service was first introduced to the residential market, users could only get a single IP address and connect a single computer to those circuits. In fact, you usually had to contact the service provider to give them the MAC address of the device you were connecting. If you wanted to change out that device, you had to call again to give them the new address. Once companies began producing inexpensive router devices that performed NAT, it was easy to disguise multiple devices behind the router.

In NAT mode, all of the LAN devices are assigned a private, nonroutable address that is only visible to other devices on the same LAN. As LAN devices need to communicate with systems on the WAN side of the network (i.e. the Internet), their address is converted to the firewall's WAN address and "tagged" with a unique port address to distinguish it from other LAN device traffic.

Source NAT

Source NAT is the most widely deployed method of address translation and provides the ability to translate a source IP address to another IP address. In this case, since we are using only the IP address of the WAN port as our new source address, we will also be changing the original source port number and performing NAPT on the packets (Figure 7.2).

Figure 7.2 Source NAT

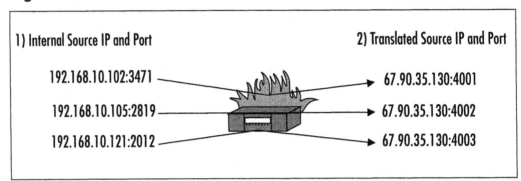

1) Internal Source IP and Port   2) Translated Source IP and Port

192.168.10.102:3471 ──────────────────────────▶ 67.90.35.130:4001

192.168.10.105:2819 ──────────────────────────▶ 67.90.35.130:4002

192.168.10.121:2012 ──────────────────────────▶ 67.90.35.130:4003

NOTE

NAT is enabled by default on SonicOS Enhanced, but if you are running the standard SonicOS software, the firewall can operate in either Transparent or NAT mode. Transparent mode allows the appliance to work as an intelligent router in that every device on the LAN network is directly addressable from the WAN using its publicly assigned address. In this mode, the SonicWALL will simply perform packet inspection on all traffic but will not insulate the LAN devices from being seen on the WAN.

To enable NAT in SonicOS Standard, go to the **Network > Settings** window and select the drop-down box on the WAN port configuration line. There are six choices, one for transparent and five with NAT. Choose the NAT option that works with your Internet service (Figure 7.3).

Figure 7.3 Setting up Source NAT (SonicOS Standard)

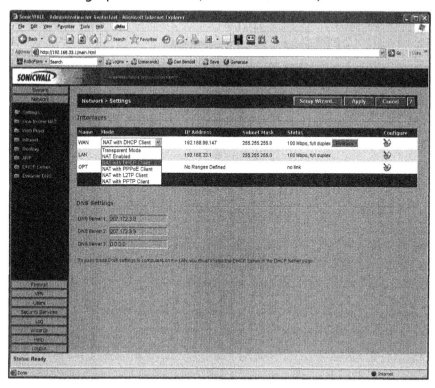

The default configuration will automatically apply the NAPT process to all traffic flowing from the LAN to the WAN, and convert all internal, private IP addresses to the IP address assigned to the WAN port.

If you do not have any resources inside your LAN that need to be accessed from the WAN, you do not have to do anything else with NAT. The firewall will automatically allow up to 254 devices (or the number of clients your appliance is allowed to support) on your LAN to access the Internet.

Destination NAT

If you have resources on your LAN that you want users outside the network to access such as a Web server or mail system, you will need to establish a mechanism for allowing inbound traffic to connect to that resource. This can be done by establishing a rule that directs all of the allowed traffic through the firewall and to the internal device (Figure 7.4).

Figure 7.4 Destination NAT

2) Translated to server's
internal private address

1) Packet's original destination address
sent to firewall's WAN IP address

192.168.10.20:25

67.90.35.130:25

In this example, we will be setting up a mail server that needs to have outside servers connect to it using the SMTP protocol, port 25. In the **Firewall > Access Rules** screen, add a new rule, and set the parameters as follows (Figure 7.5):

Action: Allow—this rule is going to permit the flow of traffic otherwise blocked by the default rules.

Service: Send E-Mail (SMTP)—the name of the service for which we want to redirect traffic.

Source: WAN—this indicates that we will be routing traffic coming from the WAN (and any address on the WAN).

Destination: 192.168.10.10—the internal address of the host providing the service. The Destination fields allow you to specify a range of addresses the traffic would be routed to if you have more than one server of that type.

Comment: Inbound mail—use this field to aid in detailing the rules purpose.

Figure 7.5 Setting up Destination NAT (SonicOS Standard)

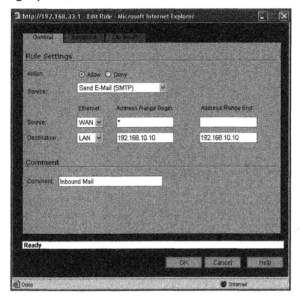

By setting the service to SMTP instead of ANY, we limit the inbound traffic to just that protocol. All other traffic sent the outside address would still be dropped.

One-to-One NAT

One-to-One NAT extends the previous two scenarios in a way that greatly increases your flexibility. If your ISP has provided you with a block of two or more public IP addresses, you can use one-to-one NAT to further regulate inbound and outbound traffic. Looking at our previous example of an internal mail server, we could use one of the additional IP addresses assigned by the ISP to specifically relate to the private address of the mail server. That is, instead of using the firewall's WAN port address that we assigned on the Network > Settings page, we can now use a separate, dedicated address for that purpose (Figure 7.6).

Figure 7.6 One-to-One NAT

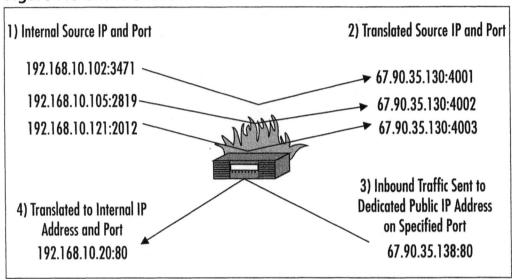

1) Internal Source IP and Port

192.168.10.102:3471

192.168.10.105:2819

192.168.10.121:2012

2) Translated Source IP and Port

67.90.35.130:4001

67.90.35.130:4002

67.90.35.130:4003

3) Inbound Traffic Sent to
Dedicated Public IP Address
on Specified Port

67.90.35.138:80

4) Translated to Internal IP
Address and Port

192.168.10.20:80

NOTE

You can only use One-to-One NAT if you selected the "NAT enabled" option in the WAN > Settings screen, as it is the only one that allows you to have multiple IP addresses assigned by your ISP. All of the other options "NAT with DHCP," "NAT with PPPoE Client," "NAT with L2TP Client," and "NAT with PPTP Client" assume you will be working with a single WAN IP address assignment.

For example, if the ISP has assigned us a block of addresses from 67.43.204.1 through 67.43.204.7 and we have established 67.43.204.1 as our firewall's WAN address, we can now add a specific One-to-One relationship using one of the other addresses in the block (Figure 7.7).

Figure 7.7 Setting up a One-to-One NAT Relationship

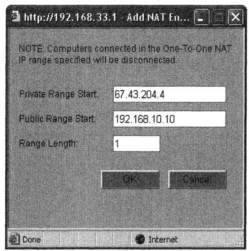

With this relationship established, we can now use the 67.43.204.4 address to refer to our mail server instead of the one we assigned to the WAN port. We still need to establish a rule in the Firewall > Access Rules screen to permit the SMTP traffic through.

Policy-Based NAT

Now that we established the basics of NAT, we can look at the powerful capabilities of the "Policy-Based NAT" feature in the Enhanced version of SonicOS. NAT Policy extends the capabilities of manipulating the traffic that flows through the firewall in dramatic ways. Now, you can redirect traffic coming in from the WAN to specific LAN devices, and policies can be established to transform the destination ports to completely different ones on the way. You can create up to 512 NAT policies on the firewall and create multiple policies for the same object. Each can be more specific than the others, and applied under very special circumstances. The more specific the policy, the higher its preference.

NOTE

NAT policies can be created to affect traffic coming and going on any of the physical interfaces, LAN, WAN or OPT, but policies can also be created that apply to VPN tunnels as long as the VPN is between two SonicWALLs running the Enhanced version of SonicOS 2.0 or later.

While most installations will create a set of standard NAT policies like the ones we discussed earlier, the flexibility of the Enhanced SonicOS NAT policy features allows you to create some unique policies.

For example, you may want to protect a number of hosts on the LAN from WAN traffic by converting standard Web packets from using the normal port 80 to a customized port on your LAN server, such as 9002 (Figure 7.8).

Figure 7.8 Custom Application of Port Address Translation

2) Translated to Internal IP
Address and Custom Port

192.168.10.20:9002

1) Inbound Traffic Sent to Public
IP Address on Specified Port

67.90.35.130:80

Alternatively, you may want to hide the identity of various LAN devices by having their IP addresses transformed to one of a range of public addresses as they access the WAN (Figure 7.9).

Figure 7.9 Many-to-Many NAT

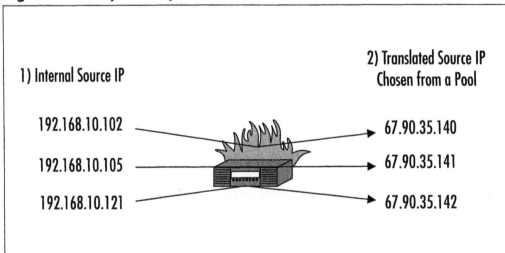

1) Internal Source IP

2) Translated Source IP
Chosen from a Pool

192.168.10.102   67.90.35.140

192.168.10.105   67.90.35.141

192.168.10.121   67.90.35.142

Now that we've seen some of the other ways NAT and PAT can be used to carefully control inbound and outbound traffic, let's look at how to create these configurations.

NAT Policy Basics

First, let's familiarize ourselves with the policy creation screen; each of the fields refers to previously defined objects such as IP addresses, defined services, or firewall interfaces (Figure 7.10).

Figure 7.10 Add NAT Policy Screen

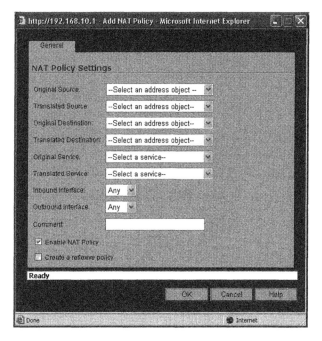

Each of the eight main fields refers to the various components of the packet that can be identified or transformed:

- **Original Source** The Source IP address of the packet entering the firewall. This entry can be a single host IP address, a range of IP addresses, or an entire IP subnet.

- **Translated Source** The firewall can change the Source IP address of the packet as it enters the device.

- **Original Destination** The IP address of the host to which the incoming packet was originally addressed.

- **Translated Destination** The address to which you want the firewall to send the packet.

- **Original Service** The port number to which the incoming packet thinks it is trying to connect.

- **Translated Service** The port number to which you want this type of traffic routed. It would be rare to change this value to anything but "Original," but you do have the ability to route standard, well-known services to private customized ports on your private servers.

- **Source Interface** The interface on the firewall on which you want the policy to look for incoming packets.

- **Destination Interface** Defines the interface on which you want the packet, once it is processed, to go out of the firewall.

- **Enable** Allows you to create the policy, but prevent it from taking effect as soon as you save it. Uncheck this box if you are not ready to use this policy but want to create it on the device.

- **Comment** Allows you to describe the policy you created for clarification. You are limited to 32 characters, and the comment will appear on the Network > Policies screen.

NOTE

The order of the NAT policies on the NAT > Policies screen will be automatically arranged by the software based on the degree of specificity of each policy. The more specific the details of the policy, the higher it will be. For example, a NAT policy that states that all LAN IP addresses are to be translated to a certain WAN address will be overridden by a policy that states a specific LAN IP address be translated to a different specific WAN IP address.

In addition, on the NAT Policies screen is a radio button that will reveal a set of special default policies that are required by the firewall and cannot be deleted or changed.

Let's look at how to create some of the more common NAT policies. We'll discuss some of the most common and useful policies here, and show you how to create some very specific configurations that may be useful.

For the purposes of these examples, we will be using some of the default objects and a number of customized ones:

- **WAN Primary IP**—67.90.35.130/255.255.255.255

- **WAN Primary Subnet**—67.90.35.128/255.255.255.240

- **LAN Primary IP**—192.16810.1/255.255.255.255

- **LAN Primary Subnet**—192.168.10.0/255.255.255.0

- **Private_Mail_Address**—192.168.10.10 (private IP address of a SMTP host on the LAN)

- **Public_Mail_Address**—67.90.35.135 (the public IP address of our mail server in DNS)

- **Outside_NAT_Pool**—67.90.35.140 - 67.90.35.140 (a pool of public IP addresses)

- **Public_Web_Address**—67.90.35.137 (the public address for our Web site)

- **Web_Server_Pool**—192.168.10.50–192.168.10.55 (a group of internal Web servers)

We will be referring to the standard "well known" port for SMTP, port 25, and a custom port 3131 for our internal mail server to listen on, Custom_Mail_Port.

NOTE

The SonicOS software allows you to create these objects on-the-fly when you are creating the NAT policy, but it is much better to identify and pre-define these objects before you need to use them.

Many-to-One NAT

For our first NAT policy, let's see how the common Many-to-One translation is created by default on the firewall. On a new installation, this will be the only default NAT policy you can edit. Go to the **Network > NAT Policy Settings** screen shown in Figure 7.11.

Figure 7.11 Creating a Many-to-One NAT Policy

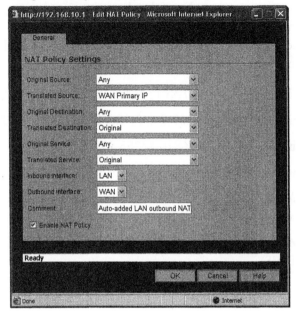

This policy can be interpreted as, "all packets coming into the LAN interface from any address going to any address on the WAN interface will have their source IP address translated into the WAN Primary IP address and sent to the original destination address. The original service will not be changed."

Many-to-Many NAT

As discussed earlier, basic Many-to-One NAT assigns a unique port number to each outbound packet to be used to track the specific session. Under these conditions, you would be limited to approximately 64,000 possible sessions (based on 64,512 possible port numbers less the reserved "well known" ports 1–1023). In the event you have to support far more than that number, you can establish a "pool" of public addresses for the firewall to use instead of just the one assigned to the WAN interface. This method provides for up to 500,000 sessions to be established.

In this case, just replace the "WAN Interface IP" object with the predefined "Outside_NAT_Pool" object, and you will have more than enough IP/ports to go around (Figure 7.12).

Figure 7.12 Creating a Many-to-Many NAT Policy

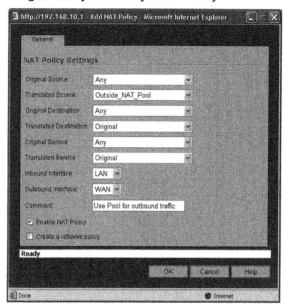

One-to-One NAT

Right after the Outbound Many-to-One policy, the Inbound One-to-One policy will be the most common. This policy is typically used to allow you to have a device on your LAN that needs to be accessed by users on the WAN. For our example, we will be hosting our own mail on an internal mail server and creating a policy that will allow other mail hosts on the Internet to send mail to our server through the firewall.

A few prerequisites are necessary, including a public IP address assigned by our ISP by which the other Internet mail servers will know us (and has been entered into our domain's DNS records as a valid Mail Exchange or MX host), and a valid access rule to allow this traffic. Keep in mind that the rules you create in the Access Rules screen must be written to the public IP address, not the private address as in earlier versions of the SonicOS (Figure 7.13).

Figure 7.13 Creating a One-to-One NAT Policy

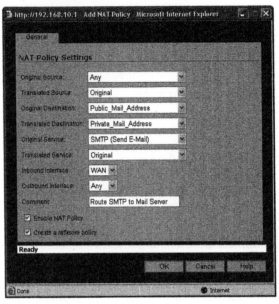

This policy can be interpreted as, "all packets coming into the WAN interface from any address going to the public address of our mail server will have the destination address translated to the private internal IP address of our mail server. The original service will not be changed."

> **WARNING**
>
> For any One-to-One NAT policy, the outbound interface must always be set to ANY, not LAN or WAN as you might think. This has to do with the way the OS analyzes the policy.

Reflexive Policies

The "Create a reflexive policy" option is a new feature that tells the system to automatically create a second, mirror policy of the one you are creating, to make sure that traffic coming from the internal device is transformed to look as though it is coming from the same public IP address. This policy can be adjusted if necessary, but it is typical of One-to-One NAT policies that you would have the IP address of any outbound traffic be converted to the IP address of the public one. If you don't use this "reflexive" policy, outbound traffic will be treated the same as traffic from any other device and get the WAN interface's IP address.

One-to-One NAT with Port Translation

We may want to consider the scenario in which your mail server uses a proprietary port for incoming messages instead of the standard port 25. If this is the case, you could also set the Translated Service field to our previously established custom port at 3131 using the object "Custom_Mail_Port" (Figure 7.14).

Figure 7.14 Creating a One-to-One NAT Policy with Port Translation

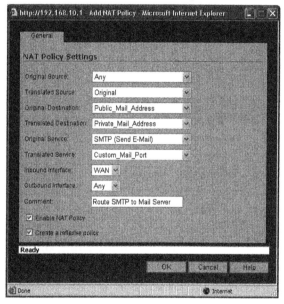

Now, in addition to the IP address being translated to the private address, the service port will be replaced with the custom one.

One-to-Many

A One-to-Many NAT policy for inbound traffic is most useful for round-robin load balancing. By mapping a single public IP address to a group of internal IP addresses assigned to a group of hosts, we can essentially spread the traffic load around.

To set up this policy, simply replace the Translated Destination with a predefined range of internal IP addresses (Figure 7.15).

Figure 7.15 Creating a One-to-Many NAT Policy

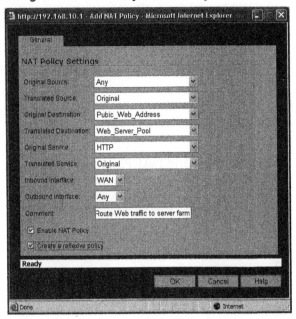

This policy will translated as, "all HTTP packets coming in from any source on the WAN and destined for the public IP address of our Web site will be routed to any of the IP addresses in the Web_Server_Pool range."

The firewall will essentially send the first connection to the first IP address, the second connection to the second IP address in the range, and so on, and then start from the first again.

Summary

NAT has always been an essential part of network design, whether for security reasons or to conserve IP addresses, and is a useful method for managing traffic flow. At its core, NAT provides the capability to hide the originating IP address of outbound traffic, thus providing an extra layer of security to protect the host's identity. NAT also provides a short-term solution to the depleting IPv4 addresses on the Internet. NAT provides the capability to use one IP for several thousand devices, thus conserving non-RFC 1918 IP addresses. With the cost of NAT devices going down each year and the increase in Internet usage, it is not surprising that NAT is a widely used feature.

The extensive flexibility of policy-based NAT of the SonicWALL Enhanced OS firmware allows the network designer to carefully sculpt a highly secure and robust environment, and introduce unique capabilities previously unavailable.

Solutions Fast Track

The Purpose of Address Translation

- ☑ Insulate LAN devices from WAN devices
- ☑ Preserve Public IP addresses
- ☑ Transform source traffic to custom destinations

SonicWALL NAT Overview

- ☑ Source NAT—Change the source information so that it appears as though it is coming from a different address or port.
- ☑ Destination NAT—Change the intended destination to some other address or port.

Policy-Based NAT

- ☑ With NAT Policy, you can redirect traffic coming in from the WAN to specific LAN devices.
- ☑ The flexibility of the Enhanced SonicOS NAT policy features allows you to create some unique policies.

☑ NAT policies can be created to affect traffic coming and going on any of the physical interfaces, LAN, WAN or OPT.

NAT Policy Basics

☑ Translates a group of source addresses to a single IP address.

☑ Useful for allowing many privately addressed internal LAN devices to access Internet WAN devices using only a single publicly routable IP address.

☑ One-to-one NAT creates a unique relationship between one WAN IP address and one LAN IP address.

☑ One-to-one NAT is useful for allowing specific inbound WAN traffic to reach an internal device.

☑ Many-to-many NAT maps the source addresses of multiple devices to a "pool" of other source addresses.

☑ Many-to-many NAT is most often used to allow a very large number of internal LAN devices to use a small number of publicly routable WAN addresses.

☑ Many-to-many NAT combines NAT and PAT to support upwards of 500,000 sessions.

☑ One-to-many NAT translates a single destination address to one of many other destination addresses.

☑ One-to-many-NAT is used to provide "load balancing" capabilities by routing traffic sent to a single publicly known IP address, such as a Web site, to a farm of internal LAN host addresses.

Frequently Asked Questions

The following Frequently Asked Questions, answered by the authors of this book, are designed to both measure your understanding of the concepts presented in this chapter and to assist you with real-life implementation of these concepts. To have your questions about this chapter answered by the author, browse to **www.syngress.com/solutions** and click on the **"Ask the Author"** form.

Q: What are the advantages of using NAT?

A: NAT conserves IP addresses, provides a hidden identity for host(s), has the capability to use nonroutable addresses from the RFC 1918 space, addresses overlapping subnets, and maintains a cohesive network.

Q: What are the advantages of using policy-based NAT over interface-based NAT?

A: The number-one reason to choose policy-based NAT over interface-based NAT is scalability. With interface-based NAT, you are limited to only performing address translation in one flow direction, only the source address can be translated, you cannot turn off PAT, and it requires all ingress traffic to be translated. With policy-based NAT, you can uniquely define address translation on a per-firewall rule definition, allowing you to control address translation flows, perform source and/or destination translation, and turn PAT on/off.

Q: How many NAT policies can I create?

A: The SonicWALL Enhanced OS allows you to create up to 512 policies.

Q: Can I manually change the priority of the policies?

A: No. The policies will be prioritized automatically by the OS based on the specificity of the policy. The more detailed a policy is, the higher its priority.

Chapter 8

Transparent Mode

Solutions in this chapter:

- **Interface Settings**

- **Understanding How Transparent Mode Works**

- **Configuring a Device to Use Transparent Mode**

- **Transparent Mode Deployment Options**

☑ Summary

☑ Solutions Fast Track

☑ Frequently Asked Questions

Introduction

Transparent mode essentially turns a layer-3 firewall into a "transparent," layer-2 "bump in a wire." An architect may be reluctant to alter the routing by adding a hop and modifying the layer-3 topology of her environment because of functional requirements, or for convenience. To implement a layer-2 device, all she needs is to schedule an outage and move some cables, and the transparent firewall deployment is akin to dropping such a bridge or switch (a multiport bridge in its own right) into her infrastructure. No routes added up or downstream, no subnetting, and no cabling considerations. Perhaps most crucial to simplicity, nodes *behind* the transparent firewall won't require re-addressing either, as they remain on the same subnet as the hosts they're firewalled from.

SonicWALL's firewalls achieve this by disabling the default NAT behavior for any IP addresses in a "transparent range." It's as simple as it sounds, and more explanation would make the description needlessly complex—in Transparent mode, addresses off any transparent interface are passed through the firewall without translation to or from the WAN interface, as though they were bridged.

Interface Settings

Before we talk about Transparent mode, some clarification about interfaces is in order. There are two types of interfaces on a SonicWALL: a/the WAN interface(s) (up to a maximum of two physical ports), which is "untrusted," and "other." These subsequent interfaces are merely additional OPT or X[1–5], usually trusted interfaces, much like the LAN interface (an additional DMZ interface, for example), and the latter X interfaces are only present on larger models. From there, an interface is assigned either an IP address statically, where the administrator actually provides the IP address, which will be translated through the firewall to the WAN IP if necessary, or the interface is "transparently" assigned; that is, not assigned at all. Contrast this with the aforementioned WAN interface. The WAN must be configured with an IP address (statically, for example) or any one of DHCP, PPPoE, L2TP, or PPTP, but make no mistake, this interface, and its zone, *will be addressed.* Your additional interfaces (OPT or X[1–5]), you may statically assign as you would a WAN interface, or as already mentioned, no assignment at all—the latter is your "transparency." These transparent zone addresses need not be translated (as they'll be bridged to the WAN "zone." It's worth noting that such a transparent zone is now essentially in the "untrusted" category (being part of, but not overlapping with, the WAN interface). This is even more real than it sounds, as any transparently assigned interface will now respond to the same IP address (or any ARP for that address) as the WAN interface would!

Permanently Assigned Interfaces

As alluded to previously, there's a "WAN" and "other" (our term) on a SonicWALL, but another way of looking at interfaces and worth considering is the notion of permanently assigned versus "user-definable" interfaces. The LAN and WAN interfaces on a SonicWALL are fixed, permanently bound to the trusted and untrusted zone types, respectively. The remaining interfaces (if you have them) can be configured and bound to any zone type, depending on the particular appliance:

- **SonicWALL PRO series:** X0—the default LAN interface.

- **SonicWALL TZ 170 series:** LAN—the single LAN interface includes all five LAN ports on the back of the TZ 170 series appliances.

- **SonicWALL PRO 1260:** LAN—the single LAN interface includes all 24 numbered ports and the uplink port on the front of the PRO 1260 security appliance.

- **SonicWALL PRO series:** X1—the default WAN interface.

- **SonicWALL PRO 1260 and SonicWALL TZ 170 series:** WAN

Source: *SonicWALL's SonicOS Enhanced 3.1 Administrator's Guide*

Then there's the category of "user-defined" interfaces, which includes the already mentioned OPT and X interfaces. These you can configure however you'd like, and they aren't terribly different from the LAN interface functionally, except that you can't make your LAN untrusted, or your WAN trusted, but you can make your "user-defined" interfaces either.

User-definable interfaces include:

- SonicWALL PRO 3060/PRO 4060/PRO 5060 security appliances include four user-definable interfaces—X2, X3, X4, and X5.

- SonicWALL PRO 2040 security appliance includes two user-definable interfaces—X2 and X3.

- SonicWALL PRO 1260 security appliance includes one user-definable interface—OPT.

- SonicWALL TZ 170 family security appliances include one user-definable interface—OPT.

Source: *SonicWALL's SonicOS Enhanced 3.1 Administrator's Guide*

Got all that? Basically, after your WAN and LAN (which are at fixed trust levels), there's other types of interfaces, variously called OPT or X1, X2, and the like, whose trust level you can change as you like. What physical ports correspond to our "fixed" or "permanently assigned" or "user-definable" ports (OPT and X2, X3,...X5, etc.) varies from appliance to appliance, but let's not allow this to confuse us. You just need to know not to expect to be able to change your WAN to transparent mode, or to transparently assign any of your non-WAN zones to the ranges of your LAN, DMZ/OPT, or anything *but* your WAN.

Understanding How Transparent Mode Works

Much too much is made of layer-2 firewalling, but a little "how" is in order, to accompany our "why and what." With Transparent mode, the SonicWALL firewall is converted from a layer-3 device to a layer-2 device, behaving a bit like a layer-2 bridge to the casual observer. In Transparent mode, the transparently assigned interface simply ARPs for the same addresses as the WAN interface. Consider Figure 8.1.

Figure 8.1 Transparent Mode ARP Cache

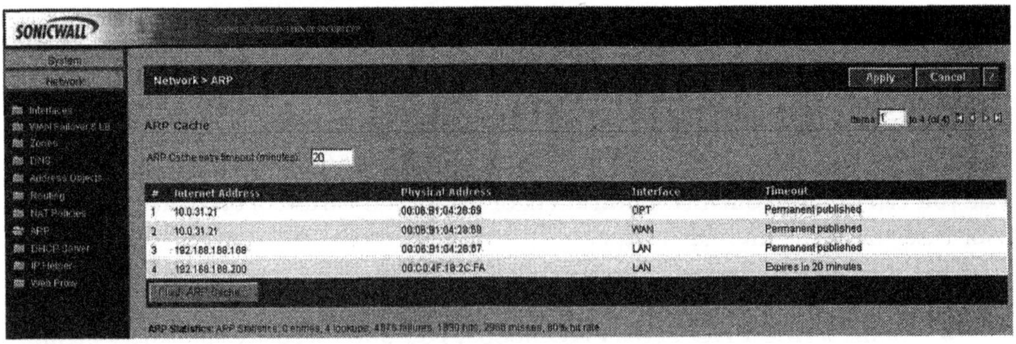

Note that both the WAN and OPT interfaces have the same IP address, but are nonetheless distinct interfaces (look closely at the last hex value of their MAC addresses).

In such a configuration, all devices on either side of the gateway are part of the same subnet. By converting the device to Transparent mode, you've segmented an existing subnet, and interpolated some firewall inspection. This isn't witchcraft; the gateway just responds to ARPs for the same IPs on two different physical interfaces. If the firewall were to remain a "traditional" layer-3 firewall, it would have to route the traffic, which would certainly require two different subnets and distinct address ranges, which may be neither possible nor desirable. A SonicWALL can take this a step further, by proxy-ARPing for "upstream" routers (on the WAN subnet) that hosts may still be configured to use as their default gateway, "transparently" avoiding unreachable gateways. Transparent mode is thus quite often the shortest distance between two points, since it requires the fewest infrastructure changes.

Configuring a Device to Use Transparent Mode

By default, an interface's traffic is translated to the WAN interface, but as we've already learned, NAT is not the goal in situations in which Transparent mode is employed. Configuring a SonicWALL firewall interface to use transparent assignment is actually quite simple, and the process doesn't really change for different types of interfaces (OPT DMZ interfaces versus LAN interfaces in Transparent mode). The process is as follows:

1. From **Network > Interfaces**, select **Configure** for an interface that's not the WAN interface (Figure 8.2).

Figure 8.2 Interface Settings Page

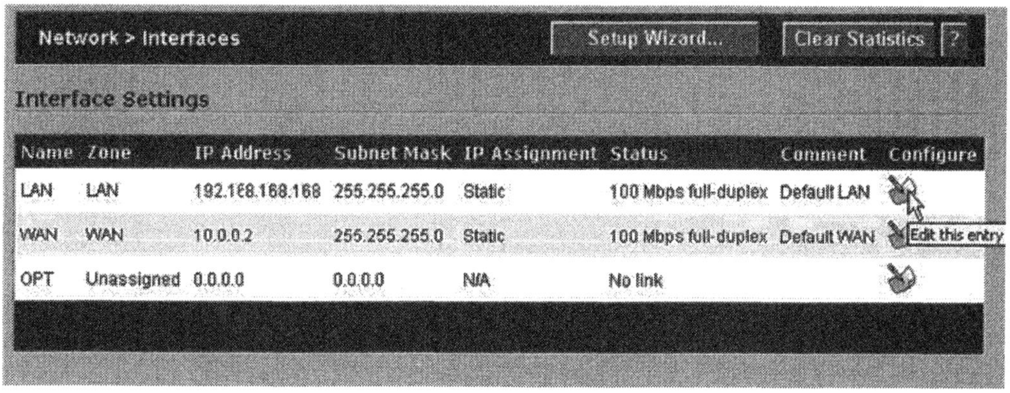

You'll get a pop-up window for the Interface Settings, from there:

2. Select **Transparent Mode** from the **IP Assignment** pull-down on the **General** tab.

3. Select the range you wish to be "transparent," which usually entails creating the transparent address object at the same time (Figure 8.3).

Figure 8.3 Editing an Interface's Settings

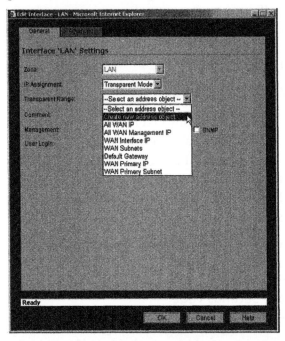

4. Make sure you've selected a range that doesn't overlap with the WAN interface and enter it using the Starting and Ending IP addresses (Figure 8.4).

Figure 8.4 Configuring a Transparent Range

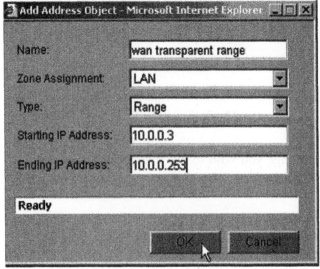

NOTE

It's worth repeating here that you shouldn't include the WAN interface IP address in the range you're assigning to a particular zone (e.g., LAN).

The result of the interface configuration should look something like Figure 8.5, regardless of the interface type (LAN, DMZ, etc.).

Figure 8.5 Interface Configured in Transparent Mode and Assigned a Transparent Range

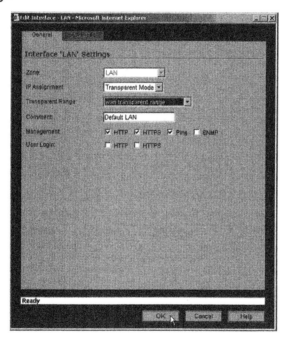

5. Confirm the configuration by looking at the ARP cache. You should see two of your physical interfaces ARPing for the same address.

Transparent Mode Deployment Options

Transparent mode offers a great deal of flexibility by providing transparent and flexible network protection for your network with the firewall. This ease of deployment *can* get us into trouble, however, if we haven't thought it through. Armed with our neat new toy, easily deployed as it is, we could attempt deployment before fully considering the implications of what we've learned so far.

Tools and Traps…

Different Interface Types

LAN, OPT/DMZ/X—all of which, except the WAN, can be configured to pass traffic "transparently," untranslated to the WAN zone.

Doing so will allow us to avoid introducing a routing hop, essentially providing firewall services for nodes by only introducing what acts as a layer-2 device, without changing next-hop (usually default) gateways for these nodes.

Sounds good so far, right? A couple of points arise in such deployments that we've already mentioned, or at least implied. First, the same "feature" we think allows us to *avoid* re-addressing issues can also *require re-addressing*. If you dropped a switch into your network, you expect hosts on all ports (potentially excluding VLAN-enabled switches) to be on the same subnet. Therefore, if your DMZ or LAN isn't using the same addressing scheme as the WAN, you either have to re-IP, or NAT (something you ostensibly were avoiding right?). So, you have to make sure that whatever zones are configured to use transparent assignment are using the same IPs as the WAN and IPs you want exposed to the outside world (and quite importantly as well, IPs that *are routable in the outside world*). Quite often, such deployments are on internal networks, but the siren call of transparent firewalling could leave you between the Scylla of re-addressing and the Charybdis of NATing, or reverting to layer-3 configurations at best. LANs may be easy to re-address, since they're usually assigned addresses with DHCP, but your DMZs, usually containing critical servers, are not. Consequently, you have to decide if you want these IPs "exposed" (albeit you have a firewall policy in front of them), or if you *can* in the event that you've chosen an RFC 1918 range for your server farm (soon to be a layer-2 DMZ) that you wish to expose to the Internet, now without a NAT.

Summary

In this chapter, we discussed how Transparent mode can provide simple, flexible, and elegant options for firewall deployments, and much sought-after transparent segmentation and inspection. Transparent mode deployments can be used to quickly and easily create a DMZ environment where none existed before, or easily secure internal Web or file servers and resources from client or end-user LAN hosts, providing internal segmentation and interpolating a security policy between these zones. The "invisible hop" of a layer-2 firewall removes the pain associated with dramatic changes to the network, including routes, default gateways, or re-addressing.

The behavior of a SonicWALL gateway in Transparent mode is different from the same device operating in layer-3 mode, and it is important to understand the differences for successful planning and deployment. NAT and routing are no longer performed, since the device's ARP behavior has changed, and its security model altered to co-opt trusted segments into the "untrusted" WAN

The final section of this chapter suggested some important planning considerations when considering layer-2 or "transparent" firewall deployments with SonicWALL.

Solutions Fast Track

Interface Settings

- ☑ A SonicWALL interface in Transparent mode transparently bridges traffic to the WAN interface.
- ☑ All interfaces, except for the WAN interface, can be configured to bridge to the WAN.

Understanding How Transparent Mode Works

- ☑ Transparent mode operates by two or more interfaces responding to ARP requests for the same IP addresses.

Configuring a Device to Use Transparent Mode

- ☑ Any user-defined interface and the "permanently assigned" LAN interface can be bridged to the WAN.

☑ User-definable interfaces consist of X and OPT interfaces, which can be assigned to various "trust levels" and bridged to the WAN in Transparent mode.

☑ The physical interface(s) (X0–X5, OPT) that map to various SonicWALL interface types vary from appliance to appliance.

Transparent Mode Deployment Options

☑ Segment internal subnets with less or minimal network configuration.

☑ Often used to provide firewall protection for internal resources, particularly small and previously unsegmented networks.

☑ Can actually force re-addressing or NATing if addresses are meant to be hidden or not routable across a public link that allows only routable addresses.

Frequently Asked Questions

The following Frequently Asked Questions, answered by the authors of this book, are designed to both measure your understanding of the concepts presented in this chapter and to assist you with real-life implementation of these concepts. To have your questions about this chapter answered by the author, browse to **www.syngress.com/solutions** and click on the **"Ask the Author"** form.

Q. What interface IP assignment modes can a SonicWALL firewall interface be assigned?

A. Static and Transparent modes.

Q. Which SonicWALL interfaces can be converted to Transparent mode?

A. LAN user-defined: OPT (usually configured as DMZ), X[1–5] (X0 is the LAN interface on Pro Series, and X1 is the WAN interface on Pro Series, otherwise X1 is an OPT on other platforms).

Q. How is ARP used to provide Transparent mode functionality?

A. Two separate physical interfaces will ARP for the same IP address, essentially switching between the two layer-2 segments.

Q. What IP address cannot be included in a transparent range?

A. The WAN IP address or any IP address assigned to another interface (e.g., LAN or other DMZ) that is also using the range and transparent assignment.

Chapter 9

Attack Detection and Defense

Solutions in this chapter:

- **Understanding the Anatomy of an Attack**
- **SonicWALL IPS**
- **SonicWALL Content Filtering**
- **Antivirus Services**

☑ **Summary**

☑ **Solutions Fast Track**

☑ **Frequently Asked Questions**

Introduction to the SonicOS Security Features

This chapter covers the details of the security features in SonicWALL appliances. These devices are packed with features that make life easier for administrators—easy to configure VPNs, built-in Dynamic Host Control Protocol (DHCP) server, advanced Network Address Translation (NAT) functionality, enhanced logging capabilities, and much more. However, a firewall's primary responsibility has always been security, keeping the bad bits out and letting the good bits in.

In addition to the strong feature set for network administration, SonicWALL appliances offer an equally strong set of protective tools. SonicWALLs have always protected networks against classic attacks such as Land, Teardrop, Ping of Death, and other network-layer=based attacks. These defensive features allow for Interface/Zone specific settings based on the level of risk Interface/Zone faces.

Moreover, while protecting at the network layer is both important and efficient, in today's world of application-layer-specific attacks, it does not provide sufficient security coverage by itself. Several optional services are available for SonicWALL appliances that provide additional security features, such as Intrusion Prevention, Content Filtering, Network Antivirus, Gateway Antivirus, Email Filtering, and Real Time Blacklists. Combine a well-defined and properly configured rule base with the optional services, and a complete picture emerges. However, what are we protecting ourselves from?

Understanding the Anatomy of an Attack

There are almost as many ways to attack a network as there are hackers who try it, but the majority of attack methods can be categorized as either automated or manual. Automated attacks cover the kinds of attacks made by self-propagating worms and other viruses. Manual attacks are generally still performed by a piece of code or other script, but the attack itself is initiated at the request of a live user, who selects his or her targets specifically. There's also a question of the competence of an attacker or complexity of an automated attack, which we will discuss.

The Three Phases of a Hack

Most attacks follow a series of phases:

- **Network reconnaissance** Initial probing for vulnerable services. Can include direct action against the target, such as port scanning, operating system (OS) fingerprinting and banner capturing, or it can be performing research about the target.

- **Exploit** The attempt to take control of a target by malicious means. This can include denying the service of the target to valid users. Generally, the goal is to achieve root-, system-, or administrative-level access on the target.

- **Consolidation** Ensuring control of the target is kept. This usually means destroying logs, disabling firewalls and antivirus software, and sometimes includes process hiding and other means of obfuscating the attacker's presence on the system. In some extreme cases, the attacker may even patch the target against the exploit he used to attack the box, to ensure that no one else exploits the target after him,

While each step may have more or less emphasis, depending on the attacker, most hacking attempts follow this general approach.

Script Kiddies

For manual attacks, the majority of events are generated by inexperienced malicious hackers, known both in the industry and the hacking underground as "script kiddies." This derogatory reference implies both a lack of maturity ("just a kid") and a lack of technical prowess (they use scripts or other pre-written code instead of writing their own). Despite these limiting factors, what they lack in quality, they more than make up for in quantity. Under a hail of arrows, even the mightiest warrior may fall. These types of attacks will generally be obvious, obnoxious, and sudden, and will usually light up your firewall or IDP (Intrusion and Detection Prevention) like a Christmas tree.

The majority of these attacks have no true intelligence behind them, despite being launched by a real person. Generally, the reconnaissance phase of these attacks will be a "recon-in-force" of a SYN packet and immediately transition to phase two by banging on your front door like an insistent vacuum cleaner salesperson. Script kiddies (also "skr1pt kiddies," "newbies," or just "newbs/noobs") glean through security Web sites like Security Focus (www.securityfocus.com), Packet Storm Security (http://packetstormsecurity.nl), and other sites that provide proof-of-concept code for exploits for new scripts to try out. Once they have these scripts, they will blindly throw them against targets—very few of these amateurs understand exactly how these hacking tools work or how to change them to do something else. Many sites that provide code realize this, and will purposely break the script so it doesn't work right, but would with a simple fix after a walk-through of the code by an experienced security professional.

Unfortunately, that only stops the new, inexperienced, or unaffiliated hacker. More commonly, hacking groups or gangs form with a few knowledgeable members at its core, with new inept recruits joining continuously. The people themselves need not live near each other in real life, but rather meet online in Internet Relay Chat (IRC) rooms and other instant messaging forums. These virtual groups will amass war chests of scripts, code snippets, and shellcode that work, thanks to the expertise of the more experienced members. Often, different hacking groups will start hacking wars, where each side attempts to outdo the other in either quantity or perceived difficulty of targets hacked in a single time span. Military targets in particular are seen as more difficult, when in fact generally the security of these sites is often well below corporate standards. Mass Website defacements are the most common result from these intergroup hacking wars, with immature, lewd, or insulting content posted to the sites.

A bright side to this problem is that many times a successful breach by these amateurs is not exploited to its fullest, since many of these hackers have no clue to exactly what sort of system they have gained access to, or how to proceed from there. To them, *owning* (a successful hack that results in a root-, administrator-, or system-level account) a *box* (a server), and modifying its presented Web page for others to see and acknowledge is generally sufficient. These attacks commonly do not proceed to phase three, consolidation.

From a protection standpoint, to defend against these attacks, it is important to keep DI and IDP signatures updated, and all systems patched, whether directly exposed to the Internet or not. Defense-in-depth is also key to ensure a successful breach does not spread. The motivation behind these groups is quick publicity, so expect hard, fast, obvious, but thorough strikes across your entire Internet-facing systems.

Black Hat Hackers

Experienced malicious hackers (sometimes called "Black Hat" hackers or just "Black Hats") tend to have a background of a script kiddy graduating from the underground cyber-gangs, a network security professional, an administrator turning to the "dark side" or a combination thereof. In fact, it is common to call law-abiding security professionals "White Hats," with some morally challenged, but generally well-intending people termed "Gray Hats." The clear delineation here is intent—

Black Hats are in it for malicious purposes, and often profit. This hat color scheme gets its roots from old Western movies and early black and white Western TV shows. In these shows, the bad guys always wore black hats, and the good guys wore white hats. Roles and morality were clearly defined. In the real world, this distinction is more muddled.

Black Hats will slowly and patiently troll through networks, looking for vulnerabilities. Generally, they have done their homework and have a good idea of the network layout and systems present before ever sending a single packet directly against your network—their phase one preparation is meticulous. A surprising amount of data can be gleaned from simple tools like the WhoIs database and Google or other Web search engines for free. Mail lists and newsgroups when data-mined for domains from a target can reveal much detail about what systems and servers are used by seeing network and system admins asking questions on how to solve server problems or configure devices for their networks, not to mention the wealth of information gleaned for social engineering. Names, titles, phone numbers, and addresses—it's all there to use by a skilled impersonator making a few phone calls and obtaining domain information, usernames, and sometimes passwords!

Notes from the Underground…

Social Engineering

Social engineering is the term used to describe the process by which hackers obtain technical information without using a computer directly to do so. Social engineering is essentially conning someone to provide you with useful information that he or she should not—whether it's something obviously important like usernames and passwords, or something seemly innocuous like the name of a network administrator or his phone number.

With a few simple pieces of valid information, some good voice acting, and proper forethought, a hacker could convince you over the phone that he or she is a new security engineer, and that the CEO is in a huff and needs the password changed now because he can't get to his e-mail or someone's going to be fired. "And that new password is what now? He needs to know it so we can log in and check it…"

Be sure to train your staff, including receptionists who answer public queries, to safeguard information to keep it out of the hands of hackers. Have authentication mechanisms to prevent impersonation.

The recon portion of the attack for a cautious Black Hat may last weeks or even months, painstakingly piecing together a coherent map of your network. When the decision to move to phase two and actively attack is finally made, the attack is quiet, slight, and subtle. They will avoid causing a crash of any services if they can help it, and will move slowly through the network, trying to avoid IDPs and other traffic logging devices. Phase three consolidation is also very common, including patching the system from further vulnerability, as they do not want some script kiddy coming in behind them and ruining their carefully laid plans.

A Black Hat's motivation is usually a strong desire to access your data—credit cards, bank accounts, social security numbers, usernames, and passwords. Other times it may be for petty revenge for perceived wrongs. Alternatively, they may want to figure out a way to divert your traffic to Web sites they control, so they can dupe users into providing these critical pieces of information—a technique known as *phishing* (pronounced like *fishing*, but with a twist). Some phishing attacks will merely copy your Web site to their own, and entice people to the site with a list of e-mails they may have lifted off your mail or database server. Sometimes, malware authors will also compromise Web sites in a manner similar to a script kiddy Web deface-ment, but instead of modifying the content on the site, they merely add additional files to it. This allows them to use the Web site itself as an infection vector for all who visit the site by adding a malicious JPEG file, Trojan horse binary, or other script into an otherwise innocuous Web site—even one protected by encryption (via Hypertext Transfer Protocol Secure, or HTTPS).

Defense against these types of attacks requires good network security design and good security policy design and enforcement. Training employees—especially IT and receptionists or other public-facing employees—about social engineering awareness and proper information control policy is paramount. For the network itself, proper isolation of critical databases and other stores of important data, combined with monitoring and logging systems that are unreachable from potentially compromised servers is key. Following up on suspicious activity is also important.

Worms, Viruses, and other Automated Malware

Mentioned in the *Notes from the Underground* sidebar, the concept for self-propagating programs is nothing new, but the practical application has only been around for the last 15 to 20 years. Since the origins of the Internet are well over 40 years old, this is significant. Indeed, in the last two to three years, malware has taken a rather nasty turn for the worst, and there's a good reason behind it.

Early worms were merely proofs-of-concept, either a "See what I can do" or some sort of glimpse at a Cyber Pearl Harbor or Internet Armageddon, and rarely had any purposefully malicious payload. This didn't keep them from being major nuisances that cost companies millions of dollars year after year. Then, however, some of the more advanced hacking groups started getting the idea that a large group of computers under a single organization's complete control might be a fun thing to have—and the concept of a zombie army was born.

Notes from the Underground…

Are You a Zombie?

The majority of machines compromised to make a zombie army are unprotected home users, directly connected to the Internet through DSL lines or cable modems. A recent study showed that while 60 percent of home Internet users surveyed felt they were safe from hackers, only 33 percent had some type of firewall. Of that minority, 72 percent were misconfigured, which means that *less than 10 percent* of home Internet users are properly protected from attack!

Furthermore, of the users who had wireless access in their homes, 38 percent used no encryption, and the 62 percent who did used wireless encryption schemes with known security flaws that could be exploited to obtain the decryption key. Essentially, every person surveyed who used wireless could be a point from which a hacker could attack—and over a third of them effortlessly.

Find out more information from the study at www.staysafeonline.info/news/safety_study_v04.pdf.

Zombies, sometimes referred to as *bots* (a group of bots is a *bot-net*), are essentially Trojan horses left by a self-propagating worm. These nasty bits of code generally phone home to either an IRC channel or other listening post system and report their readiness to accept commands. Underground hacker groups will work hard to compromise as many machines as they can to increase the number of systems under their command. Bot-nets composed of hundreds to tens of thousands of machines have been recorded. Typically, these groups use the bots to flood target servers with packets, causing a denial-of-service (DoS) attack from multiple points, creating a distributed denial of service (DDoS) attack. Nuking a person or site they don't like is fun for these people. However, the fun didn't last long.

Once a multithousand-node anonymous, controllable network became a reality, it was inevitable that economics would enter the picture, and zombie armies were sold to the highest bidder—typically spammers and organized crime. Spammers use these bots to relay spam through, so ISPs couldn't track them back to the original spammer and shut down their connection. This became so important to spammers that eventually they were contracting ethically challenged programmers to write worms for them with specific features such as mail relay and competitor Trojan horse removal. Agobot, MyDoom, and SoBig are examples of these kinds of worms. Organized crime realizes the simplicity of a cyber-shakedown and extorts high-value transaction networks such as online gambling sites for protection from DDoS attack by bot-nets under their control.

Protection from these tenacious binaries requires defense-in-depth (security checkpoints at multiple points within your network) and a comprehensive defense solution (flood control, access control, and application layer inspection). Many of the script kiddy defense methods will also work against most worms, since the target identification logic in these worms is generally limited—phase one recon is usually just a SYN to a potentially vulnerable port. This is because there is only so much space for all the worm needs to do—scanning, connecting, protocol negotiation, overflow method, shellcode, and propagation method, not to mention the backdoor Trojan. Most worms pick a target at random and try a variety of attacks against it, whether it's a valid target for the attack or not. To solve the complexity problem, many Trojans are now split into two or more parts—a small, simple propagating worm with a file transfer stub, and a second stage full-featured Trojan horse, with the *phone home*, e-mail spamming, and so forth. The first stage attacks, infects, and then loads the second stage for the heavy lifting, allowing for an effective phase three consolidation.

Information obtained by Honeypot Networks (systems designed to draw attacks away from legitimate targets and record malicious activities) shows that the average life expectancy of a freshly installed Windows system without patches connected directly to the Internet without a firewall or other protection is approximately 20 minutes. On some broadband or dial-up connections, it can take 30 minutes or longer to download the correct patches to prevent compromise by these automated attack programs. Using the Internet unprotected is a race you can't win.

Notes from the Underground…

Multivector Malware and the People Who Pay for It

Hacking (the term as used by the media for unauthorized access) is as old as computer science itself. Early on, it was mostly innocent pranks, or for learning and exploring. And while concepts for self-replicating programs were bantered around as early as 1949, the first practical viruses did not appear until the early 1980s.

These early malicious software (or *malware*) applications generally required a user's interaction to spread—a mouse button clicked, a file open, a disk inserted. By the late 1980s, however, fully automated self-replicating software programs, generally known as worms, were finally realized. These programs would detect, attack, infect, and restart all over again on the new victim without any human interaction. The earliest worms, such as the Morris Worm in 1988, had no purposeful malicious intent, but due to programming errors and other unconsidered circumstances, it still caused many problems.

The earliest worms and hacking attacks targeted a single known vulnerability, generally on a single computing platform. Code Red is a classic example—it targeted only Microsoft Windows Web servers running Internet Information Server (IIS), and specifically a single flaw in the way IIS handled ISAPI (Internet Server Application Programming Interface) extensions. And while they did significant damage, a single flaw on a single machine tends to confine the attack to a defined area, with a known, specific defense.

Unfortunately, this is no longer the case. Malware is now very complex, and the motivations for malware have changed with it. Early malware was limited to mostly pranks—file deletion, Web defacement, CD tray opening, and so on. Later, when commerce came to the Web, and valuable data such as credit card numbers and other personal information were now online and potentially vulnerable, greed became a factor in why and how malware authors wrote their code. Recently, the culprits are spammers with significant financial clout, who pay programmers to add certain features to their malware, so that spam (unsolicited e-mail), spim (unsolicited instant messages), and spyware can be spread for fun and profit.

NetSky, MyDoom, and Agobot are the newest breeds of these super-worms. New versions come out almost weekly, and certainly after any new major vulnerability announcement. They don't target just one vulnerability on one platform—they are multivector, self-propagating infectors, and will stop at nothing to infiltrate your network. Most exploit at least four different vulnerabilities, and brute force login algorithms. These worms even attack each other—NetSky and

Continued

www.syngress.com

MyDoom both remove other Trojan horses and antivirus and other security programs. A variant of Agobot attempts to overflow the FTP server left behind by a
Sasser worm infection as an infection vector.

SonicWALL IPS

SonicWALL IPS (Intrusion Prevention Service) uses a patent-pending scanning
engine to provide deep packet inspection analysis of traffic that traverses the
SonicWALL interfaces. It provides proactive defense against existing and newly discovered application and protocol vulnerabilities. The signature granularity allows
SonicWALL appliances to detect and prevent attacks based on global, attack group,
or on a per-signature basis to provide maximum flexibility and to control the
number of false-positives.

SonicWALL IPS is part of the SonicWALL Gateway Anti-Virus/Intrusion
Prevention service solution and is available to appliances running SonicOS
Enhanced. The IPS uses SonicWALL's Deep Packet Inspection Technology (DPIT).
DPIT allows the SonicWALL to look at the actual data contained in a packet, to
determine if it is malicious. DPIT also allows the SonicWALL to correctly handle
TCP fragmented byte stream inspection, as if no fragmentation has occurred.

Deep Packet Inspection Overview

DPIT enables the SonicWALL to inspect packets all the way up to the application
layer. DPIT 2.0 enables dynamic signature updates, which are pushed from the
SonicWALL Distributed Enforcement Architecture. Table 9.1 describes how DPIT
works.

Table 9.1 SonicWALL Deep Packet Inspection

1	The Pattern Definition Language Interpreter uses signatures that can be written to detect and prevent known and unknown protocols, applications, and exploits.
2	Any TCP packets that arrive out of order will be reassembled by DPIT.
3	The Deep Packet Inspection Engine's preprocessing involves nor- malization of the packet's payload. For example, an encoded HTTP request will be decoded and then checked against the sig- nature database.

Continued

Table 9.1 continued SonicWALL Deep Packet Inspection

4	Postprocessors perform actions such as passing a packet without modification, or dropping or resetting a TCP connection.
5	Deep Packet Inspection supports complete signature matching across TCP fragments without having to reassemble the fragments, unless they arrive out of order. This provides increased performance and minimizes CPU and memory consumption.

SonicWALL Intrusion Prevention Service may be applied to both inbound and outbound traffic. The signatures written for the SonicWALL are direction oriented, meaning the direction of the attack is considered when applying IPS. The SonicWALL IPS does not require the administrator to understand how and/or what signatures are applied in what direction. Configuration is as simple as specifying the Prevent All global settings for high priority attacks, medium priority attacks, and/or low priority attacks.

High priority attacks includes traffic that is always considered to be hostile. In other words, traffic of this type should never be present on the network. Common examples of high priority attacks include: DoS, DDoS, and Backdoors to name a few.

Medium priority attacks include traffic that is considered to be hostile, however, for certain environments, the traffic could be present on the network. Examples of Medium Priority attacks include: Certain FTP, Telnet, and DNS attacks.

Low priority attacks are more for informational purposes. Traffic within this category includes RPC, various Scans, and SMTP attacks.

Configuring SonicWALL IPS

Three steps must be followed when setting up the IPS on SonicWALL appliances:

1. Activate and Enable the SonicWALL IPS on the appliance.

2. Specify the global Prevent All actions under the Signature Groups Table to activate filtering against high- and medium-priority attacks.

3. Select the Interfaces (SonicOS Standard) or Zones (SonicOS Enhanced) to which IPS will be applied.

To configure SonicWALL IPS, select **Security Services | Intrusion Prevention** (Figure 9.1).

Figure 9.1 Intrusion Prevention Service Status

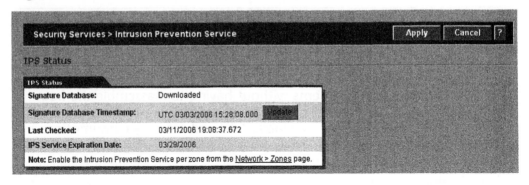

The Intrusion Prevention Service main window is divided into three sections. The first section shown in Figure 9.1 displays the status of the IPS, and includes:

- **Signature Database:** Indicates whether the signature database has been downloaded.

- **Signature Database Timestamp:** Shows the date and time of the last signature update.

- **Last Checked:** Shows the last date and time updates were checked.

The second section of the screen, shown in Figure 9.2, is used to configure the IPS Global Settings.

Figure 9.2 IPS Global Settings

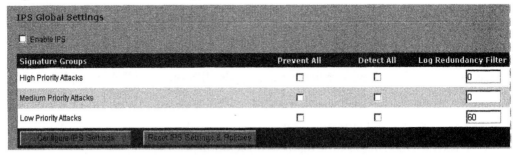

SonicWALL IPS must be enabled on the appliance by checking the **Enable IPS** checkbox. Simply checking the Enable IPS box alone does not enforce IPS; you must also configure the Prevent All and/or Detect All settings under the Signature Groups before IPS will be enforced. If Prevent All is not checked for High, Medium, or Low Priority Attacks, IPS will not be enforced on the appliance.

Typically, High Priority and Medium Priority Attacks should be configured to Prevent All. The Detect All option is used to create an entry in the SonicWALL log to inform the administrator that malicious activity was detected; however, no action is taken to prevent the traffic from traversing the SonicWALL.

The Log Redundancy Filter is used to restrict the number of identical log entries to a specific number per second. For example, if the Log Redundancy Filter is configured with a value of 30, the SonicWALL will create duplicate log entries every 30 seconds.

In addition to checking the Enable IPS checkbox and configuring the Prevent All and Detect All actions, you must also select the Interfaces or Zones that will be protected by the service.

In SonicOS Standard, IPS is applied on a per interface basis. For example, IPS may be applied to the LAN, OPT, DMZ, WAN, and/or WLAN interfaces. After selecting the interfaces that will be protected by IPS and clicking **Apply**, the IPS settings will be active on the network.

IPS is applied on a per zone basis in SonicOS Enhanced, between each zone and the WAN, and between internal zones. To enable IPS on a zone:

1. Click **Security Services | Intrusion Prevention Service**, and check the **Enable IPS** checkbox.

2. Under Signature Groups, check **Prevent All** and **Detect All** for both High and Medium Priority Attacks.

3. Click **Apply**.

4. Click **Network | Zones**, and select the **Configure** icon next to the interface or interfaces on which you would like to apply IPS.

5. On the Edit Zone page, click the **Enable IPS** checkbox.

6. Click **OK**.

The third section of the screen, shown in Figure 9.3, is used to configure the individual categories or signatures for the IPS.

Figure 9.3 IPS Policies

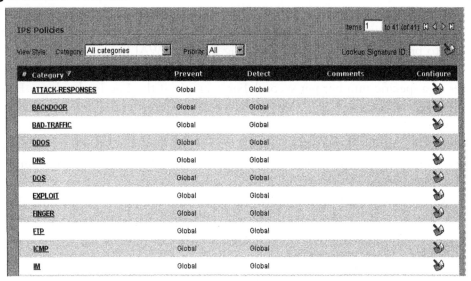

The list can be sorted by All categories, All signatures, or by individual categories. To choose the method of sorting that will be applied, click the **View Style: Category:** drop-down menu and select one of the options. The list may also be sorted by the priority of the attack types. Click the **Priority** drop-down menu and select All, High, Medium, or Low priority from the list. In addition to being able to sort the list, administrators may also query the list for a specific Signature ID by using the **Lookup Signature ID:** field.

Updating SonicWALL IPS Signatures

By default, SonicWALL appliances running IPS are configured to update once every hour. Administrators can update signatures immediately by clicking the **Update** button located in the IPS Status window.

IPS Signature Updates are secured. Upon registering the IPS Service for the appliance, a pre-shared key is created. All requests for signature updates are forced to authenticate using the pre-shared key, and use full server certificate validation via HTTPS.

Global-, Category-, and Signature-Level Policies

Administrators can configure IPS protection at the Global, Category, or Signature level to provide the most granular and flexible protection for their network environments.

- **Global** Allows configuration of IPS protection on a global level. In other words, by selecting the Prevent All action for High, Medium, and/or Low level attacks, protection against all signatures within these groups will be enforced on the appliance.

- **Category** Category-level policies allow for greater control of how the IPS service will be enforced on the appliance. Example categories include DDOS, IM, SMTP, and WEB-ATTACKS.

- **Signature** The signature-level policies provide the most granular control over the IPS service. Prevention and Detection settings for each individual signature can be applied.

Configuring Global Level Policies

Global Level policies allow for a quick and easy implementation of the SonicWALL IPS. By enabling the Prevent All and/or Detect All options for High, Medium, and Low Priority Attacks, all categories and their signatures will be enforced.

To enable Global Level IPS Policies, click the checkboxes next to **Prevent All** and/or **Detect All** for each priority of attack as shown in Figure 9.4.

Figure 9.4 IPS Global Settings

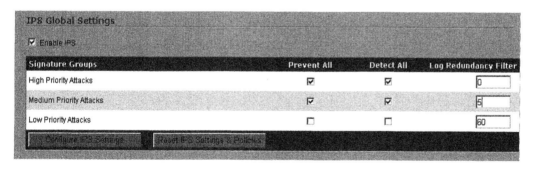

Configuring Category Policies

To configure settings for individual categories, click the **Configure** icon to the right of the category. This will display the Edit IPS Category window as shown in Figure 9.5.

Figure 9.5 The Edit IPS Category Window

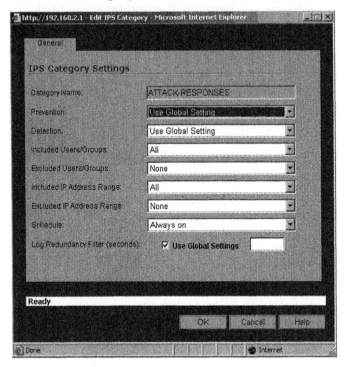

By default, the category settings will inherit the configuration of the Global Settings. Each Category can be modified to allow custom settings for the Prevention and Detection options. To change these settings, click the drop-down menu and select either **Enabled** or **Disabled**.

In addition to being able to configure the Prevention and Detection options, administrators may configure the category to include or exclude specific users and groups and/or IP address ranges. To enforce a specific category for specific users or groups, click the drop-down menu next to **Included Users/Groups** and select the user or group object from the list. The same configuration applies for excluding users or groups from a category. Select the **Excluded Users/Group** drop-down menu and select the object from the list. If specific address ranges should be included or excluded from the list, click the drop-down menu next to either **Included IP Address Range** or **Excluded IP Address Range** and select the appropriate object from the list.

Each category can also be configured to be enabled or disabled during specific times by selecting a schedule from the **Schedule:** drop-down menu.

The **Log Redundancy Filter (seconds):** field is used to override the global settings. To modify the value, clear the checkbox next to **Use Global Settings** and enter the new value in the field.

After configuring the settings for an individual category, click **OK** to save the changes. Repeat the process for each category you wish to modify.

Configuring Signature Policies

Configuring IPS policies on a per-signature basis is extremely time-consuming; however, the functionality does exist. To configure settings for a specific signature, change the **View Style: Category** option to **All Signatures**. This will display an expanded view of each category and the associated signatures. Figure 9.6 shows an example of the signature view.

Figure 9.6 IPS Signature View

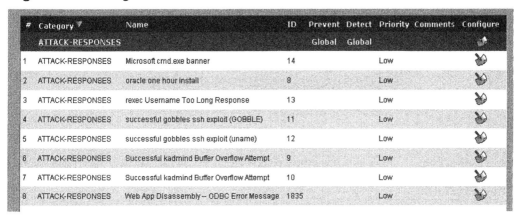

#	Category	Name	ID	Prevent	Detect	Priority	Comments	Configure
	ATTACK-RESPONSES			Global	Global			
1	ATTACK-RESPONSES	Microsoft cmd.exe banner	14			Low		
2	ATTACK-RESPONSES	oracle one hour install	8			Low		
3	ATTACK-RESPONSES	rexec Username Too Long Response	13			Low		
4	ATTACK-RESPONSES	successful gobbles ssh exploit (GOBBLE)	11			Low		
5	ATTACK-RESPONSES	successful gobbles ssh exploit (uname)	12			Low		
6	ATTACK-RESPONSES	Successful kadmind Buffer Overflow Attempt	9			Low		
7	ATTACK-RESPONSES	Successful kadmind Buffer Overflow Attempt	10			Low		
8	ATTACK-RESPONSES	Web App Disassembly -- ODBC Error Message	1835			Low		

Click the **Configure** icon to the right of the specific signature you would like to modify. This will display the **Edit IPS Signature** window as shown in Figure 9.7.

Figure 9.7 The Edit IPS Signature Settings Window

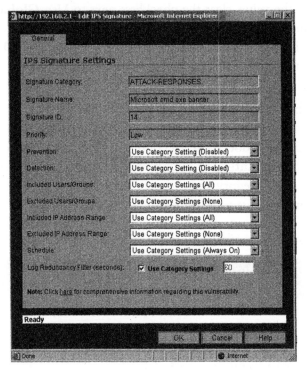

At the signature level, settings are inherited from the category level by default. To modify the settings, click the drop-down menus to the right of each parameter and select the appropriate action or object from the list.

On the bottom of each signature, a link is provided that allows administrators to obtain comprehensive information regarding each vulnerability. For example, clicking the **here** link for the signature shown in Figure 9.7 will display the page shown in Figure 9.8.

Figure 9.8 Vulnerability Information

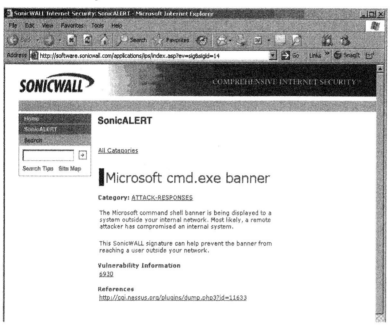

Creating and Configuring User/ Group Exclusion and Inclusion Groups

As mentioned previously, administrators can configure individual users, groups of users, or IP address ranges that will be either included or excluded from specific categories or individual signatures. For example, if you would like to create a group for Executive Management and then exclude this group from a specific category, you would first create the Executive Management group under **Users | Local Users** and click **Add User**. The Add User window will be displayed, as shown in Figure 9.9.

Figure 9.9 The Add User Dialog

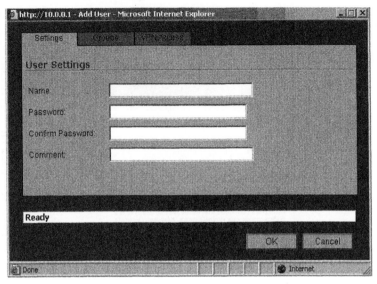

Create a user account for each of the Executive Management team members. Enter the name, password, and a comment for each user as shown in Figure 9.10.

Figure 9.10 Add User Example

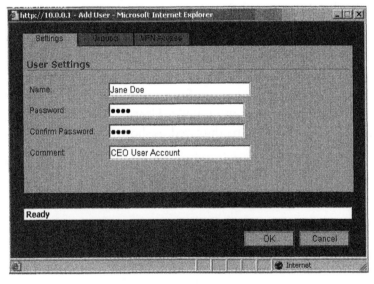

Click **OK** to create the user account. Figure 9.11 shows a list of users for our example.

Figure 9.11 Local Users

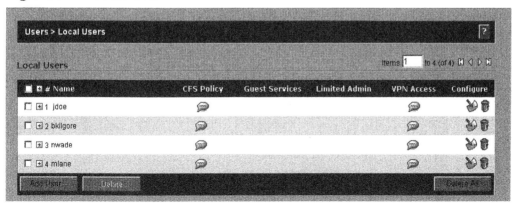

Now that we have created the user accounts for the Executive Management team, we need to create a group and add each account to it. To do so, click **Users | Local Groups** and then click **Add Group**. The Add Group window will be displayed as shown in Figure 9.12.

Figure 9.12 The Add Group Dialog

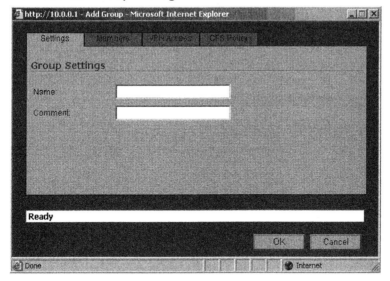

Enter the name of the group and provide a descriptive comment. Click the **Members** tab to display a list of users that can be added to the group (Figure 9.13).

Figure 9.13 The Group Members Dialog

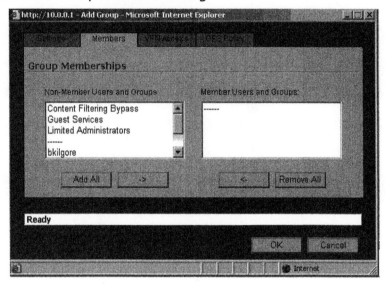

The Group Memberships window is composed of two columns: Non-Member Users and Groups and Member Users and Groups. The Non-Members Users and Groups column contains a list of existing users and groups that can be added to this group. The Member Users and Groups column lists any users and groups that have been added to the group. In our example, we will add the Executive Management user accounts to the group as shown in Figure 9.14.

Figure 9.14 Group Membership

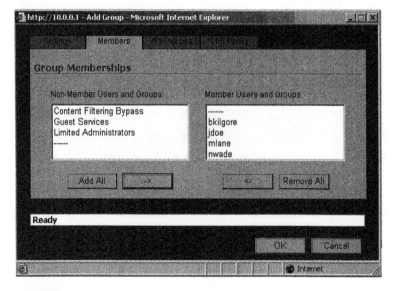

After adding the users to the group, click **OK**. Now that we have created user accounts for the Executive Management team and added them to the Executive Management group, we can configure the IPS inclusion and/or exclusion lists. In this example, we will exclude the Executive Management group from the Web Based Attacks category. To do this, click **Security Services | Intrusion Prevention Service**. Make sure **View Style: Category:** is set to **All Categories**. Scroll down to near the bottom of the IPS categories and click the **Configure** icon next to **WEB-ATTACKS.** Figure 9.15 shows the configuration options for this category.

Figure 9.15 IPS Category Settings

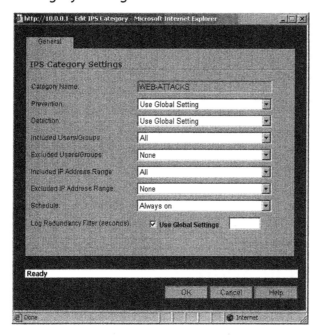

To exclude the Executive Management group from the WEB-ATTACKS category, click the **Excluded Users/Groups:** drop-down box and select the Executive Management group from the list as shown in Figure 9.16.

Figure 9.16 Configuring Exclusion Lists for IPS

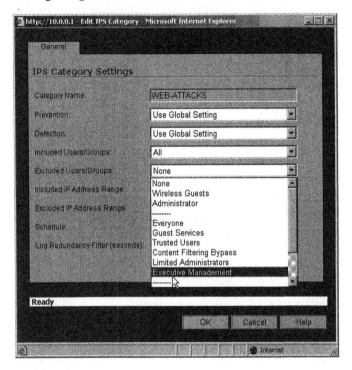

Click **OK** to save the changes. Repeat this process for each category and/or signature. The same process is used to configure Inclusion lists for users and groups to which the policy should apply.

Configuring IP Address Range Inclusion and Exclusion Lists

A second feature for creating Inclusion and Exclusion lists is to use a specific range of IP addresses, and uses the same approach as for creating User and Group Exclusion and Inclusion lists. First, an object address object defining the Range of IP addresses to include/exclude must be created. This is done on the **Network | Address Objects** page. On the **Address Objects** page, click the **Add** button under **Address Objects**. The Add Address Object window will be displayed as shown in Figure 9.17.

Figure 9.17 The Add Address Object Dialog

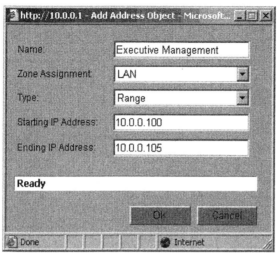

We will use our previous example of the Executive Management group. As shown in Figure 9.17, enter **Executive Management** for the Name, select the **LAN** from the Zone Assignment drop-down menu, set the **Type** to **Range**, and enter the **beginning IP Address** and **Ending IP Address** for the range. Then, click **OK** to complete the configuration.

Now that we have created the IP address range object for the Executive Management team, we can configure the IPS inclusion and/or exclusion lists. In this example, we will exclude the Executive Management range from the Web Based Attacks category. To do so, click **Security Services | Intrusion Prevention Service**. Make sure **View Style: Category:** is set to **All Categories**. Scroll down to near the bottom of the IPS categories and click the **Configure** icon next to **WEB-ATTACKS.** Figure 9.18 shows the configuration options for this category.

Figure 9.18 Edit IPS Category

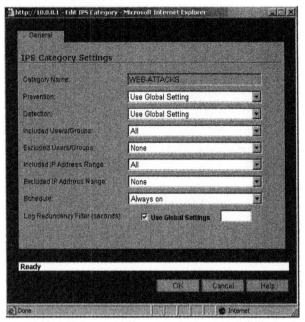

Click the drop-down list to the right of **Excluded IP Address Range** option. In the drop-down list, select the Executive Management object and then click **OK** to save the changes.

SonicWALL Content Filtering

SonicWALL Content Filtering Services (CFS) provides protection against violations of your company's Acceptable Use Policy. Administrators can enforce content filtering based on keywords, time of day, trusted and forbidden domains, and file types such as cookies, Java, and ActiveX. SonicWALL CFS is available in two versions, Standard and Premium.

SonicWALL CFS Standard is available on third-generation appliances, the SonicWALL TZW Wireless appliances, TZ and TZ170 appliances, and PRO 3060 and 4060 appliances. It provides 12 different categories of content filtering, integrates with ViewPoint reporting, and requires firmware version 6.5 or SonicOS Standard. CFS Standard does not provide Dynamic Rating and cannot be used to define user or group policies. In other words, CFS Standard is applied on a global basis.

SonicWALL CFS Premium is available for TZ170 and PRO series products. SonicOS Enhanced is required on the appliance to run the Premium service. The Premium version provides 56 individual categories of content filtering, allows user and/or group policies to be enforced, provides Dynamic Rating, and easily integrates into ViewPoint Reporting.

In addition to SonicWALL CFS, third-party content-filtering solutions can be integrated with SonicWALL appliances. Currently, SonicWALL supports N2H2 and Websense Enterprise solutions.

We will primarily discuss SonicWALL CFS Premium, which will cover all the CFS Standard options and the additional functionality available in the Premium version. To configure SonicWALL Content Filtering Services, browse to **Security Services | Content Filtering**. A page similar to Figure 9.19 will be displayed.

Figure 9.19 Content Filter Options

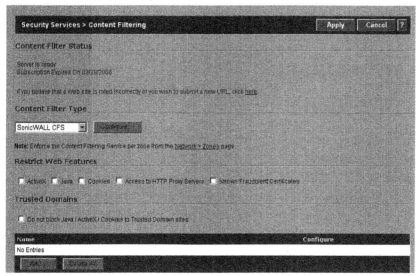

The Content Filter window is composed of six sections:

- Content Filter Status
- Content Filter Type
- Restrict Web Features
- Trusted Domains
- CFS Exclusions
- Message to Display when Blocked
- **Content Filter Status** Displays important information related to the current status of the Content Filter Service.

- **Server is ready** Indicates that the SonicWALL CFS Server is available and active.

- **Subscription Expires On** Shows the date the CFS Service subscription expires on the appliance.

- **Content Filter Type** Used to select the type of Content Filtering Service that will be enforced by the SonicWALL. Clicking the drop-down menu presents the available Content Filtering Solutions. Figure 9.20 illustrates the available options.

Figure 9.20 Content Filter Type Options

Select the Content Filter Type you would like to use from the drop-down list, and then click the **Configure** button to display relevant configuration options:

The Restrict Web Features options allow administrators to block specific Web features that are known to have security vulnerabilities or may provide attack vectors for malicious code or users. The following Web features can be blocked:

- **ActiveX** A programming language that allows scripts to be embedded in Web pages. ActiveX can be used by malicious attackers to compromise network security and/or delete files. Place a checkbox next to this option to block ActiveX controls.

- **Java** You are most likely familiar with Java applets, which are used within Web applications to perform specific functions. As with ActiveX controls, Java can be used by malicious users to exploit certain vulnerabilities that could lead to a compromise in network security. To block Java at the firewall, click the checkbox next to **Java**.

- **Cookies** Cookies are used to track Web activity and to remember certain aspects about a user's identity. For example, when you browse to a Web site and are greeted with a message that says, "Welcome Back Bob!" cookies are tracking your Web usage, which presents a compromise in user privacy. To block cookies at the firewall, simply click the checkbox next to **Cookies**.

- **Access to HTTP Proxy Servers** So you have implemented content filtering and assume that nobody can go anywhere that is not approved by the Acceptable Use Policy. Well, as you may have already figured out, where there is a will, there is a way. Users who are computer savvy may know that they can set their browser to use a Web proxy for all HTTP and HTTPS traffic to bypass the content filtering on the firewall. To prevent users from doing so, SonicWALL allows administrators to prevent access to HTTP proxy servers. To enable this feature, click the checkbox next to **Access to HTTP Proxy Servers**.

- **Known Fraudulent Certificates** Digital certificates are used to validate the identity of some Web content and files. In other words, a Web server with a certificate informs users that "It is who it says it is and here is the certificate to prove it." Uneducated users may assume that the certificate for a server is proof that any content downloaded from the server is not malicious. For example, in January 2001, VeriSign issued two certificates to an imposter masquerading as a Microsoft employee. Fraudulent certificates do exist on the Internet and pose a risk to network security. To block all known fraudulent certificates at the firewall, simply click the checkbox next to **Known Fraudulent Certificates**.

- **Trusted Domains** If you enable the ActiveX, Java, and Cookies options in Restrict Web Features, the settings are applied to all Web sites. In most cases, employees will need access to certain sites that may employ these items, and blocking access to them would interrupt legitimate access to work-related information. SonicWALL provides the capability to override the global settings and exclude certain sites from the Restrict Web Features policy.

To enable this functionality, click the checkbox next to **Do not block JAVA/ActiveX/Cookies to Trusted Domains**. This feature is only applied to domains listed under Trusted Domains. To add a Trusted Domain, click the **Add** button. This will display the **Add Trusted Domain** page as shown in Figure 9.21.

Figure 9.21 The Add Trusted Domain Page

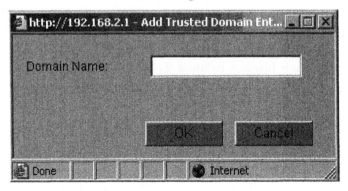

Enter the Domain name that needs to be excluded from the Restrict Web Features and then click **OK**. Once the Domain name has been added, the list will be updated (Figure 9.22).

Figure 9.22 The Trusted Domains List

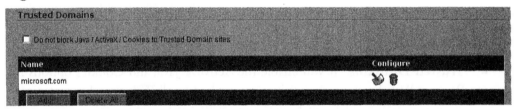

To delete a Trusted Domain from the list, simply click the **Trashcan** icon to the right of the Domain Name. If you would like to delete all the Trusted Domains from the SonicWALL, click the **Delete All** button at the bottom of the **Trusted Domains** section.

The CFS Exclusion List shown in Figure 9.23 is used to exclude a specific address range from the content filter. In high security environments, this option should not be used; all devices must comply with the Acceptable Use Policy. However, in some circumstances, it may be necessary or desired to have certain devices that are not governed by the CFS Policy.

Figure 9.23 The CFS Exclusion List

To add a range of IP addresses that will be excluded from the Content Filter Policies, click **Add**. This will display the **Add CFS Range Entry** window as shown in Figure 9.24. Enter the beginning and end IP addresses for the range and click **OK**. For example, if servers are configured with IP addresses within 10.0.0.50–10.0.0.70, you would enter 10.0.0.50 in the **IP Address From:** field, 10.0.0.70 in the **IP Address To:** field, and then click OK. This would exclude the list of IPs within this range from the Content Filter Policies.

Figure 9.24 Add CFS Exclusion Range Entry

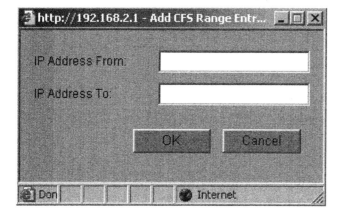

SonicWALL CFS allows administrators to use either a default or custom message that will be displayed to users when they attempt to open a Web site that is blocked by the SonicWALL CFS Policy (Figure 9.25). To enter a custom message, delete the default text and enter your custom message in the memo field. Click **Apply** to save the settings.

Figure 9.25 Message to Display for Blocked Content

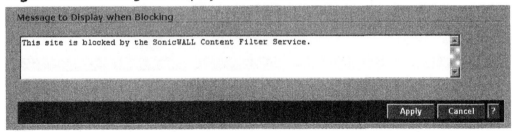

Configuring SonicWALL CFS

With the basics out of the way, we can now configure the SonicWALL Content Filtering Service settings. To do so, make sure **SonicWALL CFS** is selected in the drop-down menu under **Content Filter Type**, and then click the **Configure** button to the right of it. You will now see a window similar to Figure 9.26.

Figure 9.26 Filter Properties Window

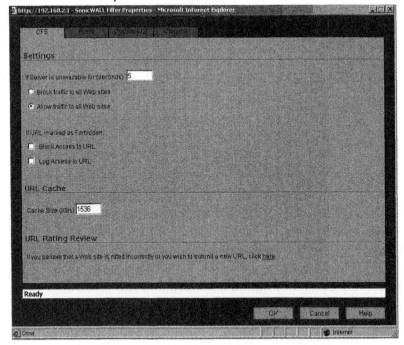

Four tabs are used to configure the CFS service, as discussed next.

CFS Tab

The CFS tab provides global options for the service. There are three sections under this tab.

Settings

- **If Server is unavailable for (seconds)** This field is used to configure the timeout value for the SonicWALL CFS server located at SonicWALL. If the CFS server is unable to be contacted by the number of seconds specified in this field, one of two options will be enforced:
  - **Block traffic to all Web sites** This is the fail-secure option. If the CFS server is unavailable, all Web traffic will be blocked by the SonicWALL. This ensures that the Acceptable Use Policy will be enforced.
  - **Allow traffic to all Web sites** In certain environments, blocking all Web traffic could interrupt business. In this case, the option to allow traffic to all Web sites provides a fail-safe option, in which all Web traffic is allowed if the CFS server is unavailable.
- **If URL marked as blocked** If a user browses to a Web site that is blocked by a certain category you have enabled on the appliance, two actions can be taken.
  - **Block Access to URL** This option blocks access to all URLs that are blocked by any category.
  - **Log Access to URL** This option will create a new entry in the Log file indicating that a violation of the policy has occurred.
- **URL Cache** The URL Cache size is used to specify the amount of memory to be allocated to storing commonly used URLs. Performance may be increased significantly by increasing the URL Cache size. However, as with any other item, there is such a thing as too much. There is no standard recommendation to what the cache size should be set to; adjust the size gradually to determine what size will work best with your network.
- **URL Rating Review** The URL Rating Review is used to submit Web sites to SonicWALL that you believe to be improperly rated by the SonicWALL. By clicking the link, you will be redirected to the SonicWALL CFS site and presented with a screen similar to that shown in Figure 9.27.

Figure 9.27 The CFS URL Rating Review Request Window

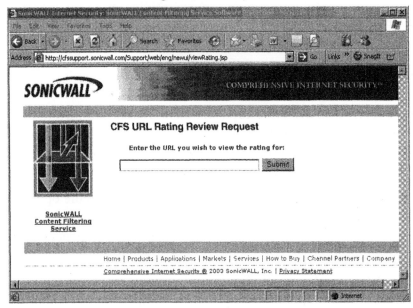

Simply enter the URL you would like reviewed and then click **Submit**. The response from SonicWALL will include information similar to that shown in Figure 9.28.

Figure 9.28 Rating Review Request Results

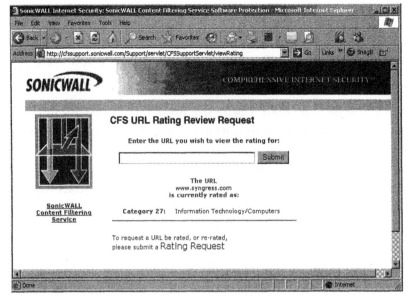

As shown in Figure 9.28, SonicWALL returns the Category number and the description of the Category for the submitted URL. If you feel that the rating returned is incorrect, you can submit a Rating Request to SonicWALL by clicking the **Rating Request** link shown at the bottom of Figure 9.28.

Policy Tab

The Policy tab is used to configure the default CFS Policy and create custom policies that can then be applied to individual users or groups. SonicWALL CFS policies use inheritance from the default policy. This means that all custom created policies inherent the filters that are configured in the default policy. With that said, SonicWALL recommends that the default policy be the most restrictive of all policies. Custom filters will then be created to grant proper privileges that are denied by the default policy. Figure 9.29 shows the Policy tab on an appliance that has no Custom Policies created.

Figure 9.29 The Policy Tab

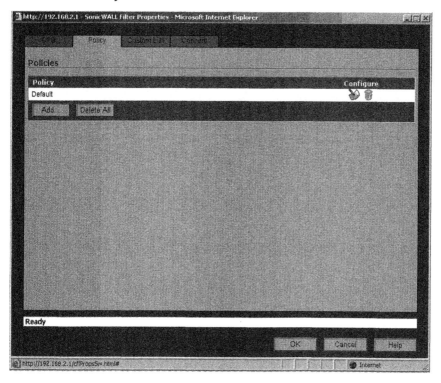

As mentioned previously, the default policy should be configured as the most restrictive of all the policies. To configure the default policy, click the **Configure**

icon to the right of **Default.** This will open the **Edit CFS Policy** window. Three tabs can be used to custom the policy.

The first tab, **Policy Name,** shown in Figure 9.30, is used to configure the Policy Name. Note: You cannot modify the default policy name.

Figure 9.30 The Policy Name Tab

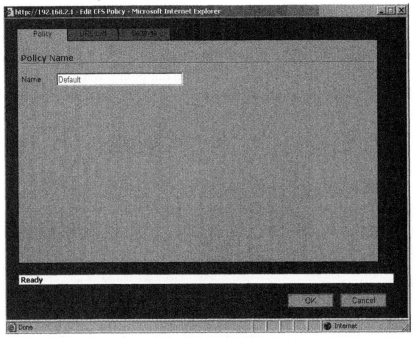

The second tab, **URL List**, is used to select the categories that will be blocked by this policy. Figure 9.31 shows the URL List screen for reference purposes.

Figure 9.31 The URL List Tab

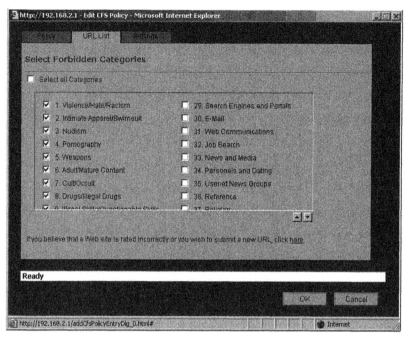

As mentioned previously, SonicWALL CFS Standard provides 12 categories and SonicWALL CFS Premium provides 56. Figure 9.31 shows an example of CFS Premium. Note the up and down arrows to the right of the screen. These are used to scroll up or down through the available categories. Typically, the Default CFS Policy will have all categories selected. This provides the greatest amount of enforcement for your Acceptable Use Policy.

To configure the Default Policy to enforce all categories, click the checkbox next to **Select all Categories**. Categories with a check mark next to them are enabled, and those without a check mark are disabled.

The third tab, **Settings**, is used to configure the Custom List Settings and Filter URLS by Time of Day options. Figure 9.32 shows an example of the Default Policy Settings window.

Figure 9.32 The Settings Tab

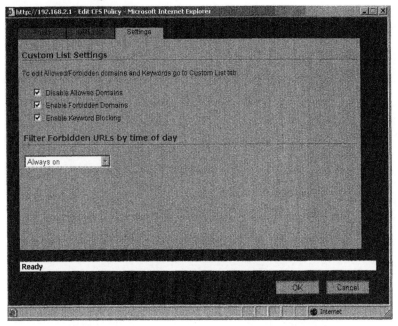

Custom List Settings allow administrators to enforce the Allowed Domains, Forbidden Domains, and Keyword Blocking options that are configured on the Custom List tab of the Content Filter window.

- **Disable Allowed Domains** Overrides the setting of allowing access to the domains entered under Allowed Domains. Remember that the default policy is the most restrictive. Custom policies will be used to grant the appropriate privileges to specific users and or groups.

- **Enable Forbidden Domains** A check box next to this option blocks access to all domain names listed under the Forbidden Domains list.

- **Enable Keyword Blocking** A check box next to this option blocks access to any site or content that contains any keywords that have been configure under the Keyword list.

The Filter Forbidden URLs by Time of Day option allows administrators to apply CFS policies based on specific schedules that have been created. In other words, if CFS is to only be applied during normal business hours, the SonicWALL can be configured to enable CFS protection Monday through Friday from 8:00 A.M. until 6:00 P.M. and disable CFS protection at any other time. The available schedules are shown in Figure 9.33.

Figure 9.33 The Filter Forbidden URLs by Time of Day Option

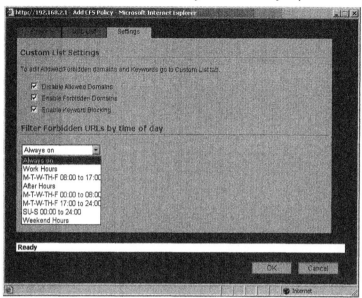

NOTE

You cannot change the Filter Forbidden URLs by time of day option for the default CFS policy. It will be configured as Always on.

Custom List Tab

Figure 9.34 shows the Custom List page.

Figure 9.34 The Custom List Page

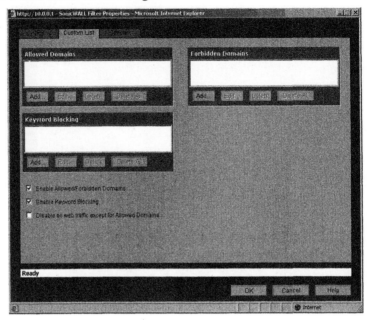

Custom lists can be created for:

- **Allowed Domains** Domains in this list will be allowed regardless of the content.

- **Forbidden Domains** Domains in this list will be blocked regardless of the content.

- **Keyword Blocking** Specified keywords will be blocked.

The following options can be enabled or disabled for the Custom Lists:

- **Enable Allowed/Forbidden Domains** A checkmark means that enforcement of the Allowed and Forbidden Domain lists is enabled.

- **Enable Keyword Blocking** A checkmark in this field enables the Keyword List.

- **Disable all Web traffic except for Allowed Domains** Enabling this option will result in blocking all Web traffic except for entries in the Allowed Domain List.

Consent Tab

The Consent options are shown in Figure 9.35.

Figure 9.35 CFS Consent Tab Settings

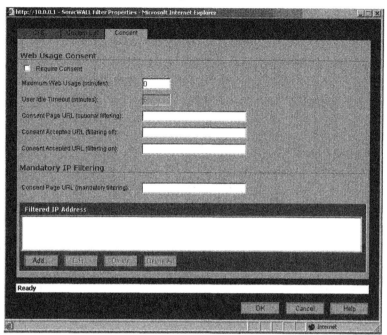

The Consent settings are used to force users to agree with the company's Acceptable Use Policy before they are allowed to browse the Web. By checking the **Require Consent** option, all users will be presented with the Consent Page specified in the Consent Page URL field.

Let's take a look at each of the fields on this page. The Maximum Web Usage (minutes) field is used to restrict Web browsing time for each user. This is useful in student lab environments, where there may be more users than available computers. A setting of zero in this field indicates that no time limitations are enforced. If the Maximum Web Usage field contains a value other than zero, the User Idle Timeout field will be available. If no users are browsing the Web before the expiration of the timeout value is reached, the SonicWALL will return to the Consent Page and require the users to agree to the Acceptable Use Policy again before being allowed to browse the Internet.

The next three fields are used to specify the Web pages that are displayed for the consent pages. The Consent Page URL (optional filtering) page is displayed anytime a user attempts to browse the Internet. The page specified in this field must be a valid URL on a Web server and be accessible by the users. The page must contain two links: one for accessing the Internet with content filtering enabled and the second for accessing the Internet with content filtering disabled. The hyperlinks for each of the links on this page will be http://LAN-IP/iAccept.html for unfiltered access and http://LAN-IP/iAcceptFilter.html for filtered access, where LAN-IP is the LAN IP address assigned to the LAN interface of the SonicWALL appliance.

After the users choose which type of access they will use, a confirmation page will be displayed to show their choices. The confirmation pages are specified in the Consent Accepted (filtering off) and Consent Accepted (filtering on) fields. Again, the values entered in these fields must be a valid URL accessible by users.

In addition to providing optional content-filtering choices for users, the Consent Page can enforce mandatory filtering for all devices or for specified devices. Users attempting to access Web content are presented with the Consent Page, which includes a link that users will click if they agree to the Acceptable Use Policy. The link must point to http://LAN-IP/iAcceptFilter.html, where LAN-IP is the IP address assigned to the SonicWALL's LAN interface.

Using the Filtered IP Address option, administrators can specify which devices content filtering will be enforced on. Up to 128 IP addresses can be specified. To select your IP addresses, click the **Add** button and enter the IP address of the computer that CFS should be enforced on. To remove a device from the list, highlight the IP address and then click the **Remove** button.

Creating Custom CFS Policies

In simple network environments, the default CFS policy may be adequate; however, in larger and more complex networks, adding Custom CFS policies provides more granular control over how CFS is enforced throughout the organization.

To create a Custom CFS Policy, browse to **Security Services | Content Filtering** and click **Configure** next to the **Content Filter Type** option. This displays the SonicWALL Filter Policies window. Select the **Policy** tab and then click **Add**. The Add CFS Policy window will be displayed as shown in Figure 9.36.

Figure 9.36 The Add CFS Policy Window

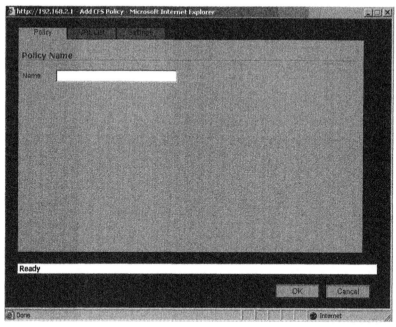

Enter a name for the policy, such as Engineering Group. Click the **URL List** tab to display the available categories for the policy. Figure 9.37 shows an example of the URL List for the CFS Premium service.

Figure 9.37 URL Forbidden Category

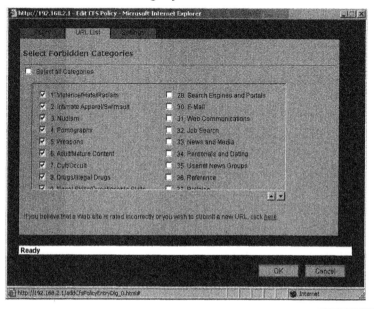

Select the specific categories that will be allowed or blocked for the Engineering Group. After you select the categories, click the **Settings** tab and enable or disable the options for Allowed Domains, Forbidden Domains, and Keyword Blocking. Select the Schedule to be used for filtering forbidden domains from the drop-down menu and then click OK to complete the policy configuration. Figure 9.38 shows the settings page.

Figure 9.38 Custom CFS Policy Settings Page

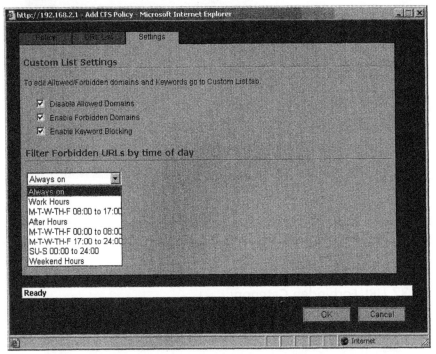

Antivirus Services

SonicWALL provides antivirus features that can be configured to provide additional protection against viruses, Trojans, worms, and other malware. Two antivirus solutions are available on SonicWALL appliances, Network Antivirus and Gateway Antivirus. Each of these solutions is discussed in more detail here.

Network Antivirus

The Network Antivirus service provides a means of enforcing the company antivirus policy network wide. Clients that do not have the antivirus software installed are denied access to Internet resources. The Network Antivirus service is based on

VirusScan AsAP. To configure Network Antivirus, go to **Security Services |
Network Antivirus**. A window similar to that shown in Figure 9.39 will appear.

Figure 9.39 The Security Services > Anti-Virus Window

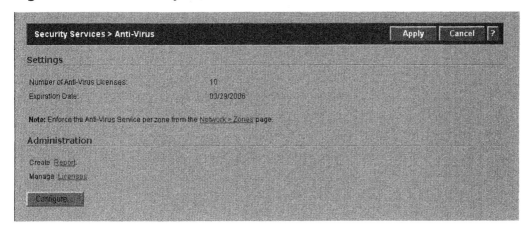

The main Anti-Virus window contains two sections, Settings and
Administration. The Settings page displays the following information:

- **Number of Anti-Virus Licenses** Displays the number of licenses available for the Network Antivirus service. In Figure 9.39, this particular appliance is licensed for 10 nodes. In other words, the Antivirus client can be
  installed on 10 devices.

- **Expiration Date** Displays the date the Network Antivirus subscription
  expires.

- **Administration** Includes options to create reports, manage the Network
  Antivirus licenses, and configure the Network Antivirus Policies.

- **Create Report** Used to create reports pertaining to the status of
  Network Antivirus Client devices. Clicking this link displays a window
  similar to that shown in Figure 9.40.

Figure 9.40 Anti-Virus Reports Authentication

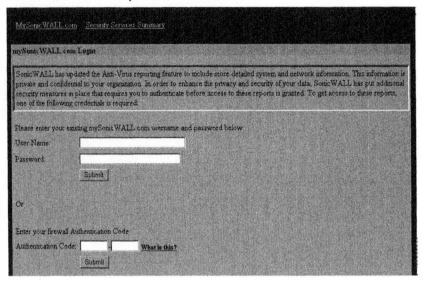

To obtain access to the reports, users must enter either the mySonicWALL user-name and password or the firewall's Authentication Code, which is displayed on the System | Status page. After successfully authenticating, the Managed VirusScan plus AntiSpyware window is displayed, as shown in Figure 9.41.

Figure 9.41 The Managed VirusScan plus AntiSpyware Window

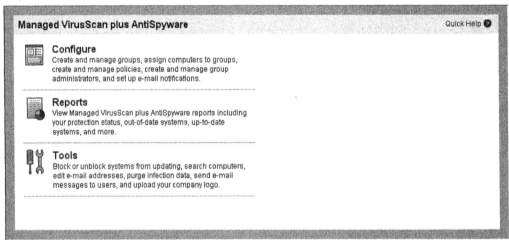

The Managed VirusScan plus AntiSpyware | Configure link shown in Figure 9.41 is used to create and manage groups, policies, administrators, and e-mail notifi-cations. You can also use it to assign computers to specific groups. Clicking this link

displays the page shown in Figure 9.42. The links on this page are used for most of your configuring, including managing groups of workstations, moving workstations between groups, and configuring the antivirus policies.

Figure 9.42 The Managed VirusScan plus AntiSpyware | Configure Link

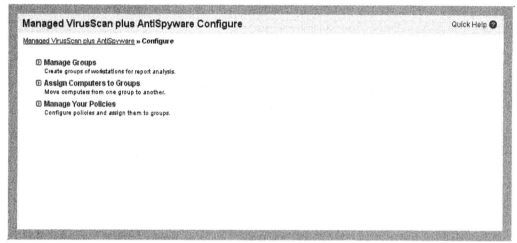

The Manage Licenses link displays information regarding the status of all licenses for the appliance (see Figure 9.43).

Figure 9.43 The Manage Licenses Page

Security Service	Status	Free Trial	Manage Service	Count	Expiration
Nodes/Users	Licensed		Upgrade	10	
Network Anti-Virus	Free Trial		Upgrade Renew Share	10	29 Mar 2006
Intrusion Prevention Service	Free Trial		Renew		29 Mar 2006
Gateway Anti-Virus	Free Trial		Upgrade Renew		29 Mar 2006
Server Anti-Virus	Not Licensed		Activate		
Gateway Anti-Spyware	Free Trial		Renew		29 Mar 2006
Content Filter	Not Licensed	Try	Activate		
Premium Content Filter	Free Trial		Renew		29 Mar 2006
E-Mail Filtering Service	Licensed				
VPN	Licensed				
Global VPN Client	Not Licensed		Activate		
Global VPN Client Enterprise	Not Licensed		Activate		
VPN SA	Licensed		Upgrade	2	
SonicOS Enhanced	Not Licensed		Activate		
Global Security Client	Not Licensed		Activate		
ViewPoint	Free Trial		Upgrade		29 Mar 2006
Comprehensive Gateway Security Suite Upgrade	Not Licensed		Activate		

You should now understand the basic configuration options for the Network Anti-Virus service, so let's look at how it actually works. Enforcing Network Anti-Virus on a particular zone ensures that all devices located on this zone have Anti-Virus protection. The first time users attempt to connect to the Internet, they will be automatically redirected to a Web page similar to the one shown in Figure 9.44.

Figure 9.44 Anti-Virus Client Installation Page

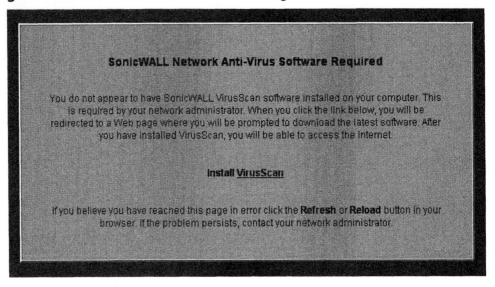

Users will click the **Install VirusScan** link to begin the installation of the client. They will not be allowed to proceed until the client is installed on their PCs. After clicking the Link, they will be presented with a window similar to the one shown in Figure 9.45.

Figure 9.45 Managed VirusScan Client Download Center

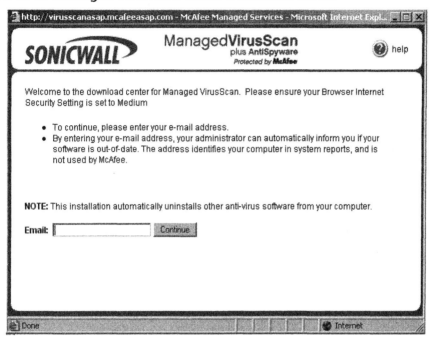

Users will be required to enter their e-mail addresses on this page. Depending on the clients' operating systems, the installation will either begin, as shown in Figure 9.46, or the users will be presented with an error message (see Figure 9.47).

Figure 9.46 Installing Managed Services Agent Status Window

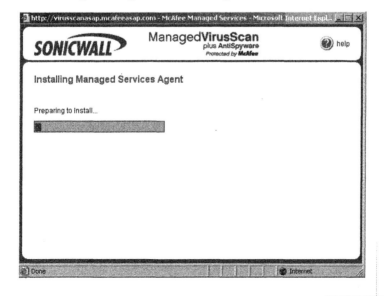

Windows XP Service Pack 2 will generate the error shown in Figure 9.47. The user must click the following message located on the top of the window: **This site might require the following ActiveX control: 'McAfee, Inc.' from 'McAfee, Inc.'. Click here to install...**

Figure 9.47 ActiveX Control Installation Warning

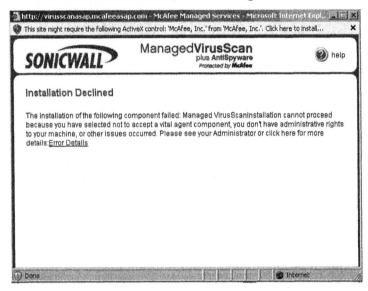

After the user clicks the link to install the ActiveX control, a confirmation dialog will be displayed, as shown in Figure 9.48.

Figure 9.48 Security Warning Dialog

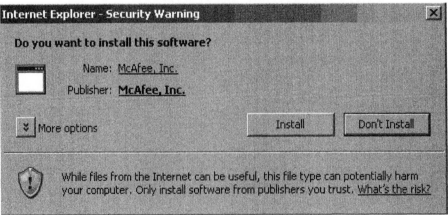

Clicking the **Install** button initiates the installation of the Anti-Virus client, and the Installing Managed Services Agent page will be displayed.

If users click **Don't Install**, the installation process is canceled, and the users will not be allowed access to Internet resources. The users will be required to repeat the installation process the next time they attempt to access the Internet.

Once the Anti-Virus software has been successfully installed, an Icon with a picture of a shield and a large V will be displayed in the System Tray (see Figure 9.49).

Figure 9.49 A System Tray Icon

SonicWALL Gateway Antivirus

The Gateway Antivirus Service (GAV) provides real-time clientless antivirus protection for devices protected by the firewall. GAV can be configured to provide protection against external and/or internal threats. HTTP, FTP, IMAP, SMTP, POP3, and TCP Stream protocols can be inspected on inbound traffic (traffic originating from outside the firewall). Only SMTP traffic is inspected on outbound traffic.

The SonicWALL GAV service provides protection against malicious software for branch/remote offices, internal network protection, file download protection, and desktop and server protection. This multitier approach provides a comprehensive and flexible framework for enforcing the corporate antivirus policy at a gateway level.

Figure 9.50 shows the main Gateway Anti-Virus window.

Figure 9.50 The Main Gateway Anti-Virus Window

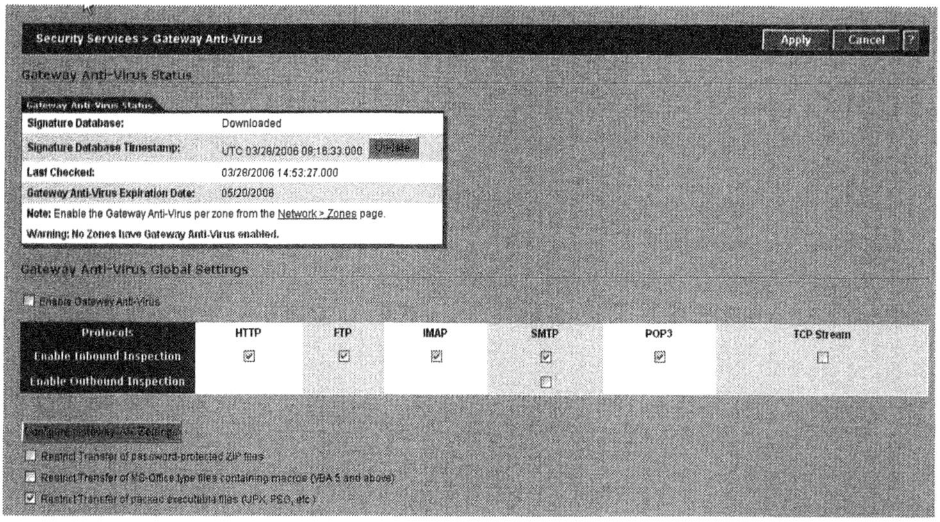

After you click the **Configure Gateway AV Settings** button, the Anti-Virus Policies window will be displayed (see Figure 9.51).

Figure 9.51 The Gateway Anti-Virus Policies Window

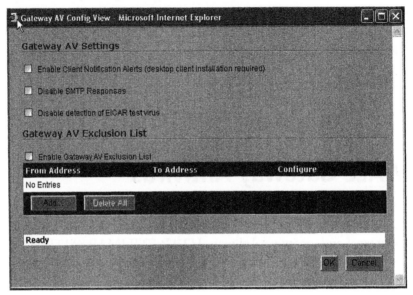

SonicWALL Anti-Spyware

A new menace threatens the security of our users. This menace is used to record Internet browsing habits, information entered into online forms, and keystrokes. It can be used to gain access to your Internet connection without your knowledge or consent and can result in degraded computer performance, invasion of privacy, loss of proprietary information, and even identify theft. The name given to this threat is spyware. Computers are often infected with spyware without users even knowing it. The most common method of infection is via downloaded programs, such as P2P applications, download managers, utilities, freeware, screensavers, and games from untrusted sources.

SonicWALL provides spyware protection at the gateway level. It not only protects devices against infection but also prevents currently infected devices from sending gathered information outbound.

Tips and Tricks...

Host-Based Anti-Spyware

From a Defense-in-Depth approach to anti-spyware protection, host-based anti-spyware software should be deployed on each end user's device; in addition, the SonicWALL AntiSpyware gateway protection should be used. If spyware somehow slips past the SonicWALL, the host-based software provides a safety net.

Enabling anti-spyware is a three-step process. First, browse to Security Services → Anti-Spyware. Enable anti-spyware by clicking the **check box** next to **Enable Anti-Spyware.** A checkmark indicates that anti-spyware is enforced. To disable anti-spyware, simply click the **check box** to clear it. The second step involved with enabling anti-spyware is to configure the appropriate settings that you would like to apply to your network. The third step is to enable anti-spyware on each zone that it will be enforced on.

Configuring Anti-Spyware

The Anti-Spyware main page has three sections. The first section, Anti-Spyware Settings, displays important information related to the status of the Anti-Spyware service. This information includes the Signature Database status, the date and time of the last update to the Signature Database, the last date and time that the SonicWALL checked for new updates, and the expiration date of the Anti-Spyware service (see Figure 9.52).

Figure 9.52 Anti-Spyware Status

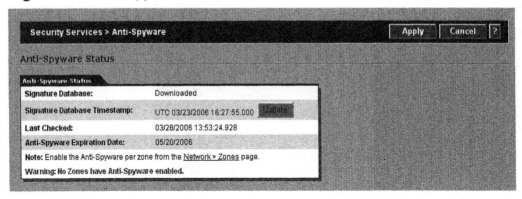

The second section of the page, Anti-Spyware Global Settings, is used to configure important settings that define how the Anti-Spyware service will function on your network. The Global Settings section is shown in Figure 9.53.

Figure 9.53 Global Settings

Anti-Spyware Global Settings			
☐ Enable Anti-Spyware			
Signature Groups	**Prevent All**	**Detect All**	**Log Redundancy Filter (seconds)**
High Danger Level Spyware	☑	☑	0
Medium Danger Level Spyware	☐	☐	0
Low Danger Level Spyware	☑	☑	0
Configure Anti-Spyware Settings Reset Anti-Spyware Settings & Policies			

Before addressing the Prevent and Detect all options, we will discuss the following individual Danger Levels assigned to spyware signatures and groups:

- **High Danger Level Spyware** Spyware with this classification is the most dangerous. Examples include keyloggers and porn dialers. Removing this spyware is extremely difficult and in some cases impossible.

- **Medium Danger Level Spyware** Spyware with this classification causes significant network and PC performance issues. Removing this spyware is extremely difficult.

- **Low Danger Level Spyware** Spyware with this classification is easily removed and poses no immediate risk to the PC and/or network.

Now we need to determine what action will be taken against each of these danger levels. The options are Prevent All and Detect All. When you enable the Prevent All action, all spyware will be blocked. Detect All, on the other hand, will detect and log all Spyware; however, no action is taken to prevent it. Because of the amount of spyware in cyberspace, using Detect All may produce significant entries in the event log. To reduce the number of identical entries, the Log Redundancy Filter can be used to specify how often identical events are logged. The value of this field is in seconds. In other words, if this value is set to five and the SonicWALL receives 10 identical entries in the five-second period, only one entry is created in the log file.

Prevent All and Detect All actions can be set at the Global, Group, or individual signature levels. To specify the actions at the Global Level, enable or disable the Prevent All and Detect All actions for the three danger levels: High, Medium, and Low.

The last section of the Anti-Spyware page, Anti-Spyware Policies, is used to view and configure the actions taken against individual Spyware groups and/or signatures. The Policies page is shown in Figure 9.54.

Figure 9.54 Anti-Spyware Policies

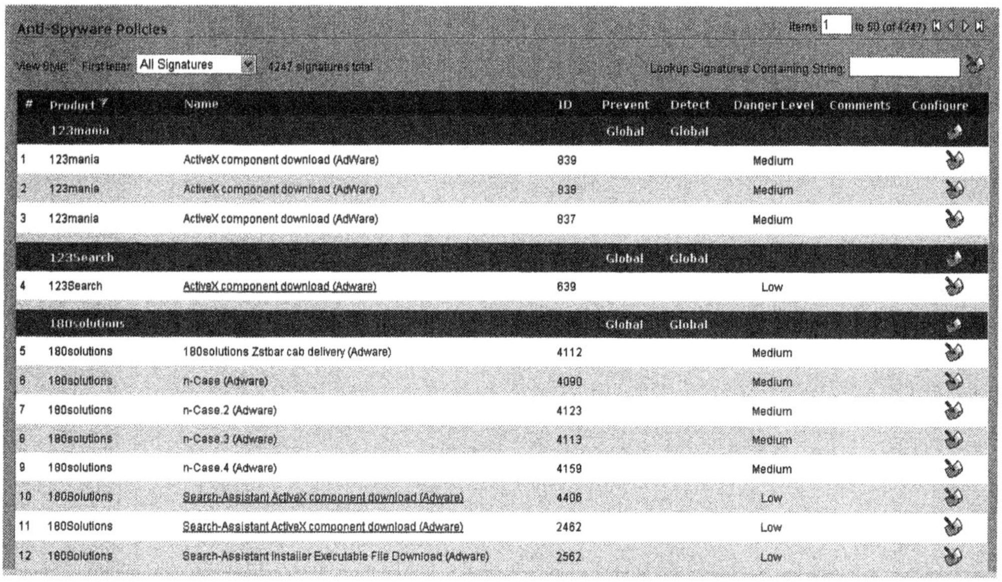

The Highlighted portion of the window is the Group, and the entries beneath the highlight are the individual signatures. To modify the action taken for either a group or signature, click the **Configure** icon to the right of it. This will display the configuration options and allow you to override the Global settings for prevention and detection. Figure 9.55 shows the available options for each group and signature.

Figure 9.55 Anti-Spyware Group/Signature Configuration Options

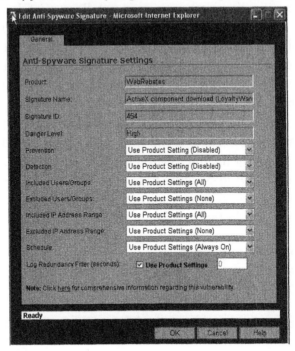

To obtain information regarding the vulnerability and, if applicable, removal instructions, click the **Click here for comprehensive information regarding this vulnerability** link, located on the bottom of the page (see Figure 9.55). This will display a page similar to the one shown in Figure 9.56.

Figure 9.56 Vulnerability Information and Removal Instructions

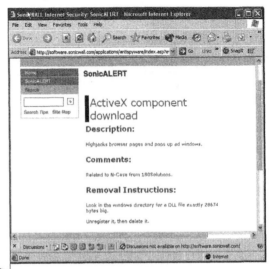

To refer back to the main Anti-Spyware page (Security Services → Anti-Spyware), click the **Configure Anti-Spyware Settings** button. The Anti-Spyware Settings dialog box will open, as shown in Figure 9.57.

Figure 9.57 The Anti-Spyware Settings Dialog Box

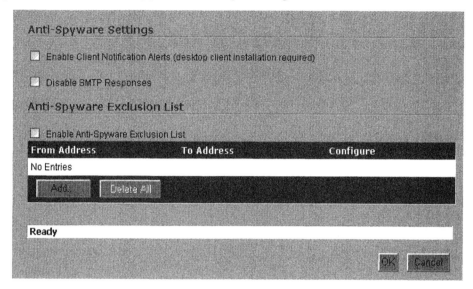

The screen is divided into two sections. The first section, Anti-Spyware Settings, is used to enable Client Notification Alerts and Disable SMTP Responses. Client Notification Alerts require client software to be installed (this software was not yet available at the time of this writing). This software will display alert notifications on client devices when the SonicWALL blocks spyware content. The Disable SMTP Responses option is used to suppress e-mail messages sent from the SonicWALL when the appliance blocks Spyware. To enable this option, select the box next to it.

The second section, Anti-Spyware Exclusion List, is used to add specific address ranges to be excluded from Anti-Spyware protection. To add a range, click the **Add** button. The Add Anti-Spyware Range Entry dialog box is displayed, as shown in Figure 9.58.

Figure 9.58 Add Anti-Spyware Range Entry

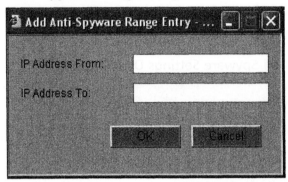

Enter the IP address of the first device in the range in the **IP Address From** field and the last device in the range in the **IP Address To** field. Click the OK button to add the range. Once you have all the ranges defined that will be excluded from Anti-Spyware protection, be sure to click the **Enable Anti-Spyware Exclusion List** option.

Finally, to enforce Anti-Spyware protection, browse to Network → Zones. Click the **Configure** icon to the right of each Zone that will have Anti-Spyware protection. In the Configure Zone dialog, click the check box under **Anti-Spyware**. A checkmark indicates that the service is enabled. To disable Anti-Spyware protection, clear the check box by clicking it.

E-Mail Filter

The E-Mail Filter, Security Services → Email Filter, enables you to selectively block or disable inbound e-mail attachments as they pass through the SonicWALL. Executables, scripts, and applications can be controlled at the gateway level.

To configure the E-Mail Filter features, browse to the Security Services → E-Mail Filter page. The page is divided into four sections: E-Mail Attachment Filtering, E-Mail Attachment Filtering Options, Warning Message, and E-Mail Blocking.

The E-Mail Attachment Filtering settings are used to either enable or disable Rapid E-Mail Attachment Filtering and/or E-Mail Attachment Filtering of Forbidden File Extensions, as well as the individual File Extensions that will be forbidden from passing through the SonicWALL appliance. Figure 9.59 shows an example of these settings.

Figure 9.59 E-Mail Filter—E-Mail Attachment Filtering

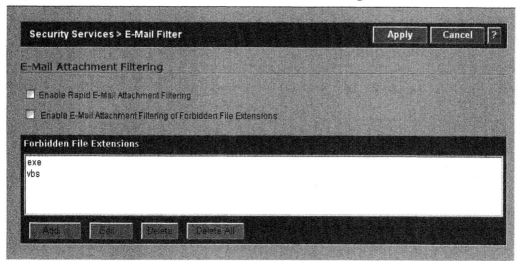

To add a new file extension to the Forbidden File Extensions list, click the **Add** button. The Add File Extension dialog box will prompt you for the extension to be added to the list (see Figure 9.60). The format is simply the extension without the leading period. For example, COM, CMD, ZIP, and so on.

Figure 9.60 Add Forbidden File Extension Dialog

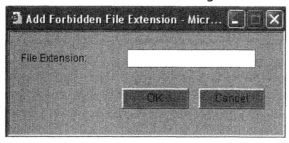

The second section of the E-Mail Filter page is E-Mail Attachment Filtering Options (see Figure 9.61). There are two options in this section:

- **Disable Forbidden File by altering the file extension and attach warning text** Selecting this option will instruct the SonicWALL to modify the extension of any attached files that contain a Forbidden File Extension and attach a Warning Message to inform the recipient that a dangerous file type has been attached to the e-mail.

- **Delete Forbidden File and attach warning text** In some cases, modifying the file extension is not acceptable. All attachments that include a Forbidden File Extension should be deleted. To delete these attachments, enable this option. The SonicWALL will inform the user by attaching the Warning Message defined in the next section.

Figure 9.61 E-Mail Attachment Filtering Options

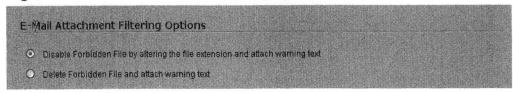

The third section of the E-Mail Filter page is the **Warning Message Text**. The text entered in this field will be attached to any e-mail that has an attachment with a Forbidden File Extension. To modify the default text, simply highlight it and begin typing the new message to be displayed. Figure 9.62 shows the default Warning Message Text.

Figure 9.62 Default Warning Message Text

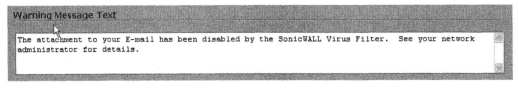

The fourth section of the E-Mail Filter page is E-Mail Blocking. There is a single option in this section, Block SMTP E-Mail fragments (Content-Type: message\partial). Enabling this option instructs the SonicWALL to block all fragmented E-Mail with a Content-Type of message\partial. Malicious users and/or malware often use this type of traffic to infect systems by dividing the message into numerous pieces in an attempt to bypass security protection controls. The pieces, which will be reassembled by the receiving client, could then be used to perform some malicious action. Figure 9.63 shows the E-Mail Blocking section of the E-Mail Filter page.

Figure 9.63 E-Mail Blocking Section

RBL Filter

Spam is a major headache. The question of how to protect your users from the inappropriate, undesired, irrelevant, and annoying messages has been in the news for some time now. Spam continues to make security headlines. Another question that is commonly asked is, What can SonicWALL do to help reduce Spam?

The answer to this question is the Real-Time Blacklist Filter Service. This service, although not as comprehensive or flexible as dedicated solutions, is a good starting place in your quest to squash Spam before it reaches your users' mailboxes. The RBL Filter uses well-known Spam databases to determine if a message is being sent from a known Spammer.

To configure the RBL Filter, browse to Security Services → RBL Filter. The page is divided into three sections: Real-Time Black List Settings, Real-Time Black List Services, and User-Defined SMTP Server Lists.

The first two sections are shown in Figure 9.64. The Real-Time Black List Settings section is used to enable or disable the RBL Filter and set the appropriate DNS servers that the SonicWALL should use. The second section, Real-Time Black List Services, is used to configure what Spam databases will be queried to determine if incoming e-mail is from a known spammer. In Figure 9.64, there are two databases configured: SPAMHaus and Sorbs.

Figure 9.64 RBL Filter

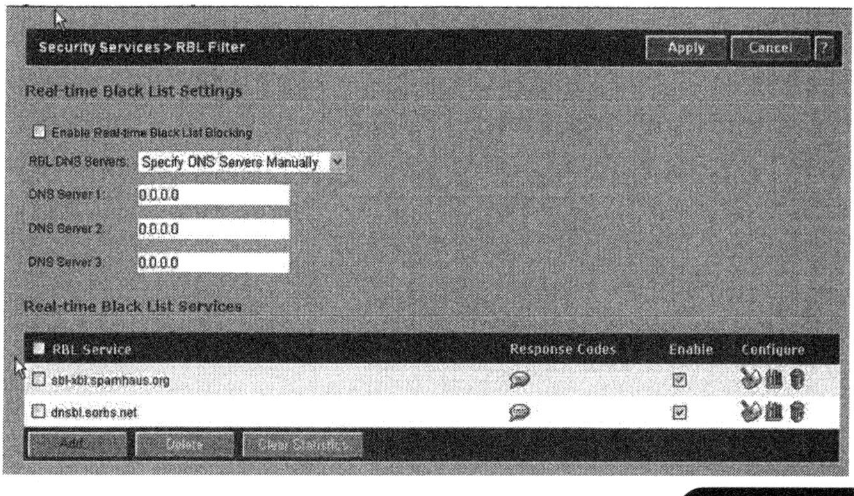

To add another Spam database, click the **Add** button. This will display the RBL Add Domain dialog box shown in Figure 9.65.

Figure 9.65 Add RBL Domain

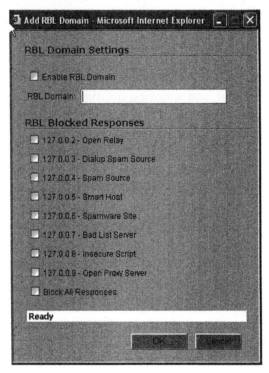

Enter the name of the RBL Domain, such as sbl-xbl.spamhaus.org, select the individual Response codes that will be used to determine what classifies messages to be Spam, and then click **OK.**

The third section of the RBL Filter page is User-Defined SMTP Server Lists, shown in Figure 9.66. This section allows administrators to define custom lists for either trusted (White List) or blocked (Black List) SMTP servers. In other words, if users are complaining about mail from a specific domain (e.g., pornadds.com), an entry can be added to the Black List to block all e-mail originating from that domain. In contrast, if a trusted domain has been listed on one of the Spam databases, and users are complaining about not receiving business-related e-mail from that domain, an entry can be added to the White List to override the result from the Spam Database query.

Figure 9.66 User-Defined SMTP Server Lists

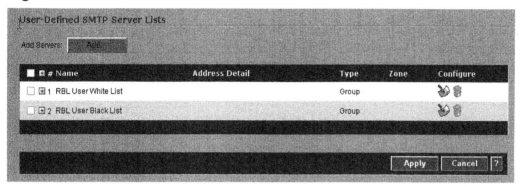

To add individual SMTP Servers to either the Black List or White List, click the **Add** button. If no Address Object has been already defined for the SMTP Server, you must create the object now. After the SMTP Server address object has been created, it must be added to either the RBL User White List or the RBL User Black List group.

To view the group members for either of the lists, click the **(+)** icon to expand the list. To delete an entry, click the **Trashcan** icon to the right of the entry. Finally, to modify an entry in the lists, click the **Configure** icon, make your changes, and then click **OK**.

Summary

Complete books are available just on the subjects covered in this chapter. However, we've managed to cover all SonicOS Security features, including Intrusion Prevention, Gateway and Network Antivirus Services, Content Filtering Services, Anti-Spyware service, Email Filter, and Real Time Blacklist features.

Solutions Fast Track

Understanding the Anatomy of an Attack

☑ Most attacks follow a series of phases: network reconnaissance, exploit, and consolidation.

☑ For manual attacks, the majority of events are generated by inexperienced malicious hackers, known both in the industry and the hacking underground as "script kiddies."

☑ A Black Hat's motivation is usually a strong desire to access your data—credit cards, bank accounts, social security numbers, usernames, and passwords. Other times it may be for petty revenge for perceived wrongs. Alternatively, they may want to figure out a way to divert your traffic to Web sites they control, so they can dupe users into providing these critical pieces of information—a technique known as *phishing*

SonicWALL IPS

☑ SonicWALL IPS uses SonicWALL's Deep Packet Inspection Technology (DPIT). DPIT allows the SonicWALL to look at the actual data contained in a packet, to determine if it is malicious.

☑ DPIT enables the SonicWALL to inspect packets all the way up to the application layer. DPIT 2.0 enables dynamic signature updates, which are pushed from the SonicWALL Distributed Enforcement Architecture.

☑ SonicWALL Intrusion Prevention Service may be applied to both inbound and outbound traffic. The signatures written for the SonicWALL are direction oriented, meaning the direction of the attack is considered when applying IPS.

SonicWALL Content Filtering

☑ SonicWALL Content Filtering Services (CFS) provides protection against violations of your company's Acceptable Use Policy. Administrators can enforce content filtering based on keywords, time of day, trusted and forbidden domains, and file types such as cookies, Java, and ActiveX. SonicWALL CFS is available in two versions, Standard and Premium.

☑ The Restrict Web Features options allow administrators to block specific Web features that are known to have security vulnerabilities or may provide attack vectors for malicious code or users.

☑ SonicWALL CFS allows administrators to use either a default or custom message that will be displayed to users when they attempt to open a Web site that is blocked by the SonicWALL CFS Policy.

Antivirus Services

☑ Two antivirus solutions are available on SonicWALL appliances, Network Antivirus and Gateway Antivirus.

☑ The Network Antivirus service provides a means of enforcing the company antivirus policy network wide. Clients that do not have the antivirus software installed are denied access to Internet resources.

☑ The Gateway Antivirus Service (GAV) provides real-time clientless antivirus protection for devices protected by the firewall. GAV can be configured to provide protection against external and/or internal threats.

Frequently Asked Questions

The following Frequently Asked Questions, answered by the authors of this book, are designed to both measure your understanding of the concepts presented in this chapter and to assist you with real-life implementation of these concepts. To have your questions about this chapter answered by the author, browse to **www.syngress.com/solutions** and click on the **"Ask the Author"** form.

Q: I am not using IPS or Gateway Anti-Virus, how can I completely disable it?

A: Browse to **Firewall | Advanced** and check the box next to **Disable Anti-Spyware, Gateway AV, and IPS Engine**.

Q: Can I enforce IPS and Anti-Spyware services for only certain PCs?

A: Yes, first enable IPS and Anti-Spyware for the Zone that contains the PCs. This enables the service for the entire Zone. To exclude certain devices from protection, enter their IP addresses in the exclusion list.

Q: What are the recommended settings for the Prevent All and Detect All options under IPS?

A: Prevent All and Detect All should be selected for both High and Medium Priority Attacks. Detect All should be selected for the Low Priority Attacks.

Q: What are the recommended settings for the Prevent All and Detect All options under Anti-Spyware?

A: Prevent All and Detect All should be selected for both the High Danger and Medium Danger levels and Detect All should be selected for the Low Danger level.

Q: I have dedicated Anti-Virus on my network. Can I also use the SonicWALL's Network Anti-Virus software?

A: Yes and No. You should never load more than one Anti-Virus application on a single device. Doing so may result in failure of both applications. While technically, you can use the existing Anti-Virus for certain PCs and the SonicWALL Network Anti-Virus for others, it is recommended to use only a single solution to simplify management.

Q: Can I load the Network Anti-Virus client on Servers?

A: No, The Network Anti-Virus client should not be loaded on Servers.

Chapter 10

Creating VPNs with SonicWALL

Solutions in this chapter:

- **Understanding IPSec**
- **IPSec Tunnel Negotiations**
- **Public Key Cryptography**
- **VPNs in SonicWALL Appliances**

☑ Summary

☑ Solutions Fast Track

☑ Frequently Asked Questions

Introduction

As you read this chapter, you will understand the concepts of virtual private networks (VPNs), how VPNs operate, and how to implement VPN tunnels using IPSec (Internet Protocol security) on SonicWALL appliances. At this time you may be thinking, "What is a VPN, and why would I need to use one?" There are several good reasons to implement VPN technology in your infrastructure, starting with security. A VPN is a means of creating secure communications over a public network infrastructure. VPNs use encryption and authentication to ensure that information is kept private and confidential. This means that you can share data and resources among several locations without the worry of data integrity being compromised.

Alone, the ability to make use of a public network to transmit data is also an advantage of VPN technology. Without using the Internet as a transport mechanism, you would have to purchase point-to-point T1s or some other form of leased line to connect multiple locations. Leased lines are traditionally expensive to operate, especially if the two points being connected are across a large geographic region. Using VPNs instead of leased lines reduces the operating cost for your company.

VPNs are also cost-effective for traveling users. Without VPNs, a traveling salesperson working outside the office might have to dial in to a modem bank at the office and incur long-distance charges for the call. A dial-up VPN is much more cost-effective, allowing the salesperson to connect to a local ISP (Internet service provider) and then access the corporate network via a VPN.

Suppose your company's corporate office has a database-driven intranet site that it wants your branch offices to be able to access, but your company does not want the rest of the world to have access to this site. Sure, you could just stick the application on an Internet-facing server and give each user a password-protected account, but the information would still be transmitted unencrypted to the user. Let's say you decide to encrypt the sessions using SSL (Secure Sockets Layer). Although this encrypts the communications, you could still face the risk of a user's login information being compromised or a possible SQL injection attack against the application itself. Wouldn't it make more sense to protect the application by not having it publicly available at all? By creating a VPN between the two sites, the branch office can access the intranet site and share resources with the corporate office, increasing productivity and maintaining a higher level of security all at the same time.

Understanding IPSec

IP security is a collection of protocols for securing communications at the IP (Internet Protocol) layer. IPSec was engineered to provide several services: privacy and confidentiality of data, origin authentication, data integrity, access control, and protection against replay attacks. IPSec is widely used for VPNs. IPSec consists of two modes, transport and tunnel. IPSec also consists of two protocols, Encapsulating Security Payload (ESP) and Authentication Header (AH). IPSec allows for manual or automatic negotiation of security associations (SAs). All this information makes up the domain of interpretation, which is used to establish security associations and Internet key exchange.

IPSec Modes

As mentioned earlier, IPSec provides us with two modes of operation: *transport mode* and *tunnel mode*. Each of these modes provides us with similar end results, but works differently to get us there. For starters, transport mode requires that both endpoints of the VPN tunnel be hosts. Tunnel mode must always be used when one endpoint is a security gateway, such as a SonicWALL appliance or router. SonicWALL appliances always provide IPSec tunnels in tunnel mode.

Transport mode encrypts only the *payload*, or data portion, of the IP packet. The header of the packet is not encrypted or altered. Think of it as a sealed envelope. You are able to see the address of whom the letter is to, but you cannot view the message delivered within. Transport and tunnel mode packets are illustrated in Figures 10.1 and 10.2.

In tunnel mode the original packet, both header and payload, is encapsulated entirely into another IP packet. This new packet has its own header, containing source and destination address information. These addresses are the actual endpoints of the tunnel. Although both modes encrypt the actual payload, tunnel mode is generally thought of to be more secure than transport mode.

Figure 10.1 Transport Mode Packet Diagram

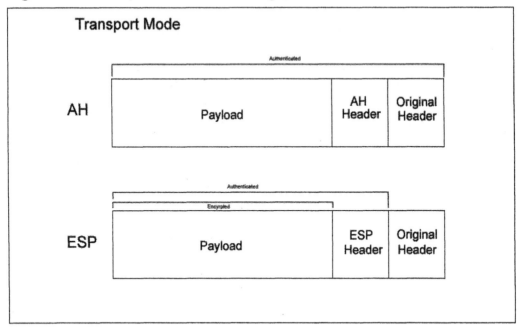

Figure 10.2 Tunnel Mode Packet Diagram

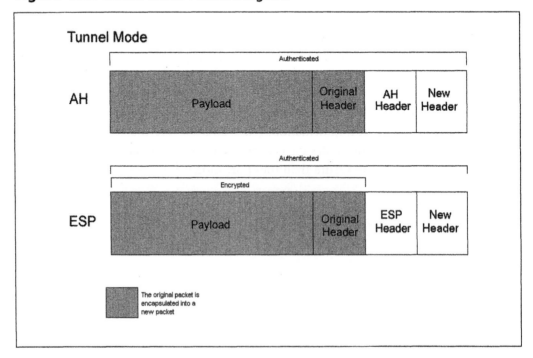

Protocols

As previously mentioned, IPSec has two methods for verifying the source of an IP packet as well as verifying the integrity of the payload contained within—Authentication Header and Encapsulating Security Payload.

Authentication header, or AH for short, provides a means to verify the source of an IP packet. It is also used to verify data integrity of the payload the packet contains. When used in transport mode, AH authenticates the IP packet's payload and portions of the IP header. When AH is used in tunnel mode, the entire internal IP header is authenticated as well as selected portions of the external IP header. AH can also protect against replay attempts. AH can be used by itself, or it can be used in conjunction with Encapsulating Security Payload.

Encapsulating Security Payload, or ESP, provides methods to ensure data privacy, source authentication, and payload integrity. ESP may also protect against replay attacks. ESP, when used in tunnel mode, encrypts the entire IP packet and attaches a new IP header to the packet. The new IP header contains all the information necessary to route your packet to its destination. ESP also allows you to choose what to do with the packet: encrypt the packet, authenticate the packet, or both. ESP, with transport mode, encrypts the IP payload, but not the IP header. Optionally, with transport mode, ESP can also authenticate the IP payload. When you are using ESP with tunnel mode, both the IP header and payload are encrypted. Like transport mode, ESP also optionally allows for authentication of the IP packet.

Key Management

Probably the most critical part of a VPN is key management and distribution. IPSec supports the use of both manual and automatic key distribution.

In manual key configurations, all security parameters are configured at both ends of the tunnel manually. Although this method works well in smaller networks, there are some issues with using manual keys. This can be especially troublesome when the key is initially distributed, since there may be no way to verify the key was not compromised before reaching its final destination. This also becomes cumbersome when you choose to change the key, which results in a need for redistribution. When using manual key VPN, the key is never changed unless the administrator chooses to change it.

To help lessen the burden on administrators, IPSec supports *Internet Key Exchange*, or IKE for short. IKE generates and negotiates keys and security associations automatically based on pre-shared secrets or digital certificates. A pre-shared secret is nothing more than a key both parties have prior to initiating the negotiations. Like manual key VPN, the pre-shared secret must be exchanged securely before use. However, unlike manual key VPNs, IKE can change the key automatically at a specified interval. This is seen as a significant security enhancement over that of manual key VPNs. We will discuss the use of pre-shared secrets later in this chapter.

IKE can also use digital certificates. During IKE negotiation, both sides generate public and private key pairs, and acquire a digital certificate. If the issuing certificate authority is trusted by both parties, the participants can verify their peer's signature by retrieving the peer's public key.

There are also several other benefits of using IKE over the use of a manual key VPN. IKE eliminates the need to manually specify the IPSec security parameters at both peers, reducing the management load on the administrator. IKE also allows for the use of anti-replay services, certification authorities, and dynamic peer authentication in IPSec VPNs, which are discussed in more detail later in this chapter.

Security Associations

Security associations (SA) is the concept used by IPSec to manage all of the parameters required to establish a VPN tunnel. In simple terms, SA is a set of parameters describing how communications are to be secured. SAs contain the following components: security keys and algorithms, mode of operation (transport or tunnel), key management method (IKE or manual key), and lifetime of the SA. IPSec stores all active security associations in a database called the *security association database* (SAD). The SAD contains all parameters needed for IPSec operation, including the keys currently in use. In order to have bidirectional communication, you must have at least two SAs, one for each direction of traffic flow.

IPSec Tunnel Negotiations

When you are using a manual key VPN for communications, negotiations are not required between the two endpoints of the VPN tunnel because all the necessary security association parameters were defined during the creation of the tunnel. When traffic matches a policy using a manual key VPN, traffic is encrypted, authenticated, and then routed to the destination gateway.

An IPSec tunnel using IKE requires two phases to complete negotiation. Phase 1 of IKE negotiation establishes a secure tunnel for negotiation of security associations. Then, during phase 2, IPSec SAs are negotiated defining the method for encrypting and authenticating user data exchange. The next section explains what happens in each phase of negotiation in detail.

Phase 1

From our previous discussion you already know that phase 1 negotiations consist of exchanging proposals on how to authenticate and secure the communications channel. Phase 1 exchanges can be done in two modes: *main mode* or *aggressive mode*.

In main mode, three two-way exchanges, or six total messages, are exchanged. During a main mode conversation, the following is accomplished:

- **First exchange** Encryption and authentication algorithms for communications are proposed and accepted.

- **Second exchange** A Diffie-Hellman exchange is done. Each party exchanges a randomly generated number, or *nonce*.

- **Third exchange** Identities of each party are exchanged and verified.

NOTE

In the third exchange, identities are not passed in the clear. The identities are protected by the encryption algorithm agreed upon in the exchange of the first two sets of messages.

In aggressive mode, the same principal objectives are completed, but are done so in a much shorter conversation. Phase 1 negotiations in aggressive mode only require that two exchanges be made, and that a total of three messages are exchanged. An aggressive mode conversation follows the following pattern:

- **First message** The initiating party proposes the security association, starts a Diffie-Hellman exchange, and sends its nonce and IKE identity to the intended recipient.

- **Second message** During the second message, the recipient accepts the proposed security association, authenticates the initiating party, sends its generated nonce, IKE identity, and its certificate if certificates are being used.

- **Third message** During the third message, the initiator authenticates the recipient, confirms the exchange, and if using certificates, sends its certificate.

In an aggressive mode exchange, the identities of communicating parties are not protected because the identities are sent during the first two messages exchanged prior to the tunnel being secured. It is also important to note that a dialup VPN user must use aggressive mode to establish an IKE tunnel.

Notes from the Underground...

What Is Diffie-Hellman?

The Diffie-Hellman (DH) key exchange protocol, invented in 1976 by Whitfield Diffie and Martin Hellman, is a protocol allowing two parties to generate shared secrets and exchange communications over an insecure medium without having any prior shared secrets. The Diffie-Hellman protocol consists of five groups of varying strength modulus. Most VPN gateways support DH Groups 1 and 2. SonicWALL appliances, however, support groups 1, 2, and 5. The Diffie-Hellman protocol alone is susceptible to man-in-the-middle attacks, however. Although the risk of an attack is low, it is recommended that you enable *Perfect Forward Secrecy* (PFS) as added security when defining VPN tunnels on your SonicWALL appliance. For more information on the Diffie-Hellman protocol, see www.rsasecurity.com/rsalabs/node.asp?id=2248 and RFC 2631 at ftp://ftp.rfc-editor.org/in-notes/rfc2631.txt.

Phase 2

Once phase 1 negotiations have been completed and a secure tunnel has been established, phase 2 negotiations begin. During phase 2, negotiation of security associations of how to secure the data being transmitted across the tunnel is completed. Phase 2 negotiations always involve the exchange of three messages. Phase 2 proposals include encryption and authentication algorithms, as well as a security protocol. The security protocol can either be ESP or AH. Phase 2 proposals can also specify whether or not to use PFS and a Diffie-Hellman group to employ. PFS is a method used to derive keys that have no relation to any previous keys. Without PFS, phase 2 keys are generally derived from the phase 1 SKEYID_d key. If an attacker was to acquire the SKEYID_d key, all keys derived from this key could be compromised. During phase 2 each side also offers its proxy ID. Proxy IDs are simply the local IP, the remote IP, and the service. Both proxy IDs must match. For example, if 1.1.1.1 and 2.2.2.2 are using the SMTP (Simple Mail Transfer Protocol) service, then the proxy ID for 1.1.1.1 would be 1.1.1.1-2.2.2.2-25 and for 2.2.2.2 it would be 2.2.2.2-1.1.1.1-25.

Damage & Defense…

Key Lifetime—Short versus Long and PFS

When planning your VPN deployment, consideration should be given to the key lifetime and perfect forward secrecy in relation to security. Since enabling PFS requires additional processing time and resources some administrators choose not to use it, instead opting for a shorter key lifetime. This, however, can be a bad practice. If a successful man-in-the-middle attack was able to discover the SKEYID_d key, all keys derived from this key could be compromised. Enabling PFS, even with a longer key life, is actually a more secure practice than having a short key life with no PFS.

Public Key Cryptography

Public key cryptography, first born in the 1970s, is the modern cryptographic method of communicating securely without having a previously agreed upon secret key. Public key cryptography typically uses a pair of keys to secure communications—a private key that is kept secret, and a public key that can be widely distributed. You should not be able to find one key of a pair simply by having the other. Public key cryptography is a form of asymmetric-key cryptography, since not all parties hold the same key. Some examples of public key cryptography algorithms include RSA, Diffie-Hellman, and ElGamal.

So how does public key encryption work? Suppose John would like to exchange a message securely with Chris. Prior to doing so, Chris would provide John with his public key. John would then take the message he wishes to share with Chris and encrypt the message using Chris's public key. When Chris receives the message, he takes his private key and decrypts the message. Chris is then able to read the message John had intended to share with him. But what if someone intercepts the message and has possession of Chris's public key? Absolutely nothing happens. When messages are encrypted using Chris's public key, they can only be decrypted using the private key associated with that public key.

PKI

PKI is the meshing of encryption technologies, services, and software together to form a solution that enables businesses to secure their communications over the Internet. PKI involves the integration of digital certificates, certificate authorities (CAs), and public key cryptography. PKI offers several enhancements to the security of your enterprise.

PKI enables you to easily verify and authenticate the identity of a person or organization. By using digital certificates, it is easy to verify the identity of parties involved in a transaction. The ease of verification of identity is also beneficial to access control. Digital certificates can replace passwords for access control, which are sometimes lost or easily cracked by experienced crackers.

Certificates

Digital certificates are nothing more than a way to verify your identity through a certificate authority using public key cryptography. SonicWALL appliances support the use of digital certificates from a wide range of vendors as a method of validating your identity during VPN negotiations with other SonicWALL appliances. There are certain steps you must take before you can use a certificate to validate your identity. First, you must generate a certificate request from within the SonicWALL appliance. When this is done, the SonicWALL appliance generates a public/private key pair. You then send a request with the public key to your certificate authority. A response, which incorporates the public key, will be forwarded to you that will have to be loaded into the SonicWALL appliance. This response generally includes three parts:

- The CA's certificate, which contains the CA's public key.
- The local certificate identifying your SonicWALL device.
- In some cases a certificate revocation list (CRL). This lists any certificates revoked by the CA.

You can load the reply into the SonicWALL device through the WebUI. Loading the certificate information into the SonicWALL gives us the following:

- Your identity can be verified using the local certificate.
- The CA's certificate can be used to verify the identity of other users.
- The CRL list can be used to identify invalid certificates.

Be sure to remember that SonicWALL appliances only support using certificates for configuring VPN tunnels from SonicWALL to SonicWALL. They are not supported for establishing VPN tunnels with the SafeNet VPN client or other software VPN clients, or with third-party VPN and firewall appliances such as NetScreen, Checkpoint, CyberGuard, or Cisco.

OCSP (CRLs)

A *certificate revocation list*, or CRL, is used to ensure that a digital certificate has not become invalid. SonicWALL appliances support the use of Online Certificate Status Protocol, or OCSP, to check for invalid certificates before connecting VPN tunnels. The OpenCA OCSP Responder is the only OCSP responder supported by SonicWALL. OCSP is a real-time method for validating digital certificates. When speaking in regards to the use of digital certificates with VPNs, the certificate is validated during phase 1 negotiations. If enabled, the SonicWALL contacts the configured remote entity to validate the certificate before negotiating the VPN tunnel. SonicWALL appliances also allow you to specify an address to refer to for OCSP.

To enable OCSP on a VPN tunnel using certificates:

1. Select **VPN | Settings**. Select the policy you wish to modify, or if creating a new policy, click **Add...** The VPN policy window will open.

2. Click the **Advanced** tab. Enable the **Enable OCSP Checking** option, and enter the URL for the SonicWALL to use to validate certificates in the **OCSP Responder URL:** box.

3. Click **OK** to save your changes.

Figure 10.3 shows the advanced settings configuration screen for a site-to-site VPN tunnel using certificates.

Figure 10.3 Advanced Settings Site-to-Site with Certificates

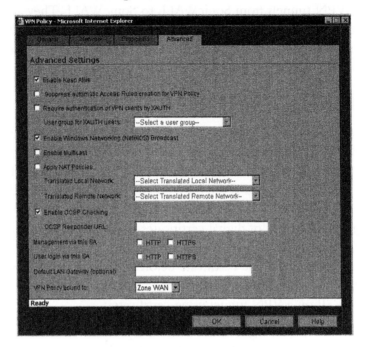

VPNs in SonicWALL Appliances

SonicWALL provides administrators with an easy-to-configure industry-standard implementation of IPSec VPN. Creating site-to-site VPN tunnels is an easy task. SonicWALL also makes it easy to deploy VPNs to your remote users and telecommuters using the SonicWALL Global VPN Client or SonicWALL Global Security Client. Every SonicWALL comes with a predefined GroupVPN policy that is designed to work seamlessly with the Global VPN client. SonicWALL makes this deployment even easier with Simple Client Provisioning, which allows the end user to connect to the SonicWALL and have the policy automatically downloaded to the client. As we go through configuration examples, you'll be able to grasp the concept of VPNs with SonicWALL appliances and see just how easy they've made VPN administration.

Site-to-Site VPNs

With SonicWALL, there are three ways to configure site-to-site VPNs when both endpoints have static IP addresses. You can use any of the following methods:

- Site-to-site VPN using a manual key.

- Site-to-site VPN using IKE with a pre-shared key (PSK).

- Site-to-Site VPN using third-party certificates.

Remember that SonicWALL appliances only support using certificates for VPN tunnels when both ends of the tunnel will be SonicWALL appliances. Either of the other two methods may be used when interoperability with other vendors is desired. Hosts behind either gateway can initiate the negotiations between the two gateways.

Site-to-site VPN tunnels require configuration on both endpoint appliances. This means that in order to complete configuration of a VPN tunnel you either need administrative access to both the local and remote VPN gateways, or you need an administrator to configure the remote end of the tunnel for you. Configuration at each endpoint is usually almost identical, except the remote and local subnets and endpoints are in reverse order.

SonicWALL uses an "almost industry-standard" default proposal configuration. The reason I say *almost* is because there is no default standard. However, many vendors all set their default proposals the same as what SonicWALL uses. The default IKE proposals used by SonicWALL for Phase 1 negotiations are main mode, Diffie-Hellman Group 2, 3DES encryption, and SHA-1 for hashing. For completing phase 2 negotiations, SonicWALL, by default, uses the ESP protocol, 3DES encryption, and SHA-1 for hashing. These options are all configurable on a per-tunnel basis, and can be tailored to your needs and desired security level.

SonicWALL also supports other methods of encryption, hashing, and so on, which can increase security, as well as make their interoperability with other vendors better. SonicWALL appliances support Diffie-Hellman groups 1, 2, and 5. Most vendors, including SonicWALL, use DH group 2 as their default group, but for the extremely paranoid or security conscious, using group 5 is an option.

SonicWALL also supports multiple encryption methods, including DES, 3DES, and multiple levels of AES, up to AES-256. Although DES is supported, it should not be used unless absolutely necessary. Over the past few years, faster processors and faster hardware have made cracking DES encryption much easier, resulting in a decrease in the ability to ensure data confidentiality when using DES.

Two methods of hashing are supported, MD5 and SHA-1. SHA-1 has become a more widely used algorithm in recent times, and has thus become the default hashing method of choice. The MD5 hash is 128 bits, versus the 160-bit length of the SHA-1 algorithm, so naturally a shorter-length hash can be attacked easier than the longer hash. There was also a demonstrated attack against an old implementation of MD5, but SonicWALL uses a different implementation of MD5 that is said to be secure. SHA-1 does require more computing horsepower than MD5, and may result in a slowdown in throughput. If throughput is an issue, or if an endpoint does not support SHA-1, MD5 can still be used and the data can still be considered secure.

Figure 10.4 shows a screenshot of the SonicWALL VPN configuration window.

Figure 10.4 SonicWALL VPN Summary Page

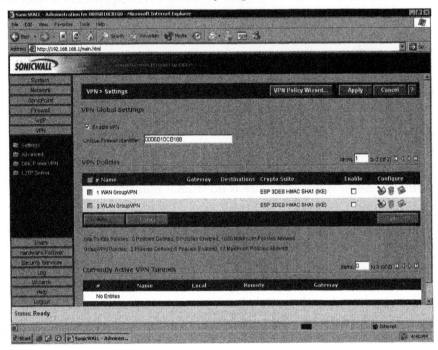

Creating a Site-to-Site VPN

Suppose we want to create a VPN tunnel from our corporate headquarters in New York to our branch office in Phoenix to provide secure access to our fileserver located on our Windows domain. We have a SonicWALL appliance at each site that will be used as our VPN gateways. We want to use the default security proposals of the SonicWALL appliances, but we want to enable Perfect Forward Secrecy using Diffie-Hellman Group 2. We will be using IKE with a pre-shared key to establish the tunnel. First, we need to establish an outline of our network addressing and VPN configuration information so that building the tunnel is easier.

Corporate Headquarters (New York)

```
SonicWALL WAN IP: 10.15.15.2
LAN Subnet: 172.16.1.0
LAN Netmask: 255.255.255.0
```

Branch Office (Phoenix)

SonicWALL WAN IP: 10.20.30.2

LAN Subnet: 172.16.9.0

LAN Netmask: 255.255.255.0

VPN Configuration Information

Security Method: IKE using Pre-shared key

Pre-shared Key: &&Our%Pre-Shared#Key^@^$

IKE Phase 1 Proposals: DH Group 2, 3DES, SHA-1

IKE Phase 2 Proposals: ESP, 3DES, SHA-1

Perfect Forward Secrecy: DH Group 2

Lifetime: 28800

Notes from the Underground...

SonicWALL Security Association Lifetimes

Many firewall/VPN vendors offer the administrator two modes for configuring security association lifetimes—time-based or data-based. Data-based lifetimes renegotiate the security associations after a specified amount of data has traversed the VPN tunnel, while time-based lifetimes renegotiate the tunnel after a specified time interval has elapsed. SonicWALL supports time-based security associations only, with their default lifetime being 28800 seconds, but this value is configurable on a per-VPN tunnel basis. If the opposing end of the VPN tunnel calls for renegotiation on a shorter life cycle than does the SonicWALL, the SonicWALL will renegotiate using the opposing gateway's requested renegotiation period.

Now that we've laid out the necessary information to build the tunnel, let's start building. It makes no difference which end of the tunnel we start with during the building process, but for our example we will start with the SonicWALL in our corporate office in New York.

Corporate Office—New York

1. Log in to the SonicWALL and click **VPN | Settings**. Locate and click the **Add...** button to open the **VPN Policy** pop-up window.

2. Since we've established we want to use a pre-shared key for security, set the **IPSec Keying Mode** to **IKE using Preshared Secret**.

3. Specify the name for the tunnel in the **Name** field. Ideally, it's a good idea to name the tunnel for the function it provides or the location it terminates. We will name our tunnel **To Phoenix Office**.

4. Input the IP address of the Phoenix firewall in the field labeled **IPSec Primary Gateway Name or Address**.

5. Enter the pre-shared secret in the **Shared Secret** field.

Figure 10.5 shows the General VPN Settings page configured as outlined in the preceding steps.

Figure 10.5 General VPN Settings—New York

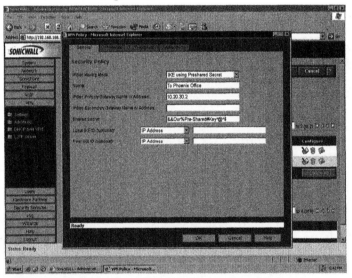

6. Click the **Network** tab to define the local and remote network ranges. Under **Local Networks**, select the radio button next to **Choose local network from list** and then select the **LAN Primary Subnet**, since this defines the New York network 172.16.1.0/24.

7. Since we have not previously defined our remote network, we will do so now. Under **Destination Networks**, select the **Choose destination network from list** option and select **Create New Address Object...** A window will open for configuring the new address object. Input the **Name**, set the **Zone Assignment** to **VPN**, set the **Type** to **Network**, and input the IP address for the Phoenix LAN and the netmask into the

fields for each. Click **OK** to save the object and select it for use. Figure 10.6 shows the address object creation, and Figure 10.7 shows the completed Network Settings tab.

Figure 10.6 Address Object Creation

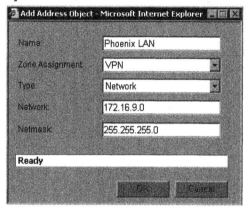

Figure 10.7 Network Settings—New York

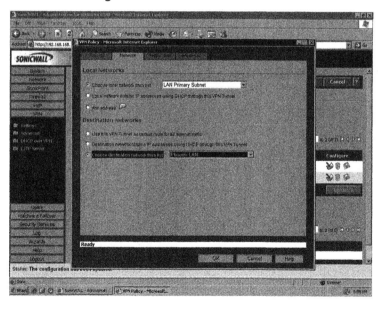

8. Click on the **Proposals** tab. The Proposals tab is where all the security proposals information is defined and configured. Because both endpoints have static IP addresses, we can use **Main Mode** for negotiation (**Exchange**). If one or our gateways has a dynamically assigned IP address,

we would need to use **Aggressive Mode** for negotiation. Since we stated that we wanted to use the default values, check to ensure the information is correct. We also outlined that we wanted to use perfect forward secrecy, so enable the **Enable Perfect Forward Secrecy** option and ensure that the value for **DH Group** is set to **Group 2**. Figure 10.8 shows our proposals configuration page.

Figure 10.8 Proposals Configuration—New York

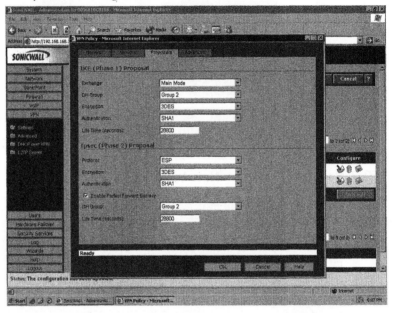

9. Select the **Advanced** tab. This is where we can configure advanced options for the VPN tunnel. To ensure that the VPN tunnel is always kept active even when no data is passing through the tunnel, enable the **Enable Keep Alive** option. If we are using a Windows-based domain or workgroup system, which may rely heavily on NetBIOS over TCP/IP (Transmission Control Protocol/Internet Protocol) broadcast messages, enable the **Enable Windows Networking (NetBIOS) Broadcast** option. This allows for Windows broadcast message to be passed across the VPN tunnel by the SonicWALL. This feature only works when there is a SonicWALL on both ends of the tunnel. Figure 10.9 shows the Advanced VPN Configuration page.

Figure 10.9 An Advanced VPN Configuration

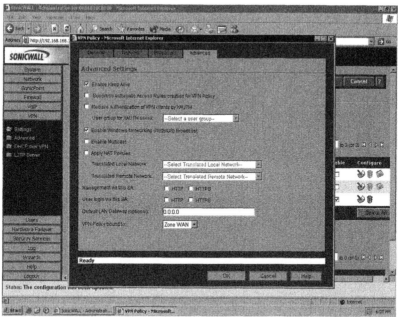

10. Click **OK** to complete the VPN tunnel configuration. You've just com-
     pleted configuration of one end of our VPN tunnel.

You will now see on the VPN status window the tunnel labeled **To Phoenix
Office**. Note in Figure 10.10 that the **To Phoenix Office** VPN tunnel is **Enabled**.
The SonicWALL is now attempting to negotiate a tunnel with the SonicWALL in
Phoenix. Now we need to log in to the Phoenix SonicWALL and configure the
other end of the VPN tunnel.

Figure 10.10 VPN Tunnel Completed

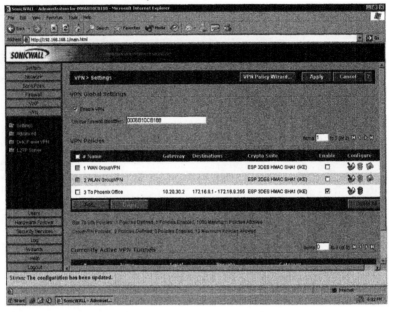

Branch Office—Phoenix

1. Log in to the Phoenix SonicWALL and select **VPN | Settings**. Click **Add...** to open the **VPN Policy** window.

2. Set the **IPSec Keying Mode** to **IKE using Preshared Secret**.

3. Specify the name for the tunnel in the **Name** field. We will name our tunnel **To New York Office.**

4. Input the IP address of the New York firewall in the field labeled **IPSec Primary Gateway Name or Address**.

5. Enter the pre-shared secret in the **Shared Secret** field. Be certain to enter the pre-shared key exactly as entered on the New York firewall.

Figure 10.11 shows the General VPN Settings page configured on our SonicWALL in Phoenix.

Figure 10.11 General VPN Settings—Phoenix

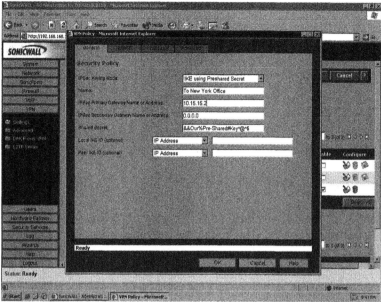
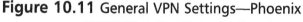

6. Click the **Network** tab to define the local and remote network ranges. Under **Local Networks**, select the **Choose local network from list** option and then select the **LAN Primary Subnet**, since this defines the Phoenix network 172.16.9.0/24.

7. Define the New York LAN as an address object on the Phoenix SonicWALL. Under **Destination Networks**, select the **Choose destination network from list** option and select **Create New Address Object...** from the drop-down list. A window will open for configuring the new address object. Input the **Name**, set the **Zone Assignment** to **VPN**, set the **Type** to **Network**, and input the IP address for the New York LAN and the netmask into the fields for each. Click **OK** to save the object and select it for use.

8. Click the **Proposals** tab. Check to ensure that all security proposals match the proposals used on our New York SonicWALL. Remember to enable perfect forward secrecy by enabling the **Enable Perfect Forward Secrecy** option and ensure that the value for **DH Group** is set to **Group 2**. Your configuration should look exactly as the configuration for the New York firewall did in Figure 10.8

9. Select the **Advanced** tab. Enable the **Enable Keep Alive** and **Enable Windows Networking (NetBIOS) Broadcast** options. Click **OK** to complete the VPN tunnel configuration.

You will now see on the VPN status window the tunnel labeled **To New York Office**. Note that this tunnel is **Enabled**. The SonicWALL is now attempting to negotiate a tunnel with the SonicWALL in New York. Since the New York SonicWALL VPN configuration has already been completed and enabled, after a few seconds you should see the tunnel listed as an active VPN tunnel under **Currently Active VPN Tunnels**.

SonicWALL GroupVPN

The SonicWALL GroupVPN is designed to make configuration and deployment of multiple VPN clients quick and easy to do. All that is required to use the GroupVPN policy is to enable it on the VPN configuration page. No policy configuration is needed. SonicWALL appliances can support up to four GroupVPN policies, one in each of the following zones: DMZ (de-militarized zone), LAN (local area network), WAN (wide area network), and WLAN (wireless LAN). The SonicWALL GroupVPN can be used only with the SonicWALL Global VPN client or the SonicWALL Global Security Client. For added security when deploying the SonicWALL GroupVPN, you should use XAUTH, LDAP (Lightweight Directory Access Protocol), or RADIUS for user authentication. Optionally, you can enable and use third-party certificates for keying.

One interesting thing about the SonicWALL GroupVPN is the ability to configure it to your desired security level. If you browse to the **VPN | Settings** page and click the **Configure** icon next to the GroupVPN you can change almost every configuration setting. On the **General** tab you can change the method for keying, either pre-shared key, or third party certificates. You can also change the pre-shared key from the default key generated by the SonicWALL. On the **Proposals** tab you can modify the Phase 1 and Phase 2 negotiations and key lifetime.

If you select the **Advanced** tab, you'll see options for **Client Authentication**. Note that the option for **XAUTH** is selected and the **User Group** is set to **Trusted Users**. This means that when the GroupVPN policy is enabled that any users who are a member of the Trusted Users group on the SonicWALL are able to access the VPN. If this option is not selected, the **Allow Unauthenticated VPN Client Access** becomes active. This allows you to select the resources that unauthenticated VPN users can access.

The final tab on the GroupVPN is the **Client** tab, which contains options for client configuration. The option **Cache XAUTH User Name and Password on**

Client allows you to specify if the remote user's password can be cached on their laptop or computer, or whether it must be re-entered each time the user accesses the VPN. Also note the option **Allow Connections to:**. This option allows you to configure what end users can do when they are connected to the VPN tunnel. They can be allowed to use the VPN tunnel and their local Internet connection normally (**Split Tunnel**), they can be allowed to access only resources behind secured gateways (**All Secured Gateways**), or they can be allowed to access only resources behind the current secured gateway (**This Gateway Only**). If **This Gateway Only** is selected, then selecting **Set Default Route as Gateway** would allow the user to have Internet access, but all traffic would be routed across the VPN rather than directly accessing the Internet. If this option is left unset, all Internet traffic would be blocked.

As mentioned earlier, SonicWALL has implemented a feature call Simple Client Provisioning. Simple Client Provisioning allows the end user to connect to the SonicWALL using the SonicWALL Global VPN client or Global Security Client and have the policy automatically downloaded to the client. By enabling the **Use Default Key for Simple Client Provisioning** option, on initial connection, aggressive mode is enabled and a default pre-shared key is used for authentication. The security policy is then downloaded automatically to the client software. This makes for easy deployment of the GroupVPN.

Deploying GroupVPN

Suppose we want our outside sales staff to use the GroupVPN policy to have access to our shared resources. We intend to deploy the SonicWALL Global VPN Client to their laptops, and we want to use XAUTH for user authentication. We've already purchased licensing for the SonicWALL Global VPN Client. To make client configuration as easy as possible, we'll use Simple Client Provisioning to automatically configure the client software with the security policy. We also want to deny our sales staff the ability to browse the Internet while they are using the VPN, and we do not want to allow caching of their password. We want to use the following security proposals:

```
Pre-share Key: $%^Group*&VPN@$#^
Phase 1: DH Group 2, AES-256, SHA-1, Default Lifetime
Phase 2: ESP, AES-256, SHA-1, Default Lifetime
Enable Perfect Forward Secrecy using DH Group 2
VPN Gateway 10.15.15.2
```

Installing the SonicWALL Global VPN Client

1. Log in to mysonicwall.com and download the SonicWALL Global VPN client. Disable any antivirus, disk protection, or firewall software you have installed. Unzip the file to the desired location and double-click **setup.exe** to begin the installation process (Figure 10.12).

2. Click **Next** until you see the license agreement. If you agree to the terms of the agreement, select **I accept the terms of the license agreement** and click **Next**.

3. Verify the install path is as desired and click **Next** to continue the installation. In most cases, the default installation path should not be changed. Click **Next** again. The installer will now copy files to their proper locations, set permissions, and install the device drivers for the SonicWALL Virtual Adapter.

4. Upon completion of the installation you will be presented with an option to **Start program automatically when users log in** and to **Launch program now**. If you want the SonicWALL Global VPN Client to start every time the user logs in, enable the first option. Otherwise, click **Finish** to complete setup and exit the installer.

Figure 10.12 SonicWALL Global VPN Client Installer

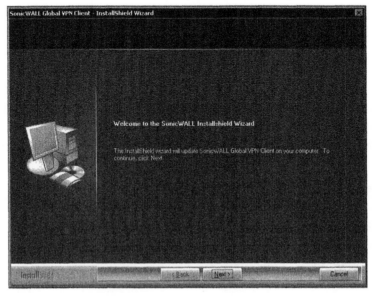

Configuring the GroupVPN Policy

1. Log in to your SonicWALL firewall and click the **VPN | Settings** tab. Click the **Configure** button next to the **WAN GroupVPN** policy to open the policy configuration window.

2. On the **General** tab, enter the desired pre-shared key.

3. Click the **Proposals** tab. Modify the proposals to match what we have established as our desired security level. Figure 10.13 shows our desired configuration.

Figure 10.13 Configuring the GroupVPN Security Proposals

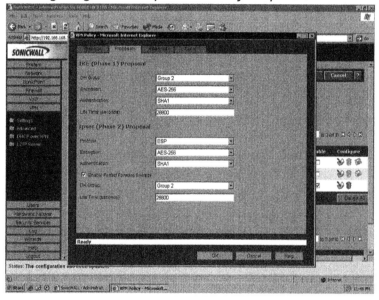

4. Click the **Advanced** tab. Ensure that the **Require Authentication of VPN Clients via XAUTH** option is selected. Figure 10.14 shows the Advanced VPN Policy screen.

Figure 10.14 Advanced GroupVPN Policy Screen

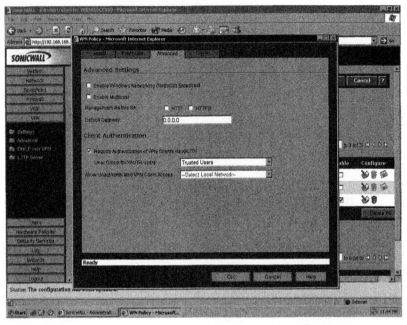

5. Click the **Client** tab. Since we do not want users to cache their passwords, ensure that **Cache XAUTH User Name and Password on Client** is set to **Never**. Since our policy also dictates we want to deny Internet access while users are using the VPN tunnel, choose the value **This Gateway Only** for the option **Allow Connections to**. Also enable **Use Default Key for Simple Client Provisioning.** Figure 10.15 shows the client configuration page.

Figure 10.15 Client Configuration GroupVPN Page

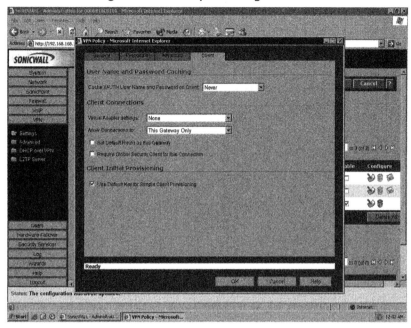

6. Click **OK** to complete and save the configuration changes we've made to the GroupVPN. Now place a checkmark in the box to the right of the policy name under the **Enable** heading to enable the policy.

Setting Up Users

Now that we've installed the Global VPN Client and configured the GroupVPN policy to our desired security level, we need to set up and configure user accounts for our remote users. User configuration is located on the **Users | Settings** page. The default authentication method is to use the Local User database, but SonicWALL supports using RADIUS, LDAP, or a combination of Local Users plus RADIUS or LDAP at the same time. In our example we will be using the local database for authentication. For detailed instructions on configuring your SonicWALL appliance to use LDAP of RADIUS for user authentication, refer to Chapter 5.

1. Select **Users | Settings**. Ensure that **Local Users** is selected as the **Authentication Method** and click **Apply**.

2. Select **Users | Local Users**. Click **Add User...** to add a new user to the database.

3. Enter the desired username and password. For our example we will add a user named **chris**. Optionally, enter a comment in the **Comment** field to describe the user. Click the **Groups** tab. You will see by default the user is a member of the **Everyone** group as well as the **Trusted Users** group. Click the tab labeled **VPN Access**. Add the desired networks we want the user to be able to access across the VPN tunnel. Click **OK** to complete creating the user.

Connecting to the VPN

Now that we've specified out security proposals for the VPN tunnel and created our user, it is time to connect and test the VPN to verify proper configuration. To test the VPN connection:

1. Start the SonicWALL Global VPN client. It is located at **Start | Programs | SonicWALL Global VPN Client**.

2. Click **File | New Connection...** to start the VPN New Connection Wizard. Click **Next** to continue.

3. You will see two options available along with an explanation of each option—**Remote Access** and **Office Gateway**. Since we will be tunneling into the network from an external location, choose **Remote Access** and click **Next**.

4. On the next screen input the IP address of the SonicWALL to which we want to connect. We will be using 10.15.15.2. Also input a name for this connection in the **Connection Name** field. For our example we will name the tunnel **Corporate Office**. Figure 10.16 shows the Global VPN client being configured with the gateway information. Click **Next** to continue to the final screen.

Figure 10.16 Global VPN Client Configuration

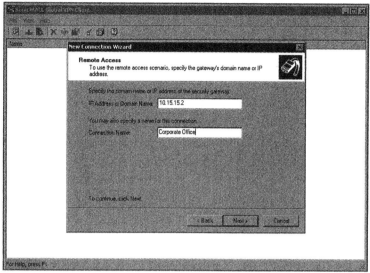

5. The last screen provides you with two options. **Create a desktop shortcut for this connection** does just as it says—places a shortcut to the connection directly on your workstation desktop. **Enable this connection when the program is launched** automatically enables the VPN tunnel upon launching the SonicWALL Global VPN client. After you've selected the options you wish to use, if any, click **Finish** to complete the configuration. You will now see the tunnel labeled Corporate Office.

6. Since we chose to use simple client provisioning to automatically download the VPN policy to the client, we will now initiate the connection to the firewall. Right-click the policy and select **Enable.** After a brief delay you will see an authentication window similar to Figure 10.17. Enter the username and password as specified for the user.

Figure 10.17 Global VPN Client Provisioning

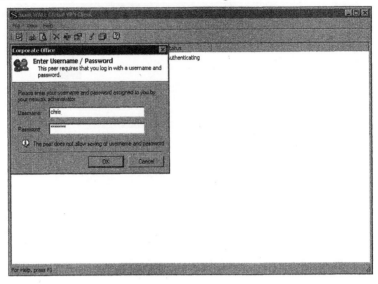

If entered successfully, the connection will continue, the policy will be provisioned and downloaded into the client, and another authentication window will appear. Again, enter the username and password as specified when the user account was set up. Once entered, the tunnel will finish its negotiations, and the **Status** will be displayed as **Connected**. Your GroupVPN tunnel is now connected. To view the security information and remote network information, double-click the VPN policy, browse to the **Status** tab, and then click **Details**. You will see security information similar to that shown in Figure 10.18.

Figure 10.18 Global VPN Status and Security Information

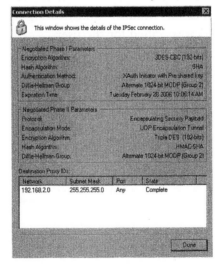

You can also monitor the VPN status by logging in to the SonicWALL. Browse to the **VPN | Settings** page. You will see a green dot on the GroupVPN tunnel under the **VPN Policies** heading. You will also see GroupVPN listed under **Currently Active VPN Tunnels,** along with the remote peer ID and the remote gateway. Figure 10.19 shows the VPN tunnel status from the SonicWALL VPN administration screen.

Figure 10.19 SonicWALL VPN Status Page

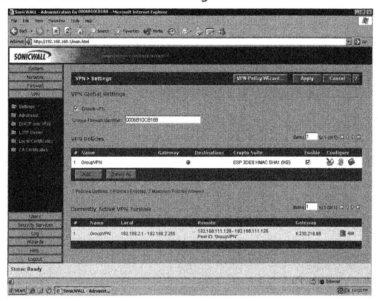

L2TP VPNs

All SonicWALL appliances have the ability to terminate L2TP (Layer 2 Tunneling Protocol) over IPSec VPN connections. L2TP over IPSec VPNs can be configured easily from within Microsoft Windows XP or Windows 2000 without the installation of any additional third-party applications. This is an ideal solution if you prefer not to license the SonicWALL Global VPN client, or if you just prefer using the native support within Microsoft Windows. You might also come across a scenario when installation of the SonicWALL Global VPN Client is not possible. You can also run both L2TP VPN tunnels and IPSec tunnels simultaneously, as well as tunnels with the SonicWALL Global VPN Client.

Notes from the Underground…

Windows 2000 Pre-Shared Key Support

Windows 2000 does not natively support using pre-shared keys for L2TP/IPSec VPNs. Before you are able to set up and connect to an L2TP VPN from a Windows 2000 machine, you must first modify the system registry. Click **Start | Run | regedit** and browse to the **HKLM\System\CurrentControlSet\Services\ Rasman\Parameters** key. Add a new value named **ProhibitIpSec** with a data type **REG_DWORD**, set the value to **1**, and the reboot the machine.

Suppose we want to use an L2TP VPN tunnel to let our Marketing manager, Bob, access the network. Bob will be using his Windows XP laptop to access the network. Since the SonicWALL L2TP server is incompatible with the Microsoft implementation of digital certificate exchange, we will be using a pre-shared key for identity.

First, we should create a user account for Bob. To create the user account:

1. Select **Users** and click **Local Users**. Click **Add User…** to add a new user to the database.

2. Enter the desired username and password; in this case the username is **Bob**. Enable the **Access from L2TP VPN client** option to enable access via L2TP. Click **OK** to complete adding the user to the local user database.

After configuring the user account, we need to configure the L2TP server on the SonicWALL. To configure the L2TP server:

1. Select **VPN** and click **L2TP Server**. Enable the **Enable L2TP server** option and click **Apply** at the top of the page. Next, click **Configure**.

2. Enter the information for your DNS (Domain Name Service) and WINS (Windows Internet Naming Service) servers into the respective fields. Under **IP Address Settings**, select **Use the Local L2TP IP Pool** and input a range of IP address to be used. It is important that this range is different than any range currently assigned to interfaces as a subnet. Click **OK** when you've completed the configuration. The SonicWALL L2TP Server is now ready for connections.

Now that we've completed the necessary configuration changes on the SonicWALL, we need to configure Bob's laptop for connecting to the SonicWALL. Windows XP has excellent support for connecting to L2TP VPN tunnels.

1. Select **Start | Settings | Control Panel** and double-click **Network Connections** Click **Create a New Network Connection**.

2. At the initial new network connection screen, click **Next**. On the **Network Connection Type** screen, choose the option **Connect to the network at my workplace** and click **Next** to continue.

3. Choose the **Virtual Private Network Connection** option and click **Next**. On the next screen, input a name for the connection. Click **Next** to proceed to the gateway information screen.

4. Input the hostname or IP address of the SonicWALL we want to connect to, and click **Next** to proceed to the final screen. Click **Finish** to complete creation of the new connection.

5. Now we need to make a few additional changes to the L2TP connection we just created. Click **Properties** and browse to the **Security** tab. Click the box labeled **IPSec Settings...** and then enable **Use pre-shared key for authentication**. Input the pre-shared key and click **OK**. Figure 10.20 shows the pre-shared key configuration.

Figure 10.20 Configuring the Windows L2TP Connection

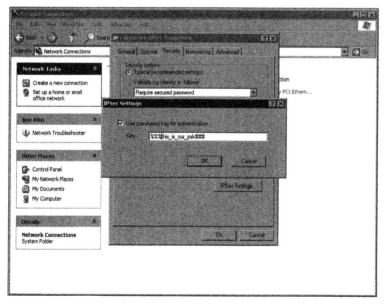

6. Click the **Networking** tab. Change the **Type of VPN** to **L2TP IPSec VPN**. Click **OK** to save the configuration changes.

7. Finally, input the username and password for the account we set up in the SonicWALL. Optionally, you can enable the connection to save the user-name and password. Click **Connect** to initiate the VPN connection.

In a few seconds the VPN tunnel will connect. You can check the properties of the VPN tunnel by clicking on the connection and looking at the **Details** tab to show IP information. Figure 10.21 shows a connected L2TP VPN. As an adminis-trator you can also monitor and disconnect any active L2TP VPN tunnels from the L2TP Server page in the SonicWALL. Figure 10.22 shows the L2TP connection status window.

Figure 10.21 The L2TP Details Window

Figure 10.22 Monitoring L2TP Connections from within the SonicWALL

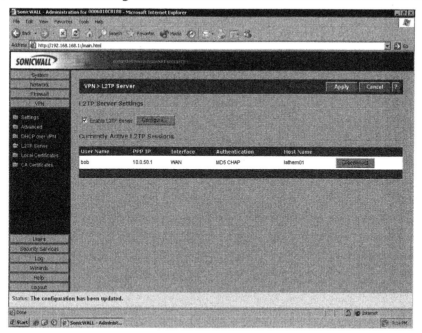

Gateway Redundancy

When VPN connectivity is a critical part of your network architecture, it is important that the tunnel's uptime be maximized. SonicWALL has included a feature
called *gateway redundancy* to provide for a second VPN gateway address.

Suppose you are creating a VPN from a branch office to the corporate office.
You have a SonicWALL at your corporate office with two WAN links terminating
on it, 10.10.10.2 and 10.20.20.2. When you create the VPN tunnel on the branch
office firewall, you would set the values for both the **IPSec Primary Gateway
Name or Address** as well as the **IPSec Secondary Gateway Name or Address**.

When the SonicWALL tries to bring the VPN up, it will first attempt to do so
on the primary gateway address. If there is a problem with bringing up the tunnel,
the firewall then attempts to utilize the secondary gateway address. The SonicWALL
might also attempt to use the secondary gateway should there be a problem with
connectivity over the first gateway address.

Summary

In the first part of this chapter we discussed VPN as a technology itself: its purpose, inner workings, and an overview of VPN in general. We learned that IPSec was designed to provide several services: privacy and confidentiality of data, origin authentication, data integrity, access control, and protection against replay attacks. We discussed how transport mode only encrypts the data portion of a packet, while tunnel mode actually encrypts the entire packet and encapsulates it in another packet.

We also mentioned that IPSec supports both manual and automatic key distribution methods. In manual key configurations, all security parameters are configured at both ends of the tunnel manually. Internet Key Exchange, or IKE for short, generates and negotiates keys and security associations automatically based on pre-shared secrets or digital certificates. IPSec uses security associations to manage all of the parameters required to establish a VPN tunnel. In simple terms, SA is a set of parameters describing how communications are to be secured.

An IPSec tunnel using IKE requires two phases to complete negotiation of the tunnel. Phase 1 of IKE negotiation establishes a secure tunnel for negotiation of security associations. Then, during phase 2, IPSec SAs are negotiated defining the method for encrypting and authenticating user data exchange.

We also discussed the use of digital certificates with SonicWALL appliances. Digital certificates are a way to verify your identity through a certificate authority using public key cryptography. SonicWALL appliances only support using certificates to create VPN tunnels from one SonicWALL appliance to another. SonicWALL also supports OCSP, a form of certificate revocation list, to ensure a certificate has not become invalid.

The default IKE proposals used by SonicWALL for Phase 1 IKE negotiations are main mode, Diffie-Hellman Group 2, 3DES encryption, and SHA-1 for hashing. For completing phase 2 negotiations, SonicWALL, by default, uses the ESP protocol, 3DES encryption, and SHA-1 for hashing. If possible, you should try to avoid using DES for any VPN tunnel configuration.

SonicWALL appliances support time-based security associations rather than data-based security associations, but this does not affect their interoperability. SonicWALL appliances will renegotiate the VPN tunnel upon request if a device at the other end has a shorter tunnel life value. When creating a SonicWALL to SonicWALL VPN tunnel, you can enable NetBIOS broadcast message to be sent through the VPN tunnel. This makes operations on Microsoft Windows domains or workgroups smoother.

The SonicWALL GroupVPN makes configuration and deployment of multiple VPN clients quick and easy; you only need to enable the default Global VPN policy. The GroupVPN can only be used with either the SonicWALL Global VPN client or the SonicWALL Global Security Client. For added security, you should use XAUTH, LDAP, or RADIUS for user authentication. The GlobalVPN allows the administrator to configure the tunnel negotiation parameters to their desired security level. SonicWALL also supports Simple Client Provisioning, which allows the end user to connect to the SonicWALL using the SonicWALL Global VPN client or Global Security Client and have the policy automatically downloaded to the client. No configuration to the client has to be manually entered.

All SonicWALL appliances have the ability to terminate L2TP over IPSec VPN connections. L2TP over IPSec VPNs can be configured easily from within Microsoft Windows XP natively, but you must use a pre-shared key rather than digital certificates for authentication. SonicWALL also allows you to run both L2TP VPN tunnels and IPSec tunnels simultaneously, as well as tunnels with the SonicWALL Global VPN Client.

SonicWALL also provides gateway redundancy in VPN configurations. This allows you to specify multiple gateways for a VPN tunnel to terminate on. In event your primary gateway loses connectivity, the SonicWALL can renegotiate the VPN tunnel on the secondary gateway. This helps to minimize VPN downtime.

Solutions Fast Track

Understanding IPSec

- ☑ IPSec was engineered to provide several services: privacy and confidentiality of data, origin authentication, data integrity, access control, and protection against replay attacks.

- ☑ IPSec provides two modes of operation: *transport mode* and *tunnel mode*.

- ☑ IPSec has two methods for verifying the source of an IP packet as well as verifying the integrity of the payload contained within—authentication header (AH) and encapsulating security payload (ESP). While ESP can encrypt and authenticate the entire packet, AH only authenticates the packet.

- ☑ IPSec supports the use of both manual keys and autokey IKE.

- ☑ Internet Key Exchange, or IKE, generates and negotiates keys and security associations automatically based on either pre-shared secrets or digital certificates.

- ☑ *Security associations* (SA) is the concept used by IPSec to manage all of the parameters required to establish a VPN tunnel, including security keys and algorithms, mode of operation (transport or tunnel), key management method (IKE or manual key), and lifetime of the SA. All of this information is stored in the security association database (SAD).

IPSec Tunnel Negotiations

- ☑ Because all security association is manually configured in a manual key VPN, negotiations are not required between the two endpoints. Traffic is simply encrypted, authenticated, and routed to the destination gateway.

- ☑ IPSec tunnels using IKE requires two phases to complete negotiation: phase 1 establishes a secure tunnel for negotiation of security associations and phase 2 IPSec SAs are negotiated defining the method for encrypting and authenticating user data exchange.

- ☑ Phase 1 exchanges can be done in two modes: main mode or aggressive mode. In main mode, six messages are exchanged, while in aggressive mode only three messages are exchanged.

- ☑ Main mode negotiations are considered more secure than aggressive mode negotiations, since the identities of the participating parties are not exchanged in the clear.

Public Key Cryptography

- ☑ Public key cryptography is the modern cryptographic method of communicating securely without having a previously agreed-upon secret key.

- ☑ Public key cryptography uses a pair of keys to secure communications—a private key that is kept secret, and a public key that can be widely distributed.

- ☑ Some examples of public key cryptography algorithms include RSA, Diffie-Hellman, and ElGamal.

☑ PKI is the meshing of encryption technologies, services, and software together to form a solution that enables businesses to secure their communications over the Internet.

☑ Digital certificates are a way to verify identities through a certificate authority (CA) using public key cryptography.

☑ Online Certificate Status Protocol, or OCSP, is the method used by SonicWALL to check and ensure that a digital certificate has not become invalid.

VPNs in SonicWALL Appliances

☑ There are three ways to configure site-to-site VPNs when both endpoints have static IP addresses: site-to-site with AutoKey IKE, third-party certificates, and manual key VPNX.

☑ A VPN can also be created between two SonicWALL appliances when one endpoint has a dynamic IP address. The negotiations of the tunnel must be initiated by the end with the dynamic IP, and aggressive mode must be used for phase 1 negotiations.

☑ When creating VPN tunnels it is advisable to always use at least 3DES for encryption and SHA-1 for hashing. If increased security is a must and throughput isn't a significant factor, consider AES-256 for encryption.

☑ Using the built-in GroupVPN policy on a SonicWALL appliance is a very simple procedure, requiring only that you enable the policy to use it out of the box.

☑ For easiest deployment of the GroupVPN, you should use XAUTH for user authentication and enable Simple Client Provisioning. This allows your users to authenticate to the SonicWALL from the SonicWALL Global VPN Client, and then the policy configuration is automatically retrieved from the SonicWALL over a secure channel.

☑ You can use the built-in SonicWALL L2TP VPN server to provide L2TP over IPSec connectivity to Windows XP without installing the SonicWALL Global VPN Client.

☑ When multiple WAN links terminate at a VPN endpoint, you can configure a secondary gateway in the VPN tunnel to provide gateway redundancy for the VPN.

Links

For more information, visit the following Web sites:

- www.ietf.org/rfc/rfc2401.txt

- www.openvalidation.org/whatisocsp/whatocsp.htm

- www.openca.org/ocspd/

- www.sonicusers.com/forum/display_forum_topics.asp?ForumID=13

- www.equinux.com/us/products/vpntracker/index.html

- www.safenet-inc.com/products/vpn/softRemote.asp

Frequently Asked Questions

The following Frequently Asked Questions, answered by the authors of this book, are designed to both measure your understanding of the concepts presented in this chapter and to assist you with real-life implementation of these concepts. To have your questions about this chapter answered by the author, browse to **www.syngress.com/solutions** and click on the **"Ask the Author"** form.

Q: Can SonicWALL firewalls establish VPN tunnels between other manufacturer's firewalls, such as Cisco PIX, NetScreen, or Snapgear?

A: Yes, SonicWALL firewalls have a broad range of compatibility modes built in. SonicWALL appliances are ICSA 1.0d certified VPN appliances, so any other appliance that is also ICSA 1.0d certified should be interoperable with SonicWALL.

Q: What encryption and hashing algorithms do SonicWALL appliances support?

A: SonicWALL appliances support Diffie-Hellman Groups 1, 2, and 5. SonicWALL appliances support DES, 3DES, AES-128, AES-192, and AES-256 for encryption algorithms. For hashing, SonicWALL appliances support MD5 and SHA-1.

Q: Can I use third-party VPN client software to connect to a VPN tunnel on a SonicWALL appliance?

A: Yes, there are many VPN client applications that can connect to a SonicWALL IKE VPN tunnel. The SafeNet VPN Client is a good example that works well with SonicWALL. In fact, the SonicWALL can export the security policy in .spd format, the format used by the SafeNet VPN Client, so it can easily be imported into the client rather than being built by hand (the SonicWALL VPN Client is a SonicWALL-branded version of this client, but is no longer distributed by SonicWALL).

Q: I want to create an IKE VPN to my SonicWALL, but I'm a Mac user. Can this be done, and if so, how?

A: Yes, you can create IKE VPN tunnels from your Mac to a SonicWALL. In fact the process is pretty simple and straightforward. A great VPN client for Mac systems is Equinux's VPN Tracker. I've used this client several times creating VPN tunnels from Mac systems, and it's a breeze to set up and configure.

Chapter 11

High Availability

Solutions in this chapter:

- **The Need for HA**

- **Configuring Hardware Failover in SonicWall Firewalls**

- **Configuring Monitoring Links**

- **Tips, Tricks, Traps, and Tuning**

- **Cabling an HA Pair**

- **How HF "Fails Over"**

☑ Summary

☑ Solutions Fast Track

☑ Frequently Asked Questions

Introduction

What is "high availability?" In the strictest sense of the word, high availability (HA) means any system designed to ensure a particular (or estimated particular) operational "uptime" in a year. Therefore, a continuously available database server would have practically no down time in any given year.

HA has essentially come to mean "redundant." System's can be designed with more reliable components, (all of which have to possess the desired Mean Time Before Failure [MTBF]) to achieve a projected 5 minutes of downtime in a given year). SonicWALL is the answer: two synchronized firewalls securing the same ingress and egress points, thus providing a redundant data path in the event that one becomes inoperable.

This chapter provides a look at the various features of SonicWALL firewalls that provide for HA. We begin with a cursory discussion of the justification for a HA network implementation. Having a rudimentary feel for the various aspects of this topic is a great help when required to justify potentially expensive, and redundant purchases to upper management. However, a truly in-depth discussion of such a broad topic is beyond the scope of this book.

After this, we examine how HA is achieved with specifically with SonicWALL firewalls. Configuration examples are provided that can be used as a baseline to architect HA solutions in your own network.

Towards the end of the chapter, we touch on some advanced configurations. Also, some potential pitfalls are considered and recommendations given on how to best mitigate them.

The Need for HA

Whether due to hardware or software faults, one fact cannot be disputed: network components fail. Much like the eventuality of death and taxes, the only real issue is *when* the problem will occur and *how much* of an impact such a failure will have. HA is about mitigating the risks of such failures and bringing them within acceptable, quantifiable bounds, which are part of a larger business strategy. Do you depend on your e-commerce Web site to be available 24 hours a day, 365 days a year? If so, your idea of acceptable network outages will be vastly different from someone whose business only relies on the network for sending and receiving occasional e-mail. Knowing your business and how it makes money is crucial when deciding which HA measures, and thus expenditures, you allocate to your resources. Management will want to make sure Information Technology (IT) is not "gold-plating" things, and you want to be prudent.

The total cost is not only measured in money, but also in time and complexity. An HA network takes longer to implement, results in more maintenance work, takes longer to gain an understanding of, and due to increased complexity, raises the risks of human error, thus countering your initial goal.

Just as one business may have more reliance on their Internet connection, a particular server, or other piece of their infrastructure, another might be completely indifferent to the uptime of the same resource. This logic comes to bear in how we implement HA. HA can be anything from a spare system in a closet, to a fully meshed, fully redundant network infrastructure with automatic failure detection and quick convergence.

Configuring Hardware Failover in SonicWALL Firewalls

Let's start by configuring a Hardware Failover (HF) pair, and then work backwards into the what, when, and where of these solutions.

Before you start your system and access the Web, look on the back of the appliance you intend to use as your backup host and write down this device's serial number (the number is also available on the box in which the firewall shipped). This serial number should be a string of 12 letters and numbers.

Hardware and Software

The HF feature set discussed in this chapter is only available on appliances running SonicOS Enhanced. HF is supported by only the PRO series of SonicWall firewalls; the TZ series does not offer HA functionality.

Before you try to build a HA pair, make sure that your intended primary and backup SonicWALL appliances are the same hardware model. Two different SonicWALL hardware platforms in a HF pair will not work.

Similarly, each SonicWALL device in a HF pair must run the same firmware version. One way to deal with this quickly is with the Synchronize Firmware feature, which synchronizes the backup device's firmware to the primary so that the two can operate as a HF pair. Be aware that if the backup device has an older version, (e.g., older than 2.5.0.5e, this synchronization will not work and you will have to manually upgrade the system's firmware.

Network Requirements

HF requires three unique, *static* addresses: one Internet Protocol (IP) for the virtual gateway IP address, a second IP for the primary's physical interface, and a third IP for the backup device's physical interface. There is a configuration option that requires only one public IP address for the WAN (essentially for the virtual IP only), but keep in mind this precludes management of the individual pair members.

SonicWALL HF does not support dynamic IP address assignment on the WAN. If you wish to implement HF, you need to negotiate static IP address assignment with your Internet Service Provider (ISP).

All SonicWALL ports must be connected together with a hub or switch (except in the case of a dedicated HA port, which is often connected directly with a crossover). Therefore, if each SonicWALL has a management WAN IP address, the respective WAN IP addresses must be in the same subnet.

Licensing and Security Services

Your SonicWALL Security Services (e.g., CFS, IPS, Gateway AntiVirus, and so on) licenses are not shared between primary and backup SonicWALL devices. They are still separate hosts, albeit configured in an HA pair, so the backup SonicWALL firewall needs its own licenses. While a heterogeneous pair will allow you to configure them as a pair, if the backup SonicWALL security appliance does not have the same subscriptions enabled, such services will be at risk in the event of a failover.

Now, assuming that your local area network (LAN), wide area network (WAN) and other interfaces are addressed and cabled, you connect your hardware pair HF-link (which should be unconfigured at this point).

Connect the HF ports on the primary SonicWALL and backup SonicWALL appliances with a crossover (CAT-5 or 6) cable. The primary and backup SonicWALL appliances require a direct connection between them. You can also cable them through a hub or switch (with a straight-through cable).

Power up the firewalls, taking care to power up the primary firewall first. At the "Hardware Failover > Settings" page on the primary SonicWALL, enter the serial number of the backup appliance that you wrote down in Step #1.

For now, we will not concern ourselves with all of the following settings; all you need to do here is check the Enable Hardware Failover and Enable Preempt Mode (see Figure 11.1). Preempting causes the primary to reassume the primary role automatically, if it comes back online after a failure.

Figure 11.1 HF Settings

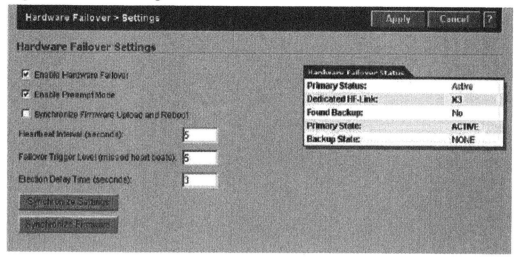

Click **Apply** to save the changes.

If everything is configured and cabled correctly, the primary SonicWALL automatically contacts the backup SonicWALL over the dedicated HF link, and configures all the settings to establish HF. The backup SonicWALL reboots and comes back in "idle" mode with its new settings.

The interface IP address for the primary (see Network > Interface) is now the virtual "floating" IP address for the pair, and nodes and traffic from that segment will use that IP address as the gateway to traverse the HA pair. To determine what IP addresses are assigned to the interfaces themselves, we will configure some additional HA settings.

Loose Ends: Configuring Monitoring Addresses and Management IPs

Now that you have a working HA configuration, there are a couple of loose ends you will want to tie up. First, now that your WAN, LAN, and other interface (except the HF link) addresses are not the virtual addresses for the pair, you will want to replace these designated addresses. From the "Hardware Failover > Monitoring page":

1. Select the **Configure** icon for an interface and enter the desired management IP addresses for the primary and backup SonicWALL appliances for that interface (see Figure 11.2).

Figure 11.2 Monitoring Settings

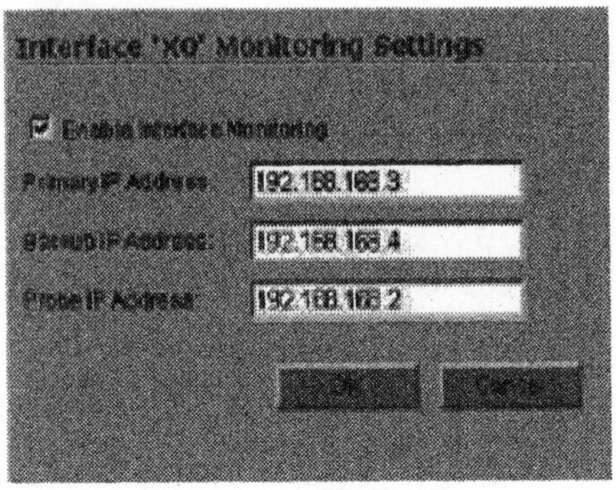

2. Click **OK**.

Relying solely on interface monitoring is usually insufficient. Mere interface monitoring would not precipitate a failover because the Ethernet link itself is up. Nonetheless, it is clear that there is no connectivity and that the pair should failover.

To address this problem, SonicWALL's HA link monitoring regularly pings specified "probe" IP addresses. If this probe address does not echo-reply, but the same address is reachable to the backup unit, failover occurs.

Configuring Monitoring Links

On the Hardware Failover > Monitoring page, select **edit** in the configure column; the Edit HA Monitoring window appears. When you check the "Enable Interface Monitoring" box and complete the fields, be sure to select a probe IP address that will be a good indicator of network availability (e.g., a next hop router). You will need to repeat this process for each interface you want to have HA.

The SonicWALL appliances will send an Internet Control Message Protocol (ICMP) echo-request to the probe address, to determine if the link is up. If both SonicWALL appliances can ping this address, all is well. If neither can successfully ping the probed address, there is no failover because the appliances will assume that the problem is with the probed host itself, and not the link in a particular interface. As mentioned said earlier, the failover condition is when only one SonicWALL can ping the probe target.

Tips, Tricks, Traps, and Tuning

Failover Function Test

The status of the HF unit is shown in the upper right corner of the management Graphical User Interface (GUI). When an initial failover occurs, the primary unit transitions to "Status: Idle." The primary unit will transition back to "Status: Active" and the backup unit will transition back to Idle when the primary comes back online *if* preempt is enabled.

1. Start a continuous ping from a host on one subnet through the firewall to a host on another network (or Internet)

2. Pull the network cable from one of your primary's interfaces.

3. Under Log > View, watch for the messages "Link is Down" and "primary firewall has transitioned to idle."

4. When the link comes back up, plug the cable back in and watch the log for "primary firewall preempting backup."

Cabling an HA Pair

Before you can configure the SonicWALL firewalls to be used in your environment, you will want to understand cabling. There are a few options available. This section covers some of the advantages and disadvantages of the most common, supported implementations. What is presented here is by no means an exhaustive treatment of cabling, switching, or spanning tree (STP), but should be enough for you to properly evaluate your own proposed architecture and make an informed decision.

The different cabling topologies discussed in this section are grouped into two broad categories: *traffic links* or *data links* and *HA links* (see Figure 11.3).

On a SonicWALL firewall, a WAN interface is connected with a straight-through cable to a hub or switch port in the same subnet as the other pair member's WAN interface. The same cabling requirements apply to LAN interfaces between the HF pair members. Because they are firewalls and not switches, your dedicated HF interface must be connected with a crossover cable if the pair members are directly connected to each other.

Figure 11.3 Cabling an HA Pair

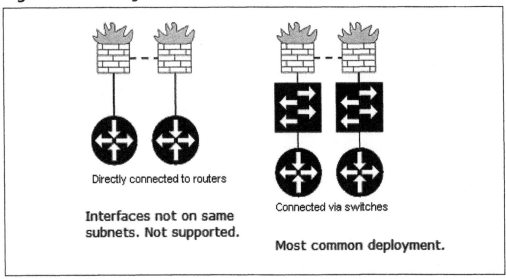

Directly connected to routers

Interfaces not on same subnets. Not supported.

Connected via switches

Most common deployment.

As far as HA traffic goes, you can connect the firewalls directly with a crossover. However, you may prefer to connect them through an Ethernet switch. If you do this and the Ethernet switch is running STP, you will want to adjust the STP settings on the switch port that the SonicWALL firewall interfaces are connected to. Since you are connecting the switch port to a host (the SonicWALL firewall) that does not participate in the STP, shortening the time until the switch interface is "forwarding" will allow for faster convergence, essentially skipping the "listening" and "learning" port modes. On a Cisco switch (i.e., portfast), you need to set this on each switch interface connected to a SonicWALL HF interface (two switch ports for the pair).See Figure 11.4. (For more details on STP, Radia Perlman's *Interconnections* is recommended.)

Figure 11.4 Another Method for Cabling an HA Pair

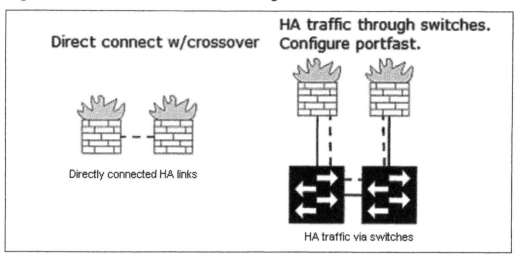

The advantages and disadvantages boil down to several advantages to directly connecting HA links:

- It is supported by SonicWALL.

- There is less likelihood of a switch failure creating problems, and there are no STP considerations.

When directly connecting the HA pair, there is a minimal chance of link failure. While switch ports rarely fail these days, it is nonetheless another point of failure. Directly connecting the firewalls removes an additional point of failure. Further, link failures are immediately detected on both firewalls.

Adding a SonicWALL Unit to a HF Configuration

To add a SonicWALL to a HF configuration, you must first make sure that the new replacement SonicWALL firewall is an identical model and that the firmware version of the replaced unit is identical to the backup firewall. You should also want to transfer your services licenses to the new unit. Next, on the backup unit (currently the primary or active firewall), export the settings file and disable HF.

1. At "Hardware Failover > Settings," uncheck "Enable Hardware Failover."

2. Connect the new soon-to-be primary and login to the unit. (Remember, since the unit is unconfigured, the management interface is located on the default IP; http://192.168.168.168). Import the settings file saved in step #1 into the new primary. In this step, the status bar may complain about licensing, but it is safe to ignore these and reboot the new primary.

3. Once the firewall has rebooted, log back in to the management interface using the LAN IP address of the primary (it will have its "old" IPs back because you have imported the settings), and then navigate to the "Hardware Failover > Settings" page and check to make sure that "Enable Hardware Failover" and "Enable Preempt Mode" are checked. The backup SonicWALL firewall should reboot; once it comes up it will go into the idle state. Check **Log > View** to ensure that all is going as expected

4. You should see that the primary status is active and the backup is now idle in the Hardware Failover Status table of the primary.

Determining When to Failover

Before going into detail about how to detect the need for a failover, let's look at a list of things that are already reason enough to fail over:

- Software crashes

- Hardware or power failure

- Link failure on monitored links, ideally gauged as the unavailability of one or more tracked "Probe" IP addresses

How HF "Fails Over"

We know that HF is the combination of one pair of SonicWALL firewalls into a single, logical device: one device is the primary SonicWALL, which actively passes all traffic (hence is "Active"), and an identical SonicWALL firewall is the backup that sits idle most of the time. In the event of a failure of the primary, the backup SonicWALL transitions to "Active" mode, and temporarily plays the role of the now down primary. Therefore, while this backup has sat idle, it has maintained itself as an exact copy of the primary through a dedicated HF link (the X3 interface on the PRO2040 series, and via the X5 interface on the PRO3060/4060/5060s) so that it can step in and take over quickly and seamlessly.

A periodic synchronization takes place over the dedicated link. There are two ways this synchronization is performed. The two units communicate "timestamps" that are used to determine their level of synchronization. In the event that the timestamps are synchronized, an incremental synchronization suffices when a change is made to the primary. This synchronization is a push to the backup. If this incremental synchronization fails, or if the timestamps between the units are out of synchronization, a complete synchronization is attempted.

Now that you know a bit about synchronization, you should have some idea of what a failover event entails. Failover occurs when security services are not available, if your physical (or logical) link detection is detected on a monitored interface, or when the primary loses power. Your failover mechanism also monitors system processes (e.g., Virtual Private Network [VPN], the Dynamic Host Configuration Protocol [DHCP] service, and Network Address Translation [NAT]). If any of these processes fail, the failover can occur, or in the event of a configuration corruption, your backup can refresh the configuration. Since the backup contains a mirror image of the primary, it also has the last known good copy of the configuration. This is the one push the backup can do to a primary: restore its configuration in the event it becomes corrupt.

Tuning

The heartbeat over the HF link is a fundamental component of SonicWALL HF and is the mechanism by which failures of the primary are detected (e.g., a software or hardware failure, service failure, or an unlikely spontaneously bad cable). There are only three configurable settings for this feature: the frequency of the heartbeats in seconds, the number of missed heartbeats (Failover Trigger Level) allowed before a failover is triggered, and "Election Delay," which is the number of seconds SonicWALL will wait to consider an interface up and stable (see Figure 11.5).

Figure 11.5 HF Settings

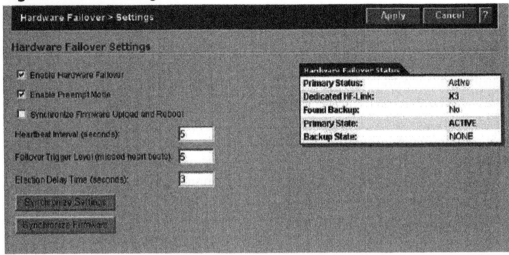

Summary

HA is a hot topic, as more importance is placed on the availability of data networks across the globe. Availability is de facto redundancy in today's designs, and SonicWALL's solution to the availability question is just that. With a link, a process, hardware, and logical monitoring, SonicWALL's offering in this arena is quite effective for cost-sensitive enterprises. There are some limitations to how the SonicWALL solution can be deployed, lacking dynamic IP support in the HA transit link (router to firewall) supports but the solution's simplicity in configuration, management, and operation makes it a boon to security staff and architects. The solution's setup takes minutes, and monitoring and repair are intuitive and straightforward. HF, in conjunction with WAN failover and load balancing support, make SonicWALL's offering a "Highly Available" contender in the SMB marketplace.

Solutions Fast Track

The Need for HA

☑ HA is a statistical statement.

☑ There are many ways to achieve HA; redundancy is only one of them and is often used synonymously.

☑ The level of availability should be dictated by your business strategy.

☑ One must consider the right balance between availability and cost.

Configuring Hardware Failure in SonicWALL Firewalls

☑ Pair members must be the exact same hardware model and firmware version.

☑ The respective interface on each pair member must reside on the same subnet.

☑ Pair members do not share licenses; therefore, pair members should have the same services and subscriptions otherwise, in the event of a failover, many services will not be available.

☑ LAN, WAN, and other interfaces must be cabled into a switch, not a router. A HA (HF-link) may be connected directly to the other pair member with a crossover cable.

☑ Only SonicOS Enhanced supports HF.

Cabling an HA Pair

☑ Using directly connected HA links is preferred.

☑ Switches add unnecessary points of failure, and potentially introduce false failures due to STP delays.

How HF "Fails Over"

☑ Backup is an exact mirror copy of the primary.

☑ The interface link state can be used to determine failover.

☑ The echo-reply from a monitored probe IP can be used to determine failover.

☑ Services and processes are also monitored.

☑ The backup can refresh a corrupt configuration on the primary, since it has an exact copy of the primary.

Chapter 12

Troubleshooting the SonicWALL

Solutions in this chapter:

- **Troubleshooting Methodology**
- **Troubleshooting Tools**
- **Network Troubleshooting**
- **SonicWALL Logs**
- **Advanced Diagnostic Routines**

☑ Summary

☑ Solutions Fast Track

☑ Frequently Asked Questions

Introduction

Troubleshooting is a fact of life in computer networking, and SonicWALL security appliances offer a selection of tools to assist with troubleshooting network access. This chapter covers different ways to track the status of packets going through the firewall.

When dealing with firewalls, it is important to remember that they often change the content of the packets going through them. It is our task to keep track of the changes and make sure they are what we intended. Most firewalls perform four main functions: packet forwarding, stateful filtering, address translation, and encryption. We tackle each of these functions differently. Troubleshooting packet forwarding can be as easy as inspecting the routing table. Address translation may require looking at a log of the traffic. Troubleshooting encryption may require analysis of a detailed packet dump. SonicWALL appliances offer specific troubleshooting tools built into the SonicOS firmware. Commands such as *ping, traceroute,* and *find network path* can help with simple connectivity troubleshooting. More advanced tools allow you to view active processes, active connections, and CPU use, to name a few.

Remember that every firewall issue is resolvable, and there is a reason behind every decision the firewall makes. We begin by looking at the process a packet undergoes as it makes its way through the firewall. Next, we review the different tools available for troubleshooting. After that, we discuss troubleshooting methods for VPNs (virtual private networks) and traffic shaping. Finally, we cover the logs the firewall creates to help us determine what the firewall is doing with our packets.

Troubleshooting Methodology

So, something is not going the way you expected it to. The first step is a sanity check. Is this a firewall issue? Are the packets making it to the firewall? Many firewall issues may actually be internal routing issues. Follow your packets from your computer through the internal network hubs, switches, and routers. It may be a good idea to sniff the traffic just outside your firewall to see what the packets look like before they get to the firewall. Every troubleshooting session begins with a plan of action. Let's outline one such plan to help us figure out what went wrong. There are seven steps to follow when troubleshooting issues.

1. **Describe the problem.** Before we can start the troubleshooting process, we need to be able to describe the problem. It is important to tackle each problem individually to solve the issue at hand.

2. **Describe the environment.** Next, we need to be able to describe which network devices we are dealing with. This step includes listing the hardware and software involved in the path of the network traffic.

3. **Determine the location of the problem.** The location of the problem is not always apparent, and we need to determine where the problem is occurring. There are several troubleshooting tools available to us to help locate the problem. This is normally done by analyzing the output of certain troubleshooting tools.

4. **Identify the cause of the problem.** Once we determine where the problem exists, we need to identify the cause of the problem. This is normally done by analyzing the output of certain troubleshooting tools.

5. **Solve the problem.** Once the cause of the problem is identified, we need to resolve the problem. This might involve physically altering the network or issuing commands to network equipment by changing the configurations. Whatever you do, keep track of what you change.

6. **Test the solution.** Recreate the issue and see if the problem is resolved. In addition, test all other services to ensure they are functioning as expected, as the fix may have affected other network traffic.

7. **Document the changes.** Documentation is one of the most important and often skipped steps in the process. A good network or security administrator keeps a detailed log of what changes are made to the network infrastructure. Keeping track of what changes are made during troubleshooting is also important because the solution might create unintended problems in other areas of the network. Keep this log handy in case other issues arise.

Troubleshooting Tools

The SonicWALL security appliance has several troubleshooting tools built in to it, and we cover the tools in detail here. Each tool has a specific purpose and should fulfill any troubleshooting need you have relating to the firewall.

Active Connections

The Active Connections Monitor allows you to monitor the current, active connections on the SonicWALL. The following list displays the following components of each active connection:

- Source IP

- Source Port

- Destination IP

- Destination Port

- Protocol

- Source Interface

- Destination Interface

- TX Bytes

- RX Bytes

You can sort the list of connections by any of the items shown by simply clicking on the column header. In addition to being able to simply monitor and sort the active connections, you can apply filters to the table to drill down to specific items of concern. For example, if you want to see all connections that are going to a specific IP address, you could apply a filter that would list only the entries with that IP as the destination. You could also apply filters that are extremely granular. For example, you may only want to see the connections from source 10.0.0.101 with the destination 10.0.0.254 using TCP port 443. This would list only the connections that match this exact criterion.

The Active Connections Monitor screen is divided into two parts. The top half of the screen is used to configure the display filters to apply to the current connections, and the bottom half displays the actual connections. We will cover the display filters first and then dive into the actual connections last. Figure 12.1 shows the available filter options.

Figure 12.1 Active Connections Monitor

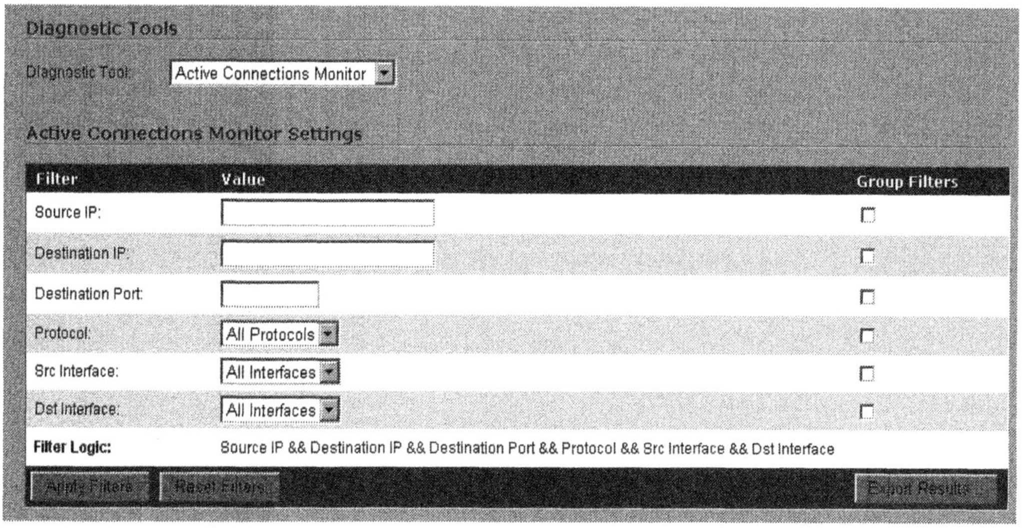

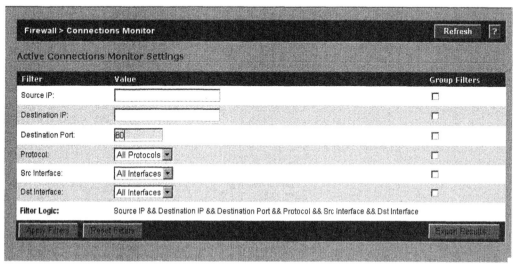

You can apply filters based on a single criterion, or you can group criteria together. Assume that you are only interested in HTTP traffic that is crossing the SonicWALL's interfaces. You would simply enter a value of **80** in the Destination Port field and then click **Apply Filters** (Figure 12.2).

Figure 12.2 Active Connections Monitor

Let's look at one more example. Assume you want to view all the active HTTP connections that are open by the device with IP address 10.0.0.103 that are going to

10.10.10.50. You would first set the individual criteria by typing **10.0.0.103** into the **Source IP** field, then **10.10.10.50** into the **Destination IP** field, and finally **80** into the **Destination Port** field. Next, place a check mark next to each of the individual entries to tell the SonicWALL you wish to group the selections together (Figure 12.3).

Figure 12.3 Active Connections Monitor

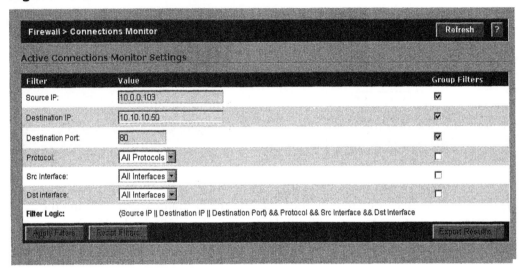

To clear the current display filters and view all active connections, click **Reset Filters**. One of the most useful functions of this tool is the Export Results… feature, which allows you to export all the active connections to either a plaintext file or a comma separated value (CSV) file. This option gives you the capability to import the data into a database or spreadsheet for more detailed analysis (Figure 12.4).

Figure 12.4 Active Connections—CSV Format

	A	B	C	D	E	F	G	H	I
1	Source IP	Source Port	Destination IP	Destination Port	Protocol	Src Interface	Dst Interface	Tx Bytes:	Rx Bytes:
2	10.0.0.202	2456	10.0.0.1	80	TCP	X0	X0	649	1188
3	10.0.0.202	2453	10.0.0.1	80	TCP	X0	X0	646	2236
4	10.0.0.202	2438	10.0.0.1	80	TCP	X0	X0	618	1164
5	10.0.0.202	2460	10.0.0.1	80	TCP	X0	X0	624	2431
6	10.0.0.202	2421	10.0.0.1	80	TCP	X0	X0	773	1562
7	10.0.0.202	2452	10.0.0.1	80	TCP	X0	X0	829	11529
8	10.0.0.202	2434	10.0.0.1	80	TCP	X0	X0	615	1183
9	10.0.0.202	2448	10.0.0.1	80	TCP	X0	X0	1358	35073

CPU Monitor

The CPU Monitor diagnostic tool displays a histogram graph of CPU use. The available time intervals are second, minute, hour, and day. In Figure 12.5, we look at the past 30 minutes of CPU use on a TZ170W appliance.

Figure 12.5 Active Connections Monitor

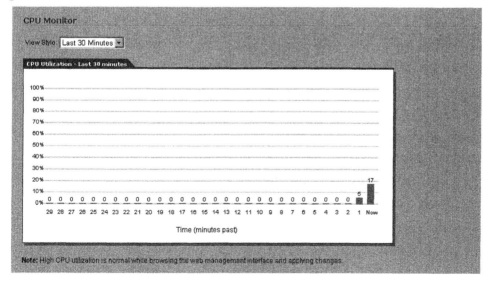

DNS Name Lookup

The DNS Name Lookup diagnostic tool is used to troubleshoot connectivity issues and/or name resolution issues. To use this tool, simple type the domain name or IP address of a device. The SonicWALL will query the DNS servers you set up during the initial configuration of the unit, and return either the IP address associated with that device or the DNS Name associated with the IP address. Figure 12.6 shows an example of DNS Name Lookup on SonicOS.

Figure 12.6 DNS Name Lookup

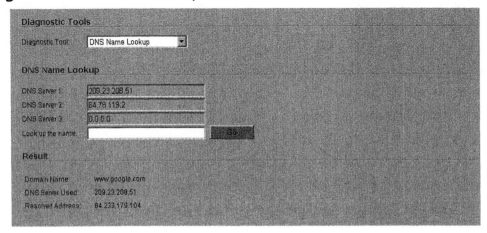

Find Network Path

Find Network Path indicates if an IP address is located on the WAN or LAN side of the SonicWALL, and is commonly used to diagnose configuration or routing issues. For example, if the results of the Find Network Path tool indicate that a computer on the Internet is located on your LAN, your problem is most likely a misconfiguration within the intranet or network settings on the SonicWALL. This tool can also be used to identify if a device is located behind a LAN network router, and if so, what the MAC address of the router is. In practice, this tool is extremely useful for troubleshooting internal routing issues within complex LANs. An example of the results from this tool is shown in Figure 12.7. The IP address that was entered into the tool was 10.0.0.100.

Figure 12.7 Find Network Path

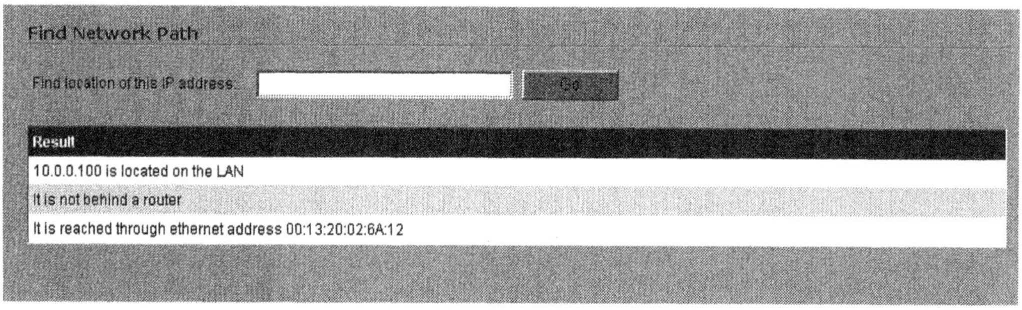

Packet Trace

The SonicWALL provides the capability to monitor traffic from a specific source as it traverses the firewall's interfaces. To truly understand what the information gathered from this tool means, you need to understand the three-way handshake. As an example, let's look at a packet trace for a connection to a Web server from a device located on the LAN. The SonicWALL is configured to trace packets from the LAN device with IP address 10.0.0.103 as shown in Figure 12.8.

Figure 12.8 Simple Packet Trace (Part 1)

Once the IP address of the device you would like to perform a trace on has been entered, simply click **Start**. The status of the Packet Trace will change from "Trace off" to "Trace active," as shown in Figure 12.9.

Figure 12.9 Simple Packet Trace (Part 2)

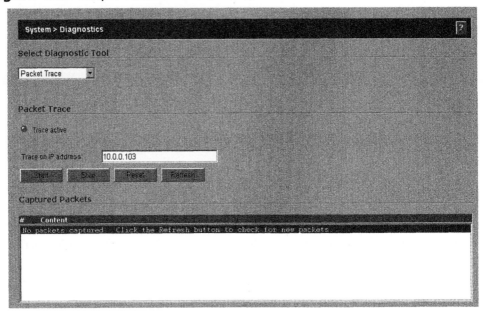

The SonicWALL will now display any packets originating from 10.0.0.103 for further analysis. We now browse to a Web site from 10.0.0.103 and then look at the packets that have been recorded by the SonicWALL. Figure 12.10 shows the results.

Figure 12.10 Example Results

```
Captured Packets

#     Content
1     TCP received on LAN [SYN]  74 bytes
2     TCP sent on LAN [SYN,ACK] 62 bytes
3     TCP received on LAN [ACK] 60 bytes
4     UDP received on LAN  81 bytes
5     UDP sent on LAN  158 bytes


Packet Detail

#:        1
Time:     02/23/2006 17:54:02.768
Content:  TCP received on LAN [SYN] 74 bytes
From:     10.0.0.103 32876 (00:11:11:d1:db:69)
To:       10.0.0.1 443 (00:06:b1:01:01:8c)
```

The first three packets captured are known as the three-way handshake. To further explain, let's look at each of the packets and their associated detail. Figure 12.11 shows the detail for the first packet received. As you can see, this is the SYN packet.

Figure 12.11 SYN Packet

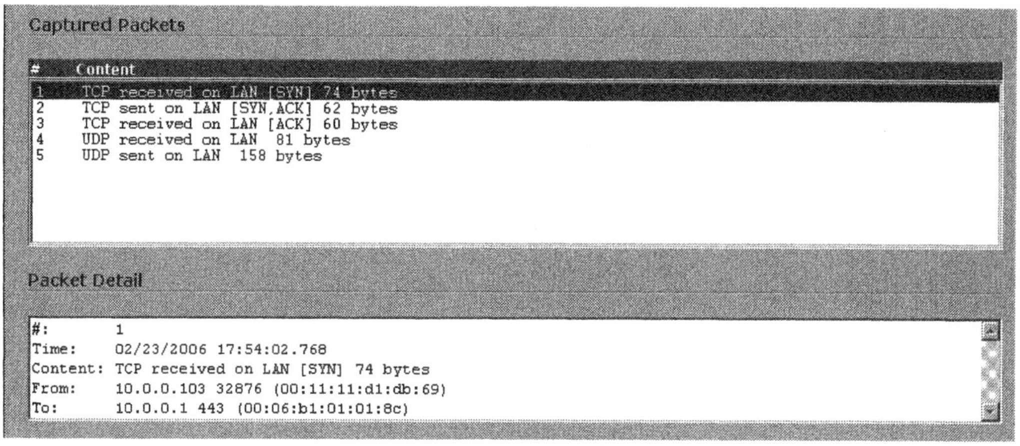

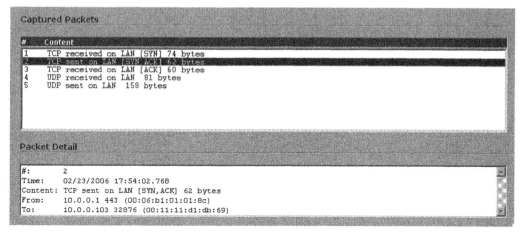

Figure 12.12 shows the SYN/ACK packet for the connection.

Figure 12.12 SYN/ACK Packet

Figure 12.13 shows the ACK packet.

Figure 12.13 ACK Packet

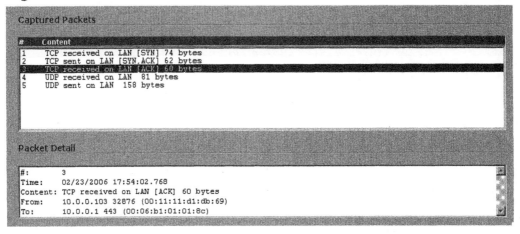

Ping

Ping is probably the most well-known troubleshooting utility in existence. The *ping* command is used to test for network connectivity, and every network operating system has a version of it pre-installed. Ping was written in December 1983 by Mike Muuss for BSD UNIX. The BSD UNIX network stack has been ported to many operating systems, including every version of Microsoft Windows. Although the name was originally derived from a sonar analogy, it is now referred to as an acronym for Packet InterNet Groper.

The functionality is simple: send an ICMP (Internet Control Message Protocol) echo-request and wait for an ICMP echo-reply. Figure 12.14 shows the result of sending a Ping request to the device with IP address 10.0.0.100.

Figure 12.14 Ping Command

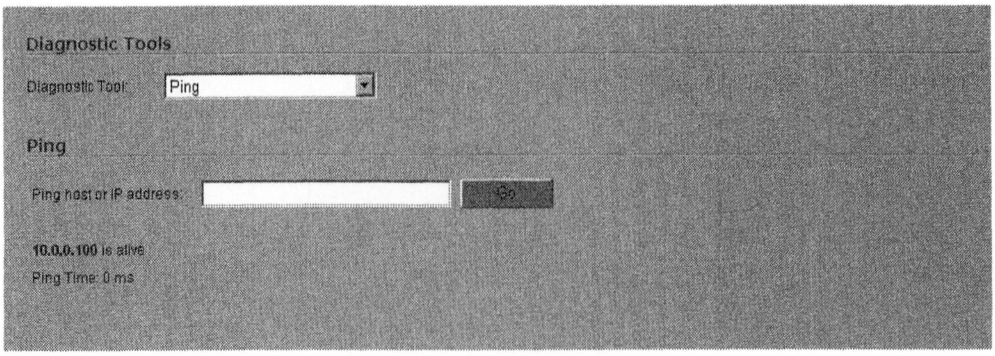

Process Monitor

The Process Monitor shows each of the running processes on the SonicWALL appliance, their priority, associated CPU use, and the system time they are using (Figure 12.15).

Figure 12.15 Process Monitor

#	Name	Function	Priority	Total%	(secs)	Current% (secs)	
1	tWebMain	0x8055a5a0	50	0.30%	12.85	0.00%	0.00
2	tAsFihWr	0x8055a5a0	128	0.21%	9.20	0.00%	0.00
3	tWdTask	0x805bb164	8	0.14%	5.97	0.00%	0.00
4	tNetTask	0x8055a5a0	50	0.05%	2.08	0.00%	0.00
5	tSonicPointPTTask	0x8055a5a0	100	0.00%	0.07	0.00%	0.00
6	tTimerTask	0x8055a5a0	50	0.00%	0.02	0.00%	0.00
7	tWebBkgnd	0x805dcee0	80	0.00%	0.02	0.00%	0.00
8	tChkCable	0x805bb164	200	0.00%	0.02	0.00%	0.00
9	tSchedObjTimer	0x805dcee0	44	0.00%	0.00	0.00%	0.00
10	tRuleTmr	0x805dcee0	44	0.00%	0.00	0.00%	0.00
11	tMyArpTask	0x805dcee0	45	0.00%	0.00	0.00%	0.00
12	tIfaceMon	0x805dcee0	46	0.00%	0.00	0.00%	0.00
13	tSarc	0x8055a5a0	47	0.00%	0.00	0.00%	0.00
14	tWdRbTask	0x8055a5a0	8	0.00%	0.00	0.00%	0.00
15	tTmrTask	0x805bb164	15	0.00%	0.00	0.00%	0.00

Real-Time Blacklist Lookup

The Real-Time Blacklist Lookup (RBL) tool, which is only available in the SonicOS Enhanced firmware, is used to test SMTP servers, DNS servers, and RBL services. Figure 12.16 illustrates the use of this tool.

Figure 12.16 Real-Time Blacklist Lookup

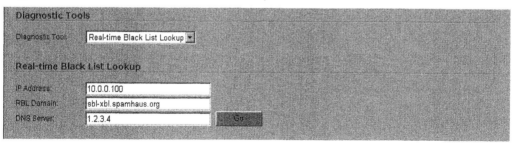

Reverse Name Resolution

While the DNS Name Lookup tool allows you to enter the fully qualified domain name (FQDN) of a host and return the IP address, the Reverse Name Resolution tool does the opposite. This tool is useful for testing DNS servers. Figure 12.17 shows an example of the results from this tool.

Figure 12.17 Reverse Name Resolution

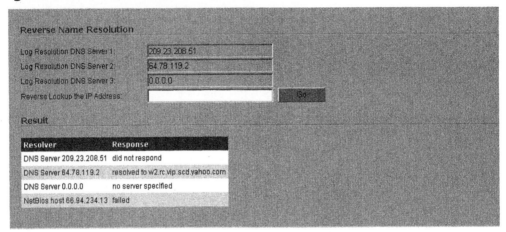

Traceroute

The traceroute tool is useful to troubleshoot multihop routing. The *traceroute* command uses the Time to Live (TTL) field of the IP protocol to get an ICMP TIME_EXCEEDED response from each gateway the packet goes through on its way to the destination. Figure 12.18 shows an example of traceroute in the SonicOS.

Figure 12.18 Traceroute

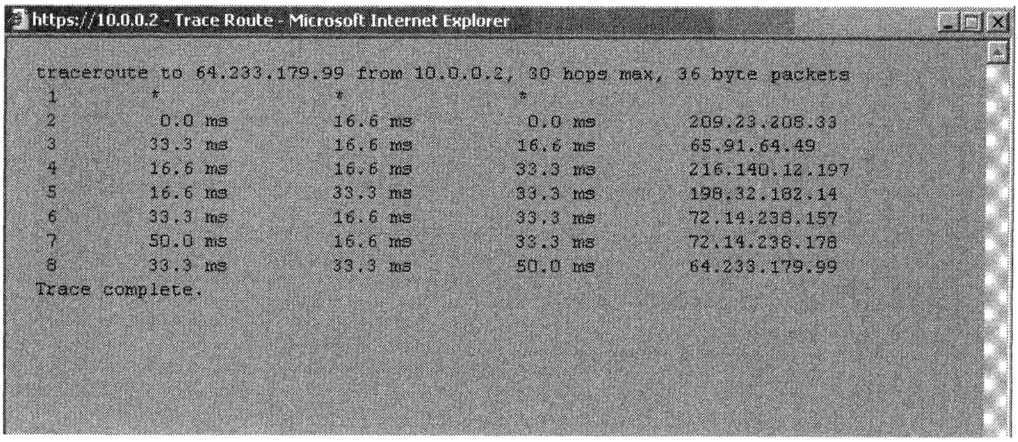

```
traceroute to 64.233.179.99 from 10.0.0.2, 30 hops max, 36 byte packets
 1        *                  *                  *
 2       0.0 ms            16.6 ms            0.0 ms         209.23.208.33
 3      33.3 ms            16.6 ms           16.6 ms         65.91.64.49
 4      16.6 ms            16.6 ms           33.3 ms         216.140.12.197
 5      16.6 ms            33.3 ms           33.3 ms         198.32.182.14
 6      33.3 ms            16.6 ms           33.3 ms         72.14.238.157
 7      50.0 ms            16.6 ms           33.3 ms         72.14.238.178
 8      33.3 ms            33.3 ms           50.0 ms         64.233.179.99
Trace complete.
```

Traceroute results should be taken with a grain of salt. Since this tool uses TTL fields in the packets, any devices that do not respond to that field will not return valid data.

ARP Cache

The Address Resolution Protocol (ARP) table of the SonicWALL appliance can be viewed by clicking **Network** and then clicking **ARP**. Figure 12.19 shows the ARP cache of the SonicWALL.

Figure 12.19 ARP Cache

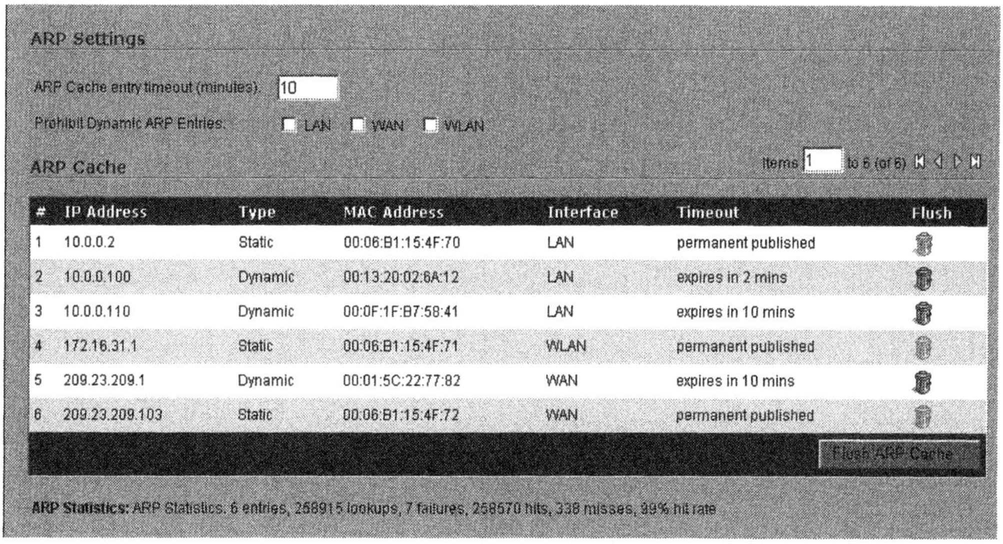

#	IP Address	Type	MAC Address	Interface	Timeout	Flush
1	10.0.0.2	Static	00:06:B1:15:4F:70	LAN	permanent published	🗑
2	10.0.0.100	Dynamic	00:13:20:02:6A:12	LAN	expires in 2 mins	🗑
3	10.0.0.110	Dynamic	00:0F:1F:B7:58:41	LAN	expires in 10 mins	🗑
4	172.16.31.1	Static	00:06:B1:15:4F:71	WLAN	permanent published	🗑
5	209.23.209.1	Dynamic	00:01:5C:22:77:82	WAN	expires in 10 mins	🗑
6	209.23.209.103	Static	00:06:B1:15:4F:72	WAN	permanent published	🗑

ARP Settings
ARP Cache entry timeout (minutes): 10
Prohibit Dynamic ARP Entries: ☐ LAN ☐ WAN ☐ WLAN

ARP Cache   Items 1 to 6 (of 6)

Flush ARP Cache

ARP Statistics: ARP Statistics: 6 entries, 258915 lookups, 7 failures, 258570 hits, 338 misses, 99% hit rate

System Status

The System Status page displays several important facts about the status of the appliance. This screen displays registration details, licensed node information, firmware version, CPU use, current system uptime, current connections, and the IP address, date, and time of the last update to the firewall. In addition, the Latest Alerts received on the SonicWALL are listed. Figure 12.20 shows the system information for the SonicWALL appliance.

Figure 12.20 System Status Information

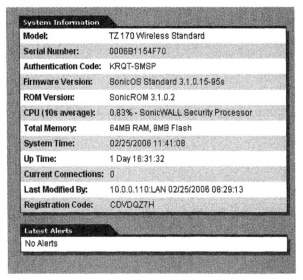

Routing Table

To view the routing table on the SonicWALL, click **Network**, **Routing**, and scroll down to the bottom of the page. The example in Figure 12.21 shows the routing table of the SonicWALL appliance.

Figure 12.21 Routing Table

Destination Network	Subnet Mask	Gateway Address	Destination Link
0.0.0.0	0.0.0.0	209.23.209.1	WAN
10.0.0.0	255.255.255.0	0.0.0.0	LAN
10.0.0.2	255.255.255.255	0.0.0.0	LAN
172.16.31.0	255.255.255.0	0.0.0.0	WLAN
209.23.209.0	255.255.255.0	0.0.0.0	WAN
209.23.209.1	255.255.255.255	0.0.0.0	WAN
209.23.209.103	255.255.255.255	0.0.0.0	LAN/WLAN
255.255.255.255	255.255.255.255	0.0.0.0	LAN

Putting It All Together

When troubleshooting the SonicWALL appliance, you can use any of the aforementioned tools to assist with resolving the issue.

Network Troubleshooting

Before you blame the firewall, you need to determine whether it is actually the root of the problem. There are several tools available for network troubleshooting. The first thing you will need is a decent packet sniffer, which is a network analyzer that will grab packets on the network and display the contents in a readable format. Ethereal (www.ethereal.com) is probably one of the best-known sniffers available and will do the job for you. The best thing about this tool is that it's free and available for both Windows and Linux platforms. Figure 12.22 shows an example of Ethereal, capturing the three-way handshake between a PC and a Web server.

Figure 12.22 Ethereal Capture of TCP Three-Way Handshake

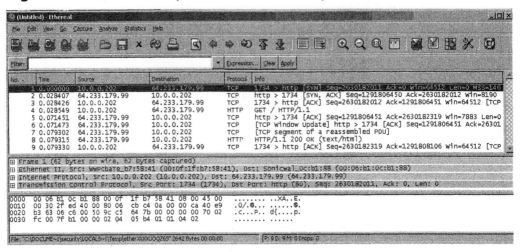

The first three packets shown in Figure 12.22 include the actual three-way handshake—[SYN], [SYN/ACK], and [ACK].

A couple of simple tests will help isolate communication problems. First, make sure the SonicWALL can ping its default gateway. The SonicWALL should also be able to ping hosts on the Internet and hosts on the internal network. If the firewall cannot reach a host, it will be difficult for a packet to reach it after going through the firewall, unless there is another firewall blocking the traffic from the firewall.

Debugging the SonicWALL Appliance

One of the most common problems experienced with firewalls is incorrect routing. If you are unable to identify where packets are going, use the Packet Trace utility or a packet sniffer such as Ethereal. Ask yourself the following questions:

- Do I have a default route?
- Is the default route pointing to the correct address and interface?
- Do I have a route to the network I am trying to get to?
- Is the route going to the correct interface?

Once you have verified that the routing is correct, the next thing to look at is the rule base. Make sure proper rules exist to allow the traffic you are trying to pass through the firewall. In addition, verify that you have selected the proper interfaces and/or zones in the rules.

The SonicWALL will log all traffic that is blocked by the firewall. Check the log file for entries pertaining to the problem traffic.

SonicWALL Logs

The SonicWALL log is a vital tool that is used to monitor potential security threats, system maintenance notices, system errors, VPN tunnel statistics, and VPN errors, to name a few. Figure 12.23 shows the System Log for SonicOS Standard.

Figure 12.23 Example of Log > View

#	Time ▼	Message	Source	Destination	Notes	Rule
1	02/25/2006 16:15:24.208	Administrator login allowed	10.0.0.110, 0, LAN (admin)	10.0.0.2, 80, LAN	admin, TCP Web (HTTP)	
2	02/25/2006 16:15:19.704	Web management request allowed	10.0.0.110, 3357, LAN	10.0.0.2, 80, LAN	TCP Web (HTTP)	
3	02/25/2006 16:15:14.528	DNS packet allowed	10.0.0.110, 1662, LAN	209.23.208.51, 53, WAN	UDP Port: 53	
4	02/25/2006 16:14:36.784	Broadcast packet dropped	10.160.8.1, 67, WAN	255.255.255.255, 68, LAN	Protocol:68	
5	02/25/2006 16:13:36.784	Broadcast packet dropped	10.160.8.1, 67, WAN	255.255.255.255, 68, LAN	Protocol:68	
6	02/25/2006 16:13:02.544	DNS packet allowed	10.0.0.100, 1028, LAN	64.78.119.2, 53, WAN	UDP Port: 53	
7	02/25/2006 16:12:36.768	Broadcast packet dropped	10.160.8.1, 67, WAN	255.255.255.255, 68, LAN	Protocol:68	
8	02/25/2006 16:11:36.784	Broadcast packet dropped	10.160.8.1, 67, WAN	255.255.255.255, 68, LAN	Protocol:68	
9	02/25/2006 16:10:36.768	Broadcast packet dropped	10.160.8.1, 67, WAN	255.255.255.255, 68, LAN	Protocol:68	
10	02/25/2006 16:09:42.624	DNS packet allowed	10.0.0.100, 1028, LAN	64.78.119.2, 53, WAN	UDP Port: 53	
11	02/25/2006 16:09:36.736	Broadcast packet dropped	10.160.8.1, 67, WAN	255.255.255.255, 68, LAN	Protocol:68	
12	02/25/2006 16:08:36.736	Broadcast packet dropped	10.160.8.1, 67, WAN	255.255.255.255, 68, LAN	Protocol:68	

View

Each entry in the log will contain a log sequence number, the date, the time, the message, source IP address, source port number, the source interface, destination IP address, destination port number, the destination interface, notes regarding the entry, and if applicable, the rule that matched the traffic. Logs can be sorted by clicking on the header column you want to sort by.

Keep in mind that if the SonicWALL loses power, the log files will be cleared, which brings up the importance of using a second device to record the log information generated by the SonicWALL. We will discuss two options that are commonly used to accomplish this.

One additional item on this page that sometimes causes confusion is the number of log entries that are displayed. By default, only 50 log entries per page are displayed. Use the navigation icons to view additional log entries (Figure 12.24).

Figure 12.24 Viewing Log Entries

Table 12.1 lists the navigation icons and their purpose.

Table 12.1 Log Navigation Icons

⏮	Move to the beginning of the log file (newest entries)
◁	Previous 50 entries
▷	Next 50 entries
⏭	Move to the end of the log file (oldest entries)

Syslog

Syslog was originally developed for UNIX-based systems. "Messages" are sent from devices configured to use Syslog, to a specified server that stores the information for later analysis. With that said, using a Syslog server ensures that all log entries will be stored and retained regardless of whether the SonicWALL is power cycled. This feature is available on almost every network device available today. The Syslog data generated by SonicWALL appliances includes every connection source and destination IP address, IP service type, and the number of bytes transferred. The SonicOS allows up to three Syslog servers to be specified. It is good security practice to configure all devices that allow Syslog to send data to at least one Syslog server. Syslog is configured under the Log Automation options, which we will cover shortly.

The Syslog Standard, RFC 3164, states that Syslog packets will be a maximum of 1024 bytes in length. There is no specified minimum length for packets. Each Syslog message will be composed of at least three key parts:

- PRI

- HEADER

- MESSAGE

The PRI field is used to indicate the priority of a message. This 8-bit value contains two important pieces of information, the Facility and Severity. The first three least-significant bits (LSBs) contain the Severity code. Using three bits allows for eight different values. Table 12.2 lists the Severity Codes available in the Syslog protocol.

Table 12.2 Syslog Severity Codes

Value	Severity
0	Emergency – System is unusable
1	Alert – Immediate Action is required
2	Critical – Critical condition detected
3	Error – Error condition detected
4	Warning – Warning condition detected
5	Notice – Normal, however significant condition detected
6	Informational – Informational message, no action needed
7	Debug – Verbose message used for debugging purposes

The remaining five bits contain the Facility code. Using five bits results in 24 different values, shown in Table 12.3.

Table 12.3 Syslog Facility Codes

Value	Facility
0	Kernel Messages
1	User-Level Messages
2	Mail System
3	System Daemons
4	Security / Authorization Messages
5	Messages Generated Internally by Syslog Daemon
6	Line Printer Subsystem
7	Network News Subsystem
8	UUCP Subsystem
9	Clock Daemon
10	Security / Authorization Messages
11	FTP Daemon
12	NTP Subsystem
13	Log Audit
14	Log Alert
15	Clock Daemon
16	Local Use 0
17	Local Use 1
18	Local Use 2
19	Local Use 3
20	Local Use 4
21	Local Use 5
22	Local Use 6
23	Local Use 7

Let's look at a typical Syslog message, captured using Ethereal (Figure 12.25).

Figure 12.25 Example Syslog Packet Capture

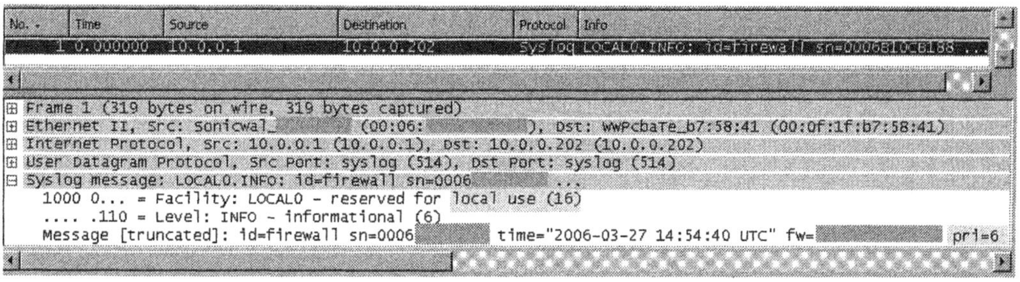

(Note: Certain fields have been marked out to protect the innocent.)

If you are familiar with how the PRI value is normally calculated, you are probably wondering why it does not add up correctly. The answer is simple. As mentioned earlier, the Syslog protocol was designed for UNIX-based systems. The calculations for the PRI value assume that the messages received will contain various Facility and Severity codes. The RFC states that the PRI value is calculated by multiplying the Facility code by 8 and then adding the value of the Severity code to the result.

For example, in Figure 12.25, the value for PRI would have been calculated to be ((Local Use 0 X 8) + Informational). Using Tables 12.2 and 12.3, we see that Local Use 0 has a value of 16 and the Severity code for Informational is 6, so we would calculate the PRI value ((16 x 8) + 6), which gives us 134.

So, why does the message shown in Figure 12.26 have a PRI value of only 6? Looking at Figure 12.25 again, the pri=6 shown is actually part of the MSG (Message); it is not the actual PRI field used by the Syslog protocol. The value of the field shown in the Message is always equal to the Severity code for SonicWALL appliances. This can be confusing, since the actual PRI value is not displayed. The actual value of PRI can be viewed by looking at the raw packet (Figure 12.26).

Figure 12.26 Example Raw Syslog Packet

```
0000  00 0f 1f b7 58 41 00 06  b1 0c b1 88 08 00 45 00   ....XA.. ......E.
0010  01 10 5f 3f 40 00 40 11  c5 d3 0a 00 00 01 0a 00   .._?@.@. ........
0020  00 ca 02 02 02 02 00 fc  9e b6 3c 31 33 34 3e 69   ........ ..<134>i
0030  64 3d 66 69 72 65 77 61  6c 6c 20 73 6e 3d 30 30   d=firewa ll sn=00
0040  30 36 42 31 30 43 42 31  38 38 20 74 69 6d 65 3d   06██████ 88 time=
0050  22 32 30 30 36 2d 30 33  2d 32 37 20 31 35 3a 35   "2006-03 -27 15:5
0060  31 3a 35 37 20 55 54 43  22 20 66 77 3d 32 31 36   1:57 UTC " fw=216
0070  2e 34 35 2e 31 38 30 2e  31 32 33 20 70 72 69 3d   ████████   pri=
0080  36 20 63 3d 30 20 6d 3d  38 30 35 20 6d 73 67 3d   6 c=0 m= 805 msg=
0090  22 49 6e 74 65 72 66 61  63 65 20 73 74 61 74 69   "Interfa ce stati
00a0  73 74 69 63 73 20 72 65  70 6f 72 74 22 20 6e 3d   stics re port" n=
00b0  35 31 35 30 34 20 69 66  3d 58 30 20 75 63 61 73   51504 if =X0 ucas
00c0  74 52 78 3d 31 36 38 33  39 38 35 20 62 63 61 73   tRx=1683 985 bcas
00d0  74 52 78 3d 31 31 31 32  38 39 20 62 79 74 65 73   tRx=1112 89 bytes
00e0  52 78 3d 31 36 37 32 35  32 38 32 30 20 75 63 61   Rx=16725 2820 uca
00f0  73 74 54 78 3d 31 36 38  37 37 35 31 20 62 63 61   stTx=168 7751 bca
0100  73 74 54 78 3d 32 33 32  30 39 39 20 62 79 74 65   stTx=232 099 byte
0110  73 54 78 3d 31 37 39 33  38 33 38 36 32 33         sTx=1793 838623
```

The value of 134, just as we had calculated, is shown between the < > brackets.

The HEADER portion of a Syslog message is 8 bits and must contain visible, printable characters. There are two fields contained in the HEADER: TIMESTAMP and HOSTNAME. TIMESTAMP is the local time and uses the format Mmm DD for the date, where Mmm is the abbreviation for the month in English and HH:MM:SS for the time. The HOSTNAME field contains the hostname or the IPv4 or IPv6 address of the device from which the message originated.

The MSG portion of a Syslog message makes up the rest of the packet, and usually contains information pertaining to the process that created the message and a description of what occurred. MSG is composed of two fields, TAG and CONTENT. The TAG field contains the name of the process or application that generated the message. The CONTENT field contains information regarding the details of the message.

Now let's put it all together. Figure 12.27 shows an example Syslog message received from a SonicWALL appliance. It has been parsed for readability.

Figure 12.27 Example Syslog Message

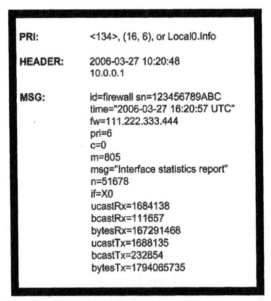

```
PRI:        <134>, (16, 6), or Local0.Info

HEADER:     2006-03-27 10:20:48
            10.0.0.1

MSG:        id=firewall sn=123456789ABC
            time="2006-03-27 16:20:57 UTC"
            fw=111.222.333.444
            pri=6
            c=0
            m=805
            msg="Interface statistics report"
            n=51678
            if=X0
            ucastRx=1684138
            bcastRx=111657
            bytesRx=167291468
            ucastTx=1688135
            bcastTx=232854
            bytesTx=1794065735
```

Now that you understand the basics of the Syslog protocol, you need to set up a Syslog server to receive messages. There are plenty of choices when it comes to choosing Syslog server software. Syslog is included with almost every version of UNIX-based operating systems. Freeware, shareware, and commercial software are available for Windows-based platforms. One of the more well-known Syslog server applications is Kiwi Syslog Daemon (www.kiwisyslog.com). There are two versions of Kiwi available: a limited freeware version and a fully featured registered version.

Figure 12.28 shows a snapshot of Kiwi receiving Syslog messages from a SonicWALL 3060 appliance.

Figure 12.28 Kiwi Syslog Screenshot

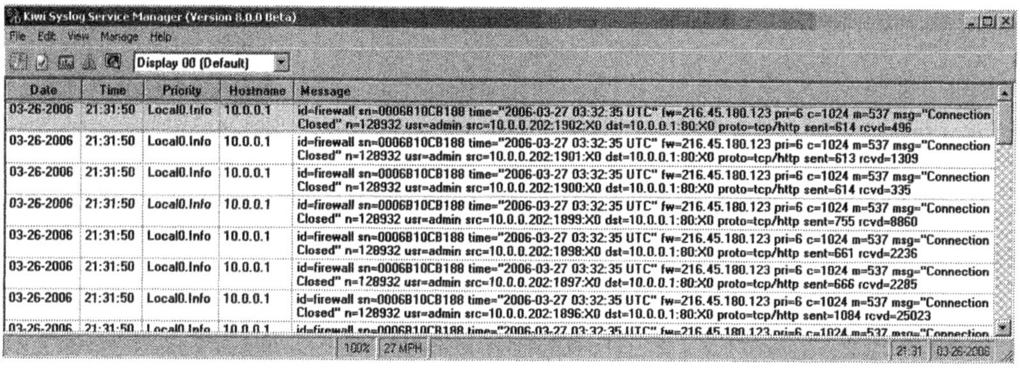

Kiwi displays Syslog entries in an easy-to-read format. Each entry listed will be in the form shown in Table 12.4.

Table 12.4 Kiwi Syslog Display Format

Item	Description
Date	The date the entry was received, in the format of MM-DD-YYYY
Time	The time the entry was received, in the format of HH:MM:SS
Priority	The level of urgency assigned to the entry. (See Table 4.x for info)
Hostname	The Hostname / IP address of the device that send the Syslog data
Message	Contains critical information regarding why the entry was created (See Table 4.x)

ViewPoint

SonicWALL ViewPoint is a stand-alone application that is specifically designed to receive the Syslog data from an appliance, analyze it, and produce graphical reports. For organizations that have only one SonicWALL appliance, ViewPoint is the way to go.

If your organization has multiple SonicWALL appliances, the Enterprise version of ViewPoint also includes the capability to manage the appliances from a single, central console. This product is called SonicWALL Global Management Server (SGMS) and is extremely powerful for multi-unit management and reporting. SGMS is discussed in detail in Chapter 13, "Enterprise SonicWALL Management."

Category

Multiple categories can be enabled to assist with monitoring, troubleshooting, and general SonicWALL maintenance. In SonicOS Standard, a number of categories can be enabled. SonicOS Enhanced provides more advanced logging capabilities and additional categories from which to choose.

The categories available in SonicOS Standard are listed in Table 12.5.

Table 12.5 SonicOS Standard Log Categories

802.11b Management	Legacy category
Attacks	Legacy category
Blocked Java Etc	Legacy category
Blocked Web Sites	Legacy category
Denied LAN IP	Legacy category
Dropped ICMP	Legacy category
Dropped TCP	Legacy category
Dropped UDP	Legacy category
Network Debug	Legacy category
System Errors	Legacy category
System Maintenance	Legacy category
User Activity	Legacy category
VPN Tunnel Status	Legacy category
WLAN IDS	WLAN IDS activity

The categories available in SonicOS Enhanced are listed in Table 12.6.

Table 12.6 SonicOS Enhanced Log Categories

Authenticated Access	Administrator, user, and guest account activity
BOOTP	BOOTP activity
Crypto Test	Crypto algorithm and hardware testing
DHCP Relay	DHCP central and remote gateway activity
DHCP Client	DHCP client protocol activity
DDNS	Dynamic DNS activity
Firewall Hardware	Firewall hardware error conditions

Continued

Table 12.6 continued SonicOS Enhanced Log Categories

Firewall Rule	Firewall rule modifications
PPP	Generic PPP activity
GMS	GMS status event
High Availability	High Availability activity
Firewall Event	Internal firewall activity
L2TP Client	L2TP client activity
L2TP Server	L2TP server activity
Intrusion Prevention	Logged events
Firewall Logging	Logging events and errors
Multicast	Multicast IGMP activity
Network Access	Network and firewall protocol access activity
Network	Network ARP, fragmentation, MTU activity
Network Traffic	Network traffic reporting events
PPP Dial-Up	PPP dial-up activity
PPPoE	PPPoE activity
PPTP	PPTP activity
Remote Authentication	RADIUS/LDAP server activity
RBL	Real-time Black List activity
RIP	RIP activity
Security Services	Security services activity
SonicPoint	SonicPoint activity
VOIP	VOIP H.323/RAS, H.323/H.225, H.323/H.245, activity
VPN	VPN activity
VPN Client	VPN Client activity
VPN IKE	VPN IKE activity
VPN IPSec	VPN IPSec activity
VPN PKI	VPN PKI activity
WAN Failover	WAN failover activity
Wireless	Wireless activity

Automation

The Log > Automation tab is used to configure mail settings that are used to send log files and alerts. An example of the Automation page is shown in Figure 12.29.

Figure 12.29 Log Automation Options

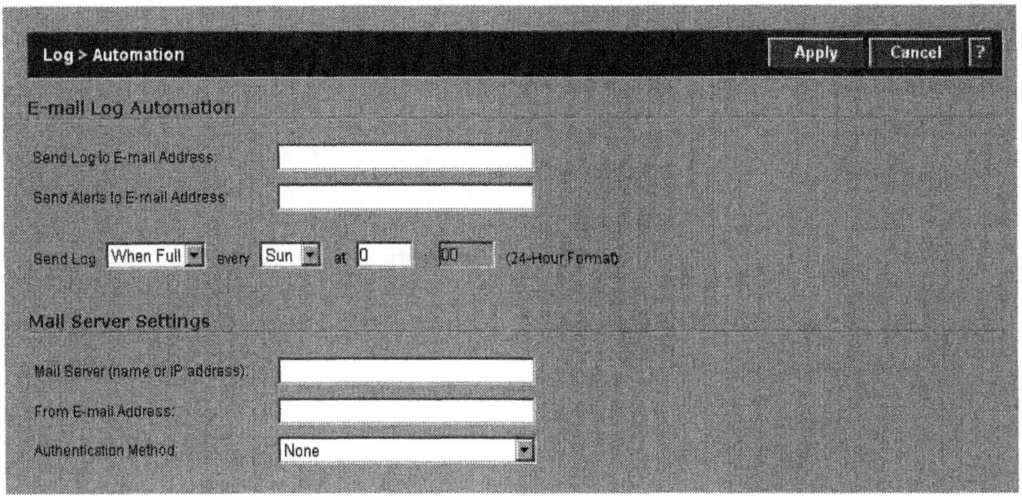

Two sections need to be configured for log automation to function properly. The first includes the following:

Send Log to Email Address: The destination address, usually the firewall administrator to whom the log files will be e-mailed.

Send Alerts to E-mail Address: The destination e-mail address to which alerts are sent. Alerts are e-mailed immediately after they occur.

Send Log schedule: The frequency in which log files are sent can be scheduled as follows:

■ Daily

■ Weekly

■ When Full

If you choose to set this option to Daily, you must specify the time that logs will be sent. When you set this option to Weekly, choose the date and time that logs will be sent. If you choose When Full, log files will be sent as soon as they are full.

The second section of the Log Automation is used to specify the Mail Server that logs will be sent through and the e-mail address they will be coming from. In other words, if the mail server on your LAN has the IP address 10.0.0.25 and you would like the e-mails to be sent from sonicwall@your_domain.com, you would simply enter this information into the Mail Server Settings fields. Figure 12.30 shows how our demo SonicWALL is configured.

Figure 12.30 Example Log > Automation Setup

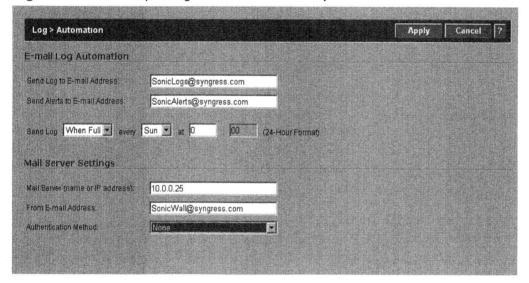

Authentication Method includes two options. In most configurations, this is set to None; however, if you would prefer to use POP, set this option to **POP Before SMTP**. After completing the configuration, click **Apply**.

Name Resolution

SonicWALL provides the capability to perform name resolution within the log entries. Caution should be used when enabling this functionality, as the SonicWALL will query DNS and attempt to resolve all IP addresses logged to their FQDN. The available options for Name Resolution are (Figure 12.31):

- None
- DNS
- NetBIOS
- DNS then NetBIOS

Figure 12.31 An Example of Enabling Name Resolution

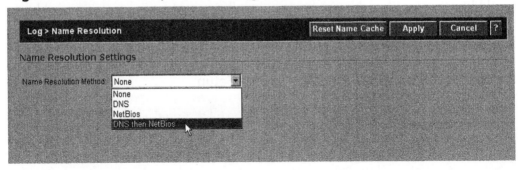

Reports

The SonicWALL appliance provides the capability to perform a rolling-analysis of the event logs. The reports that can be generated from this data include the top 25 Web sites visited, the top 25 IP addresses consuming the most bandwidth, and the top 25 services that are consuming the most bandwidth. This information can be used to tune the appliance's performance.

This feature should only be used to perform general troubleshooting, or for a quick snapshot of the activity on the network. You should not leave these options enabled on a permanent basis, as they will consume valuable memory and CPU resources on the appliance. Figure 12.32 shows an example of the options available for Data Collection reports.

Figure 12.32 Data Collection/Reports

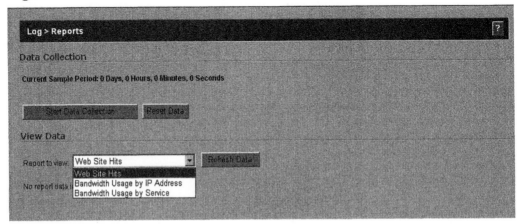

ViewPoint

ViewPoint provides dynamic, real-time, graphical, and historical reports regarding firewall activities. To enable ViewPoint reporting on your SonicWALL appliance, simply navigate to the **ViewPoint** tab under the **Log** options. Check **Enable ViewPoint Settings** under the **ViewPoint** tab and then add the **FQDN** or **IP address** of the **ViewPoint server**. We discuss ViewPoint in detail in Chapter 13.

Additional Tools

Other tools that can be used to help isolate network problems are Multi-Router Traffic Graphing (MRTG) and Getif.

MRTG is a freeware application available from http://people.ee.ethz.ch/~oetiker/webtools/mrtg/ that is used to monitor the traffic load on network links. For example, it can be used to monitor the load on a specific switch port, an uplink port, firewall interface, or router interface. The application uses SNMP to retrieve information from the monitored device and formats the information into graphical charts that are displayed in a Web browser. Figure 12.33 shows an example chart for traffic on a SonicWALL PRO 3060 appliance.

Figure 12.33 MRTG Example Graph

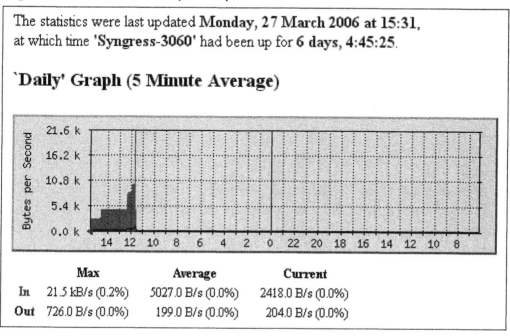

Getif is also a freeware tool (available at www.wtcs.org/snmp4tpc/getif.htm) and is used to retrieve information from SNMP enabled devices and display the information in a readable format. It can also be used to create graphs that illustrate the traffic conditions on specific interfaces. Figure 12.34 shows a screenshot of Getif listing the Interfaces on a SonicWALL PRO 3060 appliance.

Figure 12.34 Getif Listing Interfaces

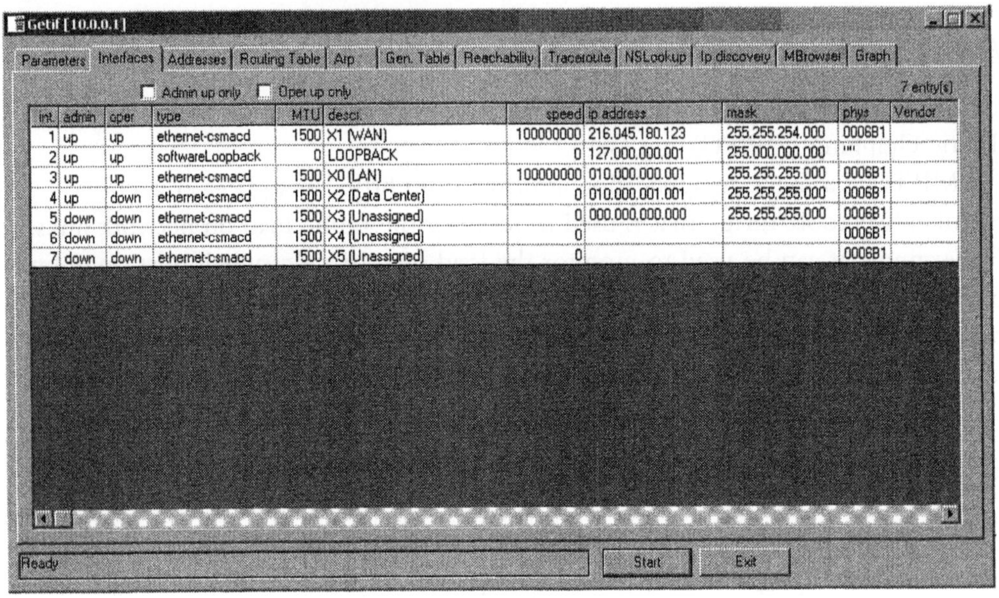

Getif [10.0.0.1]

Parameters | Interfaces | Addresses | Routing Table | Arp | Gen. Table | Reachability | Traceroute | NSLookup | Ip discovery | MBrowser | Graph

☐ Admin up only ☐ Oper up only   7 entry(s)

Int.	admin	oper	type	MTU	desci.	speed	ip address	mask	phys	Vendor
1	up	up	ethernet-csmacd	1500	X1 (WAN)	100000000	216.045.180.123	255.255.254.000	0006B1	
2	up	up	softwareLoopback	0	LOOPBACK	0	127.000.000.001	255.000.000.000		
3	up	up	ethernet-csmacd	1500	X0 (LAN)	100000000	010.000.000.001	255.255.255.000	0006B1	
4	up	down	ethernet-csmacd	1500	X2 (Data Center)	0	010.000.001.001	255.255.255.000	0006B1	
5	down	down	ethernet-csmacd	1500	X3 (Unassigned)	0	000.000.000.000	255.255.255.000	0006B1	
6	down	down	ethernet-csmacd	1500	X4 (Unassigned)	0			0006B1	
7	down	down	ethernet-csmacd	1500	X5 (Unassigned)	0			0006B1	

Ready   Start   Exit

Advanced Diagnostics

Before continuing, please beware that any changes made on the following pages could result in unintentional problems or failure of the SonicWALL. These options should only be changed when instructed to do so by SonicWALL Technical Support.

With that said, an undocumented diagnostics page on SonicWALL appliances contains additional features and diagnostic routines. SonicWALL does not and will not support these settings. To access the page, browse to http://lan-ip-address/diag.html, where lan-ip-address is the IP address of the LAN (X0) interface. This will display the Disclaimer page as shown in Figure 12.35.

Figure 12.35 Disclaimer

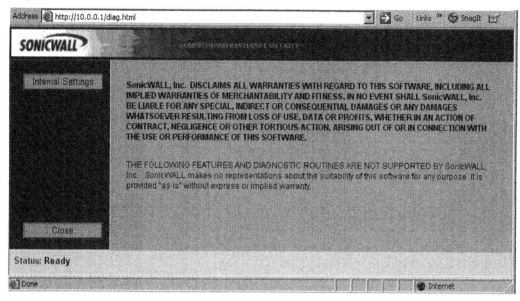

To view the settings available, click **Internal Settings**. The Internal Settings page will be displayed (Figures 12.36 through 12.40). We will not cover the purpose of the settings included on this page, but if you are like us, you want to know everything about every configurable option available on your firewall. While there is actually only a single page, multiple figures are used to help make the options easier to read.

Figure 12.36 Internal Settings (Part 1)

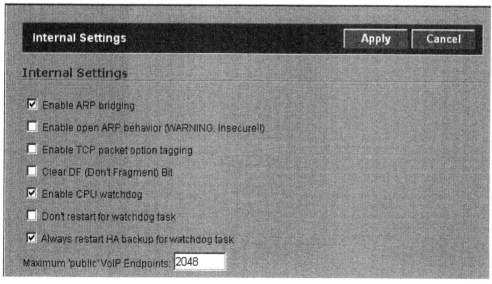

Figure 12.37 Internal Settings (Part 2)

☑ Enable inbound VPN hardware acceleration (if available)

☑ Enable outbound VPN hardware acceleration (if available)

☑ Enable Asymmetric algorithm (DH and RSA) hardware acceleration (if available)

☐ Do not adjust TCP MSS option for VPN traffic

☑ FTP bounce attack protection

☑ IP Spoof checking

☐ Override Default Route VPN for WAN HTTP(S) Management (Does not work if Apply NAT and Firewall Rules is enabled for this policy)

☐ Use Standby Management SA

☑ Allow SGMS to preempt a logged in administrator

Figure 12.38 Internal Settings (Part 3)

☑ Use interoperable IKE DH exchange

☐ Disable Gateway AV POP3 Auto Deletion

☐ Disable Gateway AV POP3 UIDL Rewriting

☐ Enable HTTP Byte-Range requests with Gateway AV

☐ Enable FTP 'REST' requests with Gateway AV

☐ Fragment VPN packets after applying ESP

☑ Allow LCP requests to PPPOE Server

☐ Log LCP Echo Requests and Replies between client and server

☑ Disconnect the PPPOE client if the server does not send traffic for `5` minutes

Figure 12.39 Internal Settings (Part 4)

☐ Disable SonicSetup/Setuptool Server

☑ Enforce Host Tag Search with for CFS

Online Help URL: `help.mysonicwall.com/help.asp`

Post authentication user redirect URL:

Minimum HTTP header length (0 to disable): `0`

More aggressive email filter filename scanning: ☑

Trace message level: `Warning ▼`

Figure 12.40 Internal Settings (Part 5)

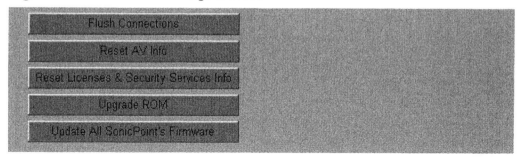

As you can see, there are numerous options, features, and diagnostic routines available on this page. However, changing any information should only be done if you *fully* understand the consequences.

Technical Support Report

The Technical Support Report (commonly referred to as the TSR) is used to generate a text-based report containing configuration and diagnostic information for the SonicWALL. If you have ever contacted SonicWALL Technical Support, you know that they will ask for the serial number and a copy of the TSR (in that order). Four optional check boxes are used to include or exclude information from the report

- VPN Keys
- ARP Cache
- DHCP Bindings
- IKE Info

Checking these options will include the relevant information in the report. Figure 12.41 shows the options and command button used to create the TSR.

Figure 12.41 Technical Support Report

It is recommended that you download a copy of the report from your SonicWALL and review the information that it contains. Figure 12.42 shows the type of information you can expect to find.

Figure 12.42 Technical Support Report Contents

```
   Valid Packets:                     2466510
   Connections Opened:                65009
   Connections Closed:                59158
   Connections Refused:               0
   Connections Aborted:               5923
   Connection Handshake Errors:       0
   SYN Flood Current Events:          0
   SYN Flood Total Events:            0
   Invalid SYN Flood Cookies:         0
   Max Incomplete Connections:        6
   Total Incomplete Connections:      421
   Average Incomplete Conn. Samples:  529
   Blacklisted Current Events:        0
   Blacklisted Total Events:          0
   Blacklisted Packets:               0


SYN Flood Protection:

   SYN-Proxy Mode:                    Never Proxy
   SYN-Proxy SACK Enabled:            Off
   SYN-Proxy Threshold:               300
   SYN-Proxy Override MSS:            Off
   SYN-Proxy Manual MSS:              1460
   SYN-Blacklisting:                  Off
   SYN-Blacklist Threshold:           1000
   Never Blacklist WAN Machine:       Off
   Never Blacklist SW Mgmt Traffic:   Off




-------------------------inetstatShow------------------------------------
Active Internet connections (including servers)
PCB        Proto Recv-Q Send-Q  Local Address      Foreign Address     (state)
--------   ----- ------ ------  ----------------   -----------------   -------
eef666c    TCP      0     7156  10.0.0.1.80        10.0.0.202.2573     ESTABLISHED
eef6144    TCP      0        0  10.0.0.1.80        10.0.0.202.2572     TIME_WAIT
eef62d0    TCP      0        0  0.0.0.0.443        0.0.0.0.0           LISTEN
eef624c    TCP      0        0  0.0.0.0.80         0.0.0.0.0           LISTEN
```

SonicWALL LED Behavior

One question commonly asked by SonicWALL firewall administrators is, "what does the Alert LED mean?" To help explain the different behaviors of the Alert and Test LEDs, refer to Table 12.6.

Table 12.6 SonicWALL LED Behavior for PRO 3060 / 4060 Appliances

Event	Power LED	Test LED	Alarm LED
ROM	Green	Yellow	Off
Reset Switch Sensed	Green	Red Blinking	Red Blinking
Safemode (Entered)	Green	Red	Off
Firmware (Loading)	Green	Yellow	Yellow Blinking
System (Up / Normal)	Green	Off	Yellow
Minor Alarm	Green	Off	Yellow Blinking
Major Alarm	Green	Off	Red Blinking
Voltage Askew	Green	Red Blinking	Off
Fan Failure	Green	Off	Red
Thermal Yellow	Green	Yellow	Red
Thermal Red	Green	Red	Red
Thermal Shutdown	Off	Off	Off

Power (Green)	Yellow Blinking	
Yellow - Solid	Red Blinking	
Red - Solid	Off	

Summary

In this chapter, we covered various ways to troubleshoot network traffic passing through the SonicWALL appliance. We discussed the various tools at our disposal and tips for troubleshooting different functions available through SonicOS.

Several troubleshooting tools are built in to SonicOS:

- **Ping** To test connectivity.

- **Traceroute** To find the path a packet takes through a network.

- **Packet Trace** To capture and analyze packet contents as they traverse the SonicWALL.

- **Find Network Path** To identify potential routing misconfigurations on the LAN.

The SonicWALL firewall provides comprehensive logging capabilities. SonicWALL owners have the ability to customize the type of events that the appliance logs, the ability to send logs and alerts to specific e-mail addresses, and the option of forwarding all connections crossing the firewall to up to three external Syslog servers.

ViewPoint is a stand-alone Syslog server that is designed to gather Syslog data from a SonicWALL appliance and generate dynamic, real-time, and historical reports detailing the activity of the traffic that traverses the SonicWALL.

Solutions Fast Track

Troubleshooting Methodology

☑ Many firewall issues may actually be internal routing issues. Follow your packets from your computer through the internal network hubs, switches, and routers. It may be a good idea to sniff the traffic just outside your firewall to see what the packets look like before they get to the firewall.

☑ There are seven steps to follow when troubleshooting issues.

☑ The seven steps of the troubleshooting methodology will help you describe the problem and the environment in which the problem occurs; determine the location of the problem, identify the problem; and solve it; test your solution; and document what changes are made to the network infrastructure.

Troubleshooting Tools

☑ Each SonicWALL tool has a specific purpose and should fulfill any troubleshooting need you have relating to the firewall.

☑ To truly understand what the information gathered from the Packet Trace tool means, you need to understand the three-way handshake.

☑ The Address Resolution Protocol (ARP) table of the SonicWALL appliance can be viewed by clicking **Network** and then clicking **ARP**.

Network Troubleshooting

☑ A couple of simple tests will help you isolate communication problems.

☑ One of the most common problems experienced with firewalls is incorrect routing. If you are unable to identify where packets are going, use the Packet Trace utility or a packet sniffer such as Ethereal.

☑ The SonicWALL will log all traffic that is blocked by the firewall. Check the log file for entries pertaining to the problem traffic.

SonicWALL Logs

☑ The SonicWALL log is a vital tool that is used to monitor potential security threats, system maintenance notices, system errors, VPN tunnel statistics, and VPN errors.

☑ Keep in mind that if the SonicWALL loses power, the log files will be cleared, which brings up the importance of using a second device to record the log information generated by the SonicWALL.

☑ Using a Syslog server ensures that all log entries will be stored and retained regardless of whether the SonicWALL is power cycled.

Advanced Diagnostic Routines

☑ The Technical Support Report (commonly referred to as the TSR) is used to generate a text-based report containing configuration and diagnostic information for the SonicWALL.

☑ Four optional check boxes (VPN Keys, ARP Cache, DHCP Bindings, and IKE Info) are used to include or exclude information from the Technical Support Report.

Frequently Asked Questions

The following Frequently Asked Questions, answered by the authors of this book, are designed to both measure your understanding of the concepts presented in this chapter and to assist you with real-life implementation of these concepts. To have your questions about this chapter answered by the author, browse to **www.syngress.com/solutions** and click on the **"Ask the Author"** form.

Q: I cannot ping the SonicWALL from my PC. Did I do something wrong?

A: Not necessarily. The SonicWALL, like other firewalls, can be configured to not respond to ping requests from clients, but by default this is blocked. To enable ping on a specific interface, choose the check box next **to Ping on the Network → Interface → Edit Interface** page.

Q: Someone told me that WinPcap drivers need to be downloaded and installed before Ethereal will work on Windows platforms. Is this true?

A: No, the latest release of Ethereal includes the WinPcap drivers and does not need to be downloaded. Ethereal will install this for you automatically.

Q: Can I configure the SonicWALL to forward Syslog messages to multiple servers?

A: Yes, you can configure multiple Syslog and SNMP servers on SonicWALL appliances.

Q: I installed a new Internet router that was preconfigured with the same IP and subnet mask of the old unit to facilitate a quick swap, but now I can no longer get to the Internet. Why?

A: The most probable cause is ARP. The hardware and IP addresses of each device on the network are used by switches, routers, firewalls, and other network equipment. The ARP Cache on such equipment contains a list of devices with their matching hardware and IP addresses. When the new router was plugged into the network, the IP address was the same as the old unit; however, the MAC address was different. When devices attempt to communicate with each other, they are ultimately using the MAC address, and therefore the problem arises. The ARP Cache of all devices that communicate with the Internet router (in this case, the SonicWALL) needs to be cleared. If this problem occurred on the LAN, then all switches, servers, PCs, or routers and the SonicWALL will need to have their ARP Cache flushed, be rebooted, or suffer until the entries in the cache expire.

Q: I noticed that my WAN interface auto-negotiated 10 Mbps at half duplex with the router. To increase performance, the interface was forced to 100 Mbps full duplex. I can no longer reach the Internet, what's going on?

A: Before forcing an interface to a specific speed and/or duplex, you need to check a couple of things. The first is to make sure that the device connected to that interface can indeed support the new settings. Second, the speed and/or duplex must be forced on both ends of the connection. The problem is almost certainly that the Internet router only supports 10 Mbps at half duplex, especially if it is an older model. Set the SonicWALL's WAN interface back to auto-negotiate and everything should function normally. If the problem persists, reboot both the SonicWALL and the Internet router.

Q: My network security was compromised, and upper management determined the best course of action would be to simply turn off the SonicWALL to isolate our LAN. We are now trying to determine how the compromise occurred by looking at the SonicWALL logs; however, the only log entries present are from the time the SonicWALL was powered back on. Where did the logs go?

A: This is a common question. All log and alert entries are stored in memory on the SonicWALL. If the appliance loses power, the logs and alerts are cleared. This stresses the point of using SonicWALL ViewPoint, a third-party Syslog server, or better yet, *both*, to record all activity on the SonicWALL appliance.

Q: My SonicWALL was rebooting itself every 20 minutes. The unit was replaced, but the new unit continues to do the same thing. What's wrong?

A: The next time the unit reboots, wait a few minutes and then export the Active Connections to a CSV file. Open the CSV file and sort it by Source IP Address. Look through the entries and identify any device with an abnormal amount of connections open. Also, look at the port numbers the connections are using. The problem is most likely a rapidly spreading worm or some other piece of malware. The infected devices will open hundreds or in some cases thousands of connections through the SonicWALL and eventually exhaust the connection cache. At this point, the SonicWALL will reboot, which will clear the connections. This particular situation can occur in networks where limited or no control over end-user devices exists; for example, the inability to enforce anti-virus, anti-spyware, and other security controls. To help reduce the impact of situations such as this, refer to the Security Services available for SonicWALL appliances, which are covered in Chapter 9, "Attack Detection and Defense." The use of these tools will greatly reduce the impact of such problems.

Q: The Alert LED is flashing on a regular basis. What does this mean?

A: The Alert LED will flash once for each log entry that is classified as an Alert. The best way to determine what is causing the LED to flash is to review the Syslog information and look for entries.

Chapter 13

Enterprise SonicWALL Management

Solutions in this chapter:

- SonicWALL Management and Reporting
- SonicWALL Global Management System Installation and Configuration

☑ Summary

☑ Solutions Fast Track

☑ Frequently Asked Questions

SonicWALL Management and Reporting

SonicWALL provides comprehensive reporting and management solutions for SonicWALL appliances. SonicWALL ViewPoint is a stand-alone solution for gathering Syslog data and generating comprehensive graphical reports for individual SonicWALL appliances. SonicWALL Global Management System (SGMS) is an enterprise management and reporting solution capable of managing thousands of appliances. We discuss each of these solutions throughout this chapter, beginning with SonicWALL ViewPoint.

SonicWALL ViewPoint

SonicWALL ViewPoint is a comprehensive reporting solution for single SonicWALL appliances. The SonicWALL appliance is configured to send its Syslog data to the ViewPoint server's Syslog server. This data is then parsed and formatted for display. Reports can be customized and scheduled by the administrator.

SonicWALL ViewPoint Server System Requirements are:

- Microsoft Windows 2000 or Windows XP Professional Service Pack 2
- 750MHz processor
- 512MB RAM
- 85MB free hard drive space

Installation

Follow these steps to install the SonicWALL ViewPoint server software:

1. Log in as administrator and double-click the **setup.exe** icon. The Introduction screen will appear as shown in Figure 13.1.

Figure 13.1 ViewPoint Introduction

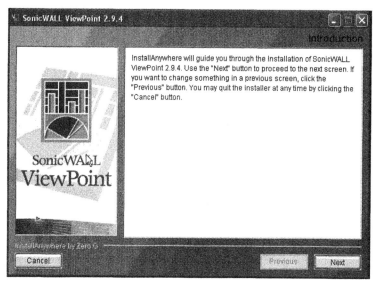

Click **Next** to continue the installation. The License Agreement window will appear as shown in Figure 13.2

Figure 13.2 License Agreement

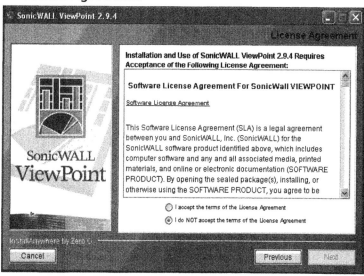

Click the radio button next to **I accept the terms of the License Agreement**. Click **Next** to proceed. The **Choose Install Folder** will appear (Figure 13.3).

Figure 13.3 The Choose Install Folder

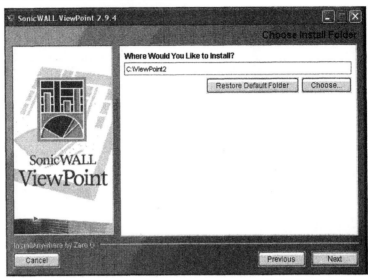

Choose the default install path or click the **Choose...** button to select a different path. Once you have configured the path, click **Next**. The SonicWALL GMS Settings window will appear as shown in Figure 13.4.

Figure 13.4 SonicWALL GMS Settings

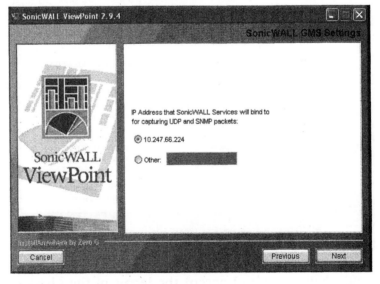

Select the radio button next to the IP address of the ViewPoint server. The IP address is used to bind the SonicWALL services to for capturing UDP and SNMP packets. After selecting the IP address, click **Next** to continue. The SonicWALL ViewPoint 2.9.4 Settings window will appear (Figure 13.5).

Figure 13.5 ViewPoint Settings

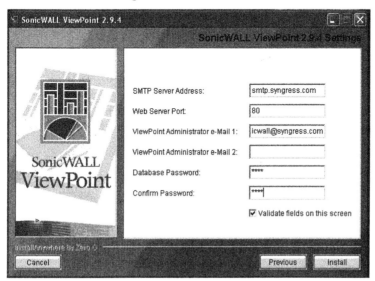

Enter the appropriate information for the SMTP Server Address, Web Server Port, Notification E-Mail Addresses, and the Database Password to use. The **Validate fields on this screen** option is used to ensure that the information entered into the fields is accurate. If the SMTP server, Web server port, or SGMS administrator e-mail addresses are undecided, make sure to clear the check box next to **Validate fields on this screen** before clicking the **Install** button. After ViewPoint is installed, the administrator can change the value of these fields. After setting the appropriate values, click **Next**. The Installing SonicWALL ViewPoint 2.9.4 status window will appear as shown in Figure 13.6.

Figure 13.6 Installation Status

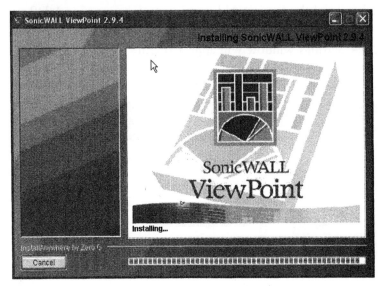

Once Phase 1 of the installation is completed, the Phase 2 Installer Launch window will appear as shown in Figure 13.7.

Figure 13.7 Phase 2 Installer Launch

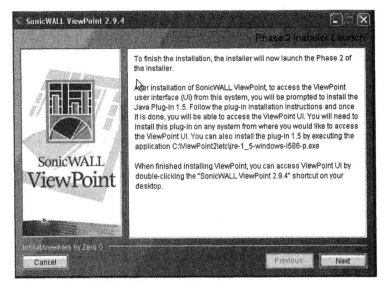

Click **Next** to begin Phase 2 of the installation process. A dialog box will appear that requires the administrator to click **OK** before continuing with the database configuration (Figure 13.8).

Figure 13.8 Phase 2 Installation

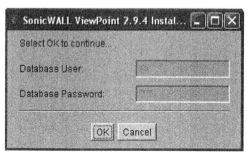

Click **OK** to continue the database configuration. After a successful installation, a dialog box will appear (Figure 13.9).

Figure 13.9 Installation Complete

Click **OK** to complete the installation process. The Install Complete window will appear as shown in Figure 13.10.

Figure 13.10 Install Complete Dialog

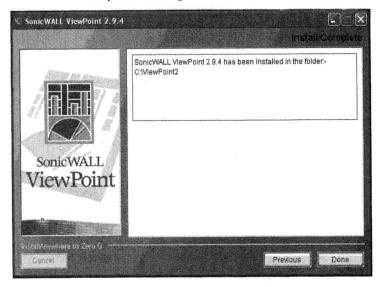

Click **Done** to end the installation wizard. Reboot the server after completing the installation.

Configuring ViewPoint

Double-click the **ViewPoint** icon on your desktop to display the ViewPoint Login screen (Figure 13.11).

Figure 13.11 ViewPoint Login Screen

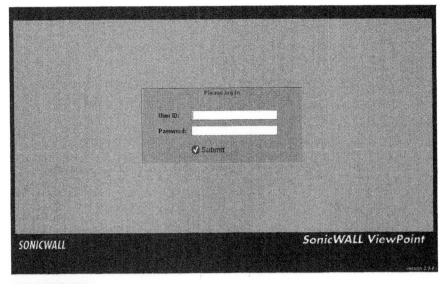

The default username is **admin** and the password is **password**. Enter the **User ID:** and **Password:** and then click the **Submit** button to log in. The Reports Panel will appear as shown in Figure 13.12.

Figure 13.12 The Reports Panel

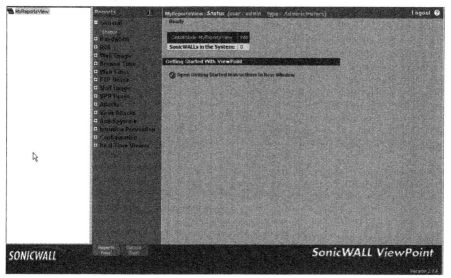

The Reports Panel is used to view Syslog data gathered from the appliance in a graphical format. The data for each of the report categories is based on historical data that has been summarized by ViewPoint. This panel also allows administrators the capability to view the Status of ViewPoint, schedule automatic reports that will be e-mailed, and view Real-Time Syslog data as it is gathered from the appliance.

The Console Panel is used to configure specific ViewPoint settings (Figure 13.13).

Figure 13.13 The Console Panel

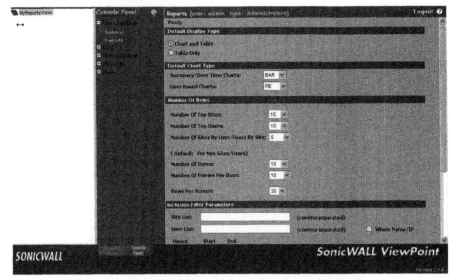

SonicWALL Global Management System Installation and Configuration

SGMS can be installed on a single server as a stand-alone product or across multiple servers to provide scalability and redundancy. The software can be installed either on a Solaris- or Windows-based server. The following operating systems are supported:

- Solaris 8
- Windows 2000
- Windows XP Professional
- Windows 2003 Server

Database Requirements

SGMS uses a database to store information about the application and the appliances it manages and monitors. The supported database platforms are:

- Oracle version 9.2.0.1
- Microsoft SQL Server 2000 with Service Pack 3 or later

Java Database Connectivity Driver

SGMS requires the use of a Java database connectivity driver (JDBC) to communicate with the database. When using Oracle as the database for SGMS, the driver is provided by the Oracle database automatically. For Windows SQL Server, SonicWALL provides the Sprinta™ 2000 JDBC driver.

Secure Communications Link

Communications between SGMS and the managed appliances use IPSec VPN tunnels. The SGMS Gateway appliance can be any VPN-enabled SonicWALL appliance; however, it is recommended that a PRO 3060 or 4060 be used.

Supported SonicWALL Appliances

The following SonicWALL appliances are supported by SGMS:

- SonicWALL TELE2/3
- TELE3 TZ, TZX, and TELE3 SP
- TZ 170, TZ 170W, and TZ 170 SP
- SOHO2/3
- XPRS and XPRS2
- PRO Series
- GX Series

Firmware Requirements

All managed SonicWALL appliances, and the SGMS Gateway appliance, must have Firmware version 6.3.1 or later installed. Earlier versions of Firmware are not supported by SGMS.

Hardware Requirements

The minimum hardware requirements for the SGMS database server are:

- 750 MHz processor
- 512MB RAM
- 80GB free hard drive space

The minimum hardware requirements for installing the SGMS Server on Windows platforms are:

- Windows 2000 Service Pack 3, Windows 2000 Professional, Windows XP Professional or Windows 2003 Server

- Microsoft Internet Explorer 6.*x* or Netscape 4.7

- 1.2 GHz processor

- 1GB RAM

- 85MB free hard drive space

The minimum hardware requirements for installing the SGMS Server on Solaris platforms are:

- Solaris 8 (English operating system) running on a SPARC hardware platform

- Netscape 4.7

- 650 MHz processor

- 1GB RAM

- Two 40GB hard drives

Network Requirements

- SGMS Server must have direct access to the Internet.

- SGMS Server must have a static IP address.

- The network connection must be able to support 1KB of bandwidth per managed appliance.

SQL Server Setup

Prior to installing SGMS, complete the following setup procedure for Microsoft SQL Server:

1. Insert the Microsoft SQL CD-ROM. The SQL Splash Screen window will appear (Figure 13.14).

Figure 13.14 SQL Server 2000 Splash Screen

2. Select **SQL Server 2000 Components**. The Install Components window will appear (Figure 13.15).

Figure 13.15 The Install Components Window

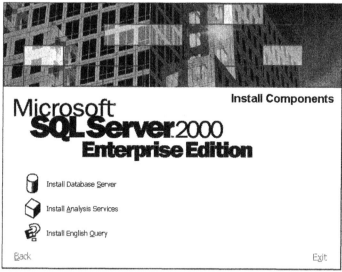

3. Choose the **Install Database Server** option. The Welcome window will appear (Figure 13.16).

Figure 13.16 SQL Server Welcome Window

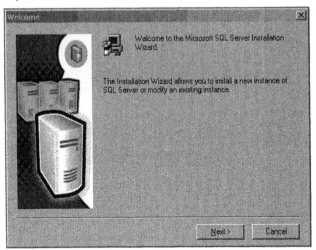

4. Click **Next**. The Computer Name window will appear. Choose **Local Computer** (Figure 13.17).

Figure 13.17 The Computer Name Window

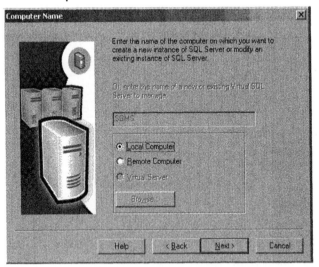

5. Click **Next** to see the Installation Selection options (Figure 13.18).

Figure 13.18 The Installation Selection Window

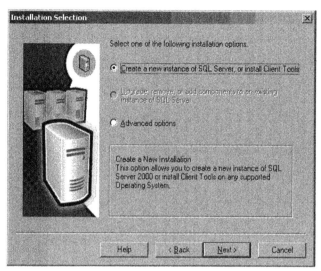

6. Choose **Create a new instance of SQL Server, or install Client Tools,** and then click **Next**. The User Information window will appear (Figure 13.19).

Figure 13.19 The User Information Window

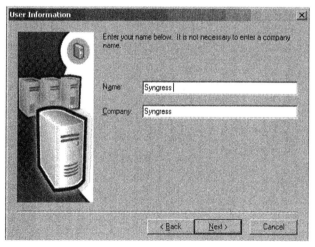

7. Enter the appropriate information in the Name and Company fields, and then click **Next** to continue the installation. After clicking **Next,** the License Agreement page will appear (Figure 13.20).

Figure 13.20 The Software License Agreement Window

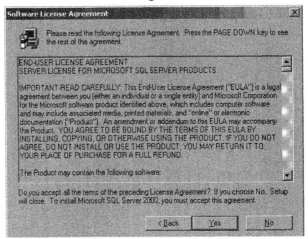

8. Click **Yes** to accept the license agreement. The Installation Definition window will appear (Figure 13.21).

Figure 13.21 The Installation Definition Window

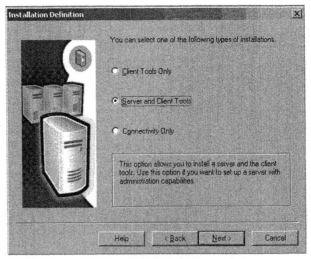

9. Choose **Server and Client Tools** and click **Next** to continue the installation. The Instance Name window will appear (Figure 13.22).

Figure 13.22 The Instance Name Window

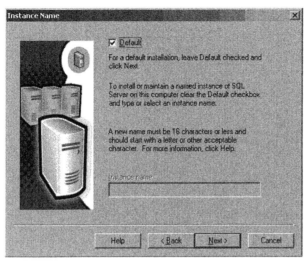

10. For new installations, leave the **Default** option checked and click **Next** to continue. The Setup Type window appears (Figure 13.23).

Figure 13.23 The Setup Type Window

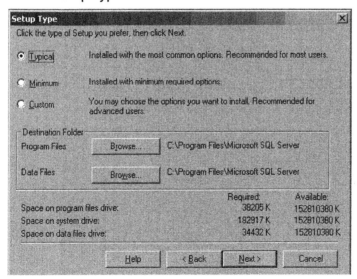

11. Select **Typical** from the available options and click **Next** to continue. You will now be prompted to enter the **Service Accounts** information as shown in Figure 13.24.

Figure 13.24 The Service Accounts Window

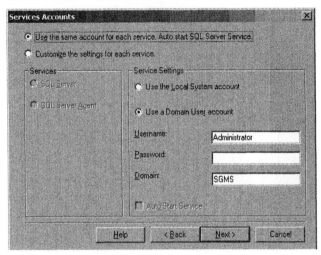

12. Enter the **username, password,** and **domain name** the Service Accounts will use. Click **Next** to continue the installation. The Authentication Mode window will appear (Figure 13.25).

Figure 13.25 The Authentication Mode Window

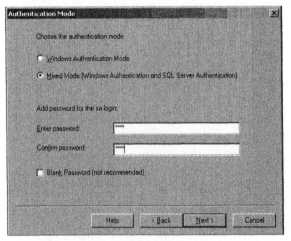

13. *Do not* choose Windows Authentication Mode. Make sure **Mixed Mode** is selected and enter the password for the sa login account. Click **Next.** The Start Copying Files window will appear (Figure 13.26).

Figure 13.26 The Start Copying Files Window

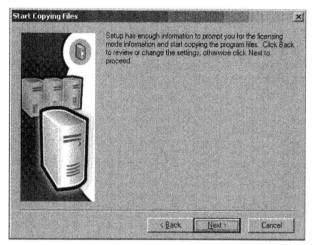

14. Click **Next** to continue. You must now choose the **Licensing Mode** as shown in Figure 13.27.

Figure 13.27 The Choose Licensing Mode Window

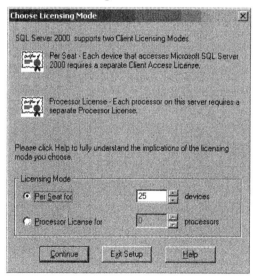

15. Choose the appropriate option for your SQL Licensing Mode, enter the number of devices or processors, and then click **Continue.** After successfully installing SQL, the Setup Complete window will appear as shown in Figure 13.28.

Figure 13.28 The Setup Complete Window

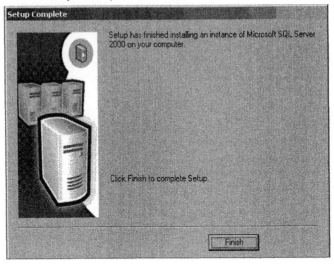

16. Click **Finish**.

After the installation of SQL Server is complete, click **Start | Programs**, and select **Enterprise Manager** from the list. Within Enterprise Manager, perform the following steps:

1. Expand the Tree View on the left side of the Enterprise Manager window. An example of the tree view is shown in Figure 13.29.

Figure 13.29 Tree View Example

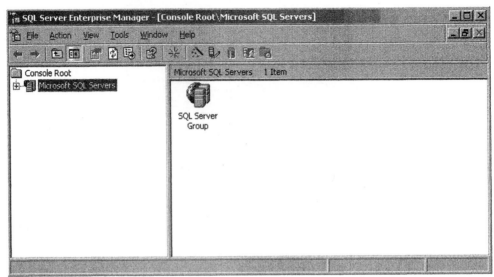

The expanded view is shown in Figure 13.30.

Figure 13.30 Expanded Tree View Example

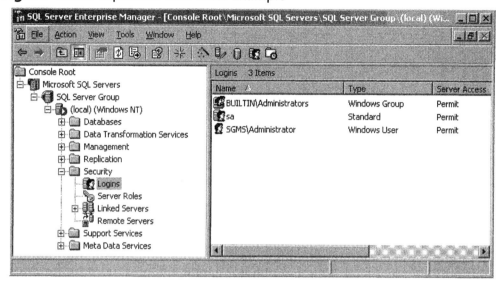

2. Right click the **Logins** icon and select **New Login** from the menu. The New Login screen will appear (Figure 13.31).

Figure 13.31 The New Login Screen

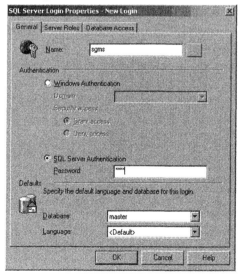

3. Enter the Login Name to create and select **SQL Server Authentication** from the Authentication section. Leave the Defaults section at its default settings. Click the **Server Roles** tab to see the Server Role options (Figure 13.32).

Figure 13.32 Server Roles Options

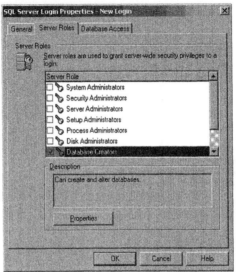

4. Check the **Database Creators** check box and then click **OK.** The Confirm Password dialog will appear (Figure 13.33).

Figure 13.33 The Confirm Password Window

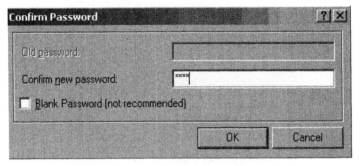

5. Retype the password and click **OK.**
6. Close Enterprise Manager.

Java Database Connectivity (JDBC) Driver

With the database server software installed and configured with the SGMS login user account, you now need to install the JDBC driver on the SGMS server. To do so:

- For Oracle, install the Oracle Client on each SGMS server that will be used. If this is a stand-alone installation, this will be installed on a single server.

- For Microsoft SQL Server 2000 or 2003, SGMS will install the Sprinta™ 2000 JDBC driver automatically.

Stand-Alone SGMS Installation

Before installing the SGMS software, administrators must determine what type of installation will be used, stand-alone or distributed. Typically, smaller organizations will choose the stand-alone installation and use a single server to manage the appliances. The downside to stand-alone implementations is the lack of firewall management redundancy and load balancing options for the managed appliances. These features are available only for distributed installations.

NOTE

While you can use a single server for both SGMS and the underlying database software, it is highly recommended to install the database on a separate server.

SGMS installation consists of two phases. The first phase installs the SGMS software on the server, and the second is used to set up the database, install SGMS services, and install the JDBC Sprinta™ driver. For a stand-alone installation, follow the steps in the next section. If you plan to use the distributed installation, see the distributed installation procedures.

Stand-Alone Installation

To install SGMS as a stand-alone, single-server solution:

1. Log in to the SGMS server as Administrator.

2. Insert the SGMS CD-ROM or browse to the location where you downloaded the SGMS software.

    ■ If you are using a CD-ROM, the installation screen will appear automatically if you have Autorun enabled.

    ■ If you downloaded SGMS, browse to the location where you saved the file and double-click **sgms.exe** to begin the installation.

    ■ For Solaris, run **sgms.bin**.

3. On the Introduction screen, click **Next** (Figure 13.34).

Figure 13.34 SGMS Introduction Screen

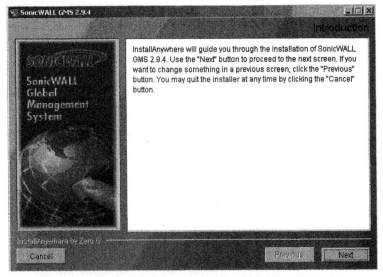

4. Read the License Agreement (Figure 13.35) and choose **I accept the terms of the License Agreement** to continue, or **I do NOT accept the terms of the License Agreement** to exit the installation.

Figure 13.35 SGMS License Agreement Screen

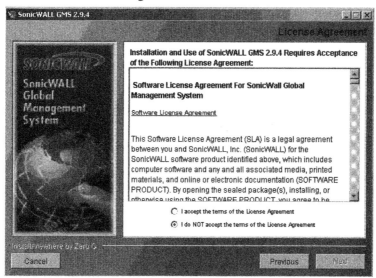

5. Read the information in the Important Database Information window (Figure 13.36), and then click **Next** to continue the installation.

Figure 13.36 Important Database Information Window

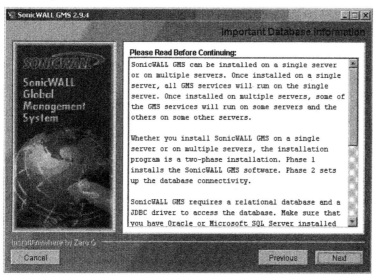

6. The Choose Install Folder window (Figure 13.37) allows you to modify the default installation path of SGMS. It is recommended to use the default path of **C:\SGMS2**. To change this location, click the **Choose** button and

browse to the folder you would like to use, or simply delete the default install path and type the location in the field. After selecting the location to use, click **Next**.

Figure 13.37 The Choose Install Folder Window

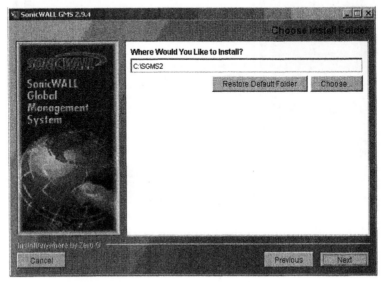

7. The next screen to appear is the SonicWALL GMS Installation Options window (Figure 13.38). There are two options available:

   ■ Install GMS Console System

   ■ Install SGMS Agent System

8. Choose **Install GMS Console System** and then click **Next** to continue.

Figure 13.38 SonicWALL GMS Installation Options Window

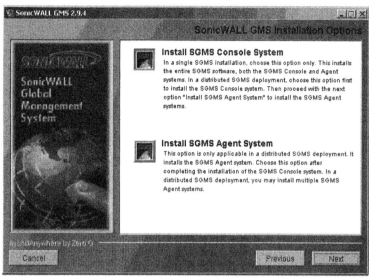

9. The SonicWALL GMS Console Options window appears (Figure 13.39). The option to **Disable Agent Installation** is only checked when performing the distributed installation. For stand-alone implementations, this should *not* be checked. Make sure it is not checked and then click **Next** to continue the installation process.

Figure 13.39 SonicWALL GMS Console Options Window

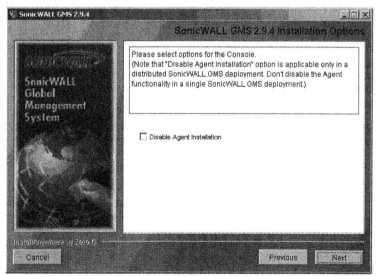

10. The SonicWALL GMS Settings window will appear. The settings on this page are used to specify critical information that will be used by SGMS, and include:

- **SMTP Server Address:** The IP address or name of the SMTP server that will be used to send e-mail alerts and reports from within SGMS. This is typically the production mail server; however, you can configure the Windows SMTP server to relay e-mail for this purpose.

- **Web Server Port:** The TCP port number that will be bound to the SGMS Tomcat Web server. If IIS is installed, it will already be bound to port 80, which is the registered port for HTTP. For SGMS to function properly, you must either change the SGMS Web server port or change the IIS HTTP port to eliminate the conflict. It is recommended that the IIS Web server be changed and SGMS be configured to use port 80 for its Web server.

- **SGMS Administrator e-Mail 1:** Enter the e-mail address for the user or distribution list that will receive alerts and notifications from the SGMS server.

- **SGMS Administrator e-Mail 2:** Enter a second e-mail address or distribution group to which e-mail alerts and notifications will be sent.

- **SGMS Gateway IP Address:** The IP address of the SonicWALL appliance that will be used as the SGMS Gateway device.

- **SGSM Gateway Password:** Enter the password for the SGMS Gateway appliance.

- **Validate fields on this screen:** This option instructs SGMS to validate each field on this screen before continuing with the installation. This ensures that information has been entered for each field and is in proper syntax.

The **SonicWALL GMS Settings** window will appear (Figure 13.40).

Figure 13.40 The SonicWALL GMS Settings Window

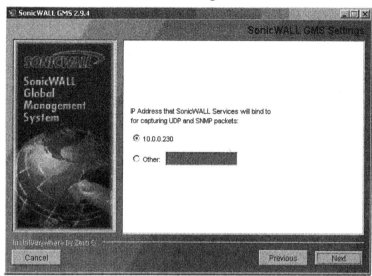

Select the IP address the SGMS services will bind to for capturing UDP and SNMP packets. Typically, this will be left at the default setting, which is the local server's IP address. Click **Next**. A second SGMS Settings page will appear, as shown in Figure 13.41.

Figure 13.41 SonicWALL GMS Settings Window

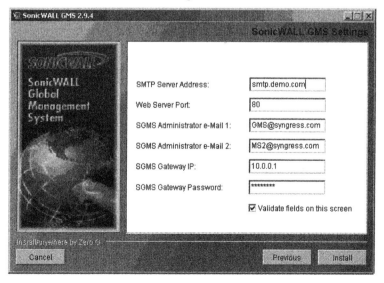

Tools & Traps…

SGMS Notification Best Practices

The SGMS Administrator E-mail address fields are used to send notifications regarding the status of SGMS and the appliances under its management. Depending on the number of appliances you are managing, a large number of e-mails may be sent. To efficiently manage the notifications sent from SGMS, you should create a mailbox specifically for this purpose. In other words, create a new mailbox named SGMS, for example. Administrators will then be granted access to this mailbox and can view the mailbox using their mail client software. This will ensure that SGMS notifications and administrators e-mail are separate from one another.

Tools & Traps…

SGMS Gateway Best Practices

The SGMS Gateway appliance is used as the communications link between the SGMS server and the managed appliances. While this device can technically be the same as the production firewall appliance, it is highly recommended that it be a dedicated appliance and, if possible, have its own Internet connection to eliminate the management overhead from the production network. It also allows you to manage the corporate production SonicWALL appliance and isolates the production network from the management traffic overhead. This ensures that mission-critical servers and services do not compete with the SonicWALL management and monitoring traffic, thus increasing performance for both.

Once you have entered the appropriate information for each field, make sure **Validate fields on this screen** is enabled and click **Next** to continue the installation process. If any errors are found with your configuration at this point, you will be prompted to fix them before the installation will continue.

If everything is okay with the configuration to this point, the Installation Status screen will appear as SGMS installs the software on your server. At this point, Phase 1 of the installation is complete and Phase 2 will begin.

As mentioned previously, SGMS is installed in two phases. Phase 1 installs the SGMS software on the server, and Phase 2 will set up the database, install SGMS services, and install the JDBC Sprinta™ 2000 driver. Upon completion of Phase 1, the Phase 2 Installer Launch window appears (Figure 13.42). Follow these steps to complete Phase 2 of the SGMS installation.

1. Click **Next** in the **Phase 2 Installer Launch** window to proceed with the installation.

Figure 13.42 The Phase 2 Installer Launch Window

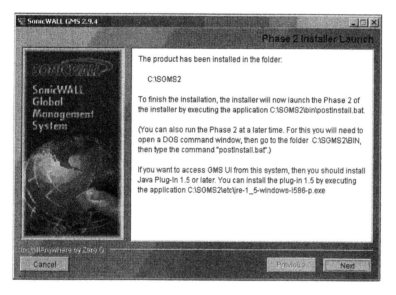

2. The Database Settings dialog box will appear with the following configuration fields (Figure 13.43):

■ **Database Vendor:** Choose the database software you plan to use, SQL or Oracle.

■ **Database Host/IP:** Enter the IP address of the database server. If the database server is installed on the same server as the SGMS server, enter **127.0.0.1**.

- **JDBC Driver:** Typically, you will accept the default entry for this field. For Oracle databases, append the IP address and port for the Oracle thin driver. Example: jdbc:oracle:thin:@ip_address:port.

- **JDBC URL:** For SQL, accept the default entry for this field. For Oracle, enter the SID in the TSN Name field.

- **Database User:** Enter the database username; for example, SGMS.

- **Database Password:** Enter the password for the database user.

3. Enter the appropriate information and click **OK** to complete Phase 2 of the installation.

Figure 13.43 The Database Settings Dialog

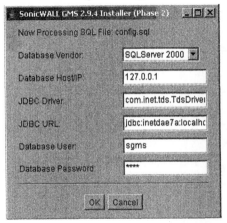

4. Restart the SGMS server.

Distributed Reporting

In larger environments, where many SonicWALL appliances are being managed, the amount of data sent to the SGMS server from managed appliances can be substantial. To offload the burden of processing report-related data, a separate server can be installed specifically for reporting capabilities. This feature is available only for SonicWALL appliances that are managed by SGMS via HTTPS.

SGMS supports two types of distributed reporting servers:

- **Summarization Only**: This option can be used with any of the management protocols supported by SGMS—HTTPS, IPSec VPN Management Tunnel, or an existing VPN tunnel. Agent servers collect Syslog data and then write the data to a mapped network drive on the reporting server. This type of reporting server does not require any special configuration.

- **Summarization and Syslog Collection**: This option only supports appliances that are managed via HTTPS by SGMS. Each appliance is configured to send its Syslog data directly to the reporting server, as opposed to using agent servers. Configuring this type of distributed reporting requires special configuration changes on the SGMS server.

To configure a Summarization and Syslog Collection Distributed Reporting server:

1. Obtain the server hardware, install and patch the operating system, and configure the Network Interface settings.

2. Follow the steps for a Fully Redundant agent installation.

3. Locate the sgmsConfig.xml file on the SGMS server and open it in a text editor.

4. Modify the entries shown in Table 13.1 so your configuration looks the same.

5. Save the sgmsConfig.xml file and exit the text editor.

6. Configure all managed appliances to use HTTPS for SGMS Management.

Table 13.1 Distributed Reporting sgmsConfig.xml Configuration Changes

scheduler.terminate	True
snmpmgr.terminate	True
syslog.terminate	True
vpnscheduler.terminate	True
vpnsummarizer.terminate	True

To forward non-HTTPS reporting traffic to the reporting server, from SGMS agent servers, make the changes listed in Table 13.2 to the sgmsConfig.xml file located on each of the agent servers.

Table 13.2 Changes to sgmsConfig.xml for Forwarding Non-HTTPS traffic to Reporting Server

Syslog-forwardToHost	Enter the IP address of the distributed reporting server
Syslog-forwardToHostPort	Enter the port number for the distributed reporting

Registering SGMS

After the installation of SGMS is complete, registration must be completed before access to the SGMS console is allowed. Follow these steps provided to complete the registration process:

1. Double-click the **SGMS** icon on your desktop. The Registration page will appear.

2. Enter your contact information into the appropriate field.

3. Enter the SGMS serial number, typically located on the SGMS CD-ROM, in the GMS Serial Number field.

4. Click **Update**.

At this point, SGMS will contact mySonicWALL.com and validate the registration information. Once SGMS is successfully registered, the initial Login screen will appear (see Figure 13.44).

Figure 13.44 Login Screen

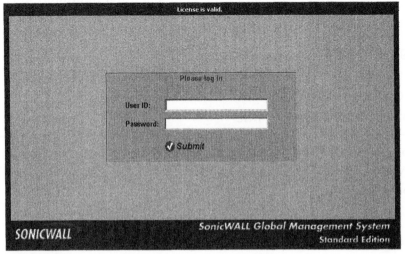

Configuring GMS

The main graphical user interface (GUI) has four panels located at the bottom of the window: Policies, Reporting, Console, and Monitor.

Policies Panel

The Policies panel is used to apply configuration changes to managed appliances. The administrator can choose to modify individual appliances, groups of appliances, or all the appliances under management from this window (Figure 13.45).

Figure 13.45 The Policies Panel

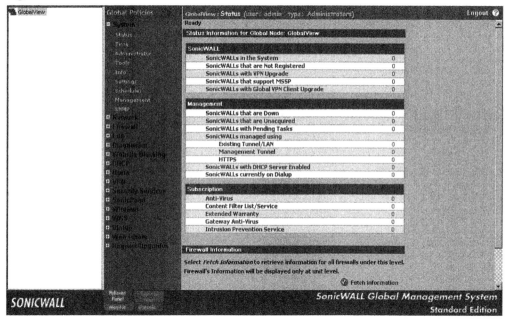

Reporting Panel

The Reporting panel displays information gathered from the managed appliances in easy-to-read graphical formats. Administrators also use this panel to configure scheduled reports for single appliances, groups of appliances, or all appliances (Figure 13.46).

Figure 13.46 The Reporting Panel

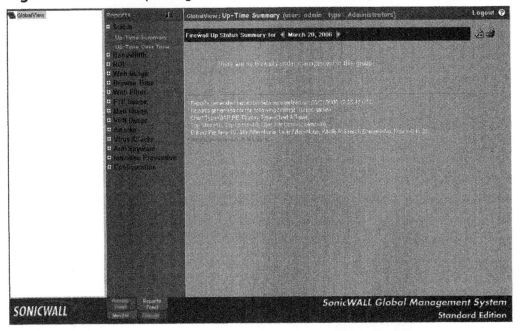

Console Panel

The Console panel is used to manage the SGMS configuration settings, which apply to the SGMS software only. Administrators use this tab to perform such tasks as managing licenses, viewing SGMS logs, creating and managing users and/or groups, modifying views, and viewing and managing pending tasks (see Figure 13.47).

Figure 13.47 The Console Panel

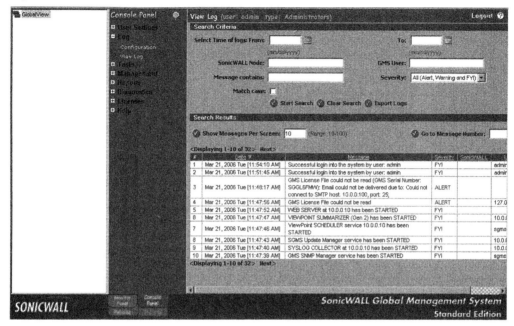

Monitoring Panel

The Monitoring panel contains several tools that are used for monitoring the status of appliances. The tools require specific licenses to enable their functionality, and include:

- GMS Navigation
- VPN Monitor
- Net Monitor
- Real–Time Syslog

Figure 13.48 shows the Monitoring panel.

Figure 13.48 The Monitoring Panel

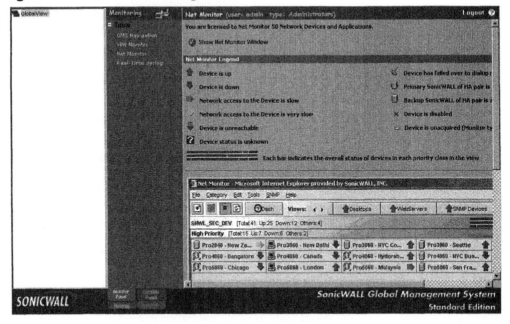

Introduction to Views

Three views can be used to filter which appliances are displayed on the GUI: Global, Group, and Unit (Figure 13.49).

Figure 13.49 The Change View Window

GlobalView pertains to all appliances under management by the SGMS server. Any configuration changes applied while in this view are distributed to all appliances. For example, if you would like to add a specific rule to specifically block certain ports a new worm uses to propagate, to all appliances, you would do this in GlobalView. To minimize the impact of changes, administrators can schedule when the updated configuration will be deployed to managed appliances.

GroupView pertains to groups of appliances, and SGMS provides the capability to group appliances based on different criteria. Changes made at the group level only affect the appliances contained in the specific group. For example, if we have ten TZ 170 appliances and five 4060 appliances, we could place these in groups to make management easier. We could then apply certain changes to only the 4060 appliances, without affecting the TZ 170 appliances.

UnitView pertains to individual appliances. Changes made in this view will only affect the individual appliance selected.

Adding SonicWALL Appliances to SGMS

To add a new appliance to SGMS, right-click the **GlobalView** icon at the top left of the screen and select **Add Unit** from the menu. The Add Unit window will appear as shown in Figure 13.50.

Figure 13.50 The Add Unit Window

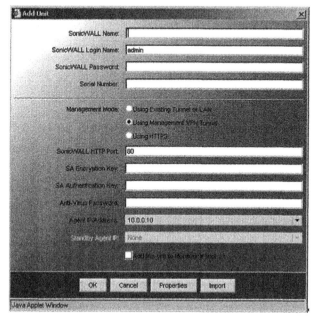

Enter a descriptive name for the appliance, the username and password for the admin account, and the SonicWALL appliance's serial number.

Select the **Management Mode** option and enter the appropriate information for the appliance.

If you choose the distributed installation option for installing SGMS, select the Agent IP Address from the drop-down menu with which this appliance will communicate. For redundant installations, select the **Standby Agent IP** from the drop-down menu.

To add this appliance to the Monitor panel, click the check box next to **Add this unit to Monitoring Tool**.

After entering the appropriate information for the appliance, click **Properties.** The Properties dialog box will appear (Figure 13.51).

Figure 13.51 The Properties Dialog

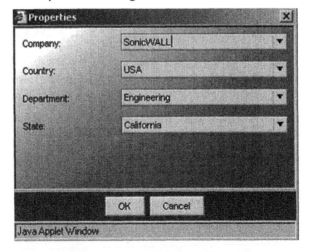

The properties for the appliance help distinguish certain characteristics about the unit, such as location information. Custom properties can be created using the Console panel. After setting the appropriate properties, click **OK**.

The appliance will now appear in the tree view at the top left of the window. Initially, the Status icon of the device indicates that SGMS is adding the unit to the display (Figure 13.52).

Figure 13.52 Tree View

Upon completion of adding the unit, the Status icon will change to a blue icon. If the appliance that has just been added is not registered under the mySonicWALL SGMS account, the icon will have a lighting bolt over the blue icon, as shown in Figure 13.53.

Figure 13.53 SonicWALL Successfully Added

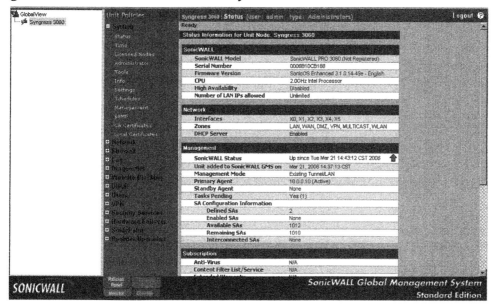

Repeat the process until all units that will be managed are added.

The Console panel is used to configure individual settings for SGMS. We will look at each of the settings available in SGMS 2.9.4.

User Settings

The User Settings window contains two links. The General window is shown in Figure 13.54. From this window, administrators can:

- Change the SGMS Admin login password
- Change the SGMS inactivity Timeout value

- Enable edit task description dialog when creating tasks feature.

- Enable Session Window Pop-Up feature

- Display the Message of the Day

Figure 13.54 The General Window

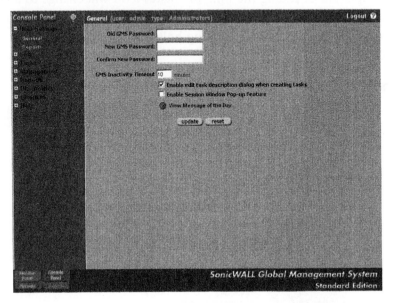

The Reports window, shown in Figure 13.55, allows administrators to configure general reporting features such as Display Type, Chart Type, Number of Items, Inclusion Filter Parameters, and so forth

Figure 13.55 The Reports Window

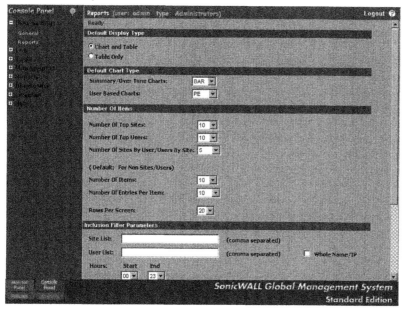

Log

The Log options are Configuration and View Log. Log → Configuration is used to specify when old logs should be deleted (Figure 13.56).

Figure 13.56 Log Options

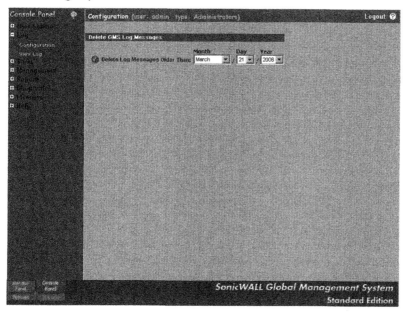

Log → View Log allows administrators to view the SGMS log file, search the log for entries using specific criteria, and configure how many log entries will be displayed on a single screen (Figure 13.57).

Figure 13.57 Log → View Log

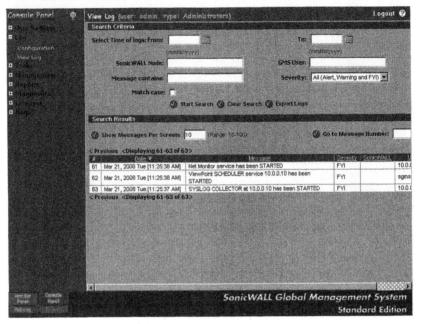

Tasks

There is only one option under the Tasks options, Schedule Tasks. The configuration options on this page are used to display certain tasks or all tasks that are scheduled to run against appliances or SGMS. Administrators can delete pending tasks, reschedule tasks, or execute the tasks immediately. Figure 13.58 shows the Scheduled Tasks window.

Figure 13.58 The Scheduled Tasks Window

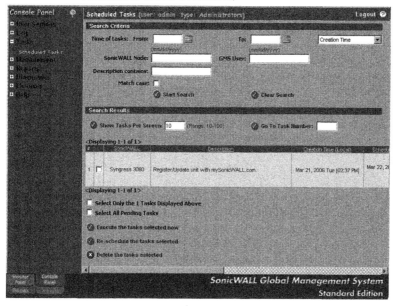

Management

There are nine options under the Management section of the SGMS Console panel.

GMS Settings

The GMS Settings window, shown in Figure 13.59, is used to configure general options of SGMS.

Figure 13.59 The GMS Settings Window

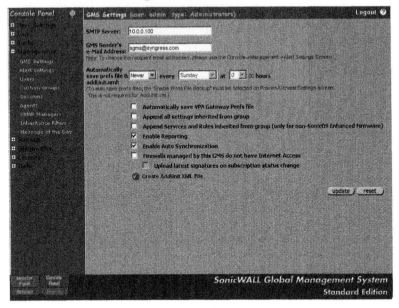

Alert Settings

The Alert Settings window allows administrators to specify specific actions that will be taken on certain events. The options include logging to the GMS Log, sending Email notifications, SNMP Traps, Syslog output, or saving to a file. Figure 13.60 shows the bottom part of the Alert Settings window.

Figure 13.60 The Alert Settings Window

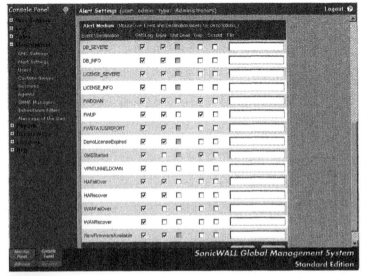

Users

The Users window provides administrators the capability to create users and groups that have access to SGMS. Users can be granted access to all features and configuration, or be restricted to specific features on a single unit. This provides for very granular access control over SGMS access. Figure 13.61 shows the default Users window.

Figure 13.61 The Users Window

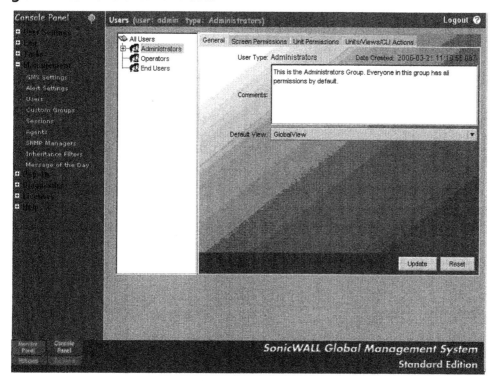

Custom Groups

Management → Custom Groups contains the grouping levels that are specified when adding new appliances. The groups defined here are listed under the Add Unit → Properties options for each appliance. To add a new group, move your mouse to the **Custom Groups** window and right-click (Figure 13.62)

Figure 13.62 Management → Custom Groups

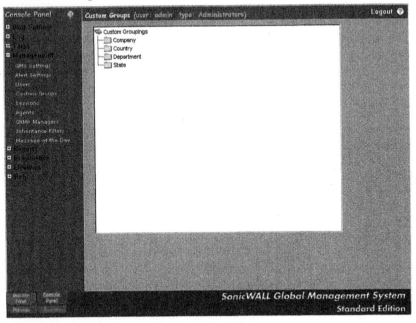

The Add Group Category dialog appears (Figure 13.63).

Figure 13.63 Add Group Category Dialog

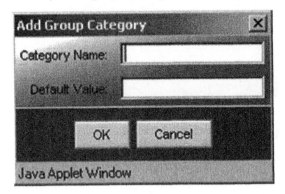

Add Group Category is used to logically group appliances by common locations or other information. Enter the Category Name and the default value that will be shown. For example, if managed appliances were spread across two regions, Northeast and Southeast, you would enter Region as the category name and either Northeast or Southeast as the default value.

The Management → Sessions window displays all active sessions on the SGMS server (Figure 13.64). Administrators can force specific sessions to end by clicking the **End selected sessions** button on this page.

Figure 13.64 The Management → Sessions Page

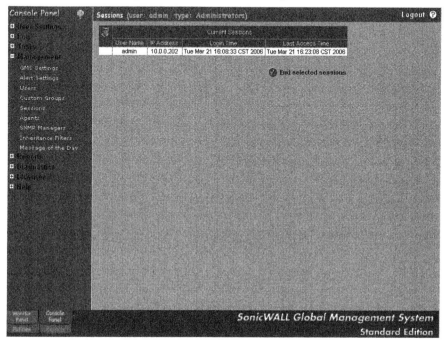

The Management → Agents page is used to configure SGMS agent servers and to specify which appliances report to what agent (Figure 13.65).

Figure 13.65 The Management → Agents Page

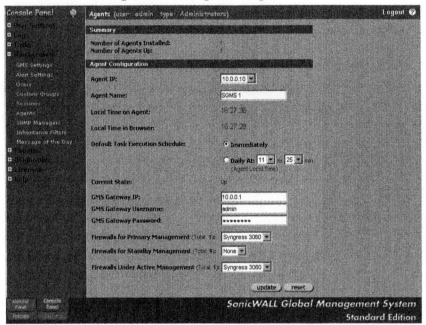

The Management → SNMP Managers page allows administrators to configure the SNMP settings for SGMS. Up to four SNMP servers can be configured to receive traps sent from appliances. In addition, you can enable or disable SNMP Trap forwarding and SNMP Trap Email features on this page (Figure 13.66).

Figure 13.66 The Management SNMP Managers Page

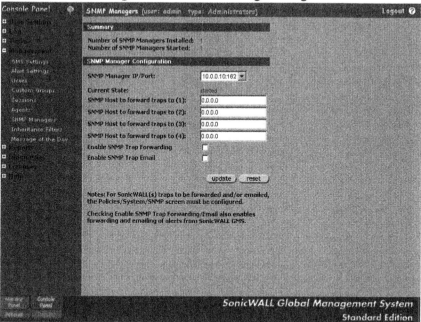

Management → Inheritance Filters, shown in Figure 13.67, is used to configure how inheritance is applied to the different configuration options on managed appliances.

Figure 13.67 The Management → Inheritance Filters Page

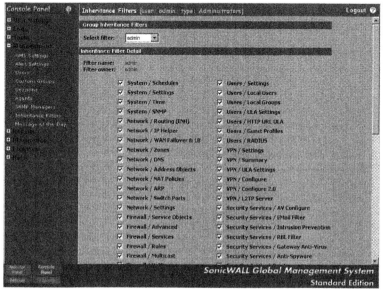

The Management → Message of the Day, shown in Figure 13.68, displays user-defined messages for specific users and groups that log in to the SGMS console. Messages can be displayed for a specific length of time and can use either plaintext or HTML format.

Figure 13.68 The Management → Message of the Day Page

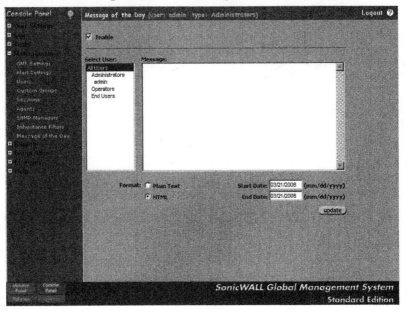

Perhaps the most important set of GMS configuration is done under Reports. The Settings options are shown in Figure 13.69 and include the amount of time (in days) raw data will be stored on the SGMS server. In addition, you have the option to enable sorting on the report tables.

Figure 13.69 The Reports → Settings Page

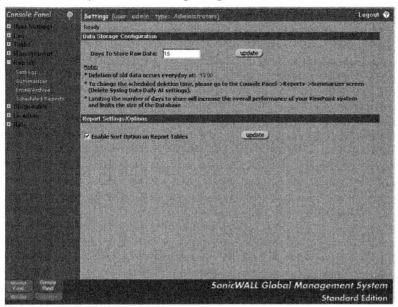

The second option under Reports is the Summarizer, which is responsible for parsing Syslog data and formatting it for reports. As shown in Figure 13.70, the Summarizer can be customized to run at specific times each day, include full URL Reporting, include ROI Reports on bandwidth use for each device or appliance, the number of days to store summarized data, and other settings that pertain to how the Summarizer functions.

Figure 13.70 The Reports → Summarizer Page

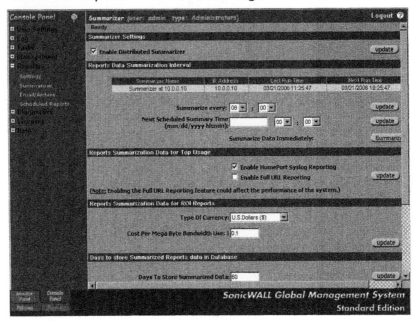

Reports → Email / Archive options include all configuration of when weekly and monthly reports will be sent, and the SGMS Web server configuration information (Figure 13.71).

Figure 13.71 The Reports → Email / Archive Page

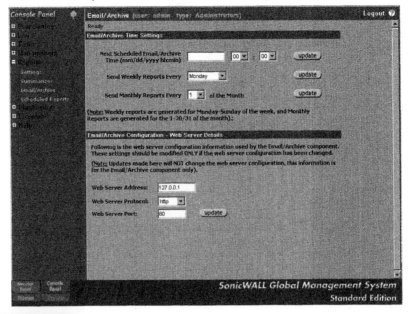

Reports → Scheduled Reports displays all the reports that have been configured to run for managed appliances. It is highly recommended that you obtain a copy of the Reporting Manual for the version of SGMS you are running to review the available options.

The Diagnostics options, shown in Figure 13.72, are used to obtain current snapshots of diagnostics information for the GMS Console, GMS Gateway, Database Information, and Agents. This information can be used to perform troubleshooting for SGMS. After a snapshot is requested and successfully processed, the results will be available under the Snapshot status page.

Figure 13.72 Diagnostics Options

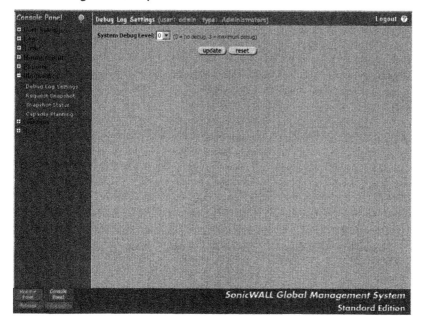

The final option under Diagnostics is Capacity Planning. Figure 13.73 shows an example of this screen and includes vital information that is used to gauge the amount of Syslog traffic that is being processed by the current server.

Figure 13.73 The Diagnostics → Capacity Planning Page

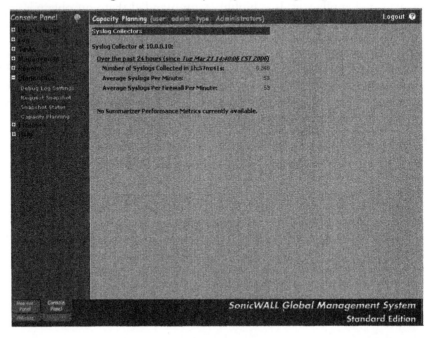

The last two options available on the Console Panel are Licenses and Help. The options available are straightforward and will not be covered. If additional information is needed, refer to the SGMS Manual available from SonicWALL.

The Monitoring panel includes additional services that can be purchased for SGMS to assist with managing and monitoring SonicWALL appliances, VPN tunnels, and GMS itself. Figure 13.74 shows the available tools.

Figure 13.74 Available Tools

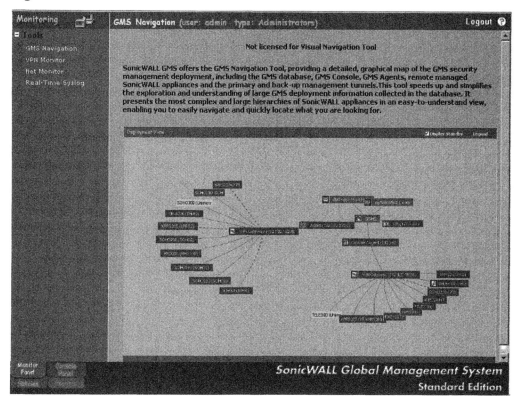

The Net Monitor page is used to configure monitoring for the managed SonicWALL products on your network (Figure 13.75).

Figure 13.75 The Net Monitor Page

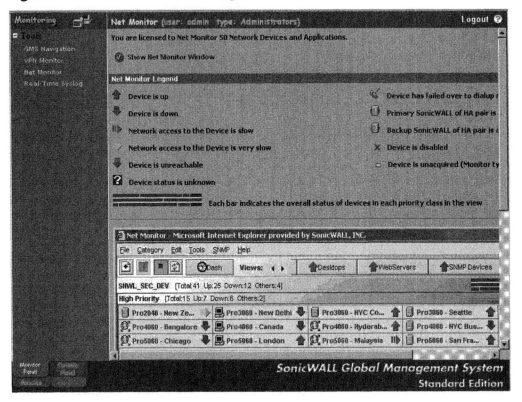

Real-Time Syslog provides access to Syslog data in real time (Figure 13.76).

Figure 13.76 The Real-Time Syslog Page

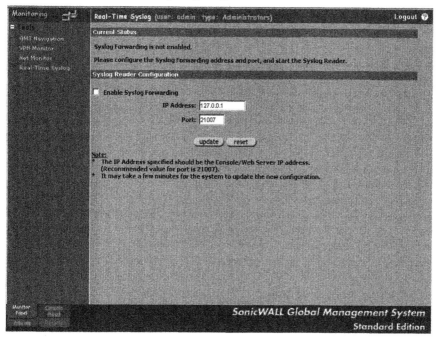

The Syslog Viewer, shown in Figure 13.77, displays collected Syslog data in real time and allows administrators to filter the displayed data.

Figure 13.77 Real-Time Syslog Viewer

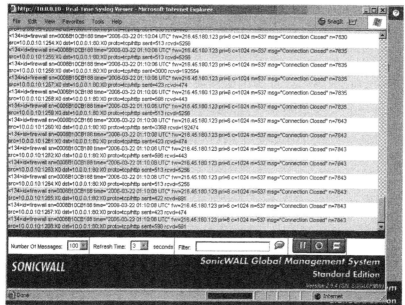

To illustrate the reporting capabilities of ViewPoint and SGMS, Figures 13.78 through 13.81 show example reports generated by SGMS. Note: ViewPoint reports will look identical.

Figure 13.78 Up-Time Over Time Example Report

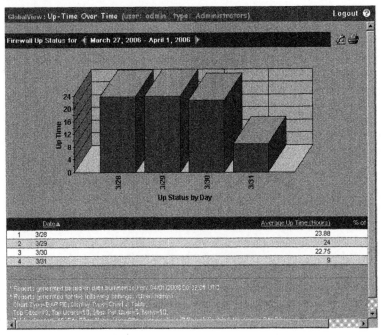

Figure 13.79 Web Usage by Browse Time Example Report

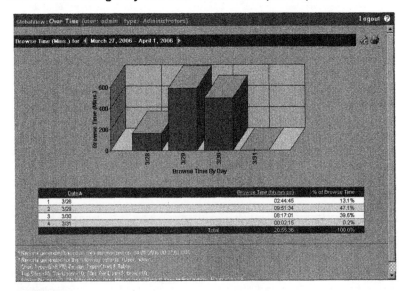

Figure 13.80 Bandwidth Over Time Example Report

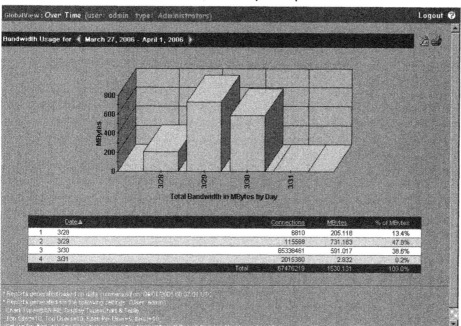

Figure 13.81 FTP Usage Over Time Example Report

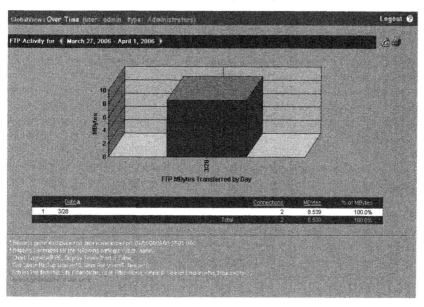

We have only touched the surface of the reporting capabilities provided by SonicWALL ViewPoint and GMS; this topic alone would require a book of its own.

Summary

SonicWALL ViewPoint and Global Management System software are extremely powerful applications that provide comprehensive reporting and management features to administrators. ViewPoint is a stand-alone solution that collects Syslog data from a SonicWALL appliance and summarizes it for report format. SGMS takes this further by allowing multiple appliances to be monitored and managed from a central console.

In this chapter, we covered the system requirements for SonicWALL ViewPoint, how to install it, and the basics of how to get around in the interface. Next, we covered the SonicWALL Global Management System software, the system requirements for the different components, how to install the software, and the basics involved with configuring the software.

The intent of this chapter was not to provide a comprehensive explanation of all the features and functions of ViewPoint and SGMS, but to merely introduce the products and provide you with the basics of how to navigate through the interfaces.

Solutions Fast Track

SonicWALL Management and Reporting

☑ The ViewPoint server requires Microsoft Windows 2000 or Windows XP Pro with Service Pack 2, a minimum of a 750 MHz processor, 512MB RAM, and 85MB free hard drive space.

☑ ViewPoint is a stand-alone solution for collecting Syslog data from SonicWALL appliances and presenting it in an easy-to-read graphical format.

☑ The ViewPoint software will install MSDE as its database to store all the data.

☑ Activity reports can be scheduled for daily, weekly, and monthly delivery via e-mail.

SonicWALL Global Management System Installation and Configuration

- ☑ SGMS can be installed on Windows or Solaris platforms and requires either Microsoft SQL 2000 or Oracle 9.2.0.1.

- ☑ SGMS can be installed as a stand-alone server or as a distributed system and provide fault tolerance and redundancy.

- ☑ The software can be scaled to manage thousands of SonicWALL appliances.

- ☑ The GMS Navigation tool displays a visual map of SGMS components and managed appliances. This service requires an additional license from SonicWALL.

- ☑ The VPN Monitor requires a valid license to function, which is not included with the SGMS license. This tool visually depicts interconnected VPN tunnels and their status.

- ☑ Net Monitor is used to display the status of SonicWALL managed appliances in a format that is easy to read.

- ☑ Real-Time Syslog Viewer is used to display incoming Syslog data in real time as it is received by the server.

Frequently Asked Questions

The following Frequently Asked Questions, answered by the authors of this book, are designed to both measure your understanding of the concepts presented in this chapter and to assist you with real-life implementation of these concepts. To have your questions about this chapter answered by the author, browse to **www.syngress.com/solutions** and click on the **"Ask the Author"** form.

Q: Is ViewPoint included with my SonicWALL appliance?

A: SonicWALL PRO 4060 and 5060 appliances are shipped with ViewPoint software. ViewPoint must be purchased for all other platforms.

Q: Can I manage my SonicWALL through ViewPoint?

A: No, ViewPoint is used specifically for reporting purposes only.

Q: How is SGMS licensed?

A: SGMS is licensed by the number of managed appliances. If you plan to manage 25 appliances, you will need a license for 25 appliances.

Q: How many SonicWALLs justify the cost of SGMS?

A: It depends. As a rule of thumb, if you have 10 or more appliances, SGMS is definitely justifiable.

Index

I

Syngress: *The Definition of a Serious Security Library*

Syn·gress (sin-gres): *noun, sing.* Freedom from risk or danger; safety. See *security*.

Configuring Netscreen Firewalls
Rob Cameron

Configuring NetScreen Firewalls is the first book to deliver an in-depth look at the NetScreen firewall product line. It covers all of the aspects of the NetScreen product line from the SOHO devices to the Enterprise NetScreen firewalls. Advanced troubleshooting techniques and the NetScreen Security Manager are also covered..

ISBN: 1--93226-639-9

Price: $49.95 US $72.95 CAN

Configuring Check Point NGX VPN-1/FireWall-1

Barry J. Stiefel, Simon Desmeules

Configuring Check Point NGX VPN-1/Firewall-1 is the perfect reference for anyone migrating from earlier versions of Check Point's flagship firewall/VPN product as well as those deploying VPN-1/Firewall-1 for the first time. NGX includes dramatic changes and new, enhanced features to secure the integrity of your network's data, communications, and applications from the plethora of blended threats which can breech your security through your network perimeter, Web access, and increasingly common internal threats.

ISBN: 1--59749-031-8

Price: $49.95 U.S. $69.95 CAN

Cisco PIX Firewalls:
Configure, Manage, & Troubleshoot
Charles Riley, Umer Khan, Michael Sweeney

Cisco PIX Firewall is the world's most used network firewall, protecting internal networks from unwanted intrusions and attacks. Virtual Private Networks (VPNs) are the means by which authorized users are allowed through PIX Firewalls. Network engineers and security specialists must constantly balance the need for air-tight security (Firewalls) with the need for on-demand access (VPNs). In this book, Umer Khan, author of the #1 best selling PIX Firewall book, provides a concise, to-the-point blueprint for fully integrating these two essential pieces of any enterprise network.

ISBN: 1-59749-004-0

Price: $49.95 US $69.95 CAN

Printed and bound by CPI Group (UK) Ltd, Croydon, CR0 4YY

03/10/2024

01040340-0018